Financialization

Max Planck Studies in Anthropology and Economy
Series editors:
Stephen Gudeman, University of Minnesota
Chris Hann, Max Planck Institute for Social Anthropology

Definitions of economy and society, and their proper relationship to each other, have been the perennial concerns of social philosophers. In the early decades of the twenty-first century these became and remain matters of urgent political debate. At the forefront of this series are the approaches to these connections by anthropologists, whose explorations of the local ideas and institutions underpinning social and economic relations illuminate large fields ignored in other disciplines.

Financialization

Relational Approaches

Edited by

CHRIS HANN AND DON KALB

berghahn
NEW YORK · OXFORD
www.berghahnbooks.com

First published in 2020 by
Berghahn Books
www.berghahnbooks.com

© 2020, 2023 Chris Hann and Don Kalb
First paperback edition published in 2023

Library of Congress Cataloging-in-Publication Data
Names: Hann, C. M., 1953- editor. | Kalb, Don, 1959- editor.
Title: Financialization : relational approaches / edited by Chris Hann and
    Don Kalb.
Description: New York : Berghahn Books, 2020. | Series: Max Planck studies
    in anthropology and economy; 6 | Includes bibliographical references and
    index.
Identifiers: LCCN 2020016091 (print) | LCCN 2020016092 (ebook) | ISBN
    9781789207514 (hardback) | ISBN 9781789207521 (ebook)
Subjects: LCSH: Financialization. | Finance--History.
Classification: LCC HG173 .F5198 2020 (print) | LCC HG173 (ebook) | DDC
    332--dc23
LC record available at https://lccn.loc.gov/2020016091
LC ebook record available at https://lccn.loc.gov/2020016092

British Library Cataloguing in Publication Data
A catalogue record for this book is available from the British Library

ISBN 978-1-78920-751-4 hardback
ISBN 978-1-80073-927-7 paperback
ISBN 978-1-78920-752-1 ebook

https://doi.org/10.3167/9781789207514

Contents

Illustrations, Figures and Tables

Illustrations

Figures

Tables

◀ Preface

CHRIS HANN

Previous volumes in this series have proven the format of bringing together half a dozen postdoctoral researchers to address a common agenda in a particular field of economic anthropology over a three-year period to be highly productive. Following investigations into rural transformations in postsocialist Eurasia (2009–2012) and the precarity of labor "on the margins of capitalism" around the world (2012–2015), "Financialization" was the label we adopted for a new cycle of projects at the Max Planck Institute for Social Anthropology between 2015 and 2018. Tristam Barrett, Charlotte Bruckermann, Natalia Buier, Dimitra Kofti, Marek Mikuš, and Hadas Weiss were the core members of this Research Group. I had three main reasons for choosing to investigate this subject.

First, the global economic crisis provoked by financial turmoil originating in the United States in 2007–2008 has demonstrated that capitalism has entered a new phase. The deeper causes and likely consequences were brilliantly outlined (with a primary focus on Western Europe) by my Max Planck colleague Wolfgang Streeck in his Adorno Lectures of 2013 (Streeck 2017). The Keynesian compromises that followed the catastrophes of the first half of the twentieth century were weakened in the 1970s, and then largely eradicated in the 1980s and 1990s. Welfare states that had contained social inequalities through redistribution based on progressive taxation were now obliged—in order to keep the system going—to ratchet up deficits on financial markets. The transformations were visible around the world. They are nowhere more conspicuous than in Britain, where Margaret Thatcher's governments oversaw a huge decline in industrial production, while the "big bang" in the City of London in 1983 prepared the ground for a roughly equivalent rise in the contribution of "financial services" to GDP. For many members of the European Union, the negative consequences of this deregulation of capitalism have been accentuated by the adoption of a common currency: the Euro. They have been manifest in the new century above all in a north–south cleavage. At the same time, despite (and in part because of) EU enlargement, the east–west divide of the Cold War era has been revived in new forms. This too is, to a significant degree, a story that hinges on finance at multiple levels (a history of "peripheral financialization," to use the terminology of Marek Mikuš in this volume). No corner of the world is unaffected—the bailout of the hegemonic power was only possible because the People's Republic of China was willing to acquire vast amounts of US debt.

No one knows for sure where all this is leading. Streeck himself has repeatedly touted the "end of capitalism." This may be premature. After all, Thorstein Veblen (among others) issued warnings about the threat posed by the "captains of finance" more than a century ago (Veblen 1904). Yet there is abundant evidence (Trump, Brexit, etc.) to corroborate Streeck's view that the compatibility of capitalism with parliamentary democracy is now being questioned in unprecedented ways. For the time being, the politics of "austerity" have triumphed. In Germany, a Social Democrat Minister of Finance is emulating his conservative predecessor by balancing the budget. But a high price is being paid, in terms of widening inequalities within countries and between them, for this desperate defense (Rakopoulos 2018). Austerity policies are increasingly reminiscent of the Dutch boy in the story who struggled to preserve the integrity of the dyke with his finger.

Despite the shock of Brexit, there is not the slightest evidence that the EU can begin to address the fundamental problems. Increasing social polarization (in particular the rise of the "plutocracy") in the developed capitalist countries is strongly associated with the increased emphasis on maximizing shareholder value, which has contributed in turn to the power of financial experts within firms and their own remarkable salaries and bonus payments. But the precise causalities here are less obvious (Godechot 2019). Is it reasonable to suppose that the one percent, who already own more assets than other human beings dream of owning, have nothing better to do with the wealth that financialization has generated for them than to feed their profits back into further speculative financial spirals?

This global conjuncture, then, was the first key factor behind the formation of our Research Group in 2015. The second was the conviction that sociocultural anthropologists have something valuable to contribute to the scholarly debates about financialization. Their contributions may take diverse forms. For example, anthropologists extend the range of contemporary comparisons beyond those that tend to dominate in the Euro-American social science literatures. They may also join up with historians to point out that, however dramatic the present phase of global crisis, capitalism has experienced many previous crises, and somehow the dykes have always been plugged. The history of debt is in any case much older than that of capitalism. David Graeber (2011) traces it back to Bronze Age Mesopotamia. Of course, there is no consensus concerning definitions of capitalism, let alone dates. But what we do know is that finance grew to be of decisive importance long before the impact of industrialization—above all in England, where the landowning aristocracy amassed debts to finance flamboyant consumption, while in the same society ordinary villagers used financial instruments for survival purposes in the face of demographic and economic fluctuations. The historical background and the path-breaking roles played by Holland and England in the emergence of financialized capitalism as we know it today are outlined by Don Kalb and Richard Robbins in the first two contributions to this volume. For Kalb, who expands the time frame to review millennia of Eurasian history, the institutions of finance were decisive in enabling the West, rather than China, to create the capitalism that transformed the planet.

The other contributors to this volume operate at a different level. They draw on the conceptual repertoires of anthropology, while borrowing freely from other disciplines whenever this helps them make sense of their empirical materials. These are diverse, but we decided at an early stage that our priority was to illuminate aspects of financialization that have remained in the shadows so far, neglected not only by other disciplines but also by those who have pioneered anthropological explorations of the world of finance by concentrating on emblematic elites, such as the traders of stocks. In contrast, we chose to pay more attention to how "ordinary people" were coping with the challenges of financialization in their households and everyday personal relations.

Here too there are historical continuities. In the era when Veblen and his Marxist contemporaries were initiating macroeconomic investigations of financial capital, we know from Viviana Zelizer's research into the dynamic expansion of the life insurance market that finance was already shaping the decisions of American households (Zelizer 1979). Yet the extent to which financial calculations penetrate human life-courses in virtually every corner of the globe nowadays is surely new. High levels of indebtedness between states are intimately bound up with unprecedented indebtedness at the micro level, where the moral ramifications are necessarily different. This volume therefore contains chapters devoted to the mundane mechanics of debt collecting in the capital of Croatia, on a provincial English housing estate, and in South African shantytowns. Other authors probe the social relations and ethical judgments associated with debt through observing court hearings, or by sitting in on meetings designed to improve "financial literacy" in a wealthy country where it remains surprisingly low, or by documenting the dramatic impact of new monetary technologies on citizens in the Global South who have never had cause to open a bank account before the coming of the neoliberal era. Questions of reception and complicity, but also of contestation and resistance, are raised throughout the volume, notably in the concluding chapters, which explore complementary aspects of the last decade of crisis in Spain with a focus on housing.

The third reason for committing the resources of the Max Planck Institute to investigate financialization was the possibility to work closely with Don Kalb, who has been a sympathetic observer of my department from its beginnings twenty years ago. I am extremely grateful to Don for the work he has invested with our group in the last few years, during which I have learned a great deal. Along the way, we profited from the stimulus of numerous guests in Halle—in particular Douglas Holmes and Karen Sykes, who visited us in July 2016. The entire group was involved in the planning and organization of a meeting in Halle in September 2018 to explore "Financialization Beyond Crisis." The authors benefited greatly on this occasion from the inputs of Laura Bear, James Carrier, Stephen Gudeman, Hadrien Saiag, and Gavin Smith. We are particularly grateful to Gavin for developing his "wrap-up" remarks into an Afterword for this book.

As always, it is a pleasure to thank Anke Meyer for assistance well beyond the call of duty in preparing the manuscript for the publisher.

Chris Hann is a Founding Director of the Max Planck Institute for Social Anthropology in Halle/Saale, and a Fellow of Corpus Christi College, Cambridge. He has published extensively on Eastern Europe, especially Hungary and Poland, both before and after the collapse of socialism. His most recent book is *Repatriating Polanyi: Market Society in the Visegrád States* (Central European University Press, 2019).

References

Godechot, Olivier. 2019. "Financialization and the Increase in Inequality." In *The Routledge International Handbook of Financialization*, ed. Philip Mader, Daniel Mertens, and Natascha van der Zwan, pp. 413–24. London: Taylor and Francis.

Graeber, David. 2011. *Debt: The First Five Thousand Years*. New York: Melville House.

Rakopoulos, Theodoros, ed. 2018. *The Global Life of Austerity: Comparing Beyond Europe*. New York: Berghahn Books.

Streeck, Wolfgang. 2017. *Buying Time: The Delayed Crisis of Democratic Capitalism*. 2nd ed. London: Verso.

Veblen, Thorstein. 1904. *The Theory of Business Enterprise*. New York: Charles Scribner's Sons.

Zelizer, Viviana A. 1979. *Morals and Markets: The Development of Life Insurance in the United States*. New York: Columbia University Press.

Introduction

Transitions to What? On the Social Relations of Financialization in Anthropology and History

<small>Don Kalb</small>

"Capitalism": a mode of production driven by private appropriation and private allocation of the social surplus. A mode of "endless" accumulation of capital. Most succinctly, and David Harvey's favorite definition: "value in motion" (Harvey 2017). "Finance": money capital. Money begetting money via the circulation of property titles and claims to future income from those titles in the form of "monetary streams" (Robbins, this volume); the driver of speculative and fictitious accumulation. "Financialization" or "financial expansion": the process by which the reproduction of societies as a whole becomes ever more dependent on finance, credit, debt, and on the logic of speculative money capital; a historical predicament in which the imperatives of finance increasingly capture and dictate the social and political forms that feed it.

Capitalism is always also a governmentality, a morality, a subjectivity. The relations to economic characteristics are never one-to-one, though, and are always partly contradictory. Moreover, since capitalism is value in motion, not defined by territory and place but by movement in space, a movement led by a succession of alliances of places and state-nations in an open ended process of accumulation, it is supremely territorially and socially uneven. This unevenness includes subjectivities, moralities, and ideologies. In world history, this unevenness combines *histories* within the wider sweep of *History*.

Financialized capitalism tends to generate governmentalities, moralities, and subjectivities, which are different from those characteristic of industrial or merchant capitalism, even while it merges with the historical sediments of these earlier and now subordinate forms. Capitalism and finance have always been as deeply political as they have been social. Indeed, they are, in the largest possible sense of the term, *relational.* That makes them even more contradictory, agonistic, and antagonistic, shot through with frictions and divisions. The "purely" economic cannot exist and has never existed, as Marx and Polanyi powerfully remind us. This is a popular intellectual fallacy derived from a "stark liberal utopia," a bourgeois myth. This myth is sustained by hegemonic actors and their preferred forms of knowledge—such as the economics discipline—precisely because its distortions engage in crucial battles for securing "the law of value" amid its ubiquitous political moments. We deploy a relational approach that assumes that value and those political moments are not narrowly "economic" or "political," but emerge out of deeply lived social relations, constituted on scales both intimate and epochal, within and against which humans live their lives and histories, indeed on which they depend for their social reproduction (for "relational approaches," see Emirbayer 1997; Kalb 1997, 2013, 2015; Kalb and Tak 2005; Pitluck, Mattioli, and Souleles 2018; Tilly 1998, 2001).

The last forty years have been a period of major financial expansion, ushering in a series of financial crises of which the consequences are still rippling through into a future that remains unknown. Throughout those credit and debt crises, global indebtedness has steadily increased. It is now, in mid-2019, around 300 percent of Gross Global Product. The financialized predicament of humanity is now more profound and more universal than ever before. Every life-course and social biography, everywhere on the globe, is willy-nilly infested with and structured by moments of financialized extraction on behalf of the owners of money capital, via public or private relations of indebtedness, or some combination. Those debts are in large part both held and owed by expanding groups that consider themselves middle classes. Their assets (housing, savings, investments, insurance policies, pensions) are growing in tandem with the wide availability of steadily cheaper credit, as in any common pyramid scheme, making the ultimate equation of costs and benefits complex and often utterly contradictory. Moreover, in some highly financialized, advanced capitalist locations, like the United States and Japan, public and private indebtedness together may reach as high as 500 percent or more. Others, like Germany, are still marked by a certain "financial repression," in public and private sectors alike, both in inherent ideologies and in practice (Weiss, this volume). The exact relations, proportions, and articulations are variegated. Some peripheral societies are still only weakly bankable. Others are becoming gradually financialized as part of an elite project, cutting out large segments of local societies from credit flows, like Azerbaijan (Barrett, this volume). Others again, like South Africa (James, this volume), India (Kar, this volume), and much of Latin America, are witnessing political projects on the Right and the Left that aim to mitigate incipient financialization with modestly redistributive transfer programs.

Those financial crises—the last one strictly speaking 2007–14, but projecting a long shadow forward—have caused social disaster and political and economic shock in many places, in particular in the social and geographic peripheries of the West, from Greece (Kofti, this volume) to Croatia (Mikuš, this volume) and Spain (Buier, Morell, this volume). The data and main events are well known, from mass dispossession of housing-collateral to mass unemployment; secular stagnation; accelerating inequalities between classes, generations, and territories; and the deep ongoing historical conundrum of the simultaneity of Quantitative Easing by central banks combined with deliberate austerity on the part of governments (with the crucial exception of China, as I shall explain below).

The crisis and its aftermaths have been a feast of accelerated learning about money, finance, and capitalism in general. Anthropology has been an active contributor to that learning, alongside history, literary studies, feminism, philosophy, sociology, and political economy. Economics, as an academic discipline and as a managerial profession for the daily running of capitalism as we know it, has found it harder to allow heterodox thinking in its midst, and yet the number of contrarian economists and their blogs has multiplied. The cumulative insights of all these scholarly endeavors are exciting. Gone is the stillness of neoliberal and neoclassical truisms perpetually recycled during the 1989–2007 *belle époque*. Some of this new writing has been explicitly anti-capitalist—the more so, it seems, since we have started to appreciate the close association of capitalism with impending environmental disaster. Capitalism cannot do without endless growth. This applies with a vengeance to indebted societies: credits are based on projected growth; otherwise, the debts can never be paid back. And so we have rightly started to talk about the "Capitalocene" rather than the Anthropocene. During the recent learning, the classics, such as Marx, Mauss, Schumpeter, Polanyi, and Keynes, have been revisited and sometimes realigned.

Added to this economic turbulence is the related and dramatic crumbling of the liberal center within Western politics; worldwide mobilizations of polarized and populist politics (Kalb and Mollona 2018); the spread of illiberal forms of rule (Kalb and Halmai 2011; Kalb 2018d), increasingly anchored in notions of civilizational difference; the reemergence of plutocracy and the escalation of inequalities (Carrier and Kalb 2015); the multiscalar political confrontations around globalization and sovereignty; the accelerating decline of Western hegemony and the rise of a China with obvious and predictably durable non-Western characteristics. All of this is profoundly interwoven with the deeper causes, mechanisms, and effects of a financialized global capitalism in crisis. Finance, then, appears both as motor, medium, and outcome of the contemporary predicament, impossible to disentangle from the wider historical social ensemble—a driver as much as an expression of contemporary global capitalism in crisis and emergent transformations. But transformations to what?

In the recent past, anthropology has often seen itself mainly as a micro-ideography of the subjectivities and practices of particular people in particular places—a tendency epitomized by the cultural turn of the 1980s and 1990s and recently again by the rise of ontology and its extreme cultural and cognitive relativism. But a few were never content with local cultural narratives and preferred to analyze the push and pull of verifiable social relations in time and space, of livelihoods and politics, thus deploying relational approaches. Some even dared to embrace explanation as against mere description. Economic anthropology and above all anthropological political economy have inclined toward this mode. The present collection features state-of-the-art articles in this latter vein. Our authors seek to discover and explain the contemporary social relations of financialization in various parts of the world, emphasizing relational forms and contestations, which are sometimes open and explicit, at other moments quasi-private and ambiguous (see also Pitluck, Mattioli, and Souleles 2018). Sometimes these forms seem decidedly local; but even then, these often turn out to be thoroughly multiscalar, from transnational interactions to hierarchy within the household. These interests depart significantly from the model that has come to be expected of the anthropology of finance. We are here not primarily concerned with "cultures of finance" or with modes of knowledge and other priorities of the somewhat misleadingly named "social studies of finance" (Ho 2009; Hertz, 1998; Zaloom, 2010; Appadurai, 2015; LiPuma, 2017). Rather than investigate finance per se, we approach financialization as a relational and uneven process over time and space. This also goes beyond earlier anthropological work on money (Parry and Bloch, 1989; Hart, 2001), which brought much insight into the cultural meanings generated through exchange practices but neglected capital and capitalism. The same can be said of recent empirical studies of indebtedness and redistribution (James, 2015; Ferguson 2015). Compared to all these authors, we are more interested in capitalism as such, in the big story that seldom emerges in other genres—even while many of our case studies engage with households and localities. Our studies are above all relational—in both the microanthropological and the macrohistorical sense—ethnographical, as well as theoretical (see Kalb and Tak 2005; Smith 2014; Di Muzio and Robbins 2016).

The more pregnant insights of anthropology often emerge from conversations between the "very micro" and "very macro" modes of enquiry (Wolf

1982, 2001; Mintz 1986; Goody 2004, 2009; Graeber 2011). David Graeber's *Debt: The Last 5000 Years* obviously stands out when it comes to finance. In this introduction, I take inspiration from Graeber's world historical gesture and mega-timeline. Graeber was inspired by Mauss. His work has centered on debt, morality, and the gift.[1] Mine will be eclectically Marxian with overtures to Polanyi, Schumpeter, and Keynes. It will be oriented toward rethinking capital, capitalism, financialization, and crisis—inevitably, then, also class, politics, and the state. And, why not, morality as a contradictory, dynamic, and agonistic aspect, fully intertwined with the pressures, politics, and relations of the day.

Money, Whence and How So?

Where does money come from? It should not come as a surprise that in the context of a powerful worldwide financial expansion, some new (old) truths have been (re)learned. Hadas Weiss's German informants would probably tell you that money is wealth coming from labor, productivity, competitiveness, and saving (Weiss, this volume). In believing this, they flexibly combine vernacular versions of a Ricardian labor theory of value with a Schumpeterian theory of competition. Some of her interlocutors may add a further "ordoliberal" element: overall societal efficiency matters for the successful accumulation of money, and therefore for mass prosperity. German society, in that vision, is like a social machine that puts a set of hard and soft public utilities to work, from morality to law to institutional design to production to social discipline. Here is German pride in a nutshell. "Germany works and competes," and seeks to do so better than others, which is why it will amass export earnings—the German mission since its unification in 1873. There is more than a whiff of vernacular mercantilism, too, in that narrative.

When I grew up in the sixties and seventies, something like this vision of money and wealth was also obtained in the Netherlands—despite a history that is deeply different from that of the neighboring German state, a history that has from its inception been merchant capitalist and overtly financialized. Compared to Germany, it is therefore historically much less equipped with a popular labor theory of value—despite a shared Protestantism. When I studied the Philips Corporation in the 1980s, with its headquarters in Eindhoven (Kalb 1997), the management had only recently stopped bringing employees together at work for "social meetings," where they would be tutored on the importance of saving part of their salaries. With the savings of the whole army of the nation's industrial employees (Philips was the largest private employer in the industrial heydays of the Netherlands, in the

1950s and 1960s, employing around 100,000 people across the country), the banking system would be enabled to transform savings into new capital cheaply, and so propel further industrial growth, which in its turn would generate higher incomes, more consumption, and more savings. Workers in Eindhoven factories believed in this theory, as did Weiss's German interlocutors. Possibly, this sensibility about wealth and money accumulating through labor, savings, and investments in material production was shared worldwide in those heady modern days, including in the socialist and the developing world. It was still believed until very recently in China. That narrative echoed the way contemporary development economics talked about modern economic growth and "take off." It reflected the actual workings and relationships of a still largely Fordist and industrializing economy amid the financial repression of those postwar days, which Keynes had so emphatically recommended. It was also regularly voiced in World Bank recommendations, and it sometimes is to this day (Robbins, this volume). The United States and the United Kingdom have always been slightly different. They are the great capitalist historical hegemons, where the stock market and private credit, and therefore speculation and debt, had played a much larger role since the early twentieth century if not earlier, both *de facto* and in the popular imagination. On the European continent, mortgages, consumer credit, and suburban private living in family owned properties, as in the United States, were not introduced on a mass scale until the 1970s; in the rest of the world, even more recently, and very unevenly.

Such vernacular theories of the production of wealth relied ultimately on a simple underlying liberal theory of money, in which money was seen as a practical invention of the market. Adam Smith, for instance, believed that men had always evinced "the propensity to barter." But barter had its limitations in practice. As societies became more complex and large-scale, so the liberal theory went, barter became an inconvenience and a drag on trade. And so, out of the natural desire for expanded exchange, money was discovered. Money, either in the form of shells, or salt, or coins, became a universal medium of exchange in the Neolithicum, five thousand years ago, when human groups had become larger and mutual contacts intensified. For such a medium to last, however, it also had to function as a reliable store and measure of value, and it had to be portable. And, thus, precious metal appeared (Graeber 2011; Goetzmann 2016).

The great city–states and empires of the Bronze Age added to those key market functions of storing and measuring value: they gave the coins their sovereign imprint and a guarantee for their value that was as good as the credibility of the king. That value was believed to reflect their weight and composition of precious metals. Here, the liberal theory of money merges fully with the "metallist" theory of currency. Humans began minting coins from copper, bronze, and increasingly silver and gold, allowing a massive expansion in the space and time horizon of exchange. Metal money and its guaranteed value also served to make the emerging and rather violent class inequalities of the Bronze Age relatively secure and durable. This was the moment of emerging powerful empires in Eurasia, from the Roman Empire in the West to India and China in the East, with their unprecedented war-making, slave trading, and widely flung commerce; their dynamic urban economies, armies, and navies. Money and violence were the glue that held them together.

In short, it was this supposedly natural logic of expanding commerce, driven by all-human propensities toward exchange, that seemed to explain the historical appearance and function of money as we know it. The market invented money. Its function was universal exchange, standard measures, and the storing of value. Precious metal was its ideal medium. Subsequently, the state emerged, which then helped to institutionalize those market currencies. The point is that, in the liberal theory, money was imagined to be "neutral," hard, honestly reflecting the real value of its metal base in the market. Not "artificial" or "distortive." And this is indeed how it appeared throughout much of European history from the Greek city–states onward. Without exception, those West Eurasian states tended to be ideologically loyal to the metallist theory of money.

What a shock, then, for a Venetian merchant in the fourteenth century to be confronted with a non-European reality that seemed to work in the opposite way. Here is Marco Polo writing about his discoveries in China; a long quotation from the passage on "How the Great Khan Causes the Bark of Trees, Made into Something Like Paper, to Pass for Money All over His Country"; this, in order to taste the full flavor of his surprise and to give a sense of context and implications:

> The emperor's mint ... is in this ... city of Cambaluc ... . You might say he has the secret of alchemy in perfection ... for he makes his money after this fashion: He makes them take of the bark of a ... mulberry tree, the leaves of which are the food of the silkworms, these trees being so numerous that whole districts are full of them. What they take is a certain fine white bast or skin ... and this they make into resembling sheets of paper, but black. When these sheets have been prepared they are cut up into pieces of different sizes. All these pieces of paper are issued with as much solemnity and authority as if they were of pure gold or silver; and on every piece a variety of officials ... have to write their names, and to put their seals. And when all is prepared duly, the chief officer deputed by the Khan smears the seal entrusted to him with vermilion, and impresses it on the paper, so that the form of the seal remains imprinted on it in red; the money is then authentic. Anyone forging it would be punished with death. And the Khan causes every year to be made such a vast quantity of this money, which costs him nothing, that it must equal in amount all the treasure of the world.

> With these pieces of paper … he causes all payments on his own account to be made; and he makes them to pass current universally over all his kingdoms and provinces and territories, and whithersoever his power and sovereignty extends. And nobody, however important … dares to refuse them on pain of death. And indeed everybody takes them readily, for wheresoever a person may go throughout the great Khan's dominions he shall find these pieces of paper current, and shall be able to transact all sales and purchases of goods by means of them just as well as if they were coins of pure gold. (quoted in Goetzmann 2016: 191–92)

Polo then continues to explain that in the lands of the Khan, foreign merchandise, gold, silver, pearls, or gems cannot be sold, except to the Khan himself. For this, he pays "a liberal price" with his paper money. "So he buys such a quantity of those precious things every year that his treasure is endless, while all the time the money he pays away costs him nothing at all." Then Polo concludes: "Now you … [know that] … the great Khan may have, and in fact has, more treasure than all the kings in the world; and you know all about it and the reason why" (quoted in Goetzmann 2016: 192).

This fragment does not mention that China's world leading paper, silk, and porcelain industries were state monopolies too, and that it was for these products that the steady stream of foreign merchants was coming. Nor does he add that these monopolies on world class luxury goods were a further support for a monetary state system that did not, as in historical Europe, run on the gold and silver controlled by wealthy merchant families or silver mine owning feudal dynasties such as that of the Fuggers. In Song China, it ran on mere state issued paper "that costs nothing," and that everyone was held to believe in and transact with.

Credit Monies and the State: Chartalism and Bourgeois Revolution

Against the background of Marco Polo's surprises in Song China, I want to shortly reflect on three issues: (1) "the state theory of money" and the theory of "credit monies"; (2) the Western amnesia of this theoretical tradition since the 1970s; and (3) its recent return, associated with the financial crisis, "Quantitative Easing," and the rise of "Modern Monetary Theory" and "finance as a franchise of public trust" (Hocket and Omarova 2017).

Song China was certainly an extreme case of "chartalism." Chartalism, or the "state theory of money," was developed by Georg Friedrich Knapp in 1905 in Germany (Knapp 1924; see also Graeber 2011), and was introduced a bit later into the English-speaking world by Alfred Mitchell-Innis. It builds on Say, Mill, Marx, and even some formulations of Adam Smith. Knapp and Innis showed that money as currency was not a special type of commodity generated within the market, as liberal theory imagined, but rather a state-based invention backed by the (potential) tax base of the sovereign. Taxation and credit, not exchange between traders, were the origins of money. "There is no question," wrote Mitchell Innes, "that credit is far older than cash" (1913; quoted in Pettifor 2017: 15). Money issued by the sovereign state was in fact a deferred and guaranteed obligation by the sovereign to arrange payment of its commodity equivalent (in gold or grain or whatnot) to the holder of this money if so demanded—as nicely shown in the Marco Polo quote. This sovereign guarantee was secured against present and future "creditable" fiscal income. The deep pocket of the state, stretched over potentially "endless" time frames and extensive territories and populations, created what we might call an "infinite security." Song China is the perfect exemplar.

The state theory of money, then, argued against market-based ideas of money and ideas that have often been associated with "metallism theory." It claimed that the state had always in principle been able to create paper money ("from nothing") by issuing it as legal tender and accepting it for tax payments and other "vertical" obligations of its subjects. Not the value of precious metal, as such, but the credit and therefore credibility of the state enabled the making of currency. The chartalist account is one that gives priority to "vertical" and tax-driven money creation versus "horizontal" commercial money. Song China is the pure type, with public paper money already circulating extensively in the thirteenth century, if not earlier— Europe had to wait to the eighteenth century—and official metal coins with little inherent value going as far back as the age of Confucius. Elements of chartalism, however, have been present in almost all official state currencies, including in classic Greece and the Roman Empire (Scheidel 2009). This was so even when the sovereign for very practical reasons chose to produce bronze or silver coins with a nominal value close to their actual value in precious metal. Maintaining a narrative of a "sound" metal base for a currency was often a necessary imperial or royal concession to powerful oligarchies controlling substantial pools of currency, and thus helped to avert civil war. Or it could be, as in the Elizabethan English case, a way to align the state structurally with mercantile interests and attract the support and wealth of international traders from more wealthy continental states.

In a capitalist context, this potentially infinite security offered by state fiscal revenue subsequently helped to set such official currencies up as the basis for credit-monies. This at least is what happened in the West of the Eurasian landmass, but apparently not, or not at the same scale, in historical China (Rosenthal and Bin Wong 2011). In the West, seigniorial actors with a secured claim on the future tax incomes of the state could begin to write out loans against interest, not only from their present money reserves, but also from their future guaranteed incomes (Vogel 2017; Di Muzio and Robbins 2016; Robbins, this volume). Credit money, then, is a claim on the future incomes of a borrower, who is now considered legally "junior" or subordinate; and it is provided by credit from a legally "senior" creditor based on the borrower's projected future revenues guaranteed by a sovereign. As Robbins points out in the next chapter of this volume, it is therefore in its core a speculative and fictitious process based on the realistic probability of a projected future, supported by the signature of the sovereign and based in the enforceable legal hierarchy between senior lenders and junior borrowers. In this way, the obstacles to capital accumulation and commerce posed by the inherently limited stock of existing precious metal were circumvented. Societies could now be flooded by credit, and this credit could sow the seeds for "endless" economic growth as well as for future tax intakes that could once again back up new cycles of credit money generation, and "endless accumulation" by the lords of finance.

For this to happen, then, the silver or gold reserves supporting the currency had to be swapped for the "infinite" tax base of the sovereign. But the sovereign, at the same time, also had to be made universally reliable in his payments to his creditors. The crown had to be subjected to binding rules. This dual move, the subjection and responsibilization of the sovereign in relation to financial claims by his "senior" creditors on his future revenues, combined with a monetary expansion driven by credit monies signed by seigniorial actors (bankers), is nothing less than the hard finance-capitalist core of what Marxists have always called the bourgeois revolution (Davidson 2017). The prime historical example of this is the Glorious Revolution in England of 1688, which overthrew the Catholic King James II and put the protestant invader William of Orange, *Stadholder* of the United Provinces (now the Netherlands), on the throne. The revolution subjected the sovereign to a parliament of landlords and merchant investors, not unlike the "raden" of bourgeois citizens in the United Provinces itself, and then went on to make the Bank of England in 1694, of which in fact the new king William was the largest investor-stakeholder (Clapham 1944; see also Robbins, this volume; and Kalb 2013, 2018b). In other words, William of Orange, the Dutch financier and military leader, attained "seniority" over King William of Orange of the United Kingdom, who was perfectly willing to bind himself as sovereign to the rules imposed by himself as a private investor.

The model itself, both of the Bank and of a sovereign subjected to a parliament of investor-citizens, and therefore subjected to "rules" and "contract," was not at all new. It was based on the prior examples of European city–states, the Dutch and Italian in particular, and perhaps going back in its basic principles to the historical city–state phenomenon more generally. Capitalism as we know it is thus historically not only based on the secure property rights of the liberals, and the dispossessed "free" labor and exploitation in production of the Marxists, but just as much, and mutually reinforcing, in the making of the capitalist-dominated state-finance nexus. This nexus between finance capital and the state is a complex set of institutionalized class relations in which capital overall dominates. It involves representation, taxation, contract, property rights, public credit, and the seigniorial banking complex, and it is ideologically expressed, as well as steadily obscured, in historical liberalism.[2]

This "Anglo-Dutch moment" (Israel 2008) then was the ultimate break with the preceding financial repression of medieval Catholic Europe. Catholic Christianity, and Islam as well, had always equated the taking of interest with illegitimate and illegal usury—illegitimate because it was an exploitation of weaker souls who were supposed to be equal under god, and associated with the widespread popular indebtedness and subsequent slavery so characteristic of the pre-Christian Roman Empire to which Christianity had been a reaction. Islam emerged from similar anti-usury concerns and allowed only participatory stakes in enterprises as well as fees on financial arrangements as a way to make money from money (see Pitluck, this volume). Christianity was, as Graeber stresses (2011), the most radical anti-money ideology coming out of the turmoil of the late Roman Empire. It was even tempted to ban the accumulation of wealth by "money making money" entirely. In the end, it entirely failed.

Central to its failure was the rise, within the fragmented feudal polity of the Holy Roman Empire, of the city–state phenomenon in Europe. Feudal competition and military rivalry in the fourteenth and fifteenth centuries made even the pope himself thoroughly indebted to the Medici of Florence. In return for the financial services to the papacy, the Medici had been allowed to sponsor not just the blasphemy of the Renaissance but also to demand a serious interest rate, previously rejected by the pope as usury. In the end of the process, the Medici themselves simply usurped and subjected the papacy by nominating one of themselves as the pope (Parks 2006), not unlike the way in which William of Orange usurped and subjected the British crown by becoming the British king. The reformation was the next step in the breakdown of anti-usury. The rise of the Dutch mercantile-financier city–state as hegemon over the European state system, expressed in the peace of Westphalia of 1648, of which it was the key broker, and then the consequent Glorious Revolution of 1688 in England, in fact a Dutch military invasion, were the long drawn out completion of the bourgeois revolution that had begun in Italy. Finance, seigniorage, and rent taking had now become powerful state making forces that were driving the rise of the Western merchant capitalist empires. It was this finance-driven expansion that produced the unprecedented militarism and war-making capacities of the northwest European states. This then drove the shift away from a Eurasian system focused on China and the East toward a transatlantic-based Western-dominated world-system, which now rapidly morphed into a *capitalist* world system.

Demise and Rebirth of the State Theory of Money

It is not hard to see how Chartalist theory could have served as an intellectual inspiration for the Keynesian revolution in economics. Keynes's *A Treatise on Money* (2011) referred explicitly to Knapp and Mitchell-Innes in its opening pages, and it laid the groundwork for his *General Theory of Employment, Interest, and Money* (2017). With the fast and wholesale demise of Keynesianism in academic departments and policy making since the late seventies, the underlying state theory of money would also disappear from public awareness. As with Keynesianism, the theory was now associated with inflation, stagflation, and an interventionist and redistributive state: the archenemy of the neoliberalism that was swiftly occupying the salons of power in these years. This attack, and then the public amnesia of the key Chartalist insights on money that followed, happened, paradoxically, while the dollar, now unlinked from gold, had in fact become an undisguised *fiat* currency—probably the first one in the history of Western hegemons to be so openly blasphemous against metallism. Key monetary authorities, now working in Lucas's "rational expectations" mode, were hell-bent on squashing any intellectual freedom that might derive from the obvious *fiat* character of contemporary money. With the aggressive stress on producing durably low inflation (see Holmes 2013; Kalb 2005), a quasi metallism immediately returned through the backdoor as gold was thrown out through the front door. The Euro was a response to the dollar leaving the gold standard (and destroying Bretton Woods), and was explicitly set up as an intra-European gold standard, overriding any possible democratic sovereign aspirations to turn fiat currencies to any wider public purpose than just following the markets (Slobodian 2018).

The neoliberal obsession with hard and sound money thus produced a willed and long-running amnesia around chartalism. Whatever neoliberalism exactly was—and this is not the place to go into that discussion—it always included a hyperactive denial of the actually existing public possibilities springing from the *fiat* character of the whole late capitalist monetary system. Global markets were the gold standard, and states and their democratic publics had to be disciplined by the possibility of harsh and immediate punishments by the markets. Global markets had primacy because they always and inevitably spoke "the truth" that democratic elites and demanding publics were liable to ignore (Slobodian 2018). Neoliberalism was, among other things, a powerful restatement of the metallist theory of money at the moment when any metal base had been openly abandoned.

David Graeber (2011) helped significantly to bring the state-theory of money back into public debate in the aftermath of the financial crunch of 2008. True, there had already emerged a neo-chartalism among hetero-dox economists in the 1990s. And in small circles, there was already some excited talk about "modern monetary theory"—an update to chartalism (Fullwiler, Kelton, and Wray 2012). Graeber, however, can be read as a precursor of the global risings of 2011—in particular Occupy Wall Street. His book enjoyed blockbuster sales worldwide. Chartalism functioned in the book primarily by suggesting that the state had always already been accountable for issues of money, credit, and debt, both for the good—popular debt forgiveness—or for the bad—imperial violence, violent accu-mulation. Graeber emphasized that the good kings of the Bronze Age would regularly wipe out popular indebtedness and produce a clean slate on behalf of the common good. In the present financial crisis, in contrast, states were scrambling to back up the failing banks of 2008 and their senior owners, and left citizens to deal with unemployment, default, and dispos-session. The sums handed over under threats of utter mayhem seemed astronomical, certainly given the decades-long neoliberal taboo on public spending. I have earlier called this the definitive moment of state capture by finance capital (Visser and Kalb 2010; Kalb 2018b). In response, parts of the stung electorate in its academic version began bringing elements of the forgotten state theory of money back, as Graeber did; including, after a while, its latest intellectual update: "modern monetary theory." These new narratives claimed that alternatives were perfectly possible and desperately required. Money and finance were a public good derived from public trust and sovereignty, at least as long as a state was borrowing and lending in its own currency and from and to its own capitalists. Long run free liquid-ity could always be made available for public purposes. Inflation could be managed, certainly when there was none as in the present context of the global surpluses of both capital and labor, combined with the political anni-hilation of labor through the globalization of capital and the capture of the state by finance.

In the context of this emerging public debate about money, credit, debt, the nation, and the state—inevitably a chapter of an even larger debate about financialized global capitalism—the Bank of England in 2014 found it expedient to explain in its own *Quarterly Bulletin* where money comes from under present conditions. The Bank's authors said 97 percent of all liquidity is nowadays generated by private bank credit loaned to debtors who are deemed credit worthy (McLeay, Radia, and Thomas 2014). The monetary authorities thus reaffirmed the credit theory of money. They thereby made an implicit bow to the state theory of money.

Paradoxically, this implicit official affirmation painfully exposed the absence of public voice in the present context. The public was only tolerated into the financial equation as the silent guarantor of it all. Neoliberalism, "rational expectations," and the deregulation of private banking had ushered in a system where the state, the nation, and its tax base had become all but captured for the purpose of guaranteeing the profit making activities of money capitalists and their higher middle class supporters. The state and the nation were expected just to sign off on the resulting escalating public guarantees; they had little say in its regulation, let alone its purposes. The money capitalists returned this free gift by openly rejecting any responsibility of their class for the national tax base by which their revenues were supposed to be guaranteed, preferring to preside over their low tax/low cost world archipelagos (Shaxson 2018) and embracing a classic cosmopolitanism of and for elites, with the people locked out. "Whose sovereignty?" they seemed to be cynically asking. Local social outcomes, meanwhile, were ever more unequal, dispossessive, disenfranchising, and plutocratic. The populist revolts that shook the political systems of the Western world and elsewhere in the course of the 2010s, moving from Left to Right over time (Kalb and Mollona 2018), may have been a surprise for the liberal *commentariat* and the ubiquitous army of policy intellectuals, but they hardly came out of the blue.

Magnifications and Contestations

Enter "Quantitative Easing." Central bankers, as shown above, must always have been quietly aware of the basic correctness of the state theory of money. The key central banker of the crisis, Ben Bernanke of the Federal Reserve, was deeply knowledgeable about the 1930s' Wall Street crash and the subsequent world-deflation. He had even written about how central banks should have reacted then (Bernanke 2016). His retrospective recommendation: massive injections of *fiat* money in order to re-inflate the stock market. Milton Friedman had once said the same (1968) and had called it "helicopter money" (see Buiter 2014). Bernanke, thus, came with the watermark of one of neoliberalism's most important thinkers. Faced with certain collapse, this gave him the necessary political credit to break the financial mold of the preceding thirty years.

When the Western financial system suffered its cardiac attack in 2008 and the economy went into a tailspin, the political class, fed on decades of neoliberalism, was unprepared to the extreme and visibly struck by disbelief.[3] Subsequently, President Obama—as unprepared as anyone else, as shown by his veneration of "behavioral economics" (with its, at that point, all but trivial embrace of "nudging" for the public good)—was allowed a large sum for public investment purposes to fight the swift decline of the economy, but many argued that this amount was simply too little, too late. European politicians were even worse. They first indulged in a round of denials that Europe had anything to do with the crisis ("American financial casino capitalism versus solid productive capitalism"). When market mayhem reached the continent, they loudly extolled collective solidarity. But after leaving the room in Brussels, they immediately began sabotaging the possibility of any collective responses (Kalb 2018a; Legrain 2014). Instead, they orchestrated a frantic sovereign competition for national budgetary soundness, lauded as the singular morally correct path to economic salvation. Particularly the Northern core proceeded proudly with imposing draconian austerity on their domestic economies. Calling this "an example for others," they began a fierce competition on the market for state debt, inevitably crushing the Southern tier of the Eurozone and the Eastern tier of the EU, states that were now going to pay much more for the financing of their debts. Greece revolted but was humiliated; Italy's Sylvio Berlusconi was unwilling, but was unceremoniously deposed by the European Council. The rifts in the EU produced by that series of fateful moments have not been healed since then. The myths that were meant to explain what was happening, why, and who was to blame have become semi-institutionalized. The initial North–South rifts within the eurozone have been overlaid by subsequent East–West conflicts within the EU, which are significantly rooted in the crisis too (Kalb 2018d), and then further sharpened by Brexit and the similarly myth-driven political chaos in Britain. When it finally dawned on the markets that the actions of European politicians could only mean that they were ready to abandon the whole Euro-project, they began betting massively against the survival of the Common Currency (the infamous "spreads in sovereign borrowing costs" and related credit default swaps). Only at that point did key European politicians retreat from the morally correct abyss, mostly under loud denunciations of those "greedy" markets and the US-dominated rating agencies.

It was in that rolling context of shock (2008–14), political paralysis, confusion, and fracture that a small coterie of powerful central bankers, led by Bernanke, took responsibility and launched, one after the other, "Quantitative Easing." Together, they pumped an equivalent of more than 25 percent of OECD GDP in fresh *fiat* monies (sovereign fictitious capital, so to speak) into the system, and thus pulled it gradually from the brink. Bond prices stabilized, stock markets turned around, banks, sovereigns, and institutional investors (Blackrock first of all) were pulled into an upward swirl. It is hard not to agree with Martin Wolf (2015) and other critical liberal commentators that QE has probably prevented a full political and economic collapse of the Western system comparable to the 1930s. A similar injection in Keynesian mode, via governments, might have done the same, and would have generated more employment, more equal effects over classes and territories, and could potentially have reversed the decades' long trend toward further inequality and the sidelining of labor (see Pettifor 2017). But clearly not even the parliamentary Lefts in the Western world were ready to take on more state debt; and in Europe, most of the social democratic Left supported austerity in principle. That potential Keynesian response was thus nowhere really on offer. Nor would finance capital, the bond market, have quietly accepted its emergence. Free gifts from Central Bankers with the politicians and the public left out stood a much better chance.

Quantitative Easing was in the end nothing but an official affirmation of financialized state capture; and indeed it worked as such. Central bankers were never supposed to plot the revolution by design. QE did prevent melt down and system wide deflation, but it left the relationships that had produced the crisis in the first place perfectly intact, gave them another lease of life—indeed magnified them. Ten years after the crash, the financial class and large property holders worldwide came away with an increase in their collective stock market value of 300 percent (as of writing in March 2019), and real estate was on the upward trajectory once more. Global public and private debt, meanwhile, had further increased to a similar 300 percent of global GDP. Inequalities had often risen further. The labor share in GDP as compared to the capitalist share continued to fall. Urban housing was becoming unaffordable for new households. The path of nonchange was clear, indisputable, and entirely unsustainable.

Some things had changed, however. US hegemony and Western dominance were now visibly collapsing. Recently challenged by the avowedly anticapitalist alliances of the Global South and the alter-globalist movement, Western capitalist hegemony was now evaporating fast—but not quite on the behest of the peasants and indigenous people of the South, allied with the working people of the North, for whom those resistances had imagined themselves to act. While QE was a financial present for stock markets and asset owners worldwide, it was the simultaneous massive Chinese monetary stimulus that did most to pull the real global economy out of its downward spiral. Chinese domestic credits were proportionally at least similar to QE in the west (see Magnus 2018). But rather than designed to sustain fictitious accumulation, Chinese credits also took the form of state-guided investments into ongoing material expansion, channeled largely through state-owned banks and state-owned enterprises, and oriented toward unprecedented urban infrastructure projects. In two years, China consumed more cement than the United States in the whole twentieth century. Its needs for oil, iron, copper, machine tools, and soja beans were gargantuan. Remember the Song Empire and think of "Socialism with Chinese characteristics," but now in its hard Keynesian state capitalist phase. After the clouds of crisis cleared, China was now the first or second national economy. It had helped to reignite economic growth in both the global North and the global South and was spending hundreds of billions of dollars on new "Silk Road" infrastructure projects anywhere in the world. It had emerged as a potential nonliberal world hegemon, if that were a possibility, and was now the de facto systemic competitor to the West (and officially recognized as such by both the United States and the EU in respectively the winter and spring of 2019—against earlier Western assumptions of liberal convergence). By mid-2019, a new Cold War seemed all but likely.

Thus, synchronized state capitalism in two starkly opposed but still kindred varieties had saved the system by greatly magnifying its credit dependence. But by seeking to restore the status quo ante, it had also changed it forever. Without those financialized state supports, the system would not work any longer. Western central banks kept loudly proclaiming their plans to return to "normal": stop buying assets, sell existing central bank assets back into the markets, and finally bring zero interest rates up to the historically expected levels of well above 3 percent. Such Western efforts, however, have steadily failed (the most recent collapsed during the drafting of this introduction, March 2019; both the FED and the ECB began QE again in September 2019). Every move toward restoration after 2015 has produced immediate signs of recession plus large stock market falls.[4] Economists who were bullish about neoliberal economic growth in the 1990s, such as Lawrence Summers, are now making a serious case that the system is seeing a return of "secular stagnation" as in the thirties, and that QE might, if continued in the present form, make things worse.[5] Financialized Western capitalism at its peak, as expressed in stock market values, has become structurally dependent on massive injections of fiat money, free liquidity, historically low interest rates, and further fictitious and speculative accumulation by and for the wealthy, made possible, fundamentally, by public underwriting of the monetary system and the plutocracy it supports. Actual economic growth, meanwhile, had become largely dependent on an ongoing Chinese material expansion driven by a similarly state-orchestrated financial expansion and a similar consequent addiction to credit, which neither the Chinese nor the global economy apparently can do without anymore. This is where we are: an East–West duet in financialized state capitalism. Both in denial—the liberal one singing the gospel of the eternal supremacy of markets and awaiting their supposedly inevitable resurrection, despite the evidence that such redemption might not happen any time soon; the other imagining itself as socialism with Chinese characteristics. Both magnanimously supportive of the imperatives of their various preferred forms of capital, and, when push comes to shove, agnostic about the further widening of class inequalities of power, wealth, and income, despite a sprinkling of rhetorical agonizing.

Recall David Graeber and his imagining of the king who intervened in market relationships in order to restore equilibrium. The king has indeed returned with a very visible hand, but not Graeber's good king of debt forgiveness. It is a king kept on a tight financial–capitalist leash, offering handfuls of new credit for nothing to ruling institutions in the hope that the ruling institutions come back to life and will lift up all boats. However, magnification of the space for public credit and finance has inevitably widened the potential space for politics too, both on the Left and the Right. In line with the comeback of chartalism, an increasingly debated body of economic thought provocatively called "Modern Monetary Theory" is now arguing that the arrival of the good king is a real possibility if only some popular sovereignty over capital is redeemed, which they picture as a mere question of free democratic choice. Modern Monetary Theory presents itself as the precise intellectual weapon for this purpose (Fullwiler, Kelton, and Wray 2012). MMT argues that modern states can in principle produce as much *fiat* money as they like without dangers of inflation. This is the ultimate rejection of neoliberal, quasi metallism. One cannot help but respond that MMT needs a serious engagement with a sophisticated labor theory of value. It is also bound to run into insurmountable problems in the current transnational context (as does and did national Keynesianism). But for now, MMT helps to underpin contemporary ideas of "people's quantitative easing" (Braun 2016)—*fiat* money injections by central banks directly into people's purses, public services, and infrastructure, rather than into the purses of money capitalists, job guarantee programs, and indeed a "Green New Deal" proposed by the Left hand of the Democratic Party in the United States. In other words, it is a monetary theory that, in conversation with Marxian, Polanyian, and Keynesian visions, might support some of the demands of the inheritors of the Left mobilizations of 2011—at least in the most sovereign core nations, hardly for the peripheries. It remains an open question whether the EU will ever award itself the "exorbitant privilege" of such sovereignty (although this might well be a necessary condition for a durable solution to its frightening problems).

On the Right, things have equally shifted. Despite the US Tea Parties of 2009–15 and the conservative ideologies of their billionaire sponsors and think tanks, metallism and the gold standard seem to have lost their shine for some. Illiberal populist rulers like Erdogan, Modi, Orbán, and, much more importantly, Donald Trump are forcing their central banks into more cheap money and costless credit. Steve Bannon, meanwhile, now a powerful investor in Right wing ideology making and supporter of international illiberal alliances, keeps associating "debasing the currency" with "debasing our citizenship." In Europe, the small competitive (and tax-dumping) nations of the North have formed a new "Hanseatic League" and continue to force a gold standard mercantilism on the rest of the EU, with the sympathy of German governments in the background. France seeks more transfers and credit facilities within and for the Eurozone as a whole. The Left–Right populist government in Italy of *Cinque Stelle* and The League pushed for monetary easing in Brussels and Frankfurt until it was dissolved in August 2019. Small country governments in the South with Leftist populist governments, like Portugal and Greece (until summer 2019), are running rather contradictory domestic policies without any longer daring to politicize Eurozone governance openly. Much of Latin America, meanwhile, is back at Right wing neoliberal orthodoxy after the demise of its China-driven pink tide. The governments of Brazil, Chile, and Argentina under Macri are once more endorsing "sound money" policies and bringing the IMF in, while Mexico is doing the same from an avowed position of Left wing sobriety. Meanwhile, prudent states in Africa, like Ghana, are borrowing on the international market for unprecedented durations of fifty to one hundred years—when a decade earlier, even loans of ten years were hard to pull off for any African state. One thing is overwhelmingly clear: the hard money hegemony of the Washington Consensus, with its demand for independent central banks, formulated in 1991, is definitely over. Contestation—intellectual, political, and popular—has become the norm.

Money, Financialization, and the Rise of Capitalism: Bourgeois Revolution #2

Every epoch generates its own theory of capitalism and puts its own accents. Locke, in the late seventeenth century, focused on the prerogatives of private property in relation to the rules of governance and the social contract. Smith and Ricardo reflected about a period of fast market expansions and widening global divisions of labor captured by notions of "commercial society," specialization, and the growing awareness that not only land but also labor and manufactures created value. Marx was witness to the spread of the factory system, the making of the working class, workers' participation in Chartism, the 1848 revolutions, the Paris Commune of 1871, and fast-paced deepening of the global divisions of labor and empire. He focused on class, exploitation in production, and the contradictions of bourgeois rule and ideology, in particular the way they both obscured and expressed the more fundamental contradictions of capital accumulation itself: fetishism. Lenin and Trotsky dealt with pervasive new forms of pro-letarianization in the periphery, alliances between workers and peasants, and the possibilities of socialist revolution in a context of imperial capitalist war making. With John Hobson, Rudolf Hilferding, and Rosa Luxemburg, there emerged a keen interest in the logics of finance and imperialism. Keynes's major works dealt with the 1930s crisis and focused on the nature of money, failures in bourgeois economics, mass unemployment, and the necessary role of the state and public credit. Polanyi studied the same crisis and theorized about the "stark utopia" of "planned" "free markets," fictitious commodities, embeddedness and disembeddedness of markets and societ-ies, and the "double movement" that emerged as societies subjected to such market utopias sought to re-embed and reregulate the markets of fictitious commodities such as labor, land, and money in particular.

The historical financial expansion that we have witnessed in the last forty years, and the crises that it keeps provoking, throw new light once again on our historical theories of capitalism. What might we have learned about the role of finance in the development of capitalism? I want to suggest that we need to rethink what could be meant with the concept of bourgeois revolution, and why that concept might be so seminal. Finance is key to that rethinking.

Let us begin by returning for a moment to thirteenth century Song China. Recall: paper money issued by the state, state monopolies on luxury productions, the Khan in benevolent control of internal markets. Not yet mentioned: a state without any debt of its own, acting as the ultimate public creditor, injecting its paper monies against low interest into society. But also a state that would not allow the rise of powerful urban oligarchies intent on limiting the power of the sovereign, weeping them out if necessary. This was a bureaucratic state, run by credentialed Confucian administra-tors from widely different backgrounds. They embodied an ethos of public service, balance, justice, and far sightedness. Although Jack Goody (2004, 2009), among others, has powerfully argued against setting up the East of Eurasia against the West of Eurasia, and vice versa, seeing them alternating in innovative evolutions—an argument that, phrased in these terms, I find convincing both in spirit and in detail—Song China had nothing that could have made it capitalist; this, despite world-leading manufactures in tiles, porcelain, paper, and textiles; dynamic cities; "free" labor and enterprising mercantile classes. All of it was there, as extensively documented by Goody and others; but in Europe, the elements combined in a different way. The class relationships, magnitude, and political role of finance capital were key in producing an ensemble in the West that could ultimately usher into historical capitalism. We are talking about conditions of possibility, not about inescapable teleological determinations.

Compare the roughly contemporaneous West-Eurasian scene of the late middle ages. One would notice the rise of an imperial Catholic Spain and a shift of the critical mass of trade from the Eastern to the Western Mediterranean, also already a projection of Spanish and Portuguese power onto the Southern Atlantic. But one would as well be struck by the rise of the Italian cities, and might already see the first signs of the emergence of another European urban landscape in the Low Countries and along the Baltic coasts. All of these were not just cities; they were full-fledged city–states. Their rise was based on their capacity not just to produce manufactures, to trade, and to accumulate mercantile wealth, nor even to lend, but also to make war. Merchant capitalism was highly armed. Urban oligarchies, as in Venice, Florence, Genova, and Amsterdam, had developed mechanisms of state and war financing that may well have been innovations on Roman financial practices, but these practices were now working in a politically deeply fragmented space, setting up systemic financial–fiscal–military competition throughout Europe and beyond. The key to their violent assent was their high tax base, used to underwrite public credit and debt, and enabled by a thoroughly monetized local economy and the wealth of the merchant houses. Merchant adventures as well as naval and military campaigns were calculated, speculative grabbing-enterprises, violent bets on bounty in the form of territory, resources, "capitulations," trade concessions, slaves, and imposed war reparations. These urban bourgeois oligarchies were already imagining themselves as something like a "civil society," and in some cultured ways, they certainly were. But they were also extremely bellicose and endlessly greedy, in particular during the periods of their violent assent. This is also true for the early relationships within the cities themselves: think of the tower landscapes of Montepulciano, Sienna, and so on, where neighbors could never be fully certain that they could actually defend their wealth against each other. Look at the historical painting collections of the Escorial in Spain, the palace of the Spanish Habsburgs in Central Castile: no theme as ubiquitous there as burning cities, either on the foreground or in the background. Perhaps these late medieval and renaissance city–states were, in financial aspects, not that different from some of the Mediterranean mercantile cities of the Antique period. But the absence of a pacifying presence such as of imperial Rome made all the difference for the wider dynamic. China never knew such protracted fundamental political fragmentation (Rosenthal and Bing Wong 2011; Goldstone 2008).

Law under the Roman Republic made a strict distinction between *imperium* and *dominium*. Dominium represented the economy of private (family) property, in which territorial power was not supposed to intervene; indeed, it was designed to support and protect it (Anderson 2013). Land was privately owned on a very large scale, and great merchant-agricultural fortunes were amassed in particular in the newer Western parts of the Empire (Banaji 2007). The monetary system of the Empire also was a pure ideological example of hard "metallism" (Scheidel 2009). Fortunes thus were safe and could be invested via sophisticated financial tools in speculative projects, including military campaigns. Rome funded part of its undertakings already via state debt. While it pacified the empire, it made private property, wealth, and monetary instruments for accumulation the essence of its legality. Under later feudalism, wealth based in private property began accumulating again; sovereign debt and monetary instruments were once more booming. But there was no ruling center, no imposed pacification. In the end, it was the speculative financiers who either put themselves on the thrones of the most competitive political units (Genova, Florence, United Provinces, United Kingdom) or simply dictated their hard conditionalities for further credit to the sovereigns (see above).

Compare again China in the time of Confucius: all the land remained ultimately the property of the sovereign, as it did elsewhere in Asia (but not in Europe, *pace* Goody). State debt did not exist. On the contrary, the state was the ultimate public creditor. Until the end of the nineteenth century, a succession of Chinese empires had remained without any state debt at all. And while cities did flourish, including their merchants, power ultimately remained with the imperial bureaucrats who cared for justice and the common wealth and used the empire's huge tax base on behalf of public welfare (Rosenthal and Bing Wong 2011).

I am hinting that the long-term possibility of bourgeois revolution(s) was inscribed into the social structures, relationships, institutions, and legality of the spaces of Western Eurasia to a markedly greater degree than in Eastern or Central zones. I am also suggesting that the key precondition to that opening was the political and military ascent of private property in its ultimate realization as speculative finance capital. There are three essential moments to this argument, and it is their combination that matters: private property and accumulation as the basic rule of politics and empire since the Greeks; the absence of a pacifying and dominating center since the fall of Rome; and the gradual subsumption of the successor Holy Roman Empire and its anti-usury imperatives to the logics of speculative finance, including crucially the rise of military–fiscal city–states in merchant capitalist mode dictating the rules of their international transactional system to everybody else.

This is not meant to be a deterministic or teleological claim, just one of possibilities, probabilities, and elective affinities. In the West, there was a violent swing between the rule of antifinance and the rule of finance; in the East, balanced and meritocratic rule by a succession of commercial-cum-public-goods–oriented empires without either the full repression (as under early feudalism) nor the actual sovereignty (as under capitalism) of finance (Rosenthal and Bin Wong 2011). This overlaps with Graeber's vision, but I align it not with a Maussian issue of morality per se. Rather, I am seeking a revisionist Marxist account that follows Banaji's (2013) very persuasive and richly informed call to take historical merchant capitalism, and indeed financial capitalism as its purest form (less studied by Banaji), more seriously—an argument further extended in Jason Moore's work (2015), which highlights the specific forms of cognition and epistemes associated with the rise of merchant capital. I would like to bring that insight into conversation with Neil Davidson's insistence that we need to think in more versatile, diversified, and deeper ways about the historical concept of the bourgeois revolution (2017). I am not at all interested in a synchronic determinist and *apriori*stic argument privileging circulation over production. Such debates are barren. Rather, I think there is space for a sophisticated idea of how credit, debt, the omnipresent advances to laborers and entrepreneurs by liquid asset owning classes in history (see Banaji 2013), and in particular the gradual usurpation of imperial (and not just urban or national) sovereignty by merchant–investor classes and outright finance capitalists—"primitive accumulators" armed to the teeth and ready and able to grab, dispossess, and regulate—finally took control not just of production itself, but of the entirety of the social reproduction of Western peoples and societies; and then, as in combined and uneven development and Trotsky's "whip of history," subjecting the world as a whole, and in always variegating and differentiating ways, to those patterned relations and logics.

For this vision to work, one must also reject all traces of methodological nationalism or any place-bound visions of social process. We are talking about long run space-making transformations in social relations, indeed class relations, that include international relations just as well as state making, institution building, and the associated legalities. The bourgeois revolution unfolded historically in the United Provinces, the UK, and France. But the making of those units was itself the outcome of an unbounded process of space making, with identifiable but shifting actors and a clear ultimate directionality. It is this century's long process that we must grasp and not fetishize the units that emerged as part of it. The drivers behind that long-run space-making process can be summarized as the bourgeois revolution. We are talking about Western Europe as a whole and a period of some three hundred years, with 1688–94 as the moment in which the rule of finance seems to have become irreversible (Israel 2008; Kalb 2013). The core of this transnational story that culminates in an unprecedented domination of the North Atlantic zone is the making of the capitalist-dominated state-finance nexus. By the mid-1850s, the finance nexus of all independent states was modeled more or less on the financialized mechanisms of the city–states and the United Kingdom. And all were geared toward setting up private property rights, creating mass fiscal bases, and allowing money and finance to force people and territories into debt, into labor, into productivity, and into the accumulation of capital. Robert Brenner (see Aston and Philpin 2010) and Eric Wolf (1982) were entirely right to insist that capital ultimately had to penetrate production, dispossess peasantries, turn them into disposable labor on variable wages, and impose the capitalist regime of value not just on the cities but also on land and labor in the countrysides and the global peripheries in order to become not just dominant but determinant. All these older Marxist insights remain valid. But that deeper penetration of capitalist logics could only happen, and indeed *did* only happen, after finance capital had subdued the summits of sovereignty in the state system, had constitutionalized any grabbing and enclosures as robust legal property rights, and had begun financing the making of global capitalist Western empires such as the United Kingdom that would ultimately outpace in overall productivity, and above all in military might, not just France, India, Russia, Persia, and the Ottoman Empire, but even China.

Jonathan Friedman has long argued that "abstract wealth" was the natural condition of capital, not "production," factories, mines, or fields. In developing their macro historical anthropology of global systems, Kajsa Ekholm-Friedman and Jonathan Friedman produced a set of publications from the late 1970s onward that were pathbreaking, though largely ignored within the anthropology discipline. They featured cycles of global financialization as a key driver of social, historical, and spatial transformation (Friedman 1978; Ekholm-Friedman and Friedman 2008; see also Kalb 2013). Their major inspiration was Rosa Luxemburg. My vision here is different, though certainly indebted to theirs. Only with Giovanni Arrighi's magnum opus (1994) did the topic of financialization cycles come back on the agenda of the historical social sciences. My account builds on his, but Arrighi, following Braudel and Marx, assumed that financialization was a recurrent response to the overaccumulation of capital in production. Harvey, too, calls capital in production the primary circuit and sees flows in the secondary and tertiary circuits as at least partially driven by overaccumulation in the first (Harvey 2007). Marxism, true to Marx's fascination with the emergence of factory production and the labor theory of value, is perhaps preprogrammed to construct such orderly sequences emanating from within production. I just want to point out here that, even within Arrighi's schema, any upcoming hegemon must be inundated with capital from a former one and thus must always already be deeply financialized, in a semidependent way, from the beginning. Many peripheral states started out as newly independent sovereign units already deeply indebted to the older capitalist networks of which they were the speculative outcome, just as the UK itself was indebted to the United Provinces, and China after 1989 to the United States.

From Big History to Histories of the Contemporary

My discussion in the preceding sections is continued in a macrohistorical vein in the following chapter by Richard Robbins, who places the United States in a direct line of development from the bourgeois revolutions of seventeenth-century Europe. The remaining chapters are more specific in their focus. The locations are mostly Eurasian, but outside the mainstream of neoliberalism.

The credit and debt structures we explore are not studied *sui-generis*, but as a set of identifiable interstitial and multiscalar relationships between finance, economics, and other institutional fields, such as states, law, religion, urban regions, environments, housing, and households. Finance seeks to order those other fields with an eye on gaining untrammeled access to value and future earnings, and securing control over the extractive monetary income streams from which it lives. Other fields, in their turn, seek influence over finance, or try to embed it at least partially into logics with a different nature and interest. It is necessary to consider a plethora of interstitial relationships. The financialization of societies always impinges on relationships between classes within the everyday life of human habitats, where credit, debt, labor, households, and public domains are reconfigured to create new fields of force in the social reproduction of societies and communities. We see class also in the widely spun spatial webs of interdependence between the conditions of local social reproduction and the demands of the often absentee lords of finance capital: class relationships are not just bound to place or bounded by the nation, but emerge within a multitiered transnational space. They take shape in social reproduction generally, not just in the labor that people have to expend for a wage in order to make such reproduction and debt payments possible. Other fields of work and care are similarly relevant (Kalb 2015; Fraser and Jaeggi 2018). Both the big history and the local histories of financialization are constituted through continuous push and pull in the relations between classes of creditors and classes of debtors. Other class segments play a role in that relationship—industrial capital is not necessarily in favor of a growing piece of the pie being eaten by finance via inflated housing costs and interest payments for its workers (Harvey 2017; Kalb 1997). Nor are states always in the pockets of capital. In the Norwegian case (Myhre, this volume), it appears almost the other way around. Financialization is therefore always a contentious story in which big or small concessions are imposed mostly on debtors, sometimes on creditors, and always with morality, law, the state, and other actors deeply involved. As a big story, it may sometimes seem to have one directionality, resulting in the increasing overall dependence of the social reproduction of societies on finance capital: the new extractivism (Mezzadra and Neilson 2019). But states are crucial intermediators, either in organizing the ways in which finance is allowed to hit the ground, or in allowing other actors to talk back. That big unfolding history has recurrently seen switches and alterations in the relational modalities of finance. These are relational contestations: either emergent, in the open, still private, or perhaps publicly silenced after prior possibilities were closed down; sometimes fuzzy, sometimes crystal clear and articulate.

The Chapters

In Chapter 1, Richard Robbins applies the concept of "monetary streams" to make visible the extent to which creditor–debtor relationships literally pervade economy and society and have replaced labor as the key to value extraction and, perhaps, to class formation. He shows that outstanding credit is heavily concentrated among the 10 percent highest earners, with the great majority of it owned by the 1 percent. Debts unsurprisingly concentrate among the 90 percent. Robbins also underlines the rather shocking fact that since the 1970s, Americans have paid more interest to finance than taxes to the state. He further discusses the legal seniority rule of creditors over debtors under liberal capitalism and notes that so far, no democratic objections to this rule have had much of an impact. His suggestion is that since debt has replaced labor as the core class relationship that sustains the contemporary US plutocracy, a debt strike would be the logical equivalent of the labor strike. The seniority rule should be one of its political targets. Robbins also powerfully illustrates the sheer unsustainability of the present system, even in its own terms. It requires perpetual and exponential economic growth to cover even just the compound interest owed to its actual owners (cf. Harvey 2017). For actual pay back of debts, he calculates a necessary growth rate of close to 15 percent—an economic absurdity, to say nothing of the ecological, social, and political implications.

Despite this being so, world governance institutions such as the World Bank are still committed to offering "financial inclusion" to the world's 1–2 billion poor people. By offering them small state transfers and micro loans, it is imagined that they can be lifted out of poverty. Sohini Kar (Chapter 2) studied the recent initiatives of the Modi government in India and summarizes them as "accumulation by saturation." Influential neoliberals such as Hernando de Soto (2001) used to celebrate the informal economy for its hidden assets, its entrepreneurial initiatives, and as a popular seedbed for capitalism. Anthropologists such as Keith Hart (2001) have also embraced money in this spirit for antibureaucratic reasons. Hindu nationalist India, however, is now planning a cashless society, where all the monetary streams will be digital and monitored by banks. The state has recently added more than 200 million accounts to its banking system through "mass account-opening drives." Kar shows that in order to make these accounts attractive for those without savings, Modi's BJP government offers a small overdraft plus life and health insurance. Despite its neoliberal provenance, the government seems keen to add its own additions to India's plethora of cash transfer programs to the poor. It expects to reduce the costs of such programs, such as the cooking gas subsidy, by setting them up as digital transfers into registered bank accounts and circumventing local corruption in the delivery of such transfers. Meanwhile, bankers are explaining to Kar that all of this only makes sense from a banker's standpoint if and when the banks can begin to offer credits to the poor via those accounts. This, of course, assumes that the government comes up with an enforceable fix for the expected rise of "non-performing loans" among the poor (see also the chapters by James, Davey, Mikuš, and Kofti). Accumulation by saturation, Kar suggests, or the "new enclosures," is about constructing the infrastructure for endless small monetary streams to continuously add to the liquidity base of India's finance capitalists. Kar is decidedly more skeptical about such "progressive" development policies than James Ferguson in his influential account of South African digitalized transfer programs (2015).

Skepticism is also expressed by Charlotte Bruckermann (Chapter 3) concerning the Chinese state's efforts to counter environmental devastation and toxic air quality at the end of history's greatest industrialization and urbanization drive through the financialization of the environment. Xi Jinping's China is developing a "green financial system" with a big role for green bonds aimed at transport, energy, recycling, and carbon markets, among others. Finance commands utopian energy as a form of white magic. In the context of exploding indebtedness of both local states and state-owned enterprises in China, the notion of realizing "ecological civilization" with the help of "green finance" gives a new shine and legitimacy to "socialism with Chinese characteristics." Bruckermann discusses how the Chinese pilot carbon markets have quickly become the second largest in the world after the EU. She also looks at what this means on the ground, in the forest communities into which green investments are supposed to flow and which are expected to reap new sources of income from "carbon offset production." In the extensive Fujian carbon forest that she studied, most of the new resources seem to have gone to nonlocal expert labor, university trained specialists in carbon measurement and bookkeeping. Manual labor tasks in the forests are now subcontracted to short-term "fluid labor pools" recruited from among the mostly elderly villagers. As in Kar's account of "accumulation by saturation," a picture emerges of a highly educated, urban carbon-network that is extracting monetary streams, now called carbon credits, from forests that in an earlier regime were tended by local worker collectives and state-owned forestry employees, some of whom once had their livelihoods guaranteed by the "iron rice bowl." Bruckermann shows how villagers talk about value, nature, labor, and life; and how they indulge in theorizing the ongoing unpaid work of both humans and nature that is offered as a free gift for, and beyond, the carbon economy.

While Modi's BJP-Hinduists and Xi Jinping's "socialists with Chinese characteristics" seek to align the elusive promises of finance with their public policy goals, Malaysia, an oil exporter, has been trying to cast part of its financial sector along the lines of Islamic ethical banking. Since the Asian crisis of the late 1990s, Malaysian governments have deliberately picked fights with US hedge funds and Goldman Sachs. This may be part of the background for the country's key role in the development of Islamic finance. As Aaron Pitluck describes (Chapter 4), Malaysia is actively engaged in promoting, producing, and regulating Islamic finance. The state has required domestic actors, from the Central Bank to individual banks, to bring in, develop, and adopt Sharia knowledge. Bonds and equities that deserve to be called Islamic have to bear the stamp of "Shariah Advisory Committees" in which "bureaucratic ethicists" and Sharia scholars discuss, improve, and eventually approve their ethical quality from the standpoint of Islam. Various transnational bodies also help to define what Islamic finance is supposed to be. Pitluck's research among Malaysian investment bankers and the Sharia specialists advising them suggests that these Councils are capable of "altering the trajectory" of conventional finance. He also concludes that the Malaysian framework enables the Councils to exert "genuine power" within investment banks. Pitluck concedes, however, that the *sukuk* market is a "moralized niche market," supported among others by the demand from the Malaysian government itself. His careful research shows that the organizational position of Sharia scholars within the investment banking process, while varying between banks and cases, is often rather weak. Their agency is more oriented toward dialogue and gradual ethical improvement of the activities of investment bankers than straightforward rule making. There is no public audit of their activities, or of their outcomes. No doubt, the trajectories of financialization can be altered. But it seems a fair hunch that without broad and active democratic pressure, Sharia scholars backed by a moderate Islamic state may find that the margins, overall, may be small. It is perhaps telling that despite the international character of the Muslim world, and the close links between Muslim societies, there is little visible international pressure toward Islamicizing finance in the Muslim world *tout court*.

In Tristam Barrett's case (Chapter 5), we meet another oil exporter: Azerbaijan. Like India and other low-income countries, Azerbaijan has been advised to work toward financial inclusion of its citizens. Nothing should be easier for an oil exporter flush with petro-dollars (oil generates 40–50 percent of GDP), one would imagine. Azerbaijan could be a canonical case for what Alessandro Mezzadra has recently called the new extractivism: using the income from classic extractivist resource exports for a new-fangled web of financial extractivism spread over the poor suburbs, benevolently labeled financial inclusion (Mezzadra and Neilson 2019). But this would be to discount the particular nature of Azerbaijan as a post-Soviet oligarchic, nationalist, privatized state-complex. Barrett sees Azerbaijan as a closed oligarchic gambling economy, epitomized by its banking sector. International banks play a minor role. Azeri banks function mainly as in-house storage and recycling bureaucracies for oligarchic oil revenue: they serve the international valorization of privatized oil wealth. Secondarily, they cultivate patronage toward the employees and friends of the billionaires by offering them mortgages and loans. Everyone else, Barrett shows, finds it hard to get a mortgage. Personal loans are mostly offered with extortionate conditions. Even such extortionate loans, however, are hard to get from the official banks, if only because few people work under formal labor contracts and thus cannot provide proof of regular income and tax payments, which are a legal requirement. Here, timing might play an unrecognized role in Barrett's account. His work suggests that in the period of 2006 to 2015, immediately preceding his field research, an explosion of popular indebtedness had taken place, much of that in foreign exchange due to the lower interest rates charged on the dollar than on the local currency of peripheral societies such as Azerbaijan (cf. Mikuš on Croatia). This lending cycle came to an abrupt end when the oil price suddenly collapsed in 2015. The local currency quickly lost 50 percent of its value, and the foreign exchange debts of citizens and banks doubled

overnight. Azerbaijan was forced to call in the IMF to refinance and con-
solidate its now deeply indebted banking sector while pacifying their powerful owners. No wonder that Barrett in these circumstances finds almost
no one in Baku having access to easy credit. Personal loans, formal and
informal, are still taken out by the majority of the population to finance life
cycle events such as the setting up of a new couple after marriage. The new
couple is given one or two renovated and refurnished rooms in the pater-
nal house or apartment. But it is not easy to get such loans on reasonable
terms. Often, trusted relationships must be mobilized. High fees and high
interest rates beyond what the state regulates are common. Barrett speaks
ironically of "domesticating finance" when he describes how problems with
paying back such overcharged loans generally result in a call on kinship and
friendship relations to bail people out (cf. the chapter by Kofti): kinship as
the credit institution of last resort in an oligarchic gamble economy where
the petrodollars get stuck at the privatized top of the pyramid and are then
recycled abroad.

It would be hard to find a greater contrast to the methods of "domesticating" a flood of petro revenues than Norway. In Azerbaijan, 20 percent of
GDP is transferred by foreign oil majors as royalties into the bank accounts
of a privatized oligarchical *rentier* state complex, while kinship serves as
the ultimate collateral for the common people. In Norway, we find a broad
national democratic consensus that the oil wealth generated among others
by its own *Statoil* (now Equinor) belongs, via taxation and dividends, to
the Norwegian nation as a whole (even though there is substantial private
exploration, and Equinor itself is increasingly aligned with private capital);
and instead of kinship, we find a sophisticated welfare state running the
largest wealth fund on earth for 5.5 million Norwegians. Norway concen-
trates its oil revenue in the Central Bank to invest it in global stocks and
equities via its Sovereign Wealth Fund. The Fund then transfers a percentage of its yearly income on those securities to the state. This amounts to 20
percent of the national budget, and it is equally disbursed over the various
ministries, subject to yearly discretion by the parliament. In Chapter 6,
Knut Christian Myhre summarily discusses the history of (and political
contestations around) the Fund in Norway. Here, there are no dictates to a
state by international markets, as in most other locations, but rather "custodial finance" functioning on behalf of the democratic Norwegian nation
and its future members, carefully procured by a universal public creditor invested in broad global portfolios with a lightly ethical and feminist
program for capitalist world governance, keen on at least rhetorically supporting a greenish transition out of the global carbon quagmire (but investing in the oil majors while Equinor continues exploring new fields farther
up North). Also of note, this largest Sovereign Wealth Fund on earth owns

around 1.5 percent of all global stocks, managed by democratic politicians and national bureaucrats, with asset managers subordinate to the democratic and consensual will of the Norwegian nation. Is Norway by now a *rentier* state, Myhre finally wonders? It is a pertinent question. He answers with a nuanced denial. First, if 20 percent of the state budget comes from the Fund's global revenues, the other 80 percent still comes from taxes. Moreover, the Fund adheres to a mission that its revenues should contribute to "the business and labor of the Norwegian nation." Hence, Myhre concludes, the Fund "affords labor" rather than allowing labor to subsist on rents. One could object that this is just how Norway has elected to mask and operationalize its *rentier* nature. Norwegian democracy in that version is doing a lot of work to obscure the inevitably *rentier*-nature of a considerable part of its contemporary financial resources. It does so precisely by investing those resources, directly and indirectly, in making the labor of its well-educated people possible according to the norms of socially necessary labor time as presently valid in the global system. *Rentier* incomes, yes, but no wish to corrupt the national capacity to labor. This must seem only morally fair for such a wealthy and happy nation, given the very substantial contributions to Norwegian society derived from the Fund. These depend, whether Norwegians like it or not, on the speculative ups and downs of the global stock-markets as well as on the lives and labor of millions of workers worldwide from which the Fund extracts its income. Norway is inevitably a *rentier* capitalist nation, albeit an apparently enlightened, fair, democratic, and hard-working one.

Hadas Weiss's Germans (Chapter 7) similarly live in practical denial of the financialized nature of German capitalism. As in the Norwegian case, this is enabled by the fact that massive German manufacturing profits are systematically routed outward, into the global stock-markets and into the sovereign debt markets of the European Union, in speculative pursuit of foreign rents. Germany as an industrial export power since its formation has always been dependent on a Western/global capitalism defined and controlled elsewhere (UK, United States)—except for a calamitous period of *Größenwahn*. This has set up the German state and nation as a paragon of shared believers in hard money and metallism theories. This might well be the deeper reason why the Euro continues to fail as a true global currency such as the US dollar, and why austerity is hardwired into the European Union. An almost constitutionalized *Inflationsangst* is part of this *gestalt*. Disciplined employers, furthermore, confront an unevenly organized industrial working class, a class that is also spread out over a plethora of low-cost countries in Eastern Europe, so as to give downward wage pressures an almost systemic character. The large rental housing sectors of post-Bismarck Germany have never been privatized, in contrast to Thatcher's Britain.

Housing costs have remained affordable, adding to the overall low costs of social reproduction in Germany. The same is true for education, health, and pensions: all organized as public goods maintained via taxes, transfers, and public choice. Surplus capital has to be moved out of this set-up swiftly, lest it would destroy it all. Weiss's chapter explains why Germany is not financialized as the Anglosaxon nations, Spain, or the Netherlands are. Financialized subjectivities are absent among participants in financial education. Instead, her informants as well as their teachers prefer to approach finance as a utility. Both the state and its subjects are attached to a moral notion of saving as a prudential act with an eye on future needs, and to prevent *Schuld* (indebtedness). As interest rates have fallen and savings cannot do that prudential work reliably anymore, Germans are advised to shift part of their household savings to equity funds. Weiss reports that they imagine these funds to be invested in German corporations that provide jobs for the German population. As the German welfare state has been reducing the scope of some of its protective functions, equity is advertised as a functional complement to a state that increasingly fails to live up to its promises. It is at this point, Weiss suggests, that an opening for a vernacular political critique emerges: capitalism and finance are unmasked as the corrupters of industrial Germany as a willed collective utility.

With Deborah James in Chapter 8, we enter the world of recognizable, neoliberal, financialized cases. Financial inclusion has been abundantly achieved. Numerous authors of our later chapters address the issues that then arise, notably debt collection (James, Davey, Mikuš, Kofti). James looks at debt advice services in the UK and South Africa, and claims, surprisingly, that within processes of financialization, there is sometimes also a new form of redistribution going on that ameliorates the worst cases of extraction. Debt advice services, in her vision, do not only help to sort out the finances of the indebted, but also sometimes fight back against financialized bureaucratic structures of routine extortionate overreach. Interestingly, under austerity in the UK, local states seem to have become precisely such an institution. In South Africa, the collusion of benefit transfer systems and easy credit within one commercial quasi-banking organization has turned supposedly private bank accounts "almost into a place of looting"—a cynical solution to the problem of loans among the poor. In the UK, some of such debt advice services are paid for by a small tax on the same financial institutions that do the extraction. In South Africa, such services are offered by NGOs, some of which are supported by mining capitalists who do not want to see their workers' lives threatened by aggressive debt collection agencies. This was a major issue in the Marikana workers' protests of 2014. James looks at the different historical and political environments in these two thoroughly financialized states and shows the different operational modus, interstitial locations, methods, and ethical motives of the debt advisors, and argues that they are more effective than one might think.

In Chapter 9, Ryan Davey takes this focus on debt advice further by zooming in on the actual interactions between advisors and their indebted clients on an English housing estate. His evaluation of such advice services is more skeptical than that of James. Instead of redistribution, he sees the conflicting moral dimensions of class operating within these interactions. The advisors are generally recruited from a deserving, disciplined, and respectable working class (or "lower middle class" in UK vernacular class taxonomy), some of them with military backgrounds, and are themselves experiencing public-sector pay freezes and possible redundancies. They have little tolerance for the consumerism and the apparent irresponsibility of the indebted. The forms that clients have to fill in, too, express a moral vision that rejects indebtedness *tout court*, except when it represents an investment in upward mobility, such as a mortgage. While advisers know in theory that precariousness is structural, in practice, they explain it as a personal moral failure to conform to normal middle class aspirations. Housing estate inhabitants return the prejudice by refusing to trust them. They would avoid asking for their help as long as they can. Davey concludes with a carefully argued rejection of the underclass-formation thesis and further reflections on class formation in general.

The next four chapters present an East European and three South European cases, all focusing on private indebtedness and the legal and moral politics of credit and debt. Marek Mikuš studies debt collection practices in Croatia. Western publics have been well informed about the Mediterranean cases but not so much about the Central-East European (CEE) ones. CEE countries have been thoroughly financialized after 2000. Western banks took over big chunks of weakly regulated banking sectors. If so allowed, they began offering foreign exchange loans and mortgages with lower interest rates than in the local currencies, borrowing the money on the international markets in a classic carry trade. Personal indebtedness in CEE, rather low until the early 2000s, was by 2008 already approaching the level of the European South (more than 40 percent of GDP; I note that this level is much higher in Northern champions of financialization like the Netherlands, the UK, or Ireland, where it is around 100 percent). What was different was that much private debt in CEE was in foreign currency. Such "forex" debts increased substantially in value against the Swiss Franc and the Euro in the course of the financial crisis (cf. Barrett on Azerbaijan, this volume). In Croatia, debt arrears are punished harshly, as Mikuš shows. Creditors have been given some powerful collection tools that entirely bypass the court system. All enforcement proceedings on nonperforming loans are centralized in one state agency for debt collection, which has the administrative authority to block bank accounts immediately and authorize regular pay back transfers, even without informing the account holder, not entirely unlike James's South African case. Creditors sometimes register a nonperforming loan even before communicating with clients, or not communicating at all. This public agency charges extortionate fees, which can easily inflate a small debt of fifty Kuna into an immediate liability five or six times the original amount. At some point in the mid-2010s, almost one in ten Croats had their bank account blocked. One might be surprised to hear that it was the EU that had insisted on streamlining debt collection and the associated legality this way, but this is not an isolated incident. The postsocialist Croatian state, desirous of European membership, was eager to submit to international demands. Some of the Zagreb-based state classes of legal specialists and accountants appear to have inserted themselves rather profitably into the resulting comprador networks. Ongoing mass outmigration, meanwhile, is often associated, both in popular stories and in actual fact, with efforts to escape debt collection. Mikuš discusses vernacular conspiracy theories of international finance bent on destroying the Croat nation; repossession blockades by Left/Right radical groups; angry neo-nationalist counter-pressures; as well as more centrist proposals for reregulation through parliament.

Dimitra Kofti's Greek case (Chapter 11) offers a sharp contrast to the Croat story of administrative efficiency and blank state support for private debt collection. Greece, after the crisis, under the Troika, was in a state of acute imposed illiquidity as money left the country to pay up for international loans. Banks were more interested in keeping going a trickle of payments from debtors rather than enforcing full repossession of houses or goods for which there was no market anyhow. Moreover, the Syriza-led Greek state had, in rejection of the Troika, vowed to defend citizens against the confiscation of their possessions. A law had been introduced already before the crisis, supported by the whole political spectrum, that secured "primary family domiciles" below a certain "real value" from creditor claims. This put the court system squarely in between citizens and creditors, exactly the opposite of what had happened in Croatia, where the courts had been cut out. Kofti describes the blurred boundaries between "private responsibility" and the social obligations of the Greek *oikos*, which were ambivalently recognized by the legal system too. Her focus is on debt, the changing relational balances within the extended kinship and friendship networks of the *oikos*, class, and the moralizing discourses of the courts and the public in Greece.

Before the great crisis, Spain was widely hailed as a model of neoliberal financialized growth. The expansion of the "ground rent frontier" was the engine of economic growth and "modernization" after the democratic transition. Finance was capitalizing on continued urbanization: investments in the construction and housing sectors, infrastructure, high-speed rail, and the making of new suburban middle class habitats for private and collective consumption—all deeply speculative processes. That regime all but collapsed after 2008. The crisis was less dramatic and less dramatically politicized than in Greece, but it still left hundreds of thousands of families dispossessed from homes that were bought against high prices, supported by an abundance of credit. Here, no governmental change took place, such as in Greece with *Syriza*, and there was no confrontation with the EU. But Spain did develop one of the major Western political movements of the 2010s, and issues of housing and dispossession were among its key drivers. The *indignados* movement subsequently generated the *Podemos* party. Affiliated local groups conquered major political positions and offices in the large cities, and ultimately drove a wedge in the party political system. But what happened outside the big cities? In Chapter 12, Natalia Buier investigates the political reactions of inhabitants of one of the best-known speculative habitats in Spain: *Valdeluz*. Situated 60 kilometers outside Madrid, it was projected as a space for high-middle-class living in a green environment near a planned railway station on the high-speed line toward Barcelona, which would reduce the time distance to central Madrid to a mere fifteen minutes. Buier describes the collapse of the project, the uninhabited spaces, major bankruptcies, stories about corruption, and a once aspiring middle class population now locked into an economically devalued and publicly infamous project disconnected from its wider environment and from the imagined futures that were its very promise. Their mobilization was not in the *Podemos* vein. It was about bringing back the growth machine, pinning hopes on the return of growth and rising exchange values, seeking to build lives around material and emotional investments into the chimera of a stable financialized capitalism.

In a second Spanish case, Marc Morell, in the last ethnographic chapter of this book, shows how the EU is supporting the development of the "sharing economy" around digital platforms for tourism such as Airbnb, and so helping the Spanish state to restart the private accumulation motor that produced the crisis in the first place. Digital "sharing," a boost for capital and assets, is driving up the prices for rental housing and real estate in Spain and on tourist islands such as Majorca in particular. He points at ruling class alliances of larger real estate owners, agency managers, neoliberal academics, and central state bureaucrats that are driving up the factual number of tourist accommodations as well as the value and price of local housing. Their politics also aims to actively reduce the public resources for social housing, crowd out lower earners from local rental markets, and keep local labor fundamentally precarious and deregulated. Finance and the crisis lurk powerfully in the background: in the aftermath of the collapse, the Spanish state sought to offload large numbers of unoccupied and repossessed housing from the banks and the large construction firms into the tourism economy by means of new rounds of credit for buy-to-rent programs, thus recapitalizing the banks and the construction sector. The need for collateral to make use of such buy-to-rent programs immediately suggests that these are aimed at the already owning middle classes, and not for others. Thus, "sharing" has turned into its opposite: a highly socially polarizing game with ownership and rents accruing primarily to a small set of larger owners, associations, and firms. Another cycle of gentrification, now platform and tourism driven, is the result, offering an opportunity for refueling the financialized and real estate based growth model of the early 2000s. Morell also describes the counter movements of local inhabitants, NGOs, and left wing academics, which have kept a certain control over the administration of Ciutat, the capital of Majorca—not to the extent though that actual regulations become enforced: the local administration has failed to build a capacity to monitor the private holiday rentals. *La lucha continúa*, Morell concludes, which is inevitably also the final message of this introduction and the book as a whole.

Acknowledgments

I am very grateful for Chris Hann's invitation in 2014 to co-lead the MPI research group on financialization. I have learned an awful lot. Thanks to our postdocs—Tristam Barrett, Charlotte Bruckermann, Natalia Buier, Dimitra Kofti, Marek Mikuš, and Hadas Weiss—for inspiring collaboration, as well as to Chris, of course. I also thank Professor Sujian Guo and his colleagues for my stay in April 2019 at the Fudan Institute for Advanced Studies, Shanghai. Several longstanding friends have kept inspiring me on the topic of capital and finance. Of these, David Harvey and Gavin Smith should be mentioned explicitly.

Don Kalb is Professor of Social Anthropology at the University of Bergen, Norway, where he leads the Frontlines of Value project. He is also Senior Researcher at Utrecht University. Until 2017, he served as Professor of Sociology and Social Anthropology at Central European University, Budapest. Recent publications include *Anthropologies of Class: Power, Practice, and Inequality* (coedited with James G. Carrier, Cambridge University Press, 2015) and *Worldwide Mobilizations: Class Struggles and Urban Commoning* (coedited with Mao Mollona, Berghahn Books, 2018).

Notes

1. One could say that Graeber combines both Marx and Mauss. This would certainly seem so from his book on value (*Towards an Anthropological Theory of Value*). But in his later work, and in *Debt*, this is much less clear. I have earlier argued that Mauss has taken the upper hand, as he has in anthropology more generally, now and in the past (see Kalb 2014, 2018c).
2. It could be argued that the best theoretician of credit money at the time was John Law, in his text "Money and Trade Considered: with a Proposal for Supplying the Nation with Money." The proposal was for a national bank for (then still independent) Scotland. Like William of Orange with the Bank of England, Law was trying to introduce "Dutch banking" to Scotland. He failed, but later succeeded spectacularly in France, only to be chased out of the country in the middle of a major financial crisis known as "the Mississippi Bubble," which happened at the same time as the "South Sea Bubble" in the British markets. One could summarize his failure as an attempt to introduce "Dutch banking" without the Dutch parliamentary institutions and class structure. William of Orange did better, realizing that they are flanking and mutually reinforcing institutions; with all the resources at his disposal, he did not need to write a treatise. See Buchan 2018; Chancellor 2019; Goetzmann 2016.
3. As was, famously, Alan Greenspan himself, the then FED president (Visser and Kalb 2010; Tooze, 2018). US politicians had been force-fed the $800 billion USD Troubled Asset Relief Program (50 percent bigger than the Pentagon budget) in the fall of 2008 by a Secretary of the Treasury, Henry Paulson, who had been the previous President of Goldman Sachs. Many, Republicans in particular , were furious that no more public money would flow to the bankers—the Tea Party of which President Trump has become the major heir had its origins in that Left/Right anger about socialism for the capitalists.
4. Martin Sandbu, "Draghi shift reveals how elusive monetary normalization remains," *Financial Times*, 12 March 2019.
5. Martin Wolf, "Monetary policy has run its course," *Financial Times*, 13 March 2019.

References

Anderson, Perry. 2013. *Passages from Antiquity to Feudalism*. London: Verso.

Appadurai, Arjun. 2015. *Banking on Words: The Failure of Language in the Age of the Derivative*. Chicago: Chicago University Press.

Arrighi, Giovanni. 2009 [1994]. *The Long Twentieth Century: Money, Power, and the Origins of Our Time*. London: Verso.

Aston, T. H., and C. H. Philpin. 2010. *The Brenner Debate: Agrarian Class Structure and Economic Development in Preindustrial Europe*. Cambridge, UK: Cambridge University Press.

Banaji, Jairus. 2007. *Agrarian Change in Late Antiquity: Gold, Labour, and Aristocratic Dominance*. Oxford: Oxford University Press.

———. 2013. *Theory as History: Essays on Modes of Production and Exploitation*. Leiden: Brill.

Bernanke, Ben. 2016. *Essays on the Great Depression*. Princeton: Princeton University Press.

Braun, Benjamin. 2016. "Speaking to the People? Money, Trust, and Central Bank Legitimacy in the Age of Quantitative Easing." *Review of International Political Economy* 23: 1064–93.

Buchan, James. 2018. *John Law: A Scottish Adventurer of the Eighteenth Century*. London: MacLehose.

Buiter, Willem. 2014. "The Simple Analytics of Helicopter Money: Why It Works— Always." *Economics* 8 (August). doi: org/10.5018/economics-ejournal.ja.2014-28. Available at SSRN: https://ssrn.com/abstract=2484853.

Carrier, James, and Don Kalb, eds. 2015. *Anthropologies of Class: Power, Practice, and Inequality*. Cambridge, UK: Cambridge University Press.

Chancellor, Edward. 2019. "The Man Who Invented Money." *New York Review of Books* LXVI, no. 7 (18 April): 47–49.

Clapham, John. 1944. *The Bank of England: A History*. Cambridge, UK: Cambridge University Press.

Davidson, Neil. 2017. *How Revolutionary Were the Bourgeois Revolutions?* Chicago: Haymarket Books.

De Soto, Hernando. 2001. *The Mystery of Capital*. London: Black Swan.

Di Muzio, Tim, and Richard Robbins. 2016. *Debt as Power*. Manchester: Manchester University Press.

Ekholm-Friedman, Kajsa, and Jonathan Friedman. 2008. *The Anthropology of Global Systems*. Vols. 1 and 2. Lanham: Altamira Press.

Emirbayer, Mustafa. 1997. "Manifesto for a Relational Sociology." *American Journal of Sociology* 103, no. 2: 281–317.

Ferguson, James. 2015. *Give a Man a Fish: Reflections on the New Politics of Distribution*. Durham: Duke University Press.

Fraser, Nancy, and Rahel Jaeggi. 2018. *Capitalism: A Conversation in Critical Theory*. London: Polity Press.

Friedman, Jonathan. 1978. "Crises in Theory and Transformations of the World Economy." *Review* (Fernand Braudel Center) 2, no. 2: 131–46.

Fullwiler, Scott, Stephanie Kelton, and Randall Wray. 2012. "Modern Monetary Theory: A Response to Critics." In *Modern Monetary Theory: A Debate*. Amherst: Political Economy Research Institute.

Goetzmann, William. 2016. *Money Changes Everything: How Finance Made Civilization Possible*. Princeton: Princeton University Press.

Goldstone, Jack. 2008. *Why Europe? The Rise of the West in World History, 1500–1850*. New York: McGraw-Hill.

Goody, Jack. 2004. *Capitalism and Modernity: The Great Debate*. London: Polity Press.
———. 2009. *The Eurasian Miracle*. London: Polity Press.

Graeber, David. 2002. *Towards an Anthropological Theory of Value: The False Coin of our Dreams*. London: Palgrave McMillan.
———. 2011. *Debt: The First 5000 Years*. Brooklyn: Melville House.

Hart, Keith. 2001. *Money in an Unequal World*. New York: Texere.

Harvey, David. 2007. *The Limits to Capital*. London: Verso.

———. 2017. *Marx, Capital, and the Madness of Economic Reason*. London: Profile Books.

Hertz, Ellen. 1998. *The Trading Crowd: An Ethnography of the Shanghai Stockmarket*. Cambridge, UK: Cambridge University Press.

Ho, Karen. 2009. *Liquidated: An Ethnography of Wall Street*. Durham: Duke University Press.

Hocket, Robert, and Saule Omarova. 2017. "The Finance Franchise." *Cornell Law Review* 102 (July): 1144–218.

Holmes, Douglas. 2013. *Economy of Words: Communicative Imperatives in Central Banks*. Chicago: Chicago University Press.

Israel, Jonathan. 2008. *The Anglo Dutch Moment: Essays on the Glorious Revolution and Its World Impact*. Cambridge, UK: Cambridge University Press.

James, Deborah. 2015. *Money from Nothing: Indebtedness and Aspiration in South Africa*. Palo Alto: Stanford University Press.

Kalb, Don. 1997. *Expanding Class: Power and Everyday Politics in Industrial Communities. The Netherlands 1850–1950*. Durham: Duke University Press.

———. 2005. "From Flows to Violence: Politics and Knowledge in the Debates on Globalization and Empire." *Anthropological Theory* 5, no. 2: 176–204.

———. 2013. "Financialization and the Capitalist Moment: Marx versus Weber in the Anthropology of Global Systems." *American Ethnologist* 40, no. 2: 258–66.

———. 2014. "Mavericks: Harvey, Graeber, and the Reunification of Anarchism and Marxism in World Anthropology." *Focaal* 69: 113–34.

———. 2015. "Introduction: Class and the New Anthropological Holism." In *Anthropologies of Class*, ed. James Carrier and Don Kalb, 1–27. Cambridge, UK: Cambridge University Press.

———. 2018a. "Austerity and 'the Discipline of Historical Context.'" In *The Global Life of Austerity: Comparing beyond Europe*, ed. Theodoros Rakopoulos, 130–49. New York: Berghahn Books (Critical Interventions).

———. 2018b. "Deep Play: Finance, Demos and Ethnos in the New Old Europe." In *The Margins of the State*, ed. Bruce Kapferer, 23–66. Canon Pyon: Sean Kingston Publishing.

———. 2018c. "Trotsky over Mauss: Anthropological Theory and the October 1917 Commemoration." *Dialectical Anthropology* 42, no. 3: 327–43.

———. 2018d. "Upscaling Illiberalism: Class, Contradiction, and the Rise of the Populist Right in Post-Socialist Central Europe." *Fudan Journal of the Humananities and Social Sciences* 11, no. 3: 303–21.

Kalb, Don, and Gabor Halmai, eds. 2011. *Headlines of Nation, Subtexts of Class: Working Class Populism and the Return of the Repressed in Neoliberal Europe*. New York: Berghahn Books.

Kalb, Don, and Mao Mollona. 2018. "Introductory Thoughts on Anthropology and Urban Insurrection." In *Worldwide Mobilizations: Class Struggles and Urban Commoning*, ed. Don Kalb and Mao Mollona, 1–30. New York: Berghahn Books.

Kalb, Don, and Herman Tak, eds. 2005. *Critical Junctions: Anthropology and History beyond the Cultural Turn*. New York: Berghahn Books.

Keynes, John Maynard. 2011 [1930]. *A Treatise on Money*. London: Martino Fine Books.
———. 2017 [1936]. *General Theory of Employment, Interest, and Money*. London: Macmillan.
Knapp, Georg Friedrich. 1924 [1905]. *The State Theory of Money*. London: Macmillan.
Legrain, Philippe. 2014. *European Spring: Why Our Economies and Politics Are in a Mess—And How to Put Them Right*. Marstongate: CB Books.
LiPuma, Edward. 2017. *The Social Life of Financial Derivatives*. Durham: Duke University Press.
Magnus, George. 2018. *Red Flags: Why Xi's China Is in Jeopardy*. New Haven: Yale University Press.
McLeay, Michael, Amar Radia, and Ryland Thomas. 2014. "Money Creation in the Modern Economy." Bank of England Quarterly Bulletin Q1. Available at SSRN: https://ssrn.com/abstract=2416234.
Mezzadra, Alessandro, and Brett Neilson. 2019. *The Politics of Operations: Excavating Contemporary Capitalism*. Durham, NC: Duke University Press.
Mintz, Sidney. 1986. *Sweetness and Power: The Place of Sugar in the Modern World*. London: Penguin.
Mitchell-Innis, Alfred. 1913. "What Is Money?" *The Banking Law Journal* (May): 377–408.
Moore, Jason. 2015. *Capitalism in the Web of Life: Ecology and the Accumulation of Capital*. London: Verso Books.
Parks, Tim. 2006. *Medici Money: Banking, Metaphysics and Art in Fifteenth Century Florence*. London: Profile Books
Parry, Jonathan, and Maurice Bloch, eds. 1989. *Money and the Morality of Exchange*. Cambridge, UK: Cambridge University Press.
Pettifor, Ann. 2017. *The Production of Money: How to Break the Power of Bankers*. London: Verso.
Pitluck, Aaron, Fabio Mattioli, and Daniel Souleles. 2018. "Finance beyond Function: Three Causal Explanations for Financialization." *Economic Anthropology* 5, no. 2: 157–71.
Rosenthal, Jean-Laurent, and R. Bin Wong. 2011. *Before and Beyond Divergence: The Politics of Economic Change in China and Europe*. Cambridge, MA: Harvard University Press.
Scheidel, Walter. 2009. "The Monetary Systems of the Han and Roman Empires." In *Rome and China: Comparative Perspectives on Ancient World Empires*, ed. Walter Scheidel, 137–209. Oxford: Oxford University Press.
———, ed. 2009. *Rome and China: Comparative Perspectives on Ancient World Empires*. Oxford: Oxford University Press.
Shaxson, Nicholas. 2018. *The Finance Curse: How Global Finance Is Making Us All Poorer*. London: Penguin.
Slobodian, Quin. 2018. *Globalists: The End of Empire and the Birth of Neoliberalism*. Cambridge, MA: Harvard University Press.
Smith, Gavin. 2014. *Intellectuals and Counter-Politics: Essays in Historical Realism*. New York: Berghahn Books.

Tilly, Charles. 1998. *Durable Inequality*. Berkeley: University of California Press.

———. 2001. "Relational Origins of Inequality." *Anthropological Theory* 1, no. 3: 355–72.

Tooze, Adam. 2018. *Crashed: How a Decade of Financial Crises Changed the World*. London: Allen Lane.

Visser, Oane, and Don Kalb. 2010. "Financialised Capitalism Soviet Style? Varieties of State Capture and Crisis." *European Journal of Sociology/Archives Europeenes de Sociology* L, no. 2: 171–94.

Vogel, Joseph. 2017. *The Ascendency of Finance*. London: Polity Press.

Wolf, Eric. 1982. *Europe and the People Without History*. Berkeley: University of California Press.

———. 2001. *Pathways of Power: Building an Anthropology of the Modern World*. Berkeley: University of California Press.

Wolf, Martin. 2015. *The Shifts and the Shocks: What We've Learned—and Have Still to Learn—from the Financial Crisis*. London: Penguin.

Zaloom, Caitlin. 2010. *Out of the Pits: Traders and Technology from Chicago to London*. Chicago: Chicago University Press.

1

Financialization, Plutocracy, and the Debtor's Economy

Consequences and Limits

RICHARD H. ROBBINS

It is our belief that if forecasts of slower real GDP growth come to pass, then it is highly likely that future real returns to capital will likewise be significantly below past historical averages.

—Dean Baker, J. Bradford DeLong, and Paul Krugman,
"Asset Returns and Economic Growth"

Beyond war, inflation, the end of the technology/productivity wave, and financial collapse, we think the most potent and short-term threat [to investors] would be societies demanding a more "equitable" share of wealth.

—*Citigroup Memo*, 2006

When financial advisors at investment bank Citigroup (Kapor et al 2006: 7), in their now notorious Plutonomy Memos, counseled their clients to maximize their rate of return on capital by investing in products and services purchased by the most wealthy, they made it plain that the financial community not only recognized the plutocratic nature of Western society but was fully willing to take advantage. At the same time, they apparently feared a rebellion by the bottom 90 percent over the continued expropriation by the 1 percent of an increasing share of the national wealth—a warning later echoed by Thomas Piketty (2014: 263).

This document was a celebration of the financialization of the global economy, where profits accrue through financial channels rather than through trade and commodity production (Arrighi 1994: 371; Krippner 2005: 174–75; 2012: 27–28). This chapter explores the origins and prerequisites of financialization—and also its consequences, notably the growth in economic inequality. I also want to examine how and why the field of economics has failed to understand the plutocratic consequences of financialization, and what sort of changes are necessary to ward off economic collapse or popular revolt.

I begin with the fact that creditors, which are banks, private investors, and debt and equity holders in general, are demanding an ever-increasing share of the world's economic output. Their power is guaranteed by the prime directive that creditors always come first; that is, before money can be spent on anything—children's welfare, public health, education, environmental preservation, poverty reduction, and so on—creditors have priority.[1] Presently, it seems nothing can change this rule: not democratic politics, not public demonstrations, not large-scale educational campaigns, and not even violent resistance. The rule has various corollaries, among them the requirement that the economy must grow perpetually and exponentially, and the requirement that more and more of daily life and its accouterments must be transformed into monetary streams to service the ever-increasing demands of creditors and investors. How this situation and creditor rule came about is a story about the history of money creation, the domination of public policy by classical economics, some linguistic legerdemain, and a cultural framework that normalizes what would otherwise be considered intolerable.

Origins and Prerequisites

To understand financialization, it is convenient to begin with the creation of the Bank of England in 1694. This is, of course, a somewhat arbitrary choice, since much went on before that time (see, e.g., Arrighi 1994). But without the financial innovation that this Bank represented, what followed could not have occurred (Kalb 2013: 261; Di Muzio and Robbins 2016). The Grand Bargain, as I'll refer to it, achieved the following:

- First, it institutionalized a means of money creation in which privately owned institutions, largely banks, create money as interest-bearing debt.
- Second, because banks create only the principle and not the interest, it locked the modern economy into exponential growth.
- Third, it ensured a steady flow of monetary resources to those who own interest-bearing financial instruments.
- Fourth, it financialized the national debt, creating a stream of payments to bond holders based primarily on the requirement that states must borrow money to operate, backed by its power to tax its citizens.

- Fifth, it set a benchmark for the expected rate of return on capital of 4 to 8 percent and served as a model for the creation of thousands more debt-based monetary streams.
- Finally, the Grand Bargain locked financial institutions and the nation–state into a partnership dedicated to maintaining economic growth at any cost.

These innovations spread to virtually all modern economies and helped fuel an unprecedented accumulation of wealth over the past three centuries. However, there are signs that they are now doing more harm than good. Each follows a relatively steady historical trajectory, but each development created problems that at this point seem insurmountable. However, understanding the history and dynamics of these developments suggest a way to counter the growing power of the plutocracy.

Money Creation as Private, Interest-Bearing Debt

The Bank of England, of course, wasn't the first bank. The origins of banking extend to antiquity. The sixteenth- and seventeenth-century Dutch were masters of finance (de Vries and van der Woude 1997). But while the Dutch brought finance to the brink of modernity, it was the English who took the final decisive step. Paper money representing metallic currency provided the essential ingredient. The scarcity of gold and silver in the sixteenth and seventeenth centuries put England at a disadvantage with its rival Spain, which was transporting boatloads of gold and silver from colonies in South America. England's coal endowment, and its pioneering of the technology to harness it, offered the potential for great increases in production. So long as money was limited to metallic coins, this potential could hardly be realized (Wennerlind 2011: 62).

Alchemy—the conversion of base metal into gold—was seen as one possible solution to the money problem. Sir Isaac Newton practiced the art with a passion. After his death in 1727, the Royal Society deemed some of his papers "not fit to be printed." Rediscovered in the middle of the twentieth century, some scholars concluded that Newton was first and foremost an alchemist (Wennerlind 2011: 44ff; Newman 2018).

Paper money provided a more practical solution. Paper had been used as a representation of gold or silver for centuries. By the thirteenth century, China was issuing cotton money that could be exchanged for gold or silver. Italians pioneered the bill of exchange, which enabled a buyer to pay a seller at another time and place in the seller's home currency. But bills of exchange or promissory notes in general were not legally transferable until the late seventeenth century, because the recipient would not be legally entitled to sue for payment. To address this problem, governments passed legislation making personal debts transferable. Consequently, like a personal check today, the debt represented by the promissory note could circulate as money.

The next ingredient in the story of debt-money involved war. Governments had always borrowed money, especially for military purposes. But in 1694, William III of England, in order to continue to conduct war against Louis the XIV of France, borrowed £1.2 million from a group of London merchants paid in notes or sealed bills rather than coins. In exchange, the King granted to the merchants a charter to found the Bank of England. The government agreed to repay the loan with £140,000 a year, an interest rate of 8 percent on the loan, plus £4,000 in management fees. It would raise the money to pay the interest through taxes. Finally, the Bank, in addition to issuing an interest-bearing debt of £1.2 million to the government, issued another £887,000 interest-bearing debt to private customers. It maintained until 1998 the exclusive right in England and Wales to issue notes as interest-bearing debt. The notes, which circulated as money, were initially supposed to be redeemable on demand for gold. Thus, the Bank of England had, in its reserves, the interest received on their loan by the government, plus a fractional reserve of coin to meet demands for an exchange of paper for coins. The creation of the Bank of England essentially completed the foundation of finance and the modern economy (Wennerlind 2011: 109).

Debt is the bedrock on which financialization rests. In 2018, including government, household, corporate, and financial debt, global debt reached $250 trillion (Dobbs et al 2015: 1; Tanzi 2018)—fueled partially by an increase in government debt, it had more than doubled over the previous fifteen years. The first problem bequeathed by the Grand Bargain is the rise of debt and the question of whether the economy can grow sufficiently to pay it off.

The Requirement for Exponential Economic Growth

Since financial institutions create only the principal of the loan, without economic growth, the interest, yield, or return on the loans, government securities, bonds, and so forth can never be realized (Werner 2014; Di Muzio and Robbins 2017). Over the long term, but particularly over the past two centuries, the growth of GDP in the global economy, especially in European offshoots (e.g., the United States and Australia) and Japan, has been spectacular: a three-hundred-fold increase in the amount of goods consumed, the number of goods produced, and the fortunes that have been made. A global citizen of today is almost nine times as wealthy as his or her counterpart some two hundred years ago; in some parts of the world, the average citizen has increased his or her wealth almost twenty-five times over the same period (see Maddison 2003). But given the explosion of global debt over the past two decades, can sufficient growth be maintained? In 2018, the ratio of global debt to economic growth was over 300 percent. In the United States, it almost doubled between 2000 and 2018 (going from 57 percent to 104 percent).

One might expect, given economists' commitment to numbers, that one of the most important pieces of data would be the rate of economic growth necessary to maintain debt-based monetary streams. However, in the economics literature, other than a paper by Dean Baker, J. Bradford DeLong, and Paul Krugman (2005) showing that the rate of return on capital depends on the rate of economic growth, there is virtual silence on the issue. A 2015 report by the global consulting agency McKinsey (Dobbs et al 2015) provides an exception by calculating necessary growth rates for selected countries to begin to pay down their sovereign debt (other categories of debt-consumer, corporate, municipal, financial were excluded from the exercise).[2] Averaging the growth rates of a group of European countries, the United States, and Japan, they found that the actual average growth rate was 1.67 percent, while the countries would have had to grow at an average rate of 3.46 percent just to begin paying back only their sovereign debts.

Since government debt constitutes less than one-third of all global debt, it is not unreasonable to suppose that to service all outstanding debts would require growth rates approaching 15 percent a year. Yet virtually all estimates of national and global growth predict a *slowing* of the rates of growth at the same time as global debt is increasing (see, e.g., IMF 2016; Piketty 2014: 206). Larry Summers, chief architect of United States economic policy under Presidents Clinton and Obama, has predicted a long period of "secular stagnation" (see Streeck 2014: 57). United States GDP, which averaged 4.4 percent from 1960 to 1989, declined to 1.9 percent between 1990 and 2019. And it was the projected decline in growth by the Trustees of the United States Social Security Trust Fund (2005) that prompted Dean Baker, Bradford DeLong, and Paul Krugman (2005) to predict lower rates of return on global investments.

Before returning to the question of why economists have failed to appreciate why growth cannot be sufficient to pay off existing debt and the social, environmental, and political consequences of that failure, let us consider who benefits from the creation of debt-based monetary streams.

A Steady Flow of Monetary Resources to the Plutocracy

As might be expected, these debts generate monetary streams that flow overwhelmingly to those who have the most interest-bearing assets at their disposal (Creutz 2010: 4). Edward N. Wolff (2012, 2013, 2017) has documented the extent of this wealth transfer (see Table 1.1). As of 2016, the top 1 percent has over 50 percent of interest-bearing assets (55.6 percent), and a significantly lower amount of debt (6.7 percent) than the bottom 90 percent (9.2 percent and 72.4 percent respectively). While numerous factors have contributed to the massive growth in inequality within countries over the past four decades (see, e.g., Piketty 2014; Milanovic 2016; Scheidel 2017), the role of financialization, particularly the control of debt-based monetary streams, has been largely neglected.

Clearly, one crucial legacy of the Grand Bargain of 1694 is a financial system in which wealth is systematically channeled from the bottom to the top. While there have been brief periods that threatened the plutocracy, these have been short-lived. When the Grand Bargain financialized the national debt, it created a stream of payments to bond holders based primarily on the requirement that states must borrow money to operate and institutionalized the prime financial rule that creditors always come first (Winters 1996; Braun 2018). Since economic growth cannot keep up with debt repayment, governments are forced into "austerity" programs to honor debt repayment to bond holders; they reduce government employment, cut education and health programs, and downsize poverty-reduction efforts.

Table 1.1. Income-generating assets and total debt by percentile of wealth—2016.

Asset type	Top 1 percent	Next 9 percent	Bottom 90 percent
Stocks and mutual funds	53.2	40.0	6.8
Financial securities	64.6	29.2	6.2
Trusts	51.4	33.2	15.4
Business equity	65.7	28.5	5.7
Nonhome real estate	40.0	42.1	17.9
Total assets for group	**55.6**	**35.2**	**9.2**
Total debt	6.7	20.9	72.4

Source: Wolff 2017, Table 2: Income.

To understand why our financial system prioritizes the rights of creditors ahead of infant health, and a whole range of societal and individual indices of well-being—food, environmental quality, health, education, shelter, etc.—we must return again to 1694 (Robbins 2018). Why would citizens accept paper notes in exchange for gold, and why would purchasers of government bonds trust the government to honor its debt? The only way to allay such anxieties (entirely justified, since government default is not uncommon historically; see Reinhart and Rogoff 2009) and ensure that bonds can be sold and/or interest rates remain payable is for governments to guarantee, at least implicitly, to prioritize debt service payments ahead of all other expenses.

William III agreed to pay the merchants from whom he borrowed to fund his war with France 8 percent interest and holders of his bonds collected approximately £96,000 yearly. Nowadays, some two to three trillion US dollars form a yearly monetary stream to the owners of global sovereign debt (see World Bank N.D.). The rate of return on investments is arguably one of the most central measures of finance. Thomas Piketty (2014) elevated its importance by making it central to his study of the growth in economic inequality with his formula "$r > g$" where "r" is the rate of return on capital and "g" is the rate of growth in the economy. While Piketty (2014: e.g., 372) attributes capital's ascendency largely to inheritance, it required also a range of legislative action to assure that the historical rate of return was maintained in the face of the ups and downs of economic growth.

If capital controllers—who, as Jeffrey Winters (1996) notes, are unelected, unappointed, and unaccountable—all wore yellow suits and met weekly in huge halls to decide where, when, and how much of their money to invest, there would be little mystery in their power. But, they don't. Most of their wealth is in the hands of wealth managers competing among each other to get the highest rate of return with the least risk for their clients (Harrington 2016). The total global assets seeking the highest rate of return, according to a Credit Suisse (2018) estimate, amounted to $317 trillion in 2018, and are projected to be $399 trillion by 2023.

Historically, the rate of return on investments, adjusted for inflation, runs from 4 to 8 percent, depending on the anticipated risk (see Piketty 2014: 52–53). A recent study (Jordà et al 2018; see also Dimson, Marsh, and Staunton 2002) of rates of return on bills, bonds, equity, and housing going back to 1870 found that housing performed best, returning 7.05 percent, stocks a 6.89 percent return, while bonds and bills returned 2.50 and 0.98 percent respectively.

Two features of investment capital concern us here. The first is the breakdown between equity and debt investment instruments, and the second is the historical trajectory of the rate of return.

Approximately 24 percent of investible assets consist of equity instruments (mostly stocks), while some 76 percent are debt-based instruments (government and corporate bonds, mortgages, credit card and student debt, etc.) (see Ro 2015). Equity instruments, while earning a higher rate of return, tend to be riskier, since the return is based on the performance of individual stocks whose ups and downs are tied largely to the material economy and the consumption of goods and services. Debt-based instruments are more secure, because, unlike most equity instruments, the rate of return is fixed and they do not depend directly on the consumption of goods and services. The two, of course, are connected, since some equity instruments are financial stocks, and consumption often requires the consumer to assume debt. The point is that, in recent decades, capital controllers prefer to invest in debt rather than in consumption, not only providing evidence of the growing importance of financialization, but arguably transforming our economy into a debt, as opposed to consumer, economy.

Second, average rates of return, highest in the early mid-twentieth century, have since fallen in the late twentieth and early twenty-first centuries (Piketty 2014: 200). If, as noted above, economic growth is slowing and will continue to slow, real return to capital might be expected to decline (see Baker, DeLong, and Krugman 2005). The question, of course, is how capital controllers, given the scope of their power, react to the threat of a reduction in the rate of return on their investments.

Maintaining Economic Growth at all Cost

As the world's most indebted entities, nation–states have a vested interest in maintaining growth and ensuring that creditors get paid. Penalties for not doing so can result in lower credit ratings, higher interest rates, and the collapse of governments. Given the political power of capital controllers, governments also come under pressure to ensure that investors receive their expected rate of return. As Benjamin Braun puts it: "when state actors transact in financial markets for governance purposes they create infrastructural entanglements, which constitute a distinct source of financial-sector power" (2018: 2). Or, more succinctly, as Braun implies, "finance always wins."

The power and interests of creditors are well illustrated in the research of Martin Gilens and Benjamin I. Page (2014, 2018) in which they systematically examine policies enacted in the United States by elected officials and compare them with those desired by the great majority of citizens. They conclude that policymaking is dominated by powerful business organizations and a small number of affluent Americans, and that when "a

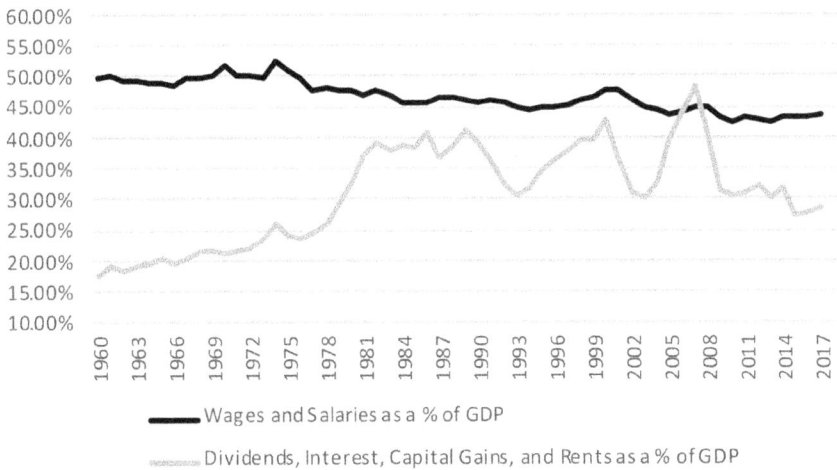

Figure 1.1. Shares of national income allocated to finance and labor. Figure created by the author.

majority of citizens disagrees with economic elites and/or with organized interests, they generally lose. Moreover, because of the strong status quo bias built into the U.S. political system, even when fairly large majorities of Americans favor policy change, they generally do not get it" (2014: 22–23).

Recent legislative action in the United States running counter to majority priorities include reducing taxes on the wealthy; reducing the power of unions; gutting government regulations or enforcement of environmental laws, labor laws, advertising, and illegal immigration; and weakening monopoly laws. As a result, since 1960, the proportion of the national income distributed as interest, dividends, capital gains, and rents (that is through finance) has steadily increased, while the proportion allocated to labor has steadily decreased at the same time as the rate of economic growth has declined (see Figures 1.1 and 1.2[3]).

In sum, then, following the Grand Bargain of 1694, which initiated the accumulation of vast wealth, humanity has been propelled on a socially and environmentally disastrous quest for unending growth. This has been accompanied by vast economic divisions both within and between countries, and by the ascendancy of capital controllers as "masters of the universe." Perhaps the most damaging and dangerous legacy is the creation of a marginalized population, evidenced in the United States not only in increases in suicides and opioid addictions, but also in growing attraction to nationalist and authoritarian regimes (see, e.g, Levitsky and Ziblatt 2019). Their roles as laborers are diminished by outsourcing, legislative actions, and mechanization; they are increasingly dismissed as consumers

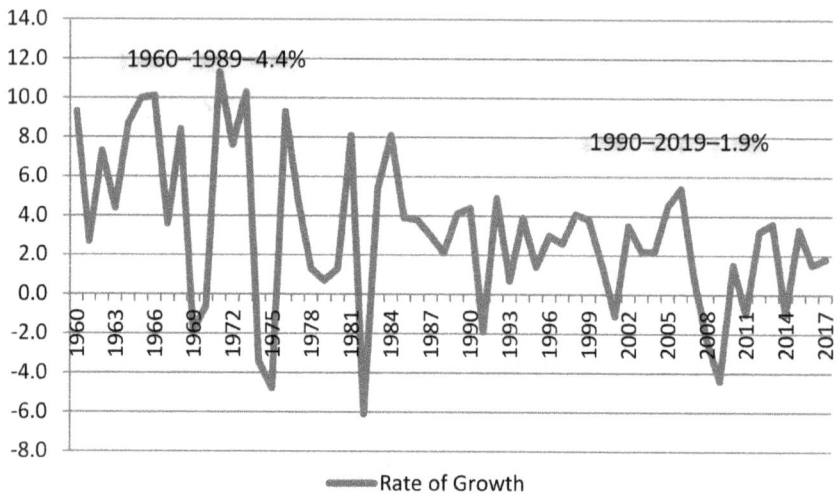

Figure 1.2. US rate of economic growth, 1960–2019. Figure created by the author.

by investors and largely ignored as voters. The vast majority is reduced to the roles of taxpayer and debtor.

The Failure of Economics

The foundation of the financialized economy coincided closely with the emergence of classical economics, whose basic premises include assuming that perpetual economic growth is the ultimate good, pronouncing the debtor as subservient to the creditor, and assuming that money is simply a substitute for barter (see Graeber 2011; Di Muzio and Robbins 2017). Consequently, economics has been slow to recognize the plutocratic consequences of the financial revolution outlined above. One of its dominant metaphors remains that of the household account (Klammer and McCloskey 1992: 145–46; McCloskey 1998: 14). The choice of a metaphor or model (Black 1962) to represent an economy is, as Stephen Gudeman (1986) notes, a cultural choice and highlights certain areas of the domain it attempts to explicate, while obscuring others. When applied to a household, for example, economic growth connotes an increase in wealth and, consequently, in well-being. Growth, after all, connotes *advancement, expansion, improvement,* and, most of all, *progress.* It contrasts with *decline, loss, stagnation,* and *diminishment.* These emotion-packed words obscure the facts of differential capital accumulation, instead postulating growth as both necessary and moral (see Friedman 2005). While most projections see growth slowing, a former chief economist of the World Bank predicts that by 2061, the economy could be growing at 20 percent a year, essentially doubling every four years (Basu 2017). The idea of perpetual growth is absurd. The growth invoked by economists is exponential, not arithmetic. For example, between 1990 and 1995, there was about a 3.6 percent annual increase in trees consumed in the United States (Howard 2007). In actual trees, that amounted to an increase of about 1.5 million trees felled over the period. If the same 3.6 percent were maintained from 2005 to 2010, the number would be 2,550,000 trees—more than a million more. The same problem applies in the case of automobiles, where sustainability is an even greater challenge. Overall production in the eighteen years between 1999 and 2017 went from some 56 million cars to over 97 million cars, an increase of *41 million cars* and an average yearly growth rate of 2.8 percent. If the industry maintained the same 2.8 percent growth rate over the next eighteen years, it would need to produce *58 million more cars* over the same period (OICA 2017).

Applying the exponential rule fifty years out for global GDP, assets, and debt, we get the results shown in Table 1.2. Since, as Milanovic (2016) suggests, the potential for inequality in a society increases as the amount of wealth increases, we can only begin to imagine what society will look like when today's children reach old age. The present economy is unsustainable in economic terms (not to mention ecological, social, and political aspects).

But exponentiality is not the only problem. Maintaining a rate of return, as David Harvey (2010: 216) notes, requires institutional investors and banks to find more and more profitable investment opportunities, more than 75 percent of which are debt instruments. Meanwhile, because future

Table 1.2. Exponential growth of GDP, financial assets, and debt in the twenty-first century (in trillions).

	2020	2030	2040	2050	2060	2070	2100
GDP (Growth rate of 3 percent)	$90	$121	$163	$218	$294	$395	$968
Assets (Growth rate of 5 percent)	$300	$489	$796	$1,297	$2,112	$3,440	$14,868
Debt (Growth rate of 4 percent)	$250	$370	$548	$811	$1,200	$1,776	$3,892

income must be channeled to pay both principal and interest, people will have less money to spend on goods and services, which induces slower economic growth (Butler 2014), as does competition for viable investments (Irwin 2014). The task of wealth managers seeking opportunities for clients to realize an acceptable rate of return relative to risk becomes increasingly difficult. As one investor put it, "If you ask me to give you the one big bargain out there, I'm not sure there is one." Investment advisors are increasingly telling their clients to "lower their expectations" (cited in Dobbs et al 2015).

"Savings" is another household metaphor that obscures more than it reveals. The "savings" metaphor conjures up images of thrifty household managers, shopkeepers, and workers regularly putting aside some of their earnings for a rainy day; but in reality, it represents creditors and investors whose investment decisions drive the global economy. The vast majorities of these "savers" are institutional investors, such as insurance companies and pension funds controlled by wealth managers whose power can disturb whole national and occasionally even global economies (Winters 1996). The metaphor conveys a false image of banks as intermediaries who simply lend out what thrifty citizens deposit, when in fact they are money creators who loan far more than they take in in deposits (Werner 2014). "Creditors" or "investors" would be more apt designations than "savers" in the textbook models of economics.

"Austerity" is a term that conveys the impression of households out-of-control, living beyond their means and, hence, morally suspect. This is not the place to expound on what is becoming a large critical literature (see, e.g., Rakopoulos 2018; Blyth 2013; Krugman 2015). Suffice to say, proposing that cutting salaries, devaluing currency, cutting pensions, privatizing the commons, and so forth will restore equilibrium by increasing income and savings is nonsense. It is another case of "finance wins."

In many ways, the very concept of financialization emerges as a complement to the household metaphor. It, too, obscures as much as it reveals. As Konczal and Abernathy note, financialization suggests a "portfolio society," where categories of social life have been securitized, and, as they put it, "we imagine every person as a little corporation set to manage his or her own investments" (2015: 5). Students, for example, take on an ever-increasing amount of debt to educate themselves. Public functions are increasingly privatized and paid for through fees, creating potential rent-seeking enterprises and further redistributing income and wealth upward. This inequality spiral saps democracy and our ability to address social problems.

Finally, inflation is another term that obscures certain economic realities. Economists talk of it in terms of keeping prices low and, in the United

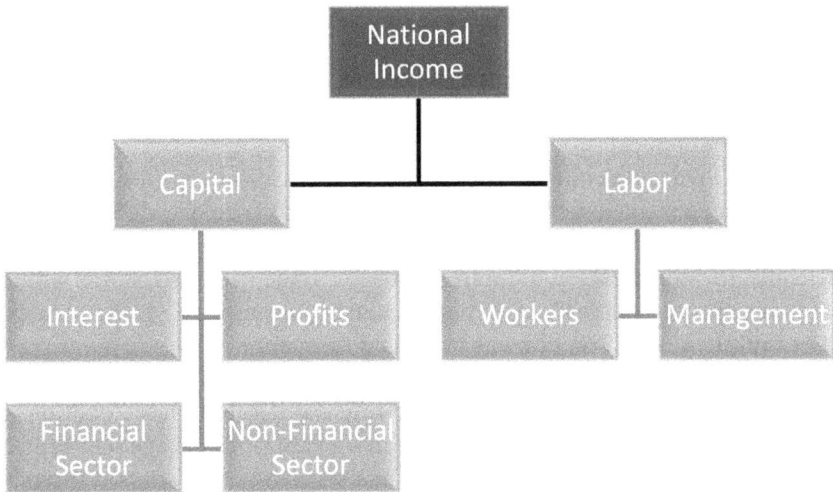

Figure 1.3. National income stream. Figure created by the author.

States, measure it with the Consumer Price Index (CPI), a measure of "the prices paid by urban consumers for a representative basket of goods and services." But rather of concern to household consumers, most of whom may benefit from price rises with wage increases, an increase in home value, or greater ease of debt repayment,[4] inflation mostly affects investors whose rate of return varies inversely with inflation.

There are other ways to conceptualize economy. I want to pose just one example, focusing again on financialization as the creation of monetary streams. A simple monetary stream is represented in Figure 1.3. National income is conventionally divided into capital and labor or wages; capital can in turn be subdivided into interest, profits, etc. Flows are shaped by various rules generally established by nation–states in laws, including taxation. In recent years, the portion going to labor in the form of wages has been cut by taxing it at a higher rate than that flowing to capital. The metaphor of a hydraulic model may be more useful than that of a household budget—a metaphor perhaps appropriate for nineteenth-century English society, but hardly befitting a modern financialized economy (cf. Gudeman 1986).

Perhaps most importantly, using a household or accounting metaphor, "debt" becomes morally repugnant. Friedrich Nietzsche once pointed out that the word for "guilt" and "sin" in German (*Schuld*) is related to the word for "debt" (*Schulden*) (see Graeber 2011: 77). The creditor assumes the position of power; while the debtor, in order to redeem her or his honor, must repay the debt, that is, justify the creditor's trust. The seriousness of the obligation, as Graeber notes, is such that in many societies, borrowers had to pledge family members or themselves as collateral. Nowadays, debt slavery and trafficking of women often takes place in the context of debt repayment. But why should ancient notions of guilt and honor play a role in modern financial transactions, particularly since paying off debt reduces the money supply?

With a hydraulic model, debt takes on very different meanings and becomes a central element of the monetary stream. In fact, debt becomes the major source of wealth. If we were to use the metaphor of monetary streams, the contribution of interest on debt to the national income would become a prominent feature of the national economy. In the United States, for example, since 1970, citizens have paid more in interest payments than they have in federal taxes (Di Muzio and Robbins 2016: 117; Robbins 2018: 102). As national economies are presently constituted, every economic transaction—the purchase of a commodity, a rent or mortgage payment, a meal at a restaurant, or payment for some service—must contain interest on someone's or something's debt (see Creutz 2010). A significant portion of income and indirect tax payments goes to service the interest on the public debt held by bondholders. Of course, since as citizens we are taxed to repay the debt, we are, quite literally, born into debt. And since the price of virtually everything includes someone's or something's debt, it is a significant factor in prices (and in taxes).[5] This fact is generally ignored by economists.

The Power of Labor and Debt

We may have reached an historical tipping point where the amount of debt and debt-based assets cannot be maintained by the declining rate of increase in economic activity. Much sovereign debt is unpayable, and the rate of the monetization of everyday life has accelerated. As Wolfgang Streeck succinctly puts it:

> Rather than restoring the protective limits to commodification that were rendered obsolete by globalization, ever new ways will be sought to exploit nature, extend and intensify working time, and encourage what the jargon calls creative finance, in a desperate effort to keep profits up and capital accumulation going. The scenario of "stagnation with a chance of bubbles" may most plausibly be imagined as a battle of all against all, punctured by occasional panics and with the playing of endgames becoming a popular pastime. (Streeck 2014: 58)

Is there a way out of this future? Many solutions have been proposed, from Thomas Piketty's (2014: 517) global wealth tax to the more ambitious proposals of Anthony Atkinson (2015) to reduce inequality in the UK.

They include raising income tax to 65 percent for the top bracket, higher taxation of capital, and the guarantee of a minimum wage. But, as Walter Scheidel (2017: 435) pointed out, even if all of Atkinson's recommendations were implemented, the Gini index of the UK would drop by only by 5.5 percentage points. In other words, even implementing apparently radical policy measures would merely reduce inequality to what it was fifty years ago. It is a similar story in the United States; over the past twenty years, Congress and courts have together cut taxes on the wealthy, passed bankruptcy bills to protect Wall Street at the expense of debtors, overseen reductions in educational budgets resulting in the tripling of student debt, privatized public functions, implemented property laws to protect the wealthy, while, at the same time, continuing to undermine protection of unions (see Konczal and Abernathy 2015: 8).

History may be the best place to look for a solution. In the United States, there were at least two periods where the seemingly inevitable rise of plutocracy celebrated in the Citigroup memos stalled. The first was the progressive era from the 1890s to the 1920s, which was marked by widespread social activism, higher voter turnout and political reform directed largely at the rising power of corporations and driven by the economic depressions of the late nineteenth and early twentieth centuries. Arguably the main champion of progressive reform was three-time Democratic nominee for President William Jennings Bryan, whose political platform included a progressive income tax, women's suffrage, the issuance of paper money by the government through a national bank, government control of corporate monopolies, public financing of elections, a limit on campaign donations, an eight-hour workday for public employees, and the support of worker's rights to organize, among other things. Alongside Theodore Roosevelt and Woodrow Wilson, Bryan was probably the most influential American politician of the period.[6]

The period from the mid-1930s to the early-1970s marked the second pause in the rise of the plutocrats. The depression of the 1930s and the election of Franklin D. Roosevelt provided the impetus for legislation to regulate banks, and came close to undoing the right of banks to create money and returning it to the government (Phillips 1999; Benes and Kumhof 2012). More importantly, it expanded the rights of workers to organize and spurred the growth of unionization in the United States. Arguably, the power of unions in the United States, and specifically the threat of workers to strike, was responsible for the rise of the middle class (Pizzigati 2012) and the retreat of the plutocrats. Then in the 1980s, the Federal Reserve Bank in the United States hiked interest rates, thus making debt more expensive, and then, building on a host of neoliberal measures, crushed the power of unions (see Mahmud 2012: 16). Union membership in the United States went from over 30 percent of the work-force to less than 10 percent. With the increase in automation, and the obstacles enacted to prevent union organization, it is difficult to see how labor today can become the impetus to reform. The shift from an economy based on material production to one based on finance has further eroded the power of labor.

Given the role of debt in a financialized economy I suggest that the old division between capitalists and laborers is being superseded by the division between creditors and debtors, or more technically, between those who earn more from interest and dividends than they pay out and those who pay out more than they take in. With debt having replaced laborer as the source of plutocratic wealth, the threat to withhold debt payments would be the equivalent to the withholding of labor. The debt strike would supplant the labor strike. Furthermore, debt strikes have several advantages over labor strikes or other forms of resistance. First, the withholding of debt payments is not illegal. Second, while potential debt strikers might fear a loss of credit, if enough people participate, creditors are not likely to want to disqualify them from future borrowing. Third, the infrastructure to repossess thousands of homes or automobiles doesn't exist. Fourth, debt strikes are nonviolent.

The major obstacle to the embrace of a debt strike is the embedded cultural meaning ascribed to the relationship between creditor and debtor. The latter is viewed as a supplicant and guilt-laden soul. The credit score has become a measure of character and worth, and the loan application a process of ritual degradation. Creditors, on the other hand, are surrounded with symbols of power—great buildings, ornate offices, and the support of the government. It is far easier in modern legislatures to pass measures to tighten bankruptcy laws or punish debtors than it is to enact laws to protect debtors and consumers.

Not only does debt dominate the modern economy, but as debt-based income streams buttress the powers of elites, the relationship between debtor and creditor in reality changes. Debt is inevitable for a normal citizen (if only for tax payments to repay the national debt). It is the chief product of the banking and financial industry that creates or controls global wealth. At this point, the debtor and the monetary streams maintained by the debtor become the foundation of the whole political economy. Without debtors laboring to sustain the income streams that flow disproportionately to the few, and above all honor their debts, the economy would cease functioning. In this sense, the wealth of the 1 percent lies in the pockets of everyone else. Lest the idea of a debt strike seem utopian, let me point out that capital does strike when threats to its rate of return rise. The debt strike was endorsed as a political tool when at least thirty members of the

U.S. House of Representatives and thirty-three U.S. Senators, attempting to force budget cuts, voted in 2013 against the government repaying its debt obligations (Montgomery and Helderman 2013). A pledge from only 20–25 percent of debtors to threaten to withhold payments would probably suffice to gain recognition and action. Such an action would have to be accompanied by specific demands: governments must reclaim the power to create money, form public banks, forgive student and Third World debt, guarantee minimum income, and so on. (see, e.g., Di Muzio and Robbins 2016: 126–34). Without such truly radical measures, meaningful change will not be effected.

Richard H. Robbins received his PhD in anthropology from University of North Carolina and has spent his entire teaching career at the State University of New York at Plattsburgh, where he is currently Distinguished Teaching Professor and Chair of the Anthropology Department. His most recent publications include *An Anthropology of Money: A Critical Analysis* (2017), *Debt as Power* (2016) (both coauthored with Tim Di Muzio), and *Global Problems and the Culture of Capitalism* (7th edition, 2018).

Notes

1. This rule is institutionalized in General Obligation Bonds, debt issued (generally by countries) that commits debtors to fund debt payments before any income is allocated elsewhere.
2. The fact that the rate of growth necessary to pay off all debts is not included in the economist's repertoire may have to do with the issue of investor confidence. If investors lose confidence in the ability of growth to realize the monetary stream expected, they may either refuse to invest or they may demand a higher return for the increased risk. This was the problem confronting England during the early stages of its financial revolution, when declines in returns led to claims that credit was unreliable, resulting in declining confidence and further falls in bond and security prices (see Wennerlind 2011: 161–96).
3. Sources: Federal Reserve Bank of St. Louis: Wages and Salaries Received: https://fred.stlouisfed.org/tags/series?t=wages. Accessed 15 January 2020.
   Federal Reserve Bank of St. Louis: Monetary Interest Paid: https://fred.stlouisfed.org/series/A2061C1A027NBEA. Accessed 15 January 2020.
   Federal Reserve Bank of St. Louis: Rate of Economic Growth: https://fred.stlouisfed.org/series/A191RL1Q225SBEA. Accessed 15 January 2020.
   Bureau of Economic Analysis: Dividends: https://apps.bea.gov/iTable/iTable.cfm?reqid=19&step=2#reqid=19&step=2&isuri=1&1921=survey. Accessed 15, January 2020.
   Department of the Treasury, Office of Tax Analysis: Capital Gains:

https://www.treasury.gov/resource-center/tax-policy/tax-analysis/Documents/Tax es-Paid-on-Capital-Gains-for-Returns-with-Positive-Net-Capital-Gains.pdf. Accessed 15 January 2020.
4. Inflation allows debtors to pay lenders back with money that is worth less than it was when originally borrowed.
5. In 2018 in the United States, interest on the national debt was 11 percent of total revenue.
6. In one of the great cautionary tales of United States political history, he was brought down by fellow progressives, in particular Clarence Darrow, his protagonist at the Scopes Trial, who had campaigned for him in 1896 (see Robbins 2009).

References

Arrighi, Giovanni. 1994. *The Long Twentieth Century.* New York: Verso.
Atkinson, Anthony B. 2015. *Inequality: What Can Be Done?* Cambridge, MA: Harvard University Press.
Baker, Dean, J. Bradford DeLong, and Paul Krugman. 2005. "Asset Returns and Economic Growth." *Brookings Papers on Economic Activity* 1: 289–330. Accessed 15 January 2020. https://www.brookings.edu/wp-content/uploads/2005/01/2005a_bpea_baker.pdf.
Basu, Kaushik. 2017. "The Global Economy in 2067." *Project Syndicate.* Accessed 17 August 2018. https://www.project-syndicate.org/commentary/long-term-global-economic-prospects-by-kaushik-basu-2017-06. Accessed 15 January 2020.
Benes, Jaromir, and Michael Kumhof. 2012. "The Chicago Plan Revisited." IMF Working Paper 13/202. August 2012. Accessed 15 January 2020. https://www.imf.org/exter nal/pubs/ft/wp/2012/wp12202.pdf.
Black, Max. 1962. *Models and Metaphors.* Ithaca: Cornell University Press.
Blyth, Mark. 2013. *Austerity: The History of a Dangerous Idea.* Oxford: Oxford University Press.
Board of Trustees of the Federal Old Age and Survivors Insurance and Disability Insurance Trust Funds. 2005. *The 2005 Annual Report of the Board of Trustees of the Federal Old Age and Survivors Insurance and Disability Insurance Trust Funds.* Washington, DC: Government Printing Office.
Braun, Benjamin. 2018. "Central Banking and the Infrastructural Power of Finance: The Case of ECB Support for Repo and Securitization Markets." *Socio-Economic Review.* DOI: 10.1093/ser/mwy008.
Butler, James. 2014. "What the Total U.S. Debt Really Looks Like and What It All Means." *Independent Voter Network.* 11 June. Accessed 15 January 2020. http://ivn.us/2014/06/11/what-is-the-real-us-total-debt.
Citigroup Memo. 2006. See Kapur, Ajay, et al., 2006.
Creutz, Helmut. 2010. *The Money Syndrome.* Peterborough, UK: Upfront Publishing.
Credit Suisse. 2018. "Global Wealth Report 2018." Accessed 15 January 2020. https://www.credit-suisse.com/corporate/en/research/research-institute/global-wealth-report.html.

de Vries, Jan, and Ad van der Woude. 1997. *The First Modern Economy: Success, Failure, and Perseverance of the Dutch Economy, 1500–1815*. Cambridge, UK: Cambridge University Press.

Dimson, Elroy, Paul Marsh, and Mike Staunton. 2002. *Triumph of the Optimists: 101 Years of Global Investment Returns*. Princeton: Princeton University Press.

Di Muzio, Tim, and Richard H. Robbins. 2016. *Debt as Power*. Manchester: Manchester University Press.

———. 2017. *An Anthropology of Money: A Critical Appraisal*. London: Routledge.

Dobbs, Richard, Susan Lund, Jonathan Woetzel, and Mina Mutafchieva. 2015. "Debt and (Not Much) Deleveraging." McKinsey & Company. Accessed 15 January 2020. https://www.mckinsey.com/global-themes/employment-and-growth/debt-and-not-much-deleveraging.

Friedman, Benjamin. 2005. *The Moral Consequences of Economic Growth*. New York: Alfred A. Knopf.

Gilens, Martin, and Benjamin I. Page. 2014. "Testing Theories of American politics: Elites, Interest Groups, and Average Citizens." *Perspective on Politics* 12: 564–81.

———. 2018. *Democracy in America? What Has Gone Wrong and What We Can Do About It*. Chicago: University of Chicago Press.

Graeber, David. 2011. *Debt: The First 5000 Years*. New York: Melville House Publishing.

Gudeman, Stephen. 1986. *Economics as Culture: Models and Metaphors of Livelihood*. Abingdon-on-Thames: Routledge & Kegan Paul.

Harrington, Brooke. 2016. *Capital Without Borders: Wealth Managers and the One Percent*. Cambridge, MA: Harvard University Press.

Harvey, David. 2010. *The Enigma of Capital: The Crises of Capitalism*. Oxford: Oxford University Press.

Howard, James L. 2007. "U.S. Timber Production, Trade, Consumption and Price Statistics 1965 to 2005." Research Paper FPL-RP-637. United States Department of Agriculture. Accessed 15 January 2020. https://www.fs.usda.gov/treesearch/pubs/50895.

International Monetary Fund (IMF). 2016. "World Economic Outlook: Subdued Demand: Symptoms and Remedies." Accessed 15 January 2020. https://www.imf.org/en/Publications/WEO/Issues/2016/12/31/Subdued-Demand-Symptoms-and-Remedies.

Irwin, Neil. 2014. "Welcome to the Everything Boom, or Maybe the Everything Bubble." *New York Times*. 7 July. Accessed 15 January 2020. https://www.nytimes.com/2014/07/08/upshot/welcome-to-the-everything-boom-or-maybe-the-everything-bubble.html.

Jordà, Òscar, Katharina Knoll, Dmitry Kuvshinov, Moritz Schularick, and Alan M. Taylor. 2018. "The Rate of Return on Everything, 1870–2015." Cesifo Working Papers no 6899. Accessed 15 January 2020. https://www.nber.org/papers/w24112.

Kalb, Don. 2013. "Financialization and the Capitalist Moment: Marx versus Weber in the Anthropology of Global Systems." *American Ethnologist* 40: 258–66.

Kapor, Ajay, Niall MacLeod, Narendra Singh, Priscilla Luk, Hao Hong, and Audrey Seybert. 2006. *Global Equity Strategy: The Plutonomy Symposium—Rising Tides*

Lifting Yachts. Accessed 15 January 2020. https://delong.typepad.com/pluton omy-3.pdf.

Klamer, Ario, and Donald McCloskey. 1992. "Accounting as the Master Metaphor of Economics." *European Accounting Review* 1, no. 1: 145–60.

Konczal, Mike, and Nell Abernathy. 2015. "Defining Financialization. Roosevelt Institute." Accessed 15 January 2020. http://rooseveltinstitute.org/defining-financialization/.

Krippner, G. R. 2005. "The Financialization of the American Economy." *Socio-Economic Review* 3, no. 2: 173–208.

———. 2012. *Capitalizing on Crisis: The Political Origins of the Rise of Finance*. Cambridge, MA: Harvard University Press.

Krugman, Paul. 2015. "The Austerity Delusion." *The Guardian*. Accessed 15 January 2020. http://www.theguardian.com/business/ng-interactive/2015/apr/29/the-austerity-delusion.

Levitsky, Steven, and Daniel Ziblatt. 2019. *How Democracies Die*. New York: Random House.

Maddison, Angus. 2003. *The World Economy: A Millennial Perspective*. Paris: Development Centre of the Organization for Economic Co-operation and Development.

Mahmud, Tayyab. 2012. "Debt and Discipline: Neoliberal Political Economy and the Working Classes." *Kentucky Law Journal* 101: 1–54.

McCloskey, Deirdre N. 1998 [1985]. *The Rhetoric of Economics*. 2nd edition. Madison: University of Wisconsin Press.

Milanovic, Branko. 2016. *Global Inequality: A New Approach for the Age of Globalization*. Cambridge, MA: Belknap Press.

Montgomery, Lori, and Rosalind S. Helderman. 2013. "House Votes to Suspend Debt Limit." *Washington Post*. Accessed 15 January 2020. https://www.washingtonpost.com/politics/hold-house-votes-to-suspend-debt-limit/2013/01/23/58f2013c-6574-11e2-85f5-a8a9228e55e7_story.html.

Newman, William. 2018. *Newton the Alchemist: Science, Enigma, and the Quest for Nature's 'Secret Fire.'* Princeton: Princeton University Press.

OICA. 2017. "International Organization of Motor Vehicle Manufacturers: Production Statistics." Accessed 15 January 2020. http://www.oica.net/category/production-statistics/2017-statistics/.

Phillips, Ronnie J. 1999. "The 'Chicago Plan' and New Deal banking reform." Working paper no. 76. Annandale-on-Hudson, NY: Levy Economics Institute of Bard College. Accessed 15 January 2020. https://doi.org/10.2139/ssrn.160989.

Piketty, Thomas. 2014. *Capital in the Twenty-First Century*. Cambridge, MA: Belknap Press.

Pizzigati, Sam. 2012. *The Rich Don't Always Win: The Forgotten Triumph Over Plutocracy that Created the American Middle Class, 1900–1970*. New York: Seven Stories Press.

Rakopoulos, Theodoros, ed. 2018. *The Global Life of Austerity: Comparing Beyond Europe*. New York: Berghahn Books.

Reinhart, Carmen M., and Kenneth S. Rogoff. 2009. *This Time Is Different: Eight Centuries of Financial Folly*. Princeton: Princeton University Press.

Ro, Sam. 2015. "Here's What the $294 Trillion Market of Global Financial Assets Looks Like." *Business Insider*. 11 February. Accessed 15 January 2020. http://www.businessinsider.com/global-financial-assets-2015-2.

Robbins, Richard H. 2009. "William Jennings Bryan and the Trial of John T. Scopes." In *Darwin and the Bible: The Cultural Confrontation*, edited by Richard H. Robbins and Mark N. Cohen, 99–116. New York: Pearson Publishers.

———. 2018. "An Anthropological Contribution to Rethinking the Relationship between Money, Debt, and Economic Growth." *Focaal: Journal of Historical and Global Anthropology* 81: 99–120.

Scheidel, Walter. 2017. *The Great Leveler: Violence and the History of Inequality from the Stone Age to the Twenty-First Century*. Princeton: Princeton University Press.

Streeck, Wolfgang. 2014. "How Will Capitalism End?" *New Left Review* 87: 35–64.

Tanzi, Alexandre. 2018. "Global Debt at Record Level." *Bloomberg Business Week*. 10 April. Accessed 15 January 2020. https://www.bloomberg.com/news/articles/2018-04-10/global-debt-at-record-level.

Trustees of the Federal Old-Age and Survivors Insurance and Disability Trust Funds. 2005. *The 2005 Annual Report of the Board of Trustees of the Federal Old-Age and Survivors Insurance and Disability Trust Funds*. Washington, DC: U.S. Government Printing Office. Accessed 6 February 2020. https://www.ssa.gov/OACT/TR/TR05/tr05.pdf.

Wennerlind, Carl. 2011. *The Casualties of Credit: The English Financial Revolution, 1620–1720*. Cambridge, MA: Harvard University Press.

Werner, Richard A. 2014. "Can Banks Individually Create Money out of Nothing?—The Theories and the Empirical Evidence." *International Review of Financial Analysis* 36: 1–19.

Winters, Jeffery A. 1996. *Power in Motion: Capital Mobility and the Indonesian State*. Ithaca: Cornell University Press.

Wolff, Edward N. 2012. "The Asset Price Meltdown and the Wealth of the Middle Class." Cambridge, MA: National Bureau of Economic Research. Accessed 15 January 2020. https://doi.org/10.3386/w18559.

———. 2013. "The Asset Price Meltdown and the Wealth of the Middle Class." *Journal of Economic Issues* 47: 333–42.

———. 2017. "Household Wealth Trends in the United States, 1962 to 2016: Has Middle Class Wealth Recovered?" Working Paper, 24085. National Bureau of Economic Research. Accessed 15 January 2020. http://www.nber.org/papers/w2408.

World Bank. N.D. Interest Payments (Current LCU) | Data. Accessed 15 January 2020. https://data.worldbank.org/indicator/GC.XPN.INTP.CN.

2

Accumulation by Saturation

Infrastructures of Financial Inclusion, Cash Transfers, and Financial Flows in India

Sohini Kar

On 28 August 2014, the Government of India, under Prime Minister Narendra Modi, launched an ambitious new program of financial inclusion: the *Pradhan Mantri Jan-Dhan Yojana* (the Prime Minister's People's Wealth Scheme, hereafter *Jan-Dhan*). *Jan-Dhan* sought to ensure that all households in India would have at least one bank account, including a debit card, giving people access to credit and savings facilities, as well as creating a new channel for welfare payments. Making "financial history," the Indian government was listed in the Guinness Book of World Records for the most number of accounts opened in a single week (Lynch 2015). By May 2016, the program had enrolled more than 210 million people through mass account-opening drives (PMJDY 2016).

In July 2015, sitting in her spacious, air-conditioned office in Mumbai, Ms. Joshi, a senior banker overseeing financial inclusion at a large public sector bank, described to me the hectic few months that followed the announcement of *Jan-Dhan*.[1] Our conversation was periodically interrupted by bank peons stopping by to drop off papers and tea, and with Ms. Joshi fielding questions from her subordinates and phone calls from her superior. Having opened these accounts—many with zero-balances (i.e., no money in the accounts)—"now the pressure is on us," Ms. Joshi explained. "We have to get in touch with these people and make sure that these accounts get funded." With customers lacking savings, the newly opened no-frills accounts would need other sources of funding, including the expansion of credit and welfare payments, to make them worth keeping on banks' books. In order for financial inclusion to be sustainable for banks, there had to be more than inclusion: flows of money in and out of the accounts were needed.

This chapter is about what happens when large numbers of poor people are financially included. How does the financial system sustain the millions of newly opened accounts? To be profitable, banks need these new accounts to generate credit. Financial inclusion allows banks to capture assets held by the poor and ultimately to expand their market for credit and "financial expropriation" (Lapavitsas 2013: 39). I suggest that financial inclusion is a process of "accumulation by saturation," a process that is triggered by the state's financial engagement with citizens, including welfare payments, flushing the financial infrastructure with newly included capital. Meanwhile, the new account holders are incorporated in an unequal way through forms of financial control.

The key to expanding financial inclusion in India has been its linkage to new and existing welfare programs. For instance, the conversion of the cooking gas subsidy into a cash transfer enabled new flows from state to citizen, rather than to wholesalers. As with other conditional and unconditional cash transfer programs that have flourished globally,[2] from the Brazilian *Bolsa Familia* (Hall 2008) and the Mexican *Prospera* (formerly *Oportunidades*) to the South African basic income grants (BIG) program (Ferguson 2015), proponents have argued that direct cash payments enable the poor to utilize the funds according to their needs, rather than as assessed by policymakers at the top (see also Banerjee and Duflo 2011; Davala et al. 2015).[3] Yet this shift to cash transfers requires understanding welfare not merely as a transaction between the state and recipient, but as a flow through the entire financial infrastructure—including the institutions that transfer benefits. This process reshapes both the economy and individual lives.

In addition to analysis of publicly available reports of *Jan-Dhan* and the cooking gas subsidy program, this chapter draws on interviews conducted in 2015 in Mumbai with commercial bankers and regulators at the central bank to understand the intersecting interests of various institutions being called upon to serve welfare.[4] I unpack the ways in which the state mediates these flows through cash-transfer–based welfare programs, and what happens as financial institutions and their infrastructures are drawn into the state's inclusive agenda.

Welfare in an Era of Austerity

India has had an expansive welfare regime through centrally sponsored schemes (CSS), which are programs supported by the central, rather than state, government. Primarily targeting poverty, these programs range from the Mahatma Gandhi National Rural Employment Guarantee

Act (MGNREGA), which offers to the rural poor one hundred days of employment, food, fertilizer, and fuel subsidies (Subramanian, Kapur, and Mukhopadhay 2008). The scale and related costs of these programs have been something of a puzzle in a neoliberal era. Scholars attribute their continued implementation to elite fears of populist uprisings and violence, should social welfare for the masses be cut (Chatterjee 2008; Gupta 2012). Since the coming to power in 2014 of the center-right National Democratic Alliance (NDA) with Modi's nationalist Bharatiya Janata Party (BJP) at the helm, however, the number of CSS has decreased from 147 to 72, and further cuts are planned in line with neoliberal rollbacks of government spending (Sahu 2015).[5]

In the midst of this fiscal contraction, the Modi government decided to move ahead rapidly with financial inclusion.[6] Speaking at the 2015 Delhi Economics Conclave, organized by the Ministry of Finance, Modi noted that his government had increased "productive public investment" in two ways: the elimination or reduction of subsidies and of "wasteful expenditure through innovative methods, like the use of technology." Speaking of financial inclusion through the *Jan-Dhan*, Modi explained that it was the backdrop for many initiatives: it "is about achieving the maximum: maximum value for every rupee spent, maximum empowerment, maximum technology, penetration among the masses." In other words, expansion of the scheme of financial inclusion could help to achieve the goals of fiscal conservatism. Financial inclusion is presented not only as an integral part of social welfare, but also as part and parcel of the government's attempts to curtail its fiscal deficit (see Bear 2015). Ironically, the retrenchment of the welfare state is coded in the language of inclusion.

The implementation of this new "maximum value" welfare system, however, requires money to flow through a complex financial network of commercial banks. The aim of *Jan-Dhan* has been to ensure that all households have not only at least one bank account, but also an indigenous RuPay debit card, which has an inbuilt accident insurance cover of Rs. 100,000 and life insurance cover of Rs. 30,000. Additionally, holders of accounts that are Aadhaar (the Indian biometric identification program) enabled will have an overdraft facility (i.e., an automatic credit facility) of up to Rs. 5,000 after the account has been satisfactorily operated for six months (PMJDY 2014). The financial infrastructure of inclusion does not simply offer a new payment channel for welfare. Rather, it draws the state into a new set of relations both with the financial sector—commercial banks and insurance companies—and with the recipients of welfare. This push for financial inclusion has been accompanied by the expansion of the government's Direct Benefit Transfer (DBT) scheme, which was launched in 2013. According to the Ministry of Finance, DBT has aimed to "ensure that benefits go to individuals' bank accounts electronically, minimizing tiers involved in fund flow thereby reducing delay in payment, ensuring accurate targeting of the beneficiary and curbing pilferage and duplication" (MIS-DBT n.d.; see also Mathur 2015).

Most scholarly debate about cash transfers has focused on either the user end or on the fiscal capabilities of the state. Little attention has been paid to how payments actually reach the poor. James Ferguson, for example, writing of unconditional basic income grants, has noted: "citizens would access their funds (in the ideal scheme) by simply swiping their national identity cards in an ATM" (2015: 30). Through basic income grants, a "neoliberally 'slim' state" could then carry out a "substantial economic intervention" (Ferguson 2015: 30) without moral policing of the poor (in terms of who deserves assistance or for what purpose it should be used). In Ferguson's argument, however, the actual payment system is bracketed outside the question of redistribution. Closer attention to what actually happens before and after the act of "swiping" shows that matters are not so simple. The financial infrastructure into which recipients are drawn and the new forms of accumulation it enables are of critical importance.

Financial Infrastructures

There were four of us in the small office of the Reserve Bank of India (RBI). While I had an appointment to meet just one person, Mr. Ramdas, he had invited two colleagues to join our conversation. Mr. Ramdas explained that the RBI was focused on "creating the infrastructure" for financial inclusion. Beyond brick and mortar branch offices, they were primarily concerned to promote digital financial services, such as those offered through the RuPay debit card, to expand outreach. The officials explained how, in building this new infrastructure, they were relying on intermediaries to create the structures through which money could be channeled. When I asked whether there would be a greater push for mobile money, which has had success in other parts of the world, given the extensive networks of mobile phones (see Maurer 2015), my interlocutors thought that in India, this would not be the case. "We have a solid banking infrastructure," Mr. Ramdas explained. The regulators preferred to focus on the existing infrastructures, and ways to expand them technologically, rather than consider a wholly new system.

Infrastructures are the "built networks that facilitate the flow of goods, people, or ideas and allow for their exchange over space" (Larkin 2013: 328). Analysis of infrastructure leads to a focus not only on the material objects but also on "the grounds on which other objects operate" (Larkin 2013: 329) and the system itself. Scholars have examined a range of networks from pipes and water delivery (Ni. Anand 2011; Von Schnitzler 2013) and housing (Lea and Pholeros 2010) to energy (Appel 2012; Collier 2011; Gupta 2015) and transportation routes (Bear 2015). These infrastructures enable new forms of technopolitics or biopolitics in the ways that material objects and technologies exert social control and produce particular kinds of power relations. They also have symbolic power in mobilizing social consciousness and political collectivities (Coleman 2014), and in the signaling of modernity and development (Khan 2006).

Closer to the concerns of this chapter, scholars in the Social Studies of Finance have pointed out how "markets' infrastructures matter" (Mackenzie 2006: 13). Financial infrastructures—trading floors, screens, computers, wires, servers, etc.— enable transactions to take place at high speeds across vast distances (Knorr Cetina 2005). They enable central banks to manage payment systems (Riles 2004) and monetary policy (Holmes 2009). Such infrastructures have changed over time, particularly with technological advancement (Zaloom 2006). But this greater speed and abstraction never eliminates the in-between of financial flows. Financial infrastructures "create the grounds on which other objects operate, and when they do so they operate as systems" (Larkin 2013: 329). Financial infrastructures produce particular assemblages—bankers, ATMs, account holders, debit cards, and regulators—that then shape the way in which individuals engage with the wider economy. If twentieth-century development pinned its hopes on massive infrastructural projects such as dams, the financial infrastructure nowadays created by programs of financial inclusion offers a different vision for the twenty-first century. In a government blog post, Sameer Sharma (2016), the Additional Secretary to the Ministry of Urban Development, writes about the potential of the *Jan-Dhan* as a "big bang" in development policy. Drawing on mathematician Martin Hairer's work and complex systems theory,[7] Sameer Sharma argues that current development and welfare programs are limited by their linear modeling. In contrast:

> Suppose, we use a tissue paper to blot spilled water and we hold one end of the paper and dip the other into the fallen water. The paper gets progressively wetter and eventually soaks up all water up to the point the water reaches our hand. There are two aspects to this, first, that this is not the same as water flowing through a pipe, which is similar to what our existing development programs assume; and, second, the next piece of tissue paper will not absorb the water in exactly the same way as the earlier one, meaning that the roll-out of the program has to take into account the context and the unique political, social and political order existing in the State. (S. Sharma 2016)

Distribution of welfare under the linear model is here conceived as analogous to a pipe delivering water. In this metaphor, water goes from the state to the recipient directly (though, as critics of the Indian welfare state have often contended, there are leakages along the way). The tissue, meanwhile, represents a quite different mechanism for transferring the fluid: it is complex and constantly changing, and, significantly, it requires saturation in order for flows to take place at all. It is the tissue analogy, Sharma suggests, that the Indian welfare system must adopt. These metaphors offer insight into the changing landscapes of welfare payment and related forms of accumulation in an era of financialization. Who benefits from these new flows?

Emergent processes of capitalist accumulation are not yet well understood (Searle 2016; Tsing 2015). Unlike "real accumulation" that increases the stock of capital by producing value and surplus value, financial accumulation "relates particularly to flows rather than stocks," (Lapavitsas 2013: 202; see also Krippner 2011). Accumulation occurs increasingly through the constant flow of capital and the expansion of loanable capital. As political economist Costas Lapavitsas argues, as households are increasingly tied into mortgages and other forms of debt, the "systemic extraction of financial profits out of the revenue of workers and other social layers" becomes a form of "financial expropriation" (2013: 39). Further, as economists Atif Mian and Amir Sufi argue, "when the rich own the stocks and bonds of a bank, they in turn own the mortgages the bank has made, and interest payments from home owners flow through the financial system to the rich" (2015: 20–21). In other words, forms of accumulation are saturated in financial transactions. Increasingly, however, it is not just wages that are subject to financial expropriation, but also welfare and social protection.

Globally, welfare programs have been "rebranded" (Dickinson 2016) in recent years to accommodate austerity regimes and neoliberal paradigms. Welfare reform in the global North has increasingly become asset-based, "neutralizing the divide between worker and investor" (Cooper 2017: 138). From pensions to social housing, forms of social welfare have increasingly been turned into forms of investment. Although welfare in the global South—with limited taxation regimes and distributive capacity—looks different (Muehlebach and Shoshan 2012; Wood and Gough 2006), it is also increasingly financialized. Financial inclusion and cash transfer programs have given rise to a new form of financialized welfare: one that enables banks or financial institutions to extract "financial value without disturbing the use values with which it is inevitably and inextricably enmeshed" (Fields 2017: 588; see also Christophers 2010). Poor people receive welfare for its use value (e.g., to pay for cooking gas or for rent), but something more takes place in the flows of finance. As the infrastructure of welfare delivery has shifted from the pipe to the tissue, the apparently simple process of transferring cash becomes part of complex financial networks. By drawing the poor and excluded into banking networks, including through cash transfers, transaction fees, and overdrafts, financial inclusion as saturation expands the terrain of financial accumulation.

Market and Payments Circuits

I met Mahua, then a woman in her thirties, in 2010 while conducting research on microfinance (Kar 2018). I had accompanied the microfinance institution's branch manager to her flat for verification of her loan application. Entering her sparse flat, she pointed to a small table and chair, where she asked me sit, saying this was a "*garib manusher bari*" (poor person's house). The branch officer went over her application, which included (though not required) a copy of her bank passbook. There was Rs. 600 (around US $10) in the account. Tracing the account details, the branch manager noted that there was little bank activity, either in terms of deposits or withdrawals; the small amount of money just sat there.

While *Jan-Dhan* will certainly result in more accounts like Mahua's, these idle accounts are not what banks desire. These accounts are costly to maintain. Only transactions that attract fees or credit initiatives can make them profitable. Mahua—like millions of Indian households—bought subsidized cooking gas as part of a longstanding government scheme. The cylinders, which had to be replaced every month or two, constituted a regular material flow in and out of the household. The transition of the cooking gas subsidy to a cash transfer enabled the state to trigger new flows.

Since the 1960s, the Indian government has promoted "clean" Liquefied Petroleum Gas (LPG) for cooking in an attempt to curb use of biomass (e.g., wood, dung) energy among the poor (Gangopadhay, Ramaswami, and Wadhwa 2005). The use of biomass for cooking has significant health effects due to indoor air pollution. The subsidy program offers all Indian households the right to purchase annually a certain number (allocated by the budget) of subsidized LPG refills. Prior to liberalization of the economy in 1991, LPG and its distribution were controlled by the state-owned energy sector. Since liberalization, however, the government has allowed private players to enter the sector. Since 2002, it has not intervened in the pricing mechanism of petroleum markets. Instead, it offered budgetary support to Oil Marketing Companies (OMCs) to cover the difference between the global market price of LPG and the price paid by Indian consumers (CAG 2016).

In November 2014, the Government of India under Modi introduced the *Pratyaksh Hanstantrit Labh Yojna* (PAHAL or the Direct Benefit Transfer for LPG Scheme), which would transfer benefits directly to the consumer.[8]

Consumers would henceforth pay the market price for the LPG cylinder, but those eligible would be subsidized through a direct benefit transfer to their bank account. As with *Jan-Dhan*, the government argued that PAHAL would curb corruption and leakages (e.g., the diversion of subsidized LPG cylinders to commercial use), weed out fake or duplicate claims, and protect the consumer (CAG 2016: 1). Simultaneously, the government launched a "Give it Up" campaign, encouraging wealthier households to voluntarily opt-out from the LPG subsidy as a form of civic duty. The savings would then fund new gas connections for households below the poverty line. In the first year, it was reported that more than 10 million consumers opted out of the subsidy program (Dutta 2016). In order to run PAHAL, however, the government needed consumers to have bank accounts into which the payments could be made. Approximately 90 percent of all registered LPG consumers are now cash transfer compliant (CAG 2016: 2), meaning that their LPG numbers are connected to a bank account. Additionally, in the process of transitioning to PAHAL, the government offered a one-off permanent advance payment to cover the cost of the first purchase of the LPG gas cylinder at the market price.

PAHAL brought together a network of institutions and actors, mediated by the financial infrastructure (see CAG 2016: 9). First, there is a market circuit or the set of transactions for purchasing the LPG cylinder on the market, where the customer places the order making a cash payment to the distributor at the market rate. The oil company sells LPG to the distributor, also at the market rate. While this first circuit is market exchange, the delivery information triggers a second circuit of capital flow or payment circuit. First, the subsidy is transferred when the OMC reports it to its central reporting server, which holds information on the consumer's Aadhaar number and bank account. Second, the transfer is reported to the government's sponsor bank, the State Bank of India, which makes the payment to the customer's bank account. For all DBT payments, including PAHAL, the government pays a transaction cost of Rs. 0.50, which is shared between the sponsor bank, the destination bank, and the payment bridge: the National Payment Corporation of India (NPCI). Finally, the customer is able to withdraw the amount as a direct cash benefit from the bank. With the introduction of PAHAL, banks have an enhanced role in managing the payment of subsidies to consumers of LPG cylinders. The financial infrastructure has become fundamental to the welfare system, while the welfare system triggers the flows necessary to expand the financial network.

The government announced the implementation of PAHAL as a resounding success, claiming that it had saved Rs. 230 billion by eliminating misuse and unnecessary subsidies. These claims were quickly criticized by the national auditor (CAG 2016). Contrary to the government's claims, the audit found that in the period from April 2015 to December 2015, only a small part of the reduction (8 percent) in the aggregate subsidy could be attributed to PAHAL. Most was due to the fall in crude prices in 2015–16 (CAG 2016: 50). Furthermore, the program had not fully succeeded in weeding out false or duplicate claims for LPG cylinders (CAG 2006: 16–34), and poor data entry by distributors was causing a high failure rate in conveying payments.[9] Some of these failures can be interpreted as growing pains of a new program. But implementation has other long-term effects in its creation and failures (see Ferguson 1994). With around 140 million consumers registered for LPG subsidies through PAHAL in its first year, the program had garnered the government a second Guinness Record for the largest cash transfer program in the world by household (PMJDY 2015). Its integration into the general program for financial inclusion meant that these new flows could generate revenue for banks and financial institutions—both through transfer fees and also credit.

Credit Links

Banks, as the mediating institution in these flows, have faced an unusual situation. *Jan-Dhan* has increased their potential market; but a large number of no-frills accounts would do nothing to improve profits. Ms. Joshi, the senior banker, relied on the flows through welfare programs like PAHAL to sustain these accounts. She expected the government to shift other welfare programs to bank account–based cash transfers.

Additionally, the government had also announced three new social security schemes: two insurance programs, and a pension program (Kar 2017). The premiums for these programs would also have to flow through the bank accounts. As Ms. Joshi further noted:

> Now what government has told is that these benefits will be available to the customer only when they pay the premium by debit to the account. So, they have to put the money [in the account]. So, the whole idea is first you give an account, then you give a [RuPay] card, you attach some social incentive there, and you are transferring all the benefits into these accounts. Flows have started. LPG subsidies started; others will start soon.

The key to sustaining the new financial inclusion program is to ensure that there is money flowing through the system. As an incentive to banks to sustain these payments, the government paid additional cash incentives to banks holding beneficiary accounts. For the rural employment scheme, as well as the maternity benefits and the pension schemes, for example, the government pays an additional fixed component of Rs. 5

and a variable Rs. 0.50 per Rs. 100 to the bank holding the beneficiary's account (Dash 2017).

The flows from welfare payments alone, however, were not enough. Ms. Joshi was not convinced of the savings potential of poor account holders. The program of financial inclusion could be sustainable only if the accounts were credit-linked:

> Unless I lend to them, the whole exercise does not make business sense; unless there are huge balances, balances to the order of [Rs.] 10,000 as the average balance of these accounts, which these people will never be able to keep. They don't have those kinds of surpluses. So, unless I credit-link them and unless I can put a collection machinery which will remain in touch with them to lend and then to recover, such that NPAs are low, this model cannot be a viable one. So, that is the long-term vision and we are actually working towards that.

The financial inclusion program offers the banks a way to observe the transaction flows of customers and create credit histories. From the banker's perspective, the ultimate goal of financial inclusion is not simply to seal leakages and provide a safe space for savings; it is to produce debt. Banks seek to lend and generate interest payments since, in the words of Ms. Joshi, "Money comes only when you lend."

The initial method of extending credit through *Jan-Dhan* is through the overdraft facility of up to Rs. 5,000.[10] *Jan-Dhan* has mandated that the purpose of these loans is to provide "hassle free credit to low-income group [sic]/underprivileged customers to meet their exigencies without insistence on security, purpose or end use of the credit" (PMJDY 2015). Overdrafts are granted to only one income-earning member of the family (i.e., one overdraft loan per household regardless of the number of accounts a household may have), preferably a woman between the ages of eighteen and sixty with regular credits from the DBT schemes (e.g., PAHAL) or other verifiable sources. Loans are at the discretion of the bank. They have to be repaid in thirty-six months, with interest rates at 2 percent above the base rate of the bank (e.g., with a base rate of 10 percent, a bank would be able to charge 12 percent interest on the overdraft). By recognizing the overdraft facility as a "priority sector," the government has encouraged this form of lending. Since bank nationalization in 1969, the government has directed banks to lend to specified sectors based on the development needs and goals of the country, particularly in agriculture and small-scale industries (Copestake 1988). This was formalized in 1972, when the RBI designated priority sectors (RBI 2014). Even after liberalization in the 1990s, all commercial banks—private/public, foreign/domestic—are still required to abide by priority lending requirements, albeit at different ratios.[11] Banks are required to meet these targets, though they have discretion as to which individuals or companies within these targeted areas to lend. In February 2015, the RBI (2015) sent a memo to all commercial banks noting that overdrafts extended by banks under *Jan-Dhan* would henceforth be considered part of banks' priority sector lending. Banks were thus additionally incentivized to fulfill their priority sector obligations through granting overdraft facilities. Once more as a result of the government's intervention, additional funds—now as credit—could flow through the financial infrastructure the state had helped to create.

Zero Balances

The process of saturation is not seamless. Government mandates for lending and opening accounts have sometimes clashed with banks' interests and profitability, and indeed regulatory concerns. First, there are the added costs that are borne by the bank when zero-balance accounts are opened and held on banks' books through the scheme. Ms. Joshi explained: "There is a cost attached to account opening, [and] there's a cost attached to card-issuance. All those costs will not be recovered. It will just go down the drain, but that is the cost one has to pay and bear with." Second, she noted: "this year [2015], my challenge is to ensure the accounts get funded and they see some traction in transactions. And then if accounts are not getting funded, I'll kind of throw them out of the system. Because then they become the source of potential trouble and I cannot deal with that risk."

Regulators at the RBI also noted that the costs of maintaining *Jan-Dhan* accounts with no revenue would be a burden on banks' balance sheets. Early in the program, then-RBI Governor Raghuram Rajan expressed concern that speed was being emphasized over the sustainability of the financial inclusion program (Staff 2014). The public sector banks spearheading much of *Jan-Dhan* have faced mounting pressures of nonperforming assets (NPAs) that have lowered banks' profitability and pose additional risks to the banking system (Gandhi 2015). In the rollout of *Jan-Dhan*, bankers expressed caution in extending overdraft credit, not only noting the lack of sufficient transactions to assess creditworthiness, but also expressing apprehension that there would be misunderstandings on the part of borrowers that they may not have to repay the overdrafts (Nu. Anand 2015). Banks, moreover, have demanded that the government create a credit guarantee fund to help cover defaults in overdrafts from *Jan-Dhan* (Kumar 2015).

In its first progress report, *Jan-Dhan* reported that 66 percent of new accounts had zero-balances. Despite the government's celebration of financial inclusion, the high proportion of zero-balance accounts remained an embarrassment. By September 2016, however, *Jan-Dhan* reported that zero-balance accounts had fallen to 24 percent, signifying the government's success in funding the nonfunded accounts. How was this possible? Journalists at the *Indian Express* newspaper (Mazoomdaar and Yadav 2016) obtained information from thirty nationalized and regional banks under the Right to Information (RTI) Act, and further investigated individual account holders in twenty-five villages and cities across six states to verify the official claims. They found that many bank officials had been making one-rupee deposits, many from their own allowances or money set aside for office maintenance. The ostensible goal was "to reduce the branch's tally of zero-balance accounts." Mazoomdar and Yadav found that as many as twenty branch managers and officials had felt under pressure from senior management to report a decline in the number of zero-balance accounts.

One of the reasons identified for the large number of zero balance accounts was the fact that many individuals opened multiple accounts in order to access the insurance policies that were bundled in with them. *Jan-Dhan* incorporated two forms of insurance with the new "no-frills" accounts: accident cover (up to Rs. 100,000) and life insurance (Rs. 30,000).[12] Both policies are available only in the frame of accounts opened under *Jan-Dhan* within a specified time period.[13] For Ms. Joshi, the bundling of life insurance was linked to the problem of zero-balance accounts, and posed a hassle for the bank. She explained:

> The only concern that we had is that the government should not have pushed that you open an account without any balance. See, when you open an account, people probably do not value that account. If you put some money in the account, you then value the account. Now, what happened when the government promised that with the card that we issue, you will get a free insurance? So people thought they can have multiple accounts. So the same family came to SBI [State Bank of India], opened an account, approached Oriental Bank of Commerce, opened an account. So the same family has multiple accounts. Now, though they do not have those kinds of surpluses they can fund as many accounts. And that is why those accounts have remained unfunded.

Thus, account holders, unsure of how the benefits worked (the intention was one insurance policy per family), opened accounts at different banks even though they were only entitled to insurance benefits from one account. Poor account holders would have little money to deposit into these different accounts. Without money in the bank, Ms. Joshi felt that people did not fully appreciate the accounts in and of themselves. They would need to be trained, in other words, to become good account holders.

Yet this "bait," as Ms. Joshi called the insurance, was simultaneously part of the strategy of creating good financial citizens through practice. For the accident insurance to be valid, an account holder would have to use her RuPay card for a financial transfer (making a payment or withdrawing cash) or nonfinancial transaction (checking the account balance without a transfer) in the ninety days prior to the accident. Originally, this period was set at forty-five days, but it was extended to ninety days in November 2015. The requirement is meant to habituate account holders into transitioning to using cards over cash. That is, in order to protect their insurance benefits—as with transferring LPG subsidies through PAHAL—account holders will slowly become accustomed to cashless transactions. The design of this program—bundling insurance with *Jan-Dhan* accounts and RuPay cards, and then requiring account holders to regularly transact with these cards—is to produce a particular kind of financial subject: a cashless one.

Cashless Subjects

While there are no limits to deposits under *Jan-Dhan*, account holders are only allowed four withdrawals or debits per month, meaning they have to carefully manage card-based payments. Banks are increasingly levying charges, imposing minimum balances, or freezing transactions when the number is exceeded (Shetty 2017). Thus, even as poor people are encouraged to use their new bank accounts and electronic payments so that their money flows into the financial system, their engagement with the financial system is constrained (see Williams 2004). Desiree Fields (2017) observes that tenants in New York City's rent-controlled housing are "unwilling subjects" of financialization, as private equity investment in housing has "swept [them] into the process without their consent," (2017: 589; see also Langley 2007). It is a similar story when new account holders are incorporated into financial networks through programs like *Jan-Dhan* and PAHAL. The poor, however, are not so much "unwilling" as unequal subjects of financialization. While banks can leverage the creditworthy poor by expanding debt, they simultaneously limit the degree to which the poor can withdraw from their own accounts while sustaining cashless transactions.

The introduction of the RuPay card and its spread through *Jan-Dhan* has been part of this push for a cashless—or as Mr. Ramdas at the RBI noted, a "less cash"—society, which the Indian government argues will reduce "black money" and increase tax revenues through electronic monitoring (M. Sharma 2016). In his critique of cash as expensive and a hindrance to monetary policy, economist Kenneth Rogoff notes that the transition to cashlessness can be facilitated through "heavily subsidized, basic debit accounts for low-income individuals.... [And] a simple idea to jump-start the process is to create debit accounts through which all government transfer payments are made" (2016: 3). The economist's recommendation neatly sums up what *Jan-Dhan* and PAHAL have been designed to accomplish.

The poor are often, quite literally, cashless subjects. As my urban poor informants in Kolkata repeatedly told me, money—including loans—did not stay long in the household, but had to be spent to cover everyday necessities such as school fees, medical bills, home repairs, and other emergencies (Kar 2018). Even when cash enters households through welfare payments, it does so momentarily, before it is dispensed. Yet technological cashlessness as enabled by *Jan-Dhan* requires an understanding of what is happening within the financial infrastructures when payments are made electronically. The utopian vision of a payment system without leakages is belied by the forms of accumulation that nestle within it. Private card companies such as Visa and MasterCard have argued against the high "cost of cash" (Visa 2016) vis-à-vis electronic payments systems. MasterCard has already been incorporated into cash transfer programs in South Africa (SASSA n.d.; Webb 2016) and Mexico (Masino and Niño-Zarazúa 2014). Visa and MasterCard compete with the indigenous Ru-Pay; seeking to profit from the shift to cashless payments, particularly in the "nondiscretionary spends," such as hospital or citizen-to-government payments by the masses (PTI 2017). In this way, payments for household expenses by the poor can become ways for private corporations, including banks that serve as intermediaries of these expenses, to capture the profits of financial transactions.[14]

The creation of sovereign currencies, argues Gustav Peebles, has led to the creation of an "inverted panopticon" whereby "in alienating the ability to safeguard economic value to the state, the state has made citizens dependent upon it" (2008: 258). With the cashless economy, citizens lose even the ability to hold a hoard of cash outside of the purview of the financial system (see also James 2015), and indeed of the state, since every transaction is traceable electronically. In India, this "inverted panopticon" has been reflected in the process of demonetization launched by Prime Minister Modi on 8 November 2016. With the elimination of bills of Rs. 500 and Rs. 1,000, more than 80 percent of the paper currency in India became worthless overnight (Dharia and Trisal 2017). Though initially rationalized as a means of targeting corruption and illegal stashes of "black money" of the wealthy, the *note-bandi* [ban], as it became popularly known, hit the poor—both urban and rural—the hardest, and crippled the informal sector (Balakrishnan 2016; Harriss-White 2017). Following critique and evidence that demonetization had done little to curb black money, Modi switched the narrative from eradicating black money to that of creating the cashless society (Staff 2016). To exchange their worthless notes, people would have to deposit them into bank accounts. Demonetization thus "pushed millions of new users onto the country's digital economic grid by virtual fiat" (Shepard 2016). Demonetization dovetailed with the government's agenda for financial inclusion and attempts to incorporate large swathes of the "unbanked" population into the formal financial infrastructure.

It is questionable whether, without the groundwork of *Jan-Dhan*, demonetization at this scale and speed would have been possible. Without recourse to the claim that most households would have a bank account to make deposits into, the government could not have proceeded with demonetization, which led to a 63 percent increase in *Jan-Dhan* accounts. Demonetization facilitated the financialization of assets that were previously parked "in unproductive physical assets" (Press Information Bureau (PIB) 2017). Despite the disruption, the Ministry of Finance announced that demonetization had "led to significant change of saving habits and formalization of assets market" (PIB 2017), stimulating the "financialisation of savings" (Singh and Behara 2017: 13) through increased investments in mutual funds and life insurance. As with PAHAL, the state had mandated new flows and expanded the financial system.

The New Enclosures

Separately and in combination, *Jan-Dhan*, PAHAL, and demonetization all functioned to bring poor households into new circuits: their cash, debts, savings, and welfare payments are meant to saturate the financial system. Once banks are brought into the project of welfare, they capitalize on the accounts as they manage their own interests. The financial infrastructure for this vision is by no means complete, as can be observed from the problem of zero-balance accounts. It needs the inputs of the neoliberal state if financial saturation is to be accomplished. Expanding the basis for debt markets by including weaker households contributes to speculative finance in general. Identified as an "enabler" for seven of the seventeen Sustainable Development Goals, financial inclusion has become a crucial component in tackling global poverty (Klapper 2016).

As Ivan Ascher (2016) has argued about the demise of the Euro-American welfare state, financialized capitalism has wrought a new kind of enclosure (see also Harvey 2011). Social welfare served as a form of commons. It was a wealth shared among citizens via redistribution. In the global South, the newly expanded financial networks, through inclusion, promise new, more efficient channels of welfare delivery. As welfare flows through the financial infrastructure, however, something very different takes place beyond the transfer of money from state to citizen. Does this matter as long as welfare is delivered to recipients? Sometimes perceived as cost-cutting and efficient, and therefore an emancipatory project for the poor, cash transfers camouflage flows of capital in the financial infrastructure that enable new forms of financial accumulation. In the new forms of accumulation by saturation, the poor may not be dispossessed; rather, their inclusion into the financial infrastructure enables new flows of capital and novel patterns of inequality.

Understanding this process requires recognizing that the payment system is neither a black box nor a simple delivery system, but rather the key ground for accumulation in the era of financialization. While financialization has often been analyzed through the lens of private speculative activities and extraction, the processes described here depend on the active role of the state. Cash transfer programs that deliver resources to poor households also allow banks new points of entry and ways of drawing capital out of the informal economy.

Acknowledgments

I am grateful to the Department of International Development at LSE for research funds that enabled this research. I would like to thank Llerena Searle and Jeremy Schmidt who read and commented on early drafts of this paper.

Sohini Kar is an anthropologist and Associate Professor in the Department of International Development at the London School of Economics and Political Science. Her research focuses on the intersection of financialialization and poverty in South Asia. She is the author of *Financializing Poverty: Labor and Risk in Indian Microfinance* (Stanford University Press, 2018).

Notes

1. Names have been changed for anonymity.
2. While conditional cash transfers (CCTs) offer cash with stipulations attached (e.g., school attendance, vaccination), basic income grants offer cash to citizens unconditionally.
3. Both Jan-Dhan and the DBT schemes were introduced under the previous centre-left Congress government, reflecting the widespread political appeal of the cash transfer programs. The Modi government has scaled up the programs at a much faster pace.

4. Interviews with representatives of financial institutions conducted during this project build on my long-term ethnographic engagement with practices of financial inclusion in India. See Kar 2018.

5. The 2015 Union Budget of the BJP/NDA government projected cuts in key social sectors such as education and healthcare (Tewari 2016). Some cuts have been made by collapsing various schemes under umbrella programs (NITI-Aayog 2015).

6. The primary government outlay for *Jan-Dhan* was to cover the life insurance component of accounts opened under the program.

7. See Cooper (2011) for discussion of the influence of complex systems on economic theory and financial regulation.

8. The move to a direct benefit transfer for LPG was first launched under the Congress government in 2011. The Direct Bank Transfer for LPG (DBTL) was launched under the NDP government in June 2013. Under the DBTL scheme, consumers had to have their Aadhaar identity number in addition to a bank account in order to avail themselves of the subsidy. This led to grievances, particularly in areas with low penetration of the new biometric identity card (CAG 2016: 5). After suspending the program briefly in March 2014, the government relaunched it in November 2014 as PAHAL.

9. The CAG (2016: 38–41) found that 64 percent of failures in transactions were attributable to errors on the distributor's side.

10. The loan amount can be the lowest of (1) four times the monthly balance, (2) 50 percent of credit summations in the account in the previous six months, or (3) Rs. 5,000 (PMJDY 2015).

11. Since liberalization, banks in India are a mix of public and private entities. In the case of public banks such as the State Bank of India, the largest public sector bank, the government is nowadays merely the largest shareholder. Nevertheless, the politics of credit in India mean that the government can enact policy more easily through public sector banks (see Kar 2018).

12. Accident insurance cover is Rs 200,000 for premium RuPay cardholders.

13. Between 2014 and 2015, the accident insurance cover was offered by HDFC Ergo; and between 2015 and 2016, it was offered by New India Assurance. The government's life insurance program was managed by the Life Insurance Company (LIC) of India.

14. As Chandrasekhar and Ghosh argue, the shift to digital payments marks a privatization of the "benefits of seigniorage" (2018: 423), or the profits of issuing currency, as intermediaries such as banks and fin-tech capture these profits.

References

Anand, Nikhil. 2011. "Pressure: The PoliTechnics of Water Supply in Mumbai." *Cultural Anthropology* 26, no. 4: 542–64.

Anand, Nupur. 2015. "Banks Go Slow on Issuing Overdraft in PMJDY Accounts." *Business Standard*. 1 September. Accessed 12 May 2017. http://www.busi

ness-standard.com/article/finance/banks-go-slow-on-issuing-overdraft-in-pmjdy-accounts-115083100905_1.html.

Appel, Hannah. 2012. "Walls and White Elephants: Oil Extraction, Responsibility, and Infrastructural Violence in Equatorial Guinea." *Ethnography* 13, no. 4: 439–65.

Ascher, Ivan. 2016. *Portfolio Society: On the Capitalist Mode of Prediction.* Brooklyn: Zone Books.

Balakrishnan, Pulapre. 2016. "The Poor Are Paying for Demonetisation." *The Wire.* 14 December. Accessed 12 May 2017. https://thewire.in/86863/the-poor-are-paying-for-the-demonetisation/.

Banerjee, Abhijit, and Esther Duflo. 2011. *Poor Economics: Rethinking Poverty and the Ways to End It.* Noida: Random House India.

Bear, Laura. 2015. *Navigating Austerity: Currents of Debt along a South Asian River.* Stanford: Stanford University Press.

Chandrasekhar, C. P., and Jayati Ghosh. 2018. "The Financialization of Finance? Demonetization and the Dubious Push to Cashlessness in India." *Development and Change* 49, no. 2: 420–36.

Chatterjee, Partha. 2008. "Democracy and Economic Transformation in India." *Economic and Political Weekly* 43, no. 16: 53–62.

Christophers, Brett. 2010. "On Voodoo Economics: Theorising Relations of Property, Value, and Contemporary Capitalism." *Transactions of the Institute of Royal Geographers* 35, no. 1: 94–108.

Coleman, Leo. 2014. "Infrastructure and Interpretation: Meters, Dams, and State Imagination in Scotland and India." *American Ethnologist* 41, no. 3: 457–72.

Collier, Stephen. 2011. *Post-Soviet Social: Neoliberalism, Social Modernity, Biopolitics.* Princeton: Princeton University Press.

Comptroller and Auditor General of India (CAG). 2016. *Report of the Comptroller and Auditor General of India on Implementation of PAHAL (DBTL) Scheme.* Report Number 25 of 2016.

Cooper, Melinda. 2011. "Complexity Theory after the Financial Crisis." *Journal of Cultural Economy* 4, no. 4: 371–85.

———. 2017. *Family Values: Between Neoliberalism and the New Social Conservatism.* Brooklyn: Zone Books.

Copestake, James. 1988. "The Transition to Social Banking in India: Promises and Pitfalls." *Development Policy Review* 6, no. 2: 139–64.

Dash, Chittaranjan. 2017. "Payment of Transaction Charges and Cash-Out Incentives on Direct Benefit Transfer (DBT) and PAHAL Transactions." Office Memorandum. 26 May. Ministry of Finance, Government of India.

Davala, Sarath, Renana Jhabvala, Mehta, Soumya Mehta, and Guy Standing. 2015. *Basic Income: A Transformative Policy for India.* London: Bloomsbury.

Dharia, Namita, and Nishita Trisal. 2017. "Introduction: Anthropology in the Age of Executive Orders." Society for Cultural Anthropology. 27 September. Accessed 18 September 2018. https://culanth.org/fieldsights/1199-introduction-anthropology-in-the-age-of-executive-orders.

Dickinson, Maggie. 2016. "Working for Food Stamps: Economic Citizenship and the Post-Fordist Welfare State in New York City." *American Ethnologist* 43, no. 2: 270–81.

Dutta, Sanjay. 2016. "PM Modi's Campaign: One Crore Households Give up LPG Subsidy." *Times of India.* 21 April. Accessed 11 September 2017. http://timesof india.indiatimes.com/india/PM-Modis-campaign-One-crore-households-give-up-LPG-subsidy/articleshow/51931982.cms.

Ferguson, James. 1994. *The Anti-Politics Machine: Development, Depoliticization, and Bureaucratic Power in Lesotho.* Minneapolis: University of Minnesota Press.

———. 2015. *Give a Man a Fish: Reflections on the New Politics of Distribution.* Durham, NC: Duke University Press.

Fields, Desiree. 2017. "Unwilling Subjects of Financialization." *International Journal of Urban and Regional Research* 44, no. 4: 588–603.

Foucault, Michel. 1991. "Governmentality." In *The Foucault Effect: Studies in Governmentality,* edited by G. Burchell, C. Gordon, and P. Miller, 87–104. Chicago: University of Chicago Press.

Gandhi, R. 2015. "Asset Reconstruction and NPA Management in India." *RBI Bulletin* (October): 73–80.

Gangopadhyay, Subhashis, Bharat Ramaswami, and Wilima Wadhwa. 2005. "Reducing subsidies on household fuels in India: How will it affect the poor?" *Energy Policy* 33, no. 18: 2326–36.

Gupta, Akhil. 2012. *Red Tape: Bureaucracy, Structural Violence, and Poverty in India.* Durham, NC: Duke University Press.

———. 2015. "An Anthropology of Electricity from the Global South." *Cultural Anthropology* 30, no. 4: 555–68.

Hall, Anthony. 2008. "Brazil's Bolsa Familia: A Double-Edged Sword?" *Development and Change* 39, no. 5: 799–822.

Harriss-White, Barbara. 2017. "Barbara Harriss-White on Demonetisation (Part 1)." *The Madras Courier.* 13 January. Accessed 15 September 2017. http://www.madras-courier.com/barbara-harriss-white-on-demonetisation-part-1/.

Harvey, David. 2011. "The Future of the Commons." *Radical History Review* 109: 101–7.

Holmes, Douglas. 2009. "Economy of Words." *Cultural Anthropology* 24, no. 3: 381–419.

James, Deborah. 2015. *Money from Nothing: Indebtedness and Aspiration in South Africa.* Stanford: Stanford University Press.

Joshi, Deepali Pant. 2006. *Social Banking: Promise, Performance and Potential.* New Delhi: Foundation Books.

Kar, Sohini. 2017. "Austerity Welfare: Social Security in the Era of Finance." *Anthropology Today* 33, no. 5: 12–15.

———. 2018. *Financializing Poverty: Labor and Risk in Indian Microfinance.* Stanford: Stanford University Press.

Khan, Naveeda. 2006. "Flaws in the Flow: Roads and Their Modernity in Pakistan." *Social Text* 24, no. 4: 87–113.

Klapper, Leora. 2016. "Financial Inclusion Has a Big Role to Play in Reaching the SDGs." *Achieving the Sustainable Development Goals: The Role of Financial Inclusion.* CGAP. 11 August. Accessed 12 September 2017. https://www.cgap.org/blog/financial-inclusion-has-big-role-play-reaching-sdgs.

Knorr Cetina, Karin. 2005. "How Are Global Markets Global? The Architecture of a Flow World." In *The Sociology of Financial Markets*, edited by Karin Knorr Cetina and Alex Preda, 38–61. Oxford: Oxford University Press.

Krippner, Greta. 2011. *Capitalizing on Crisis: The Political Origins of the Rise of Finance.* Cambridge, MA: Harvard University Press.

Kumar, K Ram. 2015. "Jan Dhan: Banks Want Fund to Help Cover Overdraft Defaults." *Hindu Business Line.* 11 January. Accessed 11 September 2017. http://www.the hindubusinessline.com/money-and-banking/jan-dhan-banks-want-fund-to-help-cover-overdraft-defaults/article6777990.ece.

Langley, Paul. 2007. "Uncertain Subjects of Anglo-American Financialization." *Cultural Critique* 65: 67–91.

Lapavitsas, Costas. 2013. *Profiting without Producing: How Finance Exploits Us All.* London: Verso.

Larkin, Brian. 2013. "The Politics and Poetics of Infrastructure." *Annual Review of Anthropology* 42: 327–43.

Lea, Tess, and Paul Pholeros. 2010. "This Is Not a Pipe: The Treacheries of Indigenous Housing." *Public Culture* 22, no. 1: 187–209.

Lindert, Kathy, Anya Linder, Jason Hobbs, and Bénédicte de la Brière. 2007. "The Nuts and Bolts of Brazil's Bolsa Família Program: Implementing Conditional Cash Transfers in a Decentralized Context." *World Bank Social Protection Discussion Paper* 0709.

Lynch, Kevin. 2015. "India Makes Financial World Record as Millions Open New Bank Accounts." *Guinness World Records.* Accessed 2 May 2017. http://www.guinness-worldrecords.com/news/2015/1/india-makes-financial-world-record-as-millions-open-new-bank-accounts.

Mackenzie, Donald. 2006. *An Engine, Not a Camera: How Financial Models Shape Markets.* Cambridge, MA: MIT Press.

Masino, Serena, and Miguel Niño-Zarazúa. 2014. "Social Service Delivery and Access to Financial Innovation: The Impact of Oportunidades: Electronic Payment System in Mexico." *World Institute for Development Economic Research (UNU-WIDER) Working Paper.* WP2014/034.

Mathur, Nayanika. 2016. *Paper Tiger: Law, Bureaucracy and the Developmental State in Himalayan India.* Delhi: Cambridge University Press.

Maurer, Bill. 2015. *How Would You Like to Pay? How Technology Is Changing the Future of Money.* Durham, NC: Duke University Press.

Mazoomdaar, Jay, and Shyamlal Yadav. 2016. "The One Rupee Trick: How Banks Cut Their Zero Balance Accounts." *Indian Express.* 13 September.

Mian, Atif, and Amir Sufi. 2015. *House of Debt: How They (and You) Caused the Great Recession, and How We Can Prevent It from Happening Again.* Chicago: University of Chicago Press.

MIS-DBT. n.d. *Direct Benefit Transfer Homepage.* Ministry of Finance, Department of Expenditure. Accessed 17 November 2018. https://web.archive.org/web/201801 05181117/http://dbtmis.planningcommission.nic.in/dbtentry/homepage.aspx.

Muehlebach, Andrea, and Nitzan Shoshan. 2012. "Post-Fordist Affect: Introduction." *Anthropological Quarterly* 85, no. 2: 317–44.

NITI-Aayog. 2015. *Report of the Sub-Group of Chief Ministers on Rationalisation of Centrally Sponsored Schemes.*

Peebles, Gustav. 2008. "Inverting the Panopticon: Money and the Nationalization of the Future." *Public Culture* 20, no. 2: 233–65.

Pradhan Mantri Jan Dhan Yojana (PMJDY). 2014. "Press Note—Launch of PMJDY, 28th August 2014." Accessed 27 May 2016. http://www.pmjdy.gov.in/FILES/PRESS/ENGLISH/28.08.2014.PDF.

———. 2015. "Overdraft up to Rs 5,000 in PMJDY Accounts." Press Information Bureau, Government of India (PIB). PAHAL-Guinness World Record. 5 December. Accessed 27 May 2016. http://pib.nic.in/newsite/PrintRelease.aspx?relid=132587.

———. 2016. "Progress Report." Accessed 15 September 2017. https://web.archive.org/web/20161119001751/http://www.pmjdy.gov.in/account.

———. 2017. "Finance Ministry: Demonetization immensely beneficial to Indian Economy and People." 30 August. Accessed 15 September 2017. http://pib.nic.in/newsite/PrintRelease.aspx?relid=170378.

Press Information Bureau (PIB), Government of India. 2017. "Finance Ministry: Demonetization Immensely Beneficial to Indian Economy and People." Accessed 4 February 2020. https://pib.gov.in/newsite/mbErel.aspx?relid=170378.

Press Trust of India (PTI). 2017. "Payment Solutions Major Visa to Focus on Mass Market in India." *Money Control.* 22 October. Accessed 20 January 2018. http://www.moneycontrol.com/news/business/payment-solutions-major-visa-to-focus-on-mass-market-in-india-2417155.html.

Reserve Bank of India (RBI). 2014. *Master Circular—Priority Sector Lending—Targets and Classification.*

———. 2015. *Priority Sector Lending—Targets and Classification—Overdraft in PMJDY Accounts.* Mumbai.

Riles, Annelise. 2004. "Real Time: Unwinding Technocratic and Anthropological Knowledge." *American Ethnologist* 31, no. 3: 392–405.

Rogoff, Kenneth. 2016. *The Curse of Cash.* Princeton: Princeton University Press.

Sahu, Prasanta. 2015. "Centrally-Sponsored Schemes to Be Reduced to 27 from 72." *The Financial Express.* 9 November.

SASSA. n.d. "You & Your New SASSA Payment Card." Accessed 20 November 2016. http://www.sassa.gov.za/index.php/knowledge-centre/category/2-publications?download=163:sassa-card-dl-booklet-sep-2013.

Searle, Llerena. 2016. *Landscapes of Accumulation: Real Estate and the Neoliberal Imagination in Contemporary India.* Chicago: University of Chicago Press.

Sharma, Mihir. 2016. "Could India Be the First to Get Rid of Cash?" *Bloomberg View.* 20 July. Accessed 13 February 2020. https://www.bloomberg.com/view/articles/2016-07-21/india-s-cashless-future.

Sharma, Sameer. 2016. "Jan Dhan Yojana—A Revolutionary Financial Inclusion Program." *MyGov Blog.* Accessed 27 May 2017. https://blog.mygov.in/jan-dhan-yojana-a-revolutionary-financial-inclusion-program/.

Shepard, Wade. 2016. "A Cashless Future Is the Real Goal Of India's Demonetization Move." *Forbes.* 14 December.

Shetty, Mayur. 2017. "Vague RBI Guidelines See Banks Cap PM's Jan Dhan Yojana Accounts." *Times of India*. Accessed 4 February 2020. https://timesofindia.india times.com/business/india-business/vague-rbi-guidelines-see-banks-cap-pms-jan-dhan-yojana-a/cs/articleshow/59432381.cms.

Singh, Bhupal, and Harendra Behera. 2017. "Impact of Demonetisation on the Financial Sector." *RBI Bulletin*. November.

Staff. 2014. "Avoid Hasty Rollout of Jan Dhan Yojana: Raghuram Rajan." *Times of India*. 16 September.

———. 2016. "From Eradicating Black Money to Cashless Economy: PM Modi's Changing Narrative since Demonetization." *The Indian Express*. 22 December.

Subramanian, Arvind, Devesh Kapur, and Partha Mukhopadhay. 2008. "The Case for Direct Cash Transfers to the Poor." *Economic and Political Weekly* 43, no. 15: 37–41.

Tewari, Saumya. 2016. "Centre's Health Education Spending Declines Over 2 Years." *IndiaSpend*. 16 March. Accessed 17 September 2017. http://www.indiaspend.com/cover-story/centres-health-education-spending-declines-over-2-years-13686.

Thomas, Hugh. n.d. "Measuring Progress Toward a Cashless Society." *Compendium*. MasterCard Advisors.

Tsing, Anna. 2015. *The Mushroom at the End of the World: On the Possibility of Life in Capitalist Ruins*. Princeton: Princeton University Press.

Visa. 2016. "Accelerating the Growth of Digital Payments in India: A Five Year Outlook." Accessed 17 September 2017. https://web.archive.org/web/20170207044154/https://www.visa.co.in/aboutvisa/research/include/Digital_Payments_India.pdf.

Von Schnitzler, Antina. 2013. "Traveling Technologies: Infrastructure, Ethical Regimes, and the Materiality of Politics in South Africa." *Cultural Anthropology* 28, no. 4: 670–93.

Webb, Christopher. 2016. "Profiting from Poverty in South Africa." *Review of African Political Economy Blog*. Accessed 16 September 2017. http://roape.net/2016/08/30/profiting-poverty-debt-finance-social-grants-south-africa/.

Williams, Brett. 2004. *Debt for Sale: A Social History of the Credit Trap*. Philadelphia: University of Pennsylvania Press.

Wood, Geoffrey, and Ian Gough. 2006. "A Comparative Welfare Regime Approach to Global Social Policy." *World Development* 34, no. 10: 1696–712.

Zaloom, Caitlin. 2006. *Out of the Pits: Traders and Technology from Chicago to London*. Chicago: University of Chicago Press.

3

Green Infrastructure as Financialized Utopia

Carbon Offset Forests in China

CHARLOTTE BRUCKERMANN

In 1949, only socialism can save China;
in 1979, only capitalism can save China;
in 1989, only China can save socialism;
in 2009, only China can save capitalism.

—Meme cited in Jinhua Guo et al.,
"Introduction: Remaking the Moral Person in a New China"

The State-Finance Nexus in China

The popular meme quoted above circulated across the Chinese Internet in early 2009 in the wake of the global financial crisis. It describes the unlikely love triangle between China and both dominant politico-economic orders of the last century: socialism and capitalism. The conflicted romance unfolds over four key dates. In 1949, the Communist Party led by Chairman Mao Zedong secured victory and national unity, ending decades of turmoil between nationalist, communist, and Japanese forces. In 1979, the Maoist era of collective production drew to a close as Deng Xiaoping forged a new path—"socialism with Chinese characteristics"—that introduced market reforms into the former command economy. Chinese policymakers were not only learning from capitalism, but also from the collapse of the Soviet bloc after 1989. In defiance of teleological predictions of marketization resulting in democratization, China subsequently solidified its communist leadership within an increasingly capitalist global order. In the wake of the financial crisis of 2007–2008, when many countries faltered under the strain of economic meltdown, China remained a bulwark of stability by safeguarding the advance of capitalism through slowing yet steady growth.

Despite the simplistic caricature of Chinese economic policy expressed in the above timeline, the meme points to the difficulty of characterizing China's trajectory within the dominant tropes of capitalism and socialism. This difficulty is compounded when we analyze the role of finance in China where the state often remains the dominant shareholder or outright owner in financial institutions (Hertz 1998). The Chinese financial landscape remains dominated by "the big four" state-owned banks, followed by the three main "policy banks" and about a dozen nation-wide incorporated banks.[1] In addition, there is a proliferating diversity of smaller regional, municipal, and rural banks, as well as foreign bank subsidiaries. Outside the formal banking sector and its regulations, yet providing similar commercial services, are a growing number of financial intermediaries often decried as "shadow banks" (*yingzi yinhang*) that offer online consumer lending, fintech wealth management services, digitalized (often app-based) asset, commodity, and stock exchanges, and peer-to-peer lending platforms.[2]

Since the global financial crisis, the Chinese government has formerly deployed debt to secure domestic growth and bolster its role as a creditor abroad through state spending. Unlike the austerity measures imposed in Europe and elsewhere, the Chinese leadership rallied around cries to establish "the new normal" (*xin changtai*) of economic rebalancing that involved investing heavily into development across the country in quasi-Keynesian fashion. This entailed moving China away from its reliance on export commodities and heavy industries, instead increasing internal demand for consumer goods, bolstering the burgeoning service sector, and spending on infrastructure, both domestically and abroad (Liu and Dunford 2016). These investments were not implemented exclusively through stimulus packages and subsidy programs. They were augmented through financializing the entire economy and in particular by offering cheap credit to local governments, thereby drawing multiple levels of governance into the state-finance nexus in unequal and uneven ways (Pan et al. 2017).

In recent decades, the state-finance nexus has shifted as the central government devolved fiscal responsibility for taxation and budgeting to the local state on an unprecedented scale (Goodman 2009). Local states struggling to make ends meet at times resorted to notoriously extractive and predatory actions, such as land grabs, commercial rezoning, and housing expropriation, as well as borrowing from banks (Bernstein and Lü 2003; Kipnis 2016). While urban areas often experienced lucrative rises in land-use prices as real estate markets thrived (Zhang 2010), rural areas were hard hit by the withdrawal of central state funds (Goodman 2009). Parallel to the increasing financialization of state policy, urban citizens often took on consumer credit and mortgages to compete on the buoyant real estate markets (M. Wang 2018), while rural citizens struggled to obtain loans secured by their more modest assets (Loubere 2018). Protests against diminishing capacities to sustain rural livelihoods and discontent over local taxes eventually led to abolition of agricultural tax in the early 2000s, a victory for farmers that further undercut the budgets of cash-strapped local governments (Kennedy 2007).

In the wake of the financial crisis, the state ordered banks to increase credit to local governments to sustain debt-fuelled growth at the subnational level (Pan et al. 2017). Simultaneously, China continued to lend internationally, overtaking Germany and Japan to become the world's top creditor.[3] While debt-to-GDP ratios of households, government, and corporations have all grown, the indebtedness of local governments and corporations has been compounded by the weak performance of state-owned-enterprises (SOEs), many of which make losses. While the central state appears to have bottomless pockets as a global creditor, local governments and SOEs have to shoulder increasing debt burdens, which constrain their room for maneuvering in local economic development.

To weather the global crisis, in November 2008, the Chinese State Council announced a 4 trillion RMB stimulus package, including 350 billion RMB earmarked for ecological and environmental projects by the National Development and Reform Commission (Fu and Si 2008).[4] The monumental dimensions of Chinese infrastructure projects in construction and transport since 2008 have caught the attention among media and academic observers alike. Yet a less conspicuous but expanding form of "infrastructure" (*jichu sheshi* or *gonggong sheshi*) for state investment is "constructing ecological civilization" (*jianshe shengtai wenming*), particularly through renewables, afforestation, and ecosystem preservation projects (J. Pan 2016).

These environmental projects bolster government legitimacy at home and abroad, as the "factory of the world" attempts an environmental cleanup by deindustrializing development and financializing ecology. These environmental projects also promise to transfer technical and financial resources to rural areas, thereby creating an economically viable and ecologically sustainable countryside. By reducing pollution, increasing renewable energy, and expanding green spaces, they contribute to decarbonization goals. Finally, they financialize the economy by tying local state and regional development bureaus to financial actors and instruments such as credits and bonds issued through banks, stock markets, and bonds indexes.

Financialization is increasingly the key driver in environmental project development in China, as the government plans to create the world's most expansive "green financial system" (SCIO 2016). Within a global political–

economic context marked by great upheavals and anxiously anticipated crises, actors in China's state-finance nexus claim to be balancing financialization with the solid growth of the "real economy" through "socialist market reforms." This rhetoric envisions the state as stabilizing the nation against crises of uncertainty (Gruin 2016; see also Ortiz 2017). The "performance legitimacy" of the party-state has long been associated with solid GDP growth since the financial crisis (Zhu 2011). Increasingly, state legitimacy also hinges on meeting the environmental demands made by ordinary citizens plagued by pollution (Lora-Wainwright 2013), an imperative gaining prominence in policies oriented toward building "ecological civilization" as a sociotechnical imaginary in China and beyond (Hansen, Li, and Svarverud 2018). Green finance thereby offers another opportunity for China to "save" the world through its socialist and capitalist triangulation: by curtailing the emission of harmful greenhouse gases and fighting anthropogenic climate change.

The Rise of Green Finance

In 2016, the Chinese government put "green finance" on the G20 agenda and issued a document unveiling the road map to a "green financial system." The plan put forward by China's most powerful ministries on 31 August included financial instruments and arrangements from the more conventional financial toolkit but emphasized ecological dimensions over profit motives (SCIO 2016). It foresaw the establishment of "green" credit, bonds, stock indexes, development funds, insurance products, and the flagship carbon markets. Within a year, having issued 230 billion RMB worth of green bonds in 2016, China became the driver of the global green bonds market (UNEP 2017: 18). By 2016, the pilot carbon markets in Beijing, Tianjin, Shanghai, Chongqing, Hubei, Guangdong, and Shenzhen exchanged quotas of 1.2 billion tons of emissions and covered 2,391 enterprises, cumulatively ranking as the second largest carbon market in the world after the EU (UNEP 2017: 23).[5]

Although standards for evaluating "greenness" vary, a common metric in the green financial system revolves around the notion of "carbon." Here, carbon does not stand for the chemical compound, but the right to emit one ton of carbon dioxide, or equivalent greenhouse gases, into the atmosphere. This metric for the quantification of environmental costs emerged from the Kyoto Protocol in 1997 that established the foundation for market-based solutions to global environmental degradation, including the exchange of emissions rights through "carbon markets" (see Hepburn 2007). At the time, China was classified as a developing country. It was therefore placed at the receiving end of Kyoto Protocol transfers of technology and finance. Developing countries could issue and sell "carbon credits" produced in domestic projects to developed, industrialized countries seeking to "offset" their emissions. These offsets included projects that reduced, avoided, or removed greenhouse gas emissions in the atmosphere through renewable energy, filtering systems, or greenhouse gas absorption in vegetation. China rapidly rose to dominate the carbon-offset sector. By October 2012, the UN had issued over 1 billion carbon credits to developing countries, with 60.1 percent hosted in China (CDM—UNFCCC 2012).[6]

As a key site for carbon credit issuing, China also became an important place for carbon trading. By the late 2000s, Beijing was a premier global location for this niche financial product (Whitington 2016). The problems that arose around carbon pricing, especially due to overallocation in the EU carbon market and global economic slowdown in the wake of the financial crisis, resulted in falling carbon prices. The attempt to establish the green financial system in China absorbs, utilizes, and capitalizes on the latent knowledge, skills, and capacities related to carbon finance in China, as avenues for monetized export of carbon credits diminish with the dismantling of global environmental treaties. The 2016 Paris Agreement ushered in a new era for global environmental governance. Considerable hopes for ecological redress were placed on finance, specifically climate finance, and China positioned itself as spearheading a new green financial system.

Labor Regimes within Financialized Nature

As economies become financialized, centers for the accumulation of capital detach from sites of production and diffuse into new spheres for the realization and circulation of value (Pitts 2017; Harvey 2018). Labor contributions diminish, rent-seeking increases, and fictitious capital proliferates (Harvey 2018). While financialization often appears as a deracinated process driven by global institutions, nation–states, and mobile elites, these processes hit the ground in uneven and sometimes tumultuous ways—not least, amongst those charged with implementing financial logics, creating financial assets, or spreading financial services.

In what follows, I examine the transformation of labor regimes in a Fujian carbon forest as an instance of financialization. My analysis is informed by anthropological literature on elites working in the financial sector (e.g., Ho 2009; Chong 2018) and by that which grapples with the installation, maintenance, and dismantling of infrastructure (e.g., Appel 2012; Bear 2015). These literatures, although instructive, are insufficient to grasp this case. The vision of the forest as an infrastructure for carbon capture forms an instance of speculating on future spatial configurations in constituting "nature" (see Harvey 1996). Extending the financial practices of risk speculation to climate change may constitute a form of "fix" for the crises of financial capital rather than a decisive step toward meeting environmental imperatives (Johnson 2015; Lohmann 2010, 2012). It is necessary to connect environmental dispossession and financialized extraction with analyses of labor exploitation to reveal how humans and the rest of nature mutually constitute life in contemporary capitalism (Moore 2016). I share Moore's (2016) concern that the devaluation of these contributions cannot be remedied by any "green arithmetic." Solutions do not lie in rethinking nature as a capitalist system, but in critiquing capitalism as a way of organizing nature (in which humanity is always already immersed).

In Fujian, the reductionist green arithmetic of creating forest carbon affects the work of residents partaking in the unfolding process of financialization of the environment on the ground. In what follows, I make the case for a grounded, emplaced analysis of regimes of labor to grasp how financialization takes root outside of cosmopolitan centers and to recognize finance's role in entrenching existing segmentation and fuelling new inequalities.

The division of labor between the state-owned forest farm's headquarters, its regional offices, and its workers in the countryside reveals how the enterprise attempted to minimalize expenditure. This process did not just happen of its own accord. It required policing environmental resources in the forestry sites, delimiting the boundaries of a managerial workforce within the state-owned forestry enterprise, hiring costly white-collar financial expertise from urban centers, and outsourcing manual labor to cheap local subcontractors. Thereby, most of the capital accumulated through carbon accumulation was actually extracted from the forest farm and channeled into cosmopolitan carbon accounting and trading services. Nonetheless, visions of the "work of nature" circulating among Fujian residents offer alternative engagements with the forests through frameworks that resist "green arithmetic" by basing their logics of labor in broader processes of social reproduction. I shall investigate each of these processes in turn before turning to a final discussion in which I argue that the conversion of the forests to function as a "green infrastructure" (*lüse sheshi*) of financial speculation exacerbates spatial inequalities and sharpens labor hierarchies.

Policing Environmental Resources

Hulin[7] was a squat, muscular man in his midtwenties with a tanned face and a dimpled smile. He wore military green ensembles and a Mao cadet cap to

Illustration 3.1. Forest guardian Hulin in front of his dormitory, emblazoned with the red characters "honest and trustworthy" (*chengxin*). Photograph by the author.

work. Like many other forest rangers in the area, Hulin was an ex-soldier. He prided himself on his patrols as a "protector of the forest" (*hulinyuan*), an official government role in every Fujian "village committee" (*cunweihui*). In addition to holding this state office, Hulin was also employed by the forestry farm and lived in the forest enterprise's office and dormitory building with an all-male team of seven. Most of the workers were young villagers with middle school degrees. They took patriotic pride in the intersection of their country's communist leadership and their province's pristine ecology, evocatively brought to life through promises of a coming "ecological civilization" (*shengtai wenming*). By integrating its forests into the carbon market, Fujian Province was a pioneer in implementing nationwide goals to financialize the environment.

Foresters like Hulin preserved the mountainous woodlands as "green infrastructure" serving the nation across three eras: first as a military installation, second as a provider of ecological services, and, most recently, as a financialized asset for carbon trading. All three visions of the forest altered local residents' interaction with the forests, but the shift toward financialization departs most profoundly from local residents' engagement with the forest.

First, according to local foresters, Maoist state policies protected Fujian forests as military terrain in the event of a Taiwanese invasion. Reflecting on the history of their lush subtropical mountainside, former soldiers turned forest guardians like Hulin described the forests as a "green wall" (*lüqiang*) that mitigated the risk from the hostile islands across the straits.

Second, in the Reform Era, forests as "ecological service providers" (*shengtai fuwu tigongzhe*) delivered clean air that resounded with environmental economics and ecological governance worldwide. Images of forests as machines filtering pollution from the atmosphere were enthusiastically appropriated by citizens, media, and the state, which pays out a variety of subsidies for environmental protection in the officially designated "ecological province."[8] To most residents, including Hulin, this translated into safeguarding their own health and livelihoods, rather than any abstract notion of protecting "nature" (*ziran*). Global environmental governance paradigms increasingly construct nature as a "service provider" akin to other forms of infrastructural installation (Jensen 2015; Carse 2012; Verran 2011). This dominant discourse extends logics of remuneration to the environment: nature becomes recast as serving humans and therefore deserves payment.

Third, the most recent reframing of the Fujian forests as green infrastructure combating greenhouse gas emission builds on logics of remunerating the environment but compounds these through the realm of green finance. The Fujian carbon market is based on the international carbon offset market in forestry (see Fiske and Paladino 2017). It is also part of the "spectacular frontier" of financialization of environmental conservation more broadly (Sullivan 2012). In 2016, the Fujian government volunteered to become one of China's emissions trading pilot zones and created a local carbon market with a central focus on forestry offsets. As forestry's measure of success shifts to carbon absorption, green infrastructures provide a financialized basis for issuing, trading, and speculating on carbon credits. This most recent set of green finance policies reconfigures the forests as green infrastructure of geoengineering that financialize the risk of regional and planetary futures.

To some Fujianese foresters, the promises of ecological civilization were being fulfilled before their very eyes. Sitting in front of his dormitory at a plastic table, smoking a cigarette and drinking green tea, Hulin explained that the new era had already arrived in his area, thanks to the great leadership of Xi Jinping, or Papa Xi (*Xi Dada*), as he affectionately referred to the President. He indicated a nearby lake:

> The lake back there, villagers are now permitted to fish with lines. But not nets or other traps. Five years ago, the water was too dirty to swim there, but now you can, no problem.... Papa Xi, he often discusses our beautiful scenery [literally: "the blue mountains and green waters," *qingshanlüshui*]. The forest company generates village income, by giving employment to villagers, and contracting the land from the village committee. If I discover somebody has broken the rules, I go to the forestry bureau, but this seldom happens, because we are very harmonious with the village committee.

For Hulin, ecological civilization bolstered communist party legitimacy. Moreover, the policy justified intervention into the ownership, exploitation, and management of ecological spaces and environmental resources beyond immediate livelihood necessities. He felt that the policy was conducive to the emergence of enlightened rural subjects:

> The coming era of ecological civilization has arrived. Papa Xi has accomplished it. Really this whole area is very beautiful now, the environment, the houses, the construction. People are finding their own work, they are becoming more self-sufficient; their mentality has been raised, especially in relation to the environment. They know about "ecological consciousness" (*shengtai yishi*). This spreads through government experiments, the pilots, and gets further disseminated through the media and the news, and this allows leaders and the people to raise their standard of living. This consciousness has really risen, and not just consciousness about protecting the environment (*huanbao yishi*), but all consciousness has risen (*shenme yishi dou tigao*). Everybody is raising their own "human quality" (*suzhi*).

As a committee member for the local state and an employee of the forestry farm, Hulin acted as a mediator vis-à-vis village residents.[9] Through negotiation, occasionally showing leniency toward minor misdemeanors, he accommodated the need to sustain local livelihoods while meeting the demands of carbon forestry. His overall project was wedged between the mundane labor of forest management and grandiose imaginaries of enlightened citizens bearing "ecological consciousness."

Corporate Restructuring in the Post-Mao Era

These ambitious aspirations for carbon finance seem a far cry from the down-to-earth business of forestry. Despite its origins as a socialist cooperative within a command economy, in recent years, the forest enterprise has adopted market-based practices of labor subcontracting and competitive bidding. Central state council directives and the loosening of legal labor safeguards since the 1980s have encouraged—and even required—state-owned enterprises to reduce their contractual workforce. By limiting permanent hires to managers and subcontracting manual labor to fluid labor pools, the state broke the Iron Rice Bowl previously enjoyed by the employees of the state-owned forestry farm.[10] In the forest enterprise, a rhetoric of kinship, belonging, and cooperation enables the enforcement and naturalization of new corporate boundaries of exclusion and hierarchical relations of inclusion.

In a county city in central Fujian, a compound of white office blocks, a canteen, guestrooms, and a tree nursery accommodate the enterprise's head office. The city is located in a valley basin that traps humidity and pollution; but through the haze, an expanse of verdant hills and forested mountains rises up into clear, blue skies. Yasen, originally established in 1958 and nowadays managing nearly 20,000 ha of forest, forests much of this land. While all Chinese land is state-owned, in some areas, the use rights lie with villages, whose representatives sign long-term contracts with Yasen. Most senior managers at Yasen are graduates from leading forestry universities. They included twenty ordinary engineers, eleven deputy senior engineers, and one senior engineer, who mostly lived in the city and make field visits as necessary. Another sixty, all-male foresters were permanent employees who worked and lived in remote dormitories, often returning to their hometowns on their days off. Most of these workers were trained in technical aspects of forestry and could supervise the hard, manual labor of those hired with short-term contracts.

As the enterprise's boss explained with regret, the forestry farm did not have the budget to recruit forest engineers at the highest level of expertise, let alone carbon finance accountants, traders, or marketers. But despite these hard times, he maintained that all employees and workers together comprised a corporate "family" (*jiating*) tied together by "human affection" (*renqing*) rather than contractual obligation. He thereby naturalized the labor hierarchies within the organization, especially along the lines of seniority and gender. More junior, and especially female, staff offered more ambivalent analyses of what it meant to work in a state-owned enterprise where "every radish has its hole" (*mei ge luobo yi ge kong*), meaning that their room for maneuver was delimited by their position in the hierarchy. Recent spending cuts had curtailed the possibilities for career advancement of junior forestry staff, but at least their lower status protected them from the staff cut-backs that had made more costly senior forest engineers redundant.

As managers attempted to streamline human resources, they also began to outsource labor at the opposite end of the labor hierarchy, turning to subcontractors to recruit manual laborers in the surrounding villages. Villagers could take up government positions as forest guardians (*hulinyuan*), or they could join work teams (*shigongdui* or *gongchengdui*) and sell their labor (*dagong*) to the forestry company. Apart from a minimal mandatory training period to satisfy insurance stipulations, the forestry company largely devolved responsibility for the treatment and payment of these workers to the labor contractor managing the team. Wages were described as erratic.

In addition, land contracting opened up new spaces for accumulation. In this county, the 176 village committees retained the ownership over the forestland use rights communally and received both an annual leasing fee and a 30 percent share of the income made by Yasen from their land. In some villages, these transfers were individualized, while in others, the committee integrated the forest company income into the government budget that paid for the rural cooperative medical coverage, educational institutions, infrastructure investment, and welfare-oriented facilities.

The market-oriented and capital-driven transformations to the enterprise since the 1980s prepared the ground for the recent process of forest financialization. From the imposition of fiscal imperatives to reduce, outsource, and diminish manual labor, it was but a short step to another form of accumulation and extraction through "carbon."

Carbon Accounting as Extraction

The impact of the forest carbon schemes on profits remained unclear due to fluctuating prices in the local emissions exchange. In any case, the initial windfall subsidy flowed primarily to the enterprise that completed the accounting and listing of the credits. Yasen hoped to earn a moderate and steady income from the sale of the credits on the emissions exchange, despite projections that carbon traders would absorb a substantial proportion of profits. In short, Yasen was itself subject to a higher-order force of extraction through its new dependence on financial expertise from carbon auditing and trading companies in the provincial capital.

One key to recasting forests as green infrastructures that absorb carbon rather than serving as ecological preservation zones or timber production sites lies in accounting (Fiske and Palladino 2017). The transformation of forests into carbon reservoirs necessitates laborious physical measurements, costly abstract calculations, and bureaucratically complex registration so that credits can be listed and sold to polluters. This accounting work justified and swallowed most of the substantial financial subsidy of 500,000 RMB from the Fujian province government. Despite completing all the formalities of carbon accounting and registration by November 2017, the forest company was still awaiting the permission to sell the credits in January 2018.

Despite employing over thirty highly skilled forestry specialists, Yasen could not change the forestry sites into facilities with quantified measures of carbon capture on its own. It had to turn to a carbon consultancy to crunch the numbers on carbon absorption and produce a document working out the sequestration over the subsequent decades. No one fully grasped the pages upon pages of equations produced in this carbon accounting exercise by the external consultants, but they also did not need to. The increase in carbon absorption from the improved forestry management would only be realized over decades. However, one definitive result of establishing the carbon offset forest was the creation of jobs for carbon calculation experts left stranded by the vanishing Kyoto Protocol Clean Development Mechanism with an exercise paid for by the provincial government subsidy.

Even the Yasen employees closest to the process of carbon financialization were wary of the process. Kuaiji, a woman in her midthirties and graduate of environmental economics, worked in Yasen's planning bureau. Responsible for preparing the documentation needed for the subsequent calculations and liaising with the outside auditor, she criticized the temporal incongruity between the slow process of accounting and listing the carbon credits, not to mention the even slower growth of the actual trees, and the rapid turnover of financial products. Moreover, she felt that the incremental process of changing "the ecological value system" (*shengtai jiazhiguan*) was not well served by the carbon forestry policy. In her view, the polluters would simply be the highest bidders on the market, concerned only to buy the cheapest carbon credits rather than investing in the future through forestry.

While an external carbon consultancy did the actual calculations, a number of Yasen employees went to the forest for several months in the summer of 2017 to measure the vegetation and thereby construct a carbon capture inventory. Groups of three to four foresters set off in the midsummer heat of July and August 2017 to take stock of the flora on sample plots selected as representative. Depending on the incline of the slope and the density of the underbrush, the work took between two and three hours at a time complete. The foresters measured the circumference and height of the trees as well as the shrubbery and underbrush with tape measures and yardsticks, bending, squatting, and stretching across the foliage. Each tree was marked with a metal tag.

For Celiang, a forester in his late twenties, measuring the plot's carbon contents changed his understanding of the forests. Due to his academic background and practical training in forestry, he had previously considered the trees as repositories of particular chemical components, including carbon and other elements. Initially, the measurement had little effect on his environmental outlook. In fact, he applauded the expansion of "close to nature" (*jin ziran*) forestry management through the carbon credit scheme at Yasen. But when he began to reflect on the peculiarity of isolating one chemical element for monetization, it seemed an absurdity. Rather than putting a price on the carbon within the forest, he felt that the forest's true value should be measured holistically as "public good" (*gongyi*). Yet by the time of my fieldwork, none of the foresters could envision alternatives to the monetization of living trees or organic processes.

The work of carbon accounting was supposed to align the absorption of carbon and the accumulation of capital in the forestry site. But this did not happen. The state subsidy for the carbon calculations was initially paid out to the forestry farm, yet was then almost immediately rechanneled toward the carbon experts doing the accounting, monitoring, and verification of the project. The extraction achieved by this process of financialization channeled the accumulation of profits back to urban centers (Mezzadra and Neilson 2017). The financialized logic of the carbon market not only facilitated extraction from the forest company to the carbon accountancy and trading firms, but also spread through the countryside by exacerbating exploitation through local labor regimes.

Subcontracting Labor through Forest Construction Teams

The carbon forest project not only opened up new channels of financial extraction from the forestry farm toward the provincial capital, but also simultaneously diffused on the ground by squeezing the labor regime of subcontracting operating at the village level. The "close to nature" principles advocated by the foresters and expanded by the carbon credits increased the labor burden for manual workers by forcing them to drag individual trees from the mountainside, rather than clear-fell the plots and pick up the timber with machinery. It also entrenched forms of exclusion from the forests and diminished local residents' capacity to profit from the forests.

Most manual labor in planting, maintaining, and felling was undertaken by temporary workers through "outsourcing" (*waibao*) to construction teams. Between one hundred and two hundred local villagers in the mountains "sold their labor" (*dagong*) to the enterprise annually. About a quarter were women. Almost all these laborers were at least middle aged. Many were considered as elders in their families, but seniority no longer translated into authority, especially for those deemed "lacking in the human quality" (*suzhi cha*) needed to be competitive on the labor market (Bruckermann 2019).

In addition to working on the green infrastructure of carbon forests, these work groups were deployed on various infrastructural developments that needed constant maintenance and repair (*xiu*). This form of labor organization originated in construction projects built with the work of migrant workers (*nongmingong*) displaced from their rural livelihoods (Thomson 2017; Swider 2015; Pun and Lu 2010). While the work in the carbon forests continued to rely on the labor of local villagers, their organization and modes of payment were increasingly aligned with a deterritorialized pool of labor. The new arrangements reduced costs for the enterprise. Moreover, some forestry employees flouted local labor rules stipulating the necessity of a labor card issued by the state in order to hire cheaper migrant laborers. The enterprise did not intervene in wage determination and employment practices and sometimes pitted villages into competition with each other as well as with migrants. Local workers complained about these precarious conditions and contrasted them with the motivation they had felt in earlier phases of infrastructure development. While the Maoist brigades relied heavily on ideological commitment and material incentives for hard labor, the shareholding system introduced in the 1980s turned village forests into a stable source of income from subsidies that complemented subsistence agriculture, township village enterprise employment, and day laboring. The construction teams of recent decades were compared unfavorably with the more horizontal distribution according to work points in the Maoist Period and village shareholding in the early Reform Era, since nowadays, the local contracting "boss" (*laoban*) held all the cards.

Duikou, a villager in his sixties, worked as a temporary laborer (*lingshigong*) as part of a work team organized by his village committee as a contractor to Yasen. His labor included planting and raising seedlings, clearing underbrush, pruning and felling trees, and hauling timber to storage sites or transport vehicles. In comparison with past forms of labor and distribution, he explained:

> In many ways, it is different, because the work team has a labor contractor (*baogongtou*), the boss (*laoban*). And he's the one who calculates, who oversees the budget, and decides how to distribute income and profits, so it is not distributed according to labor or shares; it is not equal distribution (*gongping fenpei*) or common ownership (*gongyouzhi*) in the same way.

The critique of labor extraction and resource enclosure draws on the moral logics of both the high socialist era, when distribution depended on labor contributions measured in points, and the early market era, when the villagers owned local enterprises and profits were shared between the villagers as local shareholders. Local residents did not profit from the establishment of the carbon forests through corporate accounting, nor did they anticipate payouts from the sale of its emissions credits on environmental exchanges.

The management of labor in line with financial imperatives and resource extraction echoes the broader shift toward state investment into infrastructure. Government investment to improve infrastructure, such as roads, pipes, dams, and now even forests, is generally followed by needs for maintenance. However, unlike past infrastructure labor, such as the industrialization drives of the 1950s when workers across China worked in labor brigades motivated by revolutionary fervor, material necessity, and the potential of political sanctions, the current infrastructures of deindustrialization drew labor into their remit through low wages under diminishing livelihood alternatives. As villagers compared presocialist day laboring, the Maoist brigade system, and post-Mao shareholding practices with current labor regimes, they uncovered layers of historical knowledge about the organization of work, as well as different ways of evaluating labor (see Pia 2018). In effect, some villagers elaborated their own labor theories of value. However, rather than making wholesale attacks on the extraction of surplus from the forest, their conceptualizations wove arguments about the work of human and nonhuman nature that imagined alternative, quite different labor regimes.

Mediators of Forest Evaluations

The forestry company relied on cheap, rural, and increasingly even deterritorialized labor to maintain the forests as green infrastructure. These transformations necessitated substantial work by mediators moving between incommensurable domains. Villagers voiced anxieties over the new forms of enclosure entailed by the financialization of nature and policing of environmental resources, framing their critiques through their incapacity to work within the forest and thus gain their livelihood from the green spaces. They did not make direct attacks on state ownership or rent-seeking. Instead, they based their claims to the forests on the human and nonhuman work done within its remit.

Local residents' relationship to the forests as a livelihood resource underwent many changes in the last century, as the state recast the green bounty first into a geostrategic fortress and later an atmospheric filter. The emergence of forests as financialized infrastructures marks a new phase. The appropriation of timber was forbidden, and the use of nontimber forest resources was severely curtailed. As long as no harm was done to the trees, limited hunting and fishing, the harvesting of pine resin, and collecting edible ferns, vegetables, and mushrooms were permitted. Some farmers kept chickens and bees in the forest. Villagers either consumed these nontimber forestry products themselves or sold them at local markets. Yasen employees residing in rural areas moved across multiple boundaries between the forestry farm, local politics, and village residents, frequently translating between these realms.

Mifeng, a Yasen driver, mediated these realms through his pursuit of beekeeping. Raised on a mountain range in the 1980s, after working for over a decade as a rural day laborer, he had joined Yasen in 2013 and took great satisfaction in earning a good living with the enterprise. Mifeng attracted the attention of forestry experts with his beekeeping activities in the nearby mountainside, a skill he learned from his grandfather and refined through experimentation over decades. High in the mountains, he would leave his boxes for bees to colonize in protected rock crevices, hollow tree trunks, and small caves, returning about once a year to harvest honey. He insisted his motivation for beekeeping was the desire to preserve and pass on knowledge of an ancient art. Presenting himself as a local conservationist rather than an entrepreneur pursuing financial gain, Mifeng

Illustration 3.2. Beekeeper Mifeng marveling at the bees and collecting honey from a box he wedged into a rock crevice in the mountainside the previous year. Photograph by the author.

estimated he had spread several thousand boxes across the mountainside. I met Mifeng in his capacity as a driver. When I asked about beekeeping as his "side job" (*jianchai*), he refused to quantify and calculate the exact number of boxes he had put out, the amount of work he had put in, or the potential commercial value of the honey the bees had produced.

One day in January 2018, Mifeng and I climbed up the mountains to find some of his hives perched between the cracks of a nearby rock face. As Mifeng began to pour out some of the golden honey, his face lit up with joy as he fell into a reverie on the "miraculous" (*shenqi*) production of the precious substance by the hard work and untiring labor of the bees. Exclaiming that "All we humans need to do is collect the honey, the bees diligently work to produce it, and freely share it with us," he was emphatic that the displacement of the local bee population by European varieties was the result of greedy beekeepers who kept the foreign variants due to their capacity to work "365 days a year!" Mifeng's attitude rejected an unreflective extractive thinking of humans over their environments. Instead, he upheld notions of sharing and stewardship, with the labor of bees an acknowledged part of the productive process: their gift of honey should be recognized as an outcome of their work.

Mifeng's passion for beekeeping combined global concern over nature conservation, nationalist ideologies pertaining to native fauna, and local interests in creating pristine products. This differed radically from the financialization of nature through carbon forestry. Mifeng's activities made him an ideal embodiment of the new peasant's "ecological consciousness," a possibility not lost on local and even national media covering his creative passion for high altitude forest beekeeping. Forging a vision of the "work of nature" beyond green arithmetic at the very heart of financialization, Mifeng's beekeeping formed a reclaimed pocket based around a home-grown and nonhuman labor theory of value.

Conclusion: Green Infrastructures as Financialized Utopias

Green finance allows the local and national state to integrate different kinds of workers into its project of ecological redemption. The contradictory goals of economic expansion and environmental protection are ostensibly resolved through the coupling of carbon and capital. Carbon forests transfer logics of the accumulation of capital into a financialized arena for the absorption of carbon, thereby simultaneously replicating and throwing into question regimes of economic and ecological inequality. What is at stake here are claims about the value of labor, the legitimacy of extractive capitalism, and who has rights over nature.

Green finance bridges a mismatch of temporalities between the rapid cycles of financial speculation and capital accumulation, on the one hand, and the slow growth of forests and continuous benefits of ecosystem preservation, on the other. In the classic Marxist understanding of financial credit as overcoming temporal incongruities between the production and realization of value, carbon credits emerge as a way of smoothing over this disjuncture in cycles of growth, accumulation, and exchange between forests and profits.[11] Financialization of the environment necessitates bureaucratic and technical processes of accounting that create the ecological assets underlying the system of financial trading. Carbon forests as financialized infrastructure exist at the intersection of the desire to transition to a low-carbon economy and the demand for growth by the developmentalist state.

Two overlapping scales of financial realignment are enacted through the labor of creating the Fujian carbon forest project. First, there is the modest work of carbon accounting as a bureaucratic infrastructure to quantify environmental processes and human behavior. This reveals itself to be a mixture of complex policy making, mundane measurement activities, and changing forestry practices (Fiske and Paladino 2017). Second, there is the more grandiose, even spectacular, promise of infrastructure as a kind of poetics of state-making and nation-building, where large projects herald the coming of a new era (Larkin 2013).

From the perspective of green finance, forests are rendered as assets in the form of environmental infrastructure that capture and store carbon as part of global geoengineering to reduce emissions in the atmosphere. As the commercial measure of success for forestry shifts to carbon absorption, forests provide a financialized basis for issuing, trading, and speculating on carbon credits. Nonetheless, carbon *markets*, like most contemporary markets, operate within the frame of the state. The relation between state and corporations, when it comes to taking the lead in emissions exchanges, is therefore opaque (Newell and Paterson 2010). This is compounded in the Chinese case by the state-finance nexus in general and the state ownership over the Fujian forest in particular. Questions of corporate, state, and financial capture are both more pertinent and harder to discern in the wake of high socialism (Kalb and Visser 2012).

As the forestry sector in Fujian transitioned from a state subsidy system to a geoengineered infrastructural asset valued as a carbon reservoir, to be subsequently channeled into financialized emissions exchanges, the local site was restructured according to new imperatives. The Fujian carbon offsets muddy the waters between finance and politics at various scales: the one-off subsidy of the state to create the carbon forest; the flow of this payment into the coffers of carbon experts (readily available following the demise of the Kyoto Protocol's carbon pricing schemes); and all with the intent of initiating a system that would allow (many state-owned) companies to keep polluting while buying themselves ecological redress. Carbon finance takes knowledge of environmental economics in China and channels this into a profit-generating process for financial and political elites—in this instance at the expense of local labor. Given this background, I have tried in this chapter to disentangle what exactly green finance does, both economically and ideologically, for the central state, the local government, and the everyday lives of citizens.

These reconfigurations exacerbate tensions between economic accumulation and political legitimation of the state at national and local level (Lee 2007). In a Polanyian model, we would expect laborers to look to the state to reembed the social and economic, while in a Marxist framework, labor resistance to exploitation is most commonly analyzed at points of production (Silver 2003). Chinese financialization falls between market-based capitalism and redistribution-based socialism, as capital also flows into the coffers of the central state, where it functions to secure long-term economic growth and political stability as well as to enable redistribution, despite the growing debt burden shouldered by local governments (Lee 2007; Kipnis 2016). Beyond categorical questions about socialist and capitalist tendencies, processes of financialization increasingly suffuse the Chinese economy. As in other parts of the world, the shift from an industrial to a postindustrial economic base entails that nodes of resistance not only continue in sites of production, but also emerge as disruptions in wider spheres of circulation (Clover 2016). Despite this broadening of potential points of contradiction and conflict beyond the archetypal locales of labor, managers, workers, and residents of the Fujian forests nonetheless express their critiques of green finance through labor theories of value.

In the carbon forest site, contestations over the value of work—especially in the form of self-made labor theories of value—challenge logics underpinning the endless expansion of economic growth as well as emergent forces of financial extraction. The dissonance between fixed ecologies and fluid finances allows these critiques to emerge within the heart of carbon forests as instantiations of green finance. Alternative notions of Maoist motivations, generational inheritance, and environmental stewardship suffuse these spaces, but are nonetheless incorporated into the logics of financial capitalism. The interventions of mediators, such as forest guardians, engineers, economists, and residents, far from constituting refusal or resistance, nonetheless serve to *extend* logics of labor exploitation over the human and even to the nonhuman world.

The most thoroughly financialized theory of value emerges from green expertise that frames the forest as a site of geoengineering, while forest workers reconstitute memories of brigade labor and shareholder value as ordering economic–environmental redistribution. State forest guardians recall how the forest used to be a military installation, while some small-scale forest users refuse to subject forest products to monetary quantification and capitalist exchange. The most pronounced divergence from the logic of green finance is the beekeeper who denies that the labor value of the bees can be realized through exchange. Instead, bees and humans live together in nature, symbiotically. Comparisons with day laboring, the brigade system, and shareholding practices reveal that other forms of labor organization were, and are, possible.

The new labor segmentation emerging from green finance entrenches inequalities already present in the local context by strengthening boundaries of exclusion around those able to work in, profit from, and extract rent from the carbon forests. As the boundaries of the enterprise, as well as the forest itself, become less permeable, those outside the corporation experience heightened hardship as their disposable labor is denied remuneration from the green financial system. The ideological legitimation of the state through the financialization of nature thus advances hand-in-hand with dispossession and displacement on the ground. It remains to be seen whether the state-finance nexus emerging in China can become as symbiotic to human and nonhuman nature as the advent of "ecological civilization" promises.

Acknowledgments

The patience of Chris Hann and Don Kalb enabled me to conduct several fieldwork stays and pursue different aspects of carbon finance over time. I am also very grateful to the various forestry specialists in Beijing and Fujian whose support made this rural fieldwork possible. I am thankful to all the contributors to this volume, especially Deborah James, with whom I discussed my chapter.

Charlotte Bruckermann is a Research Fellow in the Department of Social Anthropology at the University of Bergen, Norway. Her publications include *Claiming Homes: Confronting Domicide in Rural China* (Berghahn Books, 2019) and *The Anthropology of China: China as Ethnographic and Theoretical Critique* (coauthored with Stephan Feuchtwang, Imperial College Press, 2016).

Notes

1. The big four are the Bank of China, China Construction Bank, the Industrial and Commercial Bank of China, and the Agricultural Bank of China, in addition to the smaller state-owned national Bank of Communications and the Postal Savings Bank of China. The three national and international policy banks are the Agricultural Development Bank of China, China Development Bank, and Exim Bank of China. The process of diversification began in 1987 when China Merchants Bank opened as the first corporate shareholder owned bank.

2. These services are used by a variety of ambitious "investor-people" (*gumin*) (Chumley and Wang 2013). Often, however, they function to bind consumers into unsustainable debt relations or expose them to huge financial losses. Tragic stories and crowd-sourcing appeals for financial help are common in social media, where stories of debt sharks who entrap female university students (obliging them to send naked photographs of themselves with their national identity cards as collateral) garner moral outrage. There is a rich vocabulary to describe conditions of indebtedness; for example, a *fuweng* is a riches-to-rags "indebted old man" who has made bad investments; "house slavery" (*fangnu*) is the term for having to service a mortgage after the value of the property has collapsed.

3. When the mainland figure is combined with that for Hong Kong: see International Monetary Fund (n.d.).

4. This is China's comprehensive integrated development organ. The same stimulus package earmarked 280 billion RMB for housing projects, 370 billion for rural livelihood and infrastructure improvement, 180 billion for highways, railroads, and the power grid, 40 billion for health and education, 160 billion for innovation projects (including research and development), and 1 trillion for earthquake relief (Fu and Si 2008).

5. Fujian launched its regional pilot emissions trading system in September 2016, with emphasis placed on the inclusion of carbon sinks, particularly forestry carbon offset projects. In addition to the pilot carbon markets, China officially launched its unified national emissions trading system in December 2017, although actual trading is not expected to begin until 2020.

6. This refers only to the certified emissions reductions issued to developing countries through the Clean Development Mechanism.

7. All identifying names of locations, institutions, and persons have been altered to preserve anonymity.

8. From the late 1990s, Ecological Province Construction brought economic development, infrastructural engineering, ecological restoration, and social progress into unison through ambitious planning targets aimed at broad-based regional stability (Wang et al. 2015).

9. Eunice Blavascunas (2014) describes similar processes of negotiation when Polish state foresters resisted the enforcement of territorial boundaries and resource limitation in the Białowieża Forest. However, positive legacies of high socialism do not suffuse the Polish negotiations as they do in China.

10. The Iron Rice Bowl guaranteed accommodation, health insurance, care facilities, and pension benefits for state-owned "work unit" (*danwei*) employees, mainly industrial workers in urban centers (Bruckermann 2018) but also the "forestry engineers" of the state forestry farm moving between the municipal headquarters and rural forestry work.

11. A well-known problem in classical political economy between discount rates in cash flows and the growth of value in timber forests (the Faustmann formula) is arguably resolved, or at least abated, by carbon credits in green finance (see Möhring 2001; Huang and Kronrad 2001).

References

Appel, Hannah. 2012. "Offshore Work: Oil, Modularity, and the How of Capitalism in Equatorial Guinea." *American Ethnologist* 39, no. 4: 692–709.

Bear, Laura. 2015. *Navigating Austerity: Currents of Debt along a South Asian River.* Stanford: Stanford University Press.

Bernstein, Thomas, and Xiaobo Lü. 2003. *Taxation without Representation in Contemporary Rural China.* Cambridge, UK: Cambridge University Press.

Blavascunas, Eunice. 2014. "When Foresters Reterritorialize the Periphery: Post-socialist Forest Politics in Białowieża, Poland." *Journal of Political Ecology* 21, no. 1: 475–92.

Bruckermann, Charlotte. 2018. "Rumours as Moral Action: Contesting the Local State through Housing in China." *Critique of Anthropology* 38, no. 2: 188–203.

———. 2019. *Claiming Homes: Confronting Domicide in Rural China.* Oxford: Berghahn Books.

Buckingham, Kathleen, and Paul Jepson. 2013. "Forest Certification with Chinese Characteristics: State Engagement with Non-State Market-Driven Governance." *Eurasian Geography and Economics* 54, no. 3: 280–99.

Carse, Ashley. 2012. "Nature as Infrastructure: Making and Managing the Panama Canal Watershed." *Social Studies of Science* 42, no. 4: 539–63.

Chong, Kimberly. 2018. *Best Practice: Management Consultancy and the Ethics of Financialization in China.* Durham: Duke University Press.

Chumley, Lily, and Jing Wang. 2013. "'If You Don't Care for Your Money, It Won't Care for You': Chronotypes of Risk and Return in Chinese Wealth Management." In *Qualitative Research in Gambling: Exploring the Production and Consumption of Risk*, edited by Rebecca Cassidy, Andrea Pisac, and Claire Loussouarn, 202–17. London: Routledge.

Clean Development Mechanism—United Nations Framework Convention on Climate Change (CDM-UNFCCC). 2012. "CDM insights—intelligence about the CDM." Accessed 12 November 2018. https://cdm.unfccc.int/Statistics/Public/archives/201210/index.html.

Climate Bonds Initiative and Chinese Central Depository and Clearing Company (CBI and CCDC). 2018. "China Green Bond Market: Annual Report." Accessed 12 February 2019. https://www.climatebonds.net/resources/reports/china-green-bond-market-2018.

Clover, Joshua. 2016. *Riot. Strike. Riot: The New Era of Uprisings.* London: Verso.

Fiske, Shirley, and Stephanie Paladino. 2017. "Carbon Offset Markets and Social Equity: Trading in Forests to Save the Planet." In *The Carbon Fix: Forest Carbon, Social Justice and Environmental Governance,* edited by Shirley Fiske and Stephanie Paladino, 1–22. New York: Routledge.

Fu, Jing, and Tingting Si. 2008. "NDRC Reveals Details of Stimulus Package." *China Daily.* 27 November 2008. http://www.chinadaily.com.cn/bizchina/2008-11/27/content_7246758.htm.

Goodman, David. 2009. "Sixty Years of the People's Republic: Local Perspectives on the Evolution of the State in China." *The Pacific Review* 22, no. 4: 429–50.

Gruin, Julian. 2016. "The Social Order of Chinese Capitalism: Socio-economic Uncertainty, Communist Party Rule and Economic Development, 1990–2000." *Economy and Society* 45, no. 1: 24–50.

Guo, Jinhua, Arthur Kleinman, Yunxiang Yan, Jun Jing, Sing Lee, Everett Zhang, Tianshu Pan, Fei Wu. 2011. "Introduction: Remaking the Moral Person in a New China." *Deep China: The Moral Life of the Person,* edited by Jinhua Guo, Arthur Kleinman, Yunxiang Yan, Jun Jing, Sing Lee, Everett Zhang, Tianshu Pan, Fei Wu, 1–35. Berkeley: University of California Press.

Hansen, Mette Halskov, Hongtao Li, and Rune Svarverud. 2018. "Ecological Civilization: Interpreting the Chinese Past, Projecting the Global Future." *Global Environmental Change* 53: 195–203.

Harvey, David. 1996. *Justice, Nature and the Geography of Difference.* Oxford: Blackwell
———. 2018. *Marx, Capital, and the Madness of Economic Reason.* Oxford: Oxford University Press.

Hepburn, Cameron. 2007. "Carbon Trading: A Review of the Kyoto Mechanisms." *Annual Review of Environment and Resources* 32: 375–93.

Hertz, Ellen. 1998. *The Trading Crowd: An Ethnography of the Shanghai Stock Market.* Cambridge, UK: Cambridge University Press.

Ho, Karen. 2009. *Liquidated: An Ethnography of Wall Street.* Durham: Duke University Press.

Huang, Ching-Hsun, and Gary D. Kronrad. 2001. "The Cost of Sequestering Carbon on Private Forest Lands." *Forest Policy and Economics* 2, no. 2: 133–42.

International Monetary Fund. n.d. "IMF Data Access to Macroeconomic & Financial Data: Balance of Payments and International Investment Position Statistics (BOP/IIP)." Accessed 16 December 2018. https://data.imf.org/?sk=7A51304B-6426-40C0-83DD-CA473CA1FD52&sId=1484234826292.

Jensen, Casper Bruun. 2015. "Experimenting with Political Materials: Environmental Infrastructures and Ontological Transformations." *Distinktion: Journal of Social Theory* 16, no. 1: 17–30.

Johnson, Leigh. 2015. "Catastrophic Fixes: Cyclical Devaluation and Accumulation through Climate Change Impacts." *Environment and Planning A: Economy and Space* 47, no. 12: 2503–21.

Kalb, Don, and Oane Visser. 2012. "Oligarchy and State Capture: Soviet-style Mechanisms in Contemporary Finance Capitalism." In *A Handbook of Economic Anthropology,* edited by James Carrier, 571–84. Northampton, MA: Edward Elgar.

Kennedy, John James. 2007. "From the Tax-for-Fee Reform to the Abolition of Agricultural Taxes: The Impact on Township Governments in North-West China." *The China Quarterly* 189: 43–59.

Kipnis, Andrew. 2016. *From Village to City: Social Transformation in a Chinese County Seat*. Berkeley: University of California Press.

Larkin, Brian. 2013. "The Politics and Poetics of Infrastructure." *Annual Review of Anthropology* 42, no. 1: 327–43.

Lee, Ching-Kwan. 2007. *Against the Law: Labor Protests in China's Rustbelt and Sunbelt*. Berkeley: University of California Press.

Liu, Weidong, and Michael Dunford. 2016. "Inclusive Globalization: Unpacking China's Belt and Road Initiative." *Area Development and Policy* 1, no. 3: 323–40.

Lo, Alex. 2016. *Carbon Trading in China: Environmental Discourse and Politics*. New York: Palgrave Macmillan.

Lo, Alex, and Michael Howes. 2013. "Powered by the State or Finance? The Organization of China's Carbon Markets." *Eurasian Geography and Economics* 54, no. 4: 386–408.

Lohmann, Larry. 2010. "Uncertainty Markets and Carbon Markets: Variations on Polanyian Themes." *New Political Economy* 15, no. 2: 225–54.

———. 2012. "Financialization, Commodification and Carbon: The Contradictions of Neoliberal Climate Policy." *Socialist Register* 48: 85–107.

Lora-Wainwright, Anna. 2013. *Fighting for Breath: Living Morally and Dying of Cancer in a Chinese Village*. Honolulu: University of Hawai'i Press.

Loubere, Nicholas. 2018. "Indebted to Development: Microcredit as (De)marginalisation in Rural China." *The Journal of Peasant Studies* 45, no. 3: 585–609.

Mezzadra, Sandro, and Brett Neilson. 2017. "On the Multiple Frontiers of Extraction: Excavating Contemporary Capitalism." *Cultural Studies* 31, no. 2–3, 185–204.

Moore, Jason. 2016. *Capitalism in the Web of Life: Ecology and the Accumulation of Capital*. London: Verso.

Möhring, Bernhard. 2001. "The German Struggle between the '*Bodenreinertragslehre*' (land rent theory) and '*Waldreinertragslehre*' (theory of the highest revenue) Belongs to the Past —but What Is Left?" *Forest Policy and Economics* 2, no. 2: 195–201.

Newell, Peter, and Matthew Paterson. 2010. *Climate Capitalism: Global Warming and the Transformation of the Global Economy*. Cambridge, UK: Cambridge University Press.

Ortiz, Horacio. 2017. "A Political Anthropology of Finance: Profits, States, and Cultures in Cross-border Investment in Shanghai." *HAU: Journal of Ethnographic Theory* 7, no. 3: 325–45.

Pan, Fenghua, Fengmei Zhang, Shengjun Zhu, and Dariusz Wójcik. 2017. "Developing by Borrowing? Inter-Jurisdictional Competition, Land Finance and Local Debt Accumulation in China." *Urban Studies* 54, no. 4: 897–916.

Pan, Jiahua. 2016. *China's Environmental Governing and Ecological Civilization*. Berlin: Springer Verlag.

Pia, Andrea. 2018. "Memory Leaks: Local Histories of Cooperation as a Solution to Water-related Cooperation Problems." In *Cooperation in Chinese Communities:*

Morality and Practice, edited by Charles Stafford, Ellen Judd, and Eona Bell, 101–20. London: Bloomsbury.

Pitts, Frederick Harry. 2017. *Critiquing Capitalism Today: New Ways to Read Marx.* New York: Palgrave Macmillan.

Polanyi, Karl. 1944. *The Great Transformation.* New York: Farrar and Rinehart.

Pun, Ngai, and Huilin Lu. 2010. "A Culture of Violence: The Labor Subcontracting System and Collective Action by Construction Workers in Post-socialist China." *The China Journal* 64: 143–58.

SCIO (State Council Information Office of the People's Republic of China). 2016. "Guidelines for establishing the Green Financial System (*Guanyu goujian lüse jinrong tixi de zhidao yijian*)." Accessed 5 November 2018. http://www.scio.gov.cn/32344/32345/35889/36819/xgzc36825/Document/1555348/1555348.htm.

Silver, Beverly. 2003. *Forces of Labour: Workers' Movements and Globalization since 1870.* Cambridge, UK: Cambridge University Press.

Sullivan, Sian. 2012. "Banking Nature? The Spectacular Financialisation of Environmental Conservation." *Antipode* 45, no. 1: 198–217.

Swider, Sarah. 2015. "Building China: Precarious Employment among Migrant Construction Workers." *Work, Employment and Society* 29, no. 1: 41–59.

Thomson, William. 2017. "Masculinity at Its Margins: Migrant Construction Work in China." *Women's Studies Quarterly* 45, no. 4: 306–20.

UNEP ("United Nations Environment Programme.") 2017. *Establishing China's Green Financial System: Progress Report 2017.* Accessed 16 December 2018. https://wedocs.unep.org/bitstream/handle/20.500.11822/22285/China_Green_Finance_ProgressRep_ES_EN.pdf?sequence=1&isAllowed=y.

Verran, Helen. 2011. "Imagining Nature Politics in the Era of Australia's Emerging Market in Environmental Services Interventions." *The Sociological Review* 59, no. 3: 411–31.

Wang, Mengqi. 2018. "'Rigid Demand': Economic Imagination and Practice in China's Urban Housing Market." *Urban Studies* 55, no. 7: 1579–94.

Wang, Yutao, Mengxing Sun, Renqing Wang, and Feng Lou. 2015. "Promoting Regional Sustainability by Eco-Province Construction in China: A Critical Assessment." *Ecological Indicators* 51: 127–38.

Whitington, Jerome. 2016. "Carbon as a Metric of the Human." *Political and Legal Anthropology Review (PoLAR)* 39: 46–63.

Zhang, Li. 2010. *In Search of Paradise: Middle-class Living in a Chinese Metropolis.* Ithaca: Cornell University Press.

Zhu, Yuchao. 2011. "'Performance Legitimacy' and China's Political Adaptation Strategy." *Journal of Chinese Political Science* 16, no. 2: 123–40.

4

Altering the Trajectory of Finance

Meaning-Making and Control in Malaysian Islamic Investment Banks

AARON Z. PITLUCK

Introduction: Theorizing IBF

Critique presupposes understanding. One can't accurately critique—much less regulate or reform or replace—something that one doesn't understand. This truism is particularly perplexing for moral critics of finance, as well as critical social scientists and autonomous regulatory bodies, because there are wide structural asymmetries of knowledge between these outside observers and financial experts (Knorr Cetina 1999). Given the pervasive and growing influence of finance in society (Pitluck, Mattioli, and Souleles 2018), it is important for public intellectuals and the public to be capable of understanding, critiquing, and potentially controlling the finance industry. This chapter investigates the global Islamic banking and finance (IBF) industry in Malaysia to understand how moral critics are bridging these epistemic communities and attempting to alter the trajectory of finance.

Islamic finance is a moralized niche market (Fourcade and Healy 2007) with well over $2 trillion held in Islamic banks and financial instruments, primarily in thirty-two countries in Southeast Asia and West Asia (the Middle East). Approximately 3 percent of IBF is located in Muslim-minority countries (Pitluck and Adhikari 2018). What cultural practices are defined as Islamic finance (Maurer 2005: 40; Warde 2010), and what cultural practices are defined as the unmarked case of (conventional) finance (de Goede 2005) are not predefined or self-evident either from theology or economic theory. A working definition of Islamic finance emphasizes distinctive ends: it must ensure that all financed projects involve productive assets, ideally in entrepreneurial activity, and are not interpreted as prohibited by the religion, such as financing the production of alcohol or pork products. Secondly, the means to reach these ends are constrained in Islamic finance; specifically, profiting from *riba* and *gharar* (roughly translatable as usurious interest and unproductive risk respectively) are prohibited, as are profitably exploiting information asymmetries with clients or other financiers. Moreover, for-profit Islamic banks also have some social obligations, such as charitable giving. Islamic financial institutions are permitted to profit from "Shariah-compliant" banking fees for services rendered and for returns on investments. The precise operationalization of IBF varies across financial institutions and across legal jurisdictions (El-Gamal 2006; Maurer 2005; Pitluck 2013: 433; Pitluck 2016; Sloane-White 2017: ch. 6; Vogel and Hayes 1998: 72–93; Warde 2010).

Previous research in Malaysia has examined how Islamic banking and finance have been guided and promoted by decades of leadership in government, universities, think tanks, and regulatory bodies (Ariff 2017; Gomez and Jomo 1999; Lai 2014; Rethel 2010; Rudnyckyj 2019). In contrast to these "top down" explanations, my methodology examines the prosaic "bottom up" production of new forms of finance within Islamic investment banks. The novelty of this research is in examining how Islamic finance is coproduced before the ideas are assimilated and institutionalized by state actors.

This chapter demonstrates that Islamic finance is a meaning-making and control project negotiated between entrepreneurs, moral critics, and bureaucratic ethicists in small group social interactions embedded in larger assemblages of cognition and agency (c.f. Arjalies et al. 2017; Callon 1998; Knorr Cetina and Bruegger 2002). By "meaning-making," I wish to emphasize that Islamic finance's self-definition is itself inherently contested, and so identifying cultural practices as "conventional finance" or as "Islamic finance" is an ongoing meaning-making process (Pitluck 2013: 431–35). Islamic finance is also a project of control—to control not only the meaning of Islamic finance, but to control investment bankers and ultimately their clients (c.f. Pitluck 2008). The control project is inseparable from the meaning-making project; before one can be a critic of finance, much less alter the trajectory of finance by controlling an investment banker, one must understand and interpret financial instruments and services.

Drawing on this proposition, as well as ethnographic interviews in Islamic investment banks in Malaysia, I argue that the degree to which Islamic finance is a substantive altering of the trajectory of finance is contingent on a power struggle between investment bankers, Shariah scholars, and Shariah personnel within the financial service commodity chain. Shariah scholars are important and powerful critics in meaning-making

and control, but their agency is significantly shaped by areligious[1] investment bankers, by Shariah bureaucrats employed by the firm, and by
upstream clients and downstream investors and their salespeople. This
research induces five strategic factors that shape the balance of power
between the investment bankers and their critics. I conclude by speculating on the implications of these findings for other actors and social movements seeking to moralize markets and alter the trajectory of capitalism. I
suggest that the outcome of such efforts will vary from firm to firm and be
the product of a power struggle between three parties analogous to those
identified here—entrepreneurs, moral critics, and bureaucratic ethicists—
and that the balance of power is shaped, in large part, by strategic behavior
embedded in commodity chains.

Methodology and Literature Review

This paper's findings are derived from a larger, ongoing project. In 2012,
2013, and 2019, I conducted approximately fifty focused, ethnographic,
tape-recorded interviews in Malaysia with investment bankers and Islamic
experts (i.e., "Shariah scholars" and Shariah personnel) in ten investment
banks. The ethnographic interviews focus on the informants' work constructing "*sukuk*," a class of financial instrument developed over the past
quarter century as a moral replacement for sovereign and corporate bonds.
These banks form the super majority of the domestic *sukuk* market and
approximately half of the international *sukuk* market.[2] My informants held
key positions within their respective banks; the investment bankers were
typically located in the Debt Capital Markets department, while the Shariah
experts were to be found either in the Shariah Department or on the bank's
external Shariah Committee.

Investment bankers, like many professionals in markets, are insulated
from external critics by structural information asymmetries between professionals and outsiders (Abbott 1988). This exclusionary financial culture
is institutionalized by professional associations, by state support of the
professions' market power with credentialing requirements, and by post-
secondary educational institutions and on-the-job training. While this
information asymmetry can be bridged—outsiders can obtain financial
expertise and master financial practices—such knowledge changes constantly due to what financiers call "financial innovation" (Nesvetailova
2014). Consequently, outsiders cannot maintain their financial expertise
without "becoming insiders" by obtaining employment in the finance
industry. This problem is observable in regulatory agencies that supervise financial institutions (Eisenbach et al. 2015), and tensions exist even

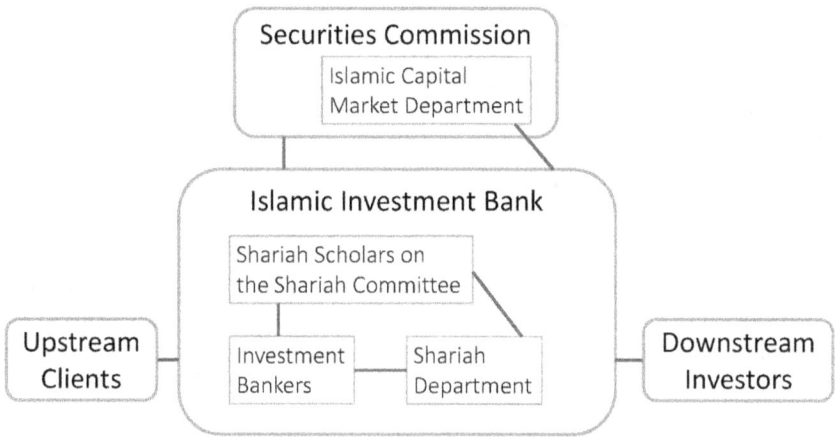

Figure 4.1. The financial commodity chain for *sukuk*. In this moralized financial service commodity chain for *sukuk*, rounded rectangles represent distinct organizations, and lines represent social interactions between key parties that shape meaning-making and control. Figure created by the author.

within the banks between financial professionals and their nonprofessional supervisors (Hardie and MacKenzie 2014; Lépinay 2007; MacKenzie 2011; Muniesa et al. 2011; Preda 2002).

This chapter draws on my ethnographic interviews to investigate how religious outsiders attempt to control financiers and alter the trajectory of finance by bridging the information asymmetries created by the finance profession.

Meaning-Making and Control within the Financial Commodity Chain

What constitutes Islamic finance is hammered out in small group social interactions embedded in financial service commodity chains (c.f. Hopkins and Wallerstein 1986). Figure 4.1 illustrates the financial commodity chain for *sukuk*, an Islamic financial instrument produced and sold by the investment banking industry. Three parties interact within the Islamic investment bank: the investment bankers employed as financial engineers, the Shariah scholars on the Shariah Committee, and the Shariah personnel employed by the bank, notably in the Shariah Department. The bank is regulated by the Securities Commission and the Central Bank, and Shariah experts are employed in the Shariah Advisory Councils of both institutions, as well as in individual departments, such as the Securities Commission's

Islamic Capital Market Department. The market for these financial services consists of the downstream investors who purchase *sukuk* and the upstream clients who hire the investment bank to raise funds by issuing (selling) *sukuk*.[3] Before turning to examine social interaction within the bank more carefully, we must consider the institutional environment in which it takes place.

Compared to global norms, Malaysian corporate governance regulations are stringent and perceived as effective (World Economic Forum 2017).[4] Malaysia also has exceptionally strong corporate governance regulations for Islamic financial institutions (in contrast to countries like Egypt, Saudi Arabia, Turkey, and the United Kingdom, where Shariah-compliance is largely unregulated by the state; see Alkhamees 2013). In Malaysia, to operate as an Islamic bank or as an Islamic subsidiary of a conventional bank, the bank must be licensed or registered as an Islamic financial institution.[5] All such firms are subject to regulatory and legal requirements beyond those of the conventional finance industry. The most salient requirement is the institutionalized position of moral critics and bureaucratic ethicists within Islamic financial institutions, as detailed in the Central Bank's *Shariah Governance Framework for Islamic Financial Institutions* (Bank Negara Malaysia 2011). In my fieldwork, I found that self-descriptions of routine banking work as well as in-depth descriptions of particular *sukuk* were always formulated to conform to the *Shariah Governance Framework*.

Islamic financial institutions must appoint a Shariah Committee to supervise the bank's management (Bank Negara Malaysia 2011).[6] In Malaysia, these positions are analogous to the corporation's board of directors insofar as the members have part-time appointments, are not employed by the bank, and have careers elsewhere (or are retired). The *Framework* requires that Shariah Committees in Malaysia are formally independent of management and report directly to the firms' boards of directors. This committee must be composed of at least five persons, all of them Muslim, the majority of whom are credentialed Islamic experts. The Shariah Committee is assured access to any of the firm's internal documents that it requires (including confidential documents), and its members are granted exemptions from legislated secrecy provisions. To promote financial independence from management, the Islamic experts' compensation is determined by the Remuneration Committee of the Board of Directors, and appointments must meet several criteria so as to avoid conflicts of interest. The reappointment, resignation, or dismissal of a Shariah Committee member must be reported to the Central Bank and its Shariah Advisory Council. All changes to the membership of the Shariah Committee (including appointments) must be approved by both the Central Bank and the Central Bank's own Shariah Advisory Council (see below). Beyond the requirements detailed in the *Framework*, banks and Shariah Committees are free to alter their organization and governance (e.g., whether the Committee makes decisions by consensus, or the specific duties of the Chair).

Shariah experts are also employed internally by the bank as full-time employees. Some of these positions are required by corporate governance regulations; for example, Islamic financial institutions must have Shariah Research and Shariah Secretariat positions to provide support for the Shariah Committee. Those appointed to these positions must have the same minimum credentialing qualifications as persons holding positions on the Shariah Committee. However, Islamic banks in Malaysia pragmatically experiment with hiring additional Shariah personnel, both for the Shariah Department and for other departments, including in Audit, Risk, or Legal.

Shariah experts are also employed in Malaysia's Central Bank (the Shariah Advisory Council in Bank Negara) and the securities market regulator (the Islamic Capital Market Department and the Shariah Advisory Council in the Securities Commission). The *Central Bank of Malaysia Act 2009* institutionalizes the Shariah Advisory Council in the Central Bank as the nation's highest authority for interpreting financial practices in the Islamic Banking and Finance sector, including civil disputes. Malaysia is one of eleven countries that have institutionalized centralized Shariah committees at the level of the Central Bank.[7] The institutional context is additionally shaped by various transnational bodies of Shariah experts, among them the Accounting and Auditing Organization for Islamic Financial Institutions (AAOIFI), the Islamic Financial Services Board (IFSB), and the International Islamic Fiqh Academy established by the Organization of Islamic Cooperation (OIC). In my Malaysian fieldwork, Shariah scholars occasionally consulted publications by these and other bodies, but this was done within the Malaysian legal context in which the Central Bank's Shariah Advisory Council is the country's highest authority for meaning-making and adjudicating control.

The Three Parties

How do (potentially non-Muslim) investment bankers make Shariah-compliant products and financial instruments? These bankers are typically termed "product sponsors" or "product specialists," or are referred to by the department in which they work. Many are like Lee,[8] a non-Muslim Chinese-Malaysian executive vice president employed in the conventional parent bank's Debt Capital Markets Department rather than the bank's

Islamic banking subsidiary. Lee is a deal-maker, engaged with the client services team at the earliest "pitch" stage of a product for a prospective client. He "works hand in hand" with what he terms an "Islamic structuring team" composed of investment bankers in his department and Shariah personnel assembled from the bank for each project based on expertise and availability. He also works quite closely with "Shariah Advisory" in the Shariah Department. From Lee's perspective, as a banker making bespoke transactions for businesses, most of which are Shariah-compliant, Shariah makes finance "quite limited." Therefore, to make a financial instrument Shariah-compliant, you must explore ways to get around things. He perceives himself as "layering in the Islamic structure" on top of "the underlying commercial intentions" of the client. He described his team in Debt Capital Markets as a "check and balance for the commercial aspect" of the transaction. For Lee, being "Shariah-compliant" means above all compliant to a client's best interests. He perceives himself as advocating for the client's economic interests, while it is the responsibility of the Shariah experts to ensure that the client and the client's investors will perceive the *sukuk* as Shariah-compliant. Generalizing from our case, we can conceptualize the investment bankers as internal entrepreneurs creating moralized markets, who are deeply concerned for the marketability and profitability of their products (c.f. Godechot 2008).

Globally, including in Malaysia, the Shariah experts who sit on corporate firms' external Shariah Committees are referred to as "Shariah scholars." This is an honorific expression rarely used to refer to Shariah experts employed full-time in firms (discussed below), who are variously described as "Shariah officers" or referred to in organizational terms (e.g., "the Shariah team" or "the Shariah Advisory"). In the language of the corporate governance literature, Shariah scholars are independent and external persons not employed by the bank, representing neither management nor shareholders. Looking outward from our case, the Shariah scholars can be understood as external moral critics with an institutionalized position in this moralized commodity chain.

In contrast to other countries, the Malaysian Central Bank stipulates that a Shariah scholar may not sit on the Shariah Committee of more than one bank or insurance company (Alkhamees 2013; Rusni Hassan et al. 2016: 52).[9] Therefore, in Malaysia, all Shariah scholars are, in the words of one such scholar, "part-timers" with full-time jobs outside of the industry—often in universities or Islamic finance think tanks—or are retired. The Shariah scholars I interviewed, without exception, did not identify as employees of the bank on whose Shariah Committee they served. They did not refer to the bank as "we." Rather, they referred to it as "the bank," "the business," "the function," or "management." Some emphasized that they were distant and critical observers of the corporation. Mohd stressed at diverse points in our interview that, as a scholar, "We are answerable to God. We believe that we cannot go against God's will. Shariah is there and we should exhaust our effort to apply all of God's orders. So we should obey the Shariah and we should be able to change our policy, our bank's policy, our legal constraints ... to God's will. That is our philosophy." He then posed the rhetorical question, "So why do you ask us to change our Shariah in order to satisfy [Central Bank] policy? They are the ones that should change policy! This always creates a sort of tension between the Shariah Committee and management."

Another Shariah scholar, Ahmad, emphasized that the bankers and Shariah scholars have independent and autonomous roles: "To them [the bankers], they just want to do it.... . To them, I don't think [the detailed requirements of Shariah] makes much difference. But they also want to comply, if possible. We are the ones who tell them whether what they want to do is complying with the Shariah or not."

However, such uncompromising positions are exceptional. Much more common among scholars employed on Shariah Committees is a relationship to the bank of pragmatic incrementalism. This is partly theological and partly political. Numerous scholars explicitly or implicitly put forward the theological argument that permissibility is the core of *muamalat* (Islamic economic jurisprudence). As al-Qaradawi (2001: 7), a scholar who is influential in Malaysia and in the Islamic world, explains, "In Islam, the sphere of things prohibited is very small, while that of things permissible is extremely vast. [Hence] ... the general principle of the permissibility of things and within the scope of Allah's favor." The other component is political. As Faruq explained:

> We need to sort of strike a balance between the readiness of the industry and what needs to be done immediately; what can be done in five years' time; what can be done in ten years' time. So the industry needs to grow. We don't want to be seen as too rigid. We don't want to be seen as too many requirements to fulfill ... a lot of things that we need to balance.

In a separate interview, his colleague on the same bank's Shariah Committee made a very similar point:

> I think that for most Islamic investors, for them they are like, "Okay, I know [Islamic finance] is not perfect but I will live with it." ... Because if you look to it twenty years ago, what was Malaysia with regard to Islamic finance? Nothing. Thirty years ago, we didn't even have Islamic finance.... . So it takes time to fine tune. And so I think that is basically one of accommodation. We know it is not perfect, but better than we were before. Hopefully, we will [get] into a better situation in the future.... . So I

know some of the things we approve are not 100 percent right, but I also know that [if] you want it to be 100 percent, it won't fly.... This is the compromise we have to do; this is the only way to do it. It is a work in progress; so we go.

When Shariah scholars described themselves in a positive light, or described others in a positive light, they tended to present themselves as engaging intellectually with the bank's products and modifying them, rather than preventing a product from materializing. For example, Harun argued that a Shariah scholar shouldn't engage in "sheikh sitting," which he imagines as "a sheikh in long white robes comes in and issues a fatwa and says this is what you have to do." It is better to be "proactive" and to "be very imaginative," to imagine the products from the perspective of what is fair to the customer as well as the bank. Ashraff emphasized that the Shariah Committee cannot simply say what is "allowable." "You cannot stop at that level. If it is not allowable, what is the alternative?"

In contrast to the views of self-described "Islamic economists" based outside of the finance industry who emphasize social justice rather than commerce (see Rudnyckyj 2017, 2019), numerous Shariah scholars paused in their narratives to emphasize that Islamic financial institutions are profit-making commercial institutions and not charities:

> There is nothing wrong with getting profit from the activities because ... even though you are an Islamic bank, [that] does not mean you are a charitable body. You are a profit-making body with some responsibilities to the shareholders, to the depositors.... Profit also is one of [our] targets but having said that ... you can get as much as possible profit gains, but you cannot ignore the Shariah side, the ethical side of it.

There are spatial and temporal limits to the capacity of the Shariah Committee, convening at least once every other month (Bank Negara Malaysia 2011: 36), with its five or so "part-timers," to evaluate and monitor bank practices to ensure that they are Shariah-compliant. For some, the responsibility weighs heavily. Irfan explained that he serves as a Shariah scholar because it is his responsibility as a human, and as part of a community. He described how he feels accountable for his work, both now and in the hereafter. "I myself, I told my colleague, if I am not comfortable, I do not want to continue. Simply because you [are] a Shariah Committee [member], you have responsibilities, and therefore you are accountable, and the responsibilities actually [are] beyond what we can bear. So if you don't do extra, are we comfortable? Are we being responsible here?"

To enable "part-timer" Shariah scholars to supervise a vast, potentially transnational Islamic Investment bank and to fulfill its obligations under the *Shariah Governance Framework*, Islamic banks employ "full-timer"

Shariah personnel to assist the Shariah scholars. Generalizing from our case, we can understand these Shariah personnel as bureaucratic ethicists (cf. Abend 2014). In Islamic banks, these employees are tasked with empowering two parties with partly conflicting interests: other bank employees such as the investment bankers and management tasked with generating revenues and minimizing costs, and the external Shariah scholars on the Shariah Committee tasked with supervising the bank to ensure it is profiting (and cost-cutting) using Shariah-compliant means. The *Shariah Governance Framework* specifies little regarding these employees, other than that Islamic financial institutions are required to provide administrative support for the Shariah Committee, and to ensure that their decisions are carried out.

Analytically, we can imagine Islamic banks as organizing their Shariah Departments on an advocacy spectrum. At one end of the spectrum, the Shariah Department is simply an advocate of management's interests. As a Shariah scholar observes of the Shariah Department with which he works, "So they, of course, they are always on the CEO's side. The CEO wants something, so they are always trying to [advocate a Shariah opinion to support] the CEO and the management."[10] At the other end of the spectrum, the Shariah Department—although not independent—may advocate on behalf of the Shariah Committee within the bank. For example, one Head of a Shariah Department, throughout our three-hour interview, consistently identified himself and his department with the bank—using the word "we," for example. However, at a crucial point in the interview, he emphasized that he perceived himself and the Shariah scholars as forming a single profession, contrasted with the management:

> Because Shariah people want to talk among themselves, it is easier to understand, compared to when they talk to outsiders. Because outsiders tend to—bankers always have secrets. They will not tell everything to Shariah scholars. So that one, we want to protect [against]. They won't tell everything to Shariah scholars, so Shariah Advisory's role is to know everything, what basically [the bankers] want out of this proposed structure.

However, even at this bank, other Shariah personnel are staffed in the product development team to ensure unconflicted Shariah advocacy on behalf of the bankers' areligious interests.

Having identified three distinct parties within Islamic investment banks that coproduce Islamic finance, we can also analytically specify three ideal-typical banks that vary according to the balance of power between these three parties. In critic-empowered banks, the scholars in the Shariah Committee are the most powerful actors in the triad and impose their interpretation of Shariah upon the bank's products and processes. In the other two ideal-types, although the Shariah Committee retains formal control over all the bank's products, in practice, the balance of power shifts to another party. In entrepreneur-empowered banks, the Shariah Committee and Shariah personnel exert minimal influence over the investment bankers whose decisions, as in a conventional bank, are determined by their professional expertise (Ho 2009; Lépinay 2011). Lastly, in the bureaucrat-empowered banks, the Shariah personnel employed by management exert the most influence over both the investment bankers and Shariah scholars. This typology is helpful in the analysis of empirical organizational contexts. In the remaining sections of this chapter, I adduce five significant factors that the parties manipulate and the consequences of the ensuing balance of power for the bank's behavior.

Manipulation of Time

The first factor shaping meaning-making and social control is the manipulation of time. In economic life, time itself is priced. In the finance industry, a significant cost of financial transactions is the price of experts' limited time and cognitive labor. Additionally, firms often have a competitive advantage if they can perform high quality temporally constrained and sequenced tasks faster than their competitors. Clients hire an investment bank to produce a *sukuk* to raise funds; the longer the process takes, the longer the delay in receiving the funds. In Malaysia, the norm is for an investment bank to produce a *sukuk* within three months of the bank receiving the client's contract—although powerful clients have been known to pressure banks to issue in as short as four or five weeks. Another motivation for issuing as quickly as possible comes into play when the bank has made assurances to the prospective client based on short-term economic forecasts. Delays in issuing a *sukuk* increase the risk that the client will not raise the funds the banker had predicted. Shariah Committee members also face temporal constraints. They are not employees, they have incompatible schedules, and their primary worksites are geographically dispersed. These constraints are magnified if some Shariah scholars on the Committee are based in the Middle East.

Throughout my interviews, the Shariah experts emphasized the intellectual challenge of interpreting and understanding complex financial products in light of the religion. In practice, their interpretive work always takes place in a social context of limited time—limited time to read and understand the financial products, and limited time to dialogue with fellow Shariah experts in the Shariah Committee or in the bank. The Shariah scholars, as "part-timers," are at a temporal disadvantage compared with the "full-timers" in the Shariah Department, from whom they "buy time" by asking the latter to conduct tasks on their behalf.

Delaying a bank's products—rather than explicitly withholding approval—may be one of the stronger and subtler forms of the Shariah Committee's power:

> Where [there is] a lot of debate, [and where] there are some disagreements, and then so the challenge is to … usually we will say, 'Let's postpone this and think more about it. Get more information. Revisit this.' And there have been products where up to three meetings we finally come to an agreement. There have been cases where they [the bank] have withdrawn the product—withdrew the proposal—because they saw the debate.

The securities market regulator is in the strongest position to manipulate time. I spoke with investment bankers at two banks who had had products approved by their Shariah Committee, only to find that the Securities Commission raised questions about the Islamic principle of the product. The ensuing delay was sufficient to force the bank to reengineer the *sukuk* by grounding it in an alternative Islamic principle.

Management uses diverse strategies to shorten the time Shariah Committee members have to review documents and deliberate. At several banks, the "standard operating procedure" was for management to submit documents to the Shariah Committee members a minimum of seven calendar days prior to the Shariah Committee meeting. However, there was substantial tension in this organizational requirement. One Shariah scholar insisted that he would not permit management to "smuggle papers" into meetings at the last minute when they were of substantive importance. Others were ready to compromise on this requirement. Working on behalf of management, the Shariah Secretariat would sometimes pressure the scholars to expedite a conclusion by referencing the remaining items on the Committee's agenda.

Agenda Setting

A second factor shaping the balance of power in meaning-making and control is agenda setting. Shariah scholars potentially exert enormous control over investment bankers in Shariah Committees. In critic-empowered banks, scholars can and do put investment bankers on their agendas and mandate their attendance. They interrogate bankers regarding products and processes and dismiss them when the committee chooses to deliberate privately. They can and do request that bankers in various departments or product development units conduct internal studies in their areas of expertise to address points of fact or concerns of the Committee. My ethnographic interviews reveal, however, that these powers are qualified by the balance of power between the Shariah scholars and other parties in the bank.

Arguably the party with the most institutionalized agenda setting power is the Shariah Department, particularly where it has a strong and prestigious Head. The Shariah Department Head acts as a gatekeeper with regard to the issues and information that reach the Shariah Committee. As one Head explained succinctly, "I am the one who decides, basically, whether the issue goes to the Shariah Committee or not." The Shariah Department creates the literal agenda for the Shariah Committee meetings. When scholars make decisions in the meetings, the Shariah Department institutionalizes them in the form of minutes. There is a tension in how detailed and accurately this translation is accomplished, particularly because many Shariah scholars rely on previous minutes to recall their own debates and decisions. There is also external pressure to create minimalist minutes because minutes can be accessed by regulators and potentially by the public.

Management, too, holds significant agenda-setting power, above all in determining the Shariah Department's size and the Shariah Scholars' compensation. Institutionalized routines can be reshaped to alter who in the bank is expected to attend the Shariah Committee meetings, and whether the Shariah Committee members are empowered to exclude these committee participants and discuss bank matters privately. In three different banks, I came across cases where management had eluded critique of its own Shariah scholars by hiring prestigious external Shariah scholars as consultants. The motivations for this varied. In one firm, key decision makers (perhaps the client) perceived the Shariah Department and Committee as too inexperienced. At the other two banks, the investment bankers or management preferred to work with one scholar rather than a committee so as to make faster decisions—a situation magnified in one case by the fact that several members of the Shariah Committee were based in the Middle East. Regardless of the motivation, the net effect of these arrangements is to disempower and deskill the firms' Shariah scholars and Shariah departments into auditors of prestigious external scholars' meaning-making. Such arrangements obviate the intentions of the Shariah corporate governance regulations, which are designed to minimize conflicts of interest and create zones of autonomy between the product development teams and the Shariah scholars.

Another strategy to circumvent the Shariah Committee's meaning-making and control is to approach each Shariah Committee member individually. This is a common practice in some banks. Typically, management insists that a decision is time sensitive, and must be decided prior to the next Shariah Committee meeting. A member of the Shariah Department approaches each Shariah Committee member individually, often in person, to solicit approval. When the Shariah Department has collected enough approvals, the decision is made and minuted at the following meeting as an interim decision. While in theory, each Shariah Committee member can telephone or email other Committee members to confer on these occasions, in practice, this strategy by management circumvents the Shariah Committee as a deliberative body. In critic-empowered banks, Shariah scholars may insist on concluding a one-on-one meeting by postponing a decision until the next Shariah Committee meeting. In Islamic investment banks with powerful Shariah Committee Heads, the latter may make decisions as a proxy for the Committee.

Management's Positioning of the Shariah Committee within the Commodity Chain

The third determinant of the balance of power between entrepreneurs, moral critics, and bureaucratic ethicists is where management positions Shariah scholars and personnel within the financial service commodity chain. Management retains considerable discretion in this strategic area. When Shariah experts are positioned earlier and further upstream in the commodity chain, they are in a stronger position to shape the outcome. The later downstream they are introduced in the commodity chain, the less influence they will have over the work of the investment bankers, unless they are willing to withhold their authorization and send the product back to the product development team, or to enter into late-stage negotiations for alternative designs with the investment bankers.

In bureaucrat-empowered banks, informants described Shariah experts employed in product development teams alongside investment bankers, providing input at the earliest imaginable stage in the creation of new products, even before the prospective client has signed a contract with the investment bank, while the scholars are positioned at the end of the commodity chain. As one investment banker described this relationship, his financial engineers worked with the "Islamic Team" to develop financial instruments and products with an eye toward "[getting] the approval of the Shariah scholars." In such banks, by the time the final product reaches the Shariah Committee, there are unlikely to be many Shariah issues, and therefore little room for creative input into the resulting structure. As one Shariah Committee member at this bank explained, "We are just tweaking here and there because . . . [if] the Shariah Department is actually playing its role efficiently and effectively, then our work will be lessened." The Shariah Department would not bring any products to the Shariah Committee where there were "obvious problems.... . They would only bring it to us if they feel okay, there is no issues.... . The Shariah Committee ... doesn't want to be looking at everything, so in many ways, we are guided by the Shariah Department." This balance of power can be subtle; at this particular bank, the Shariah Committee is provided preliminary sketches of new products for "in principle approval" very early in the process; however, the scholars rarely supply feedback at this stage.

In contrast, at critic-empowered banks, the Shariah Committee is substantively incorporated early in the commodity chain. For example, at one bank, a Shariah scholar discussed the extensive discussions that the Shariah Committee had on a proposed product. The investment banker's description was consonant with this. He described creating new products as "an iterative process" in which he is telephoning or meeting with Shariah experts daily. "Sometimes we deal with them too much, lah!" and then he laughs. He also emphasizes that creative ideas sometimes arise among the Shariah scholars: "When it comes to innovative structures, they will definitely speak to us and talk to us from a commercial perspective to see if that works, if we can sell it to the market."

At an entrepreneur-empowered bank, the investment bankers elude and disempower the bank's Shariah scholars and personnel by having recourse to external Shariah scholars as described above. "Quite frankly," one investment banker explained, "the only reason we need to go back to [our] Shariah [Committee] is because we need their endorsement of the structures, even if it is a typical structure that has been used over and over again. But because of the [Securities Commission] requirements, we need Shariah advisement for each submission. We therefore need to appoint or consult them technically [at the end of the process]."

External Support

A strikingly unusual characteristic of Islamic finance in Malaysia is the role that financial regulators play in standardization. For example, as of February 2020, the Shariah Advisory Council in the Central Bank has issued fourteen Shariah Standards. As described on the Council's website, "Shariah Standards outline the principles, pillars and conditions of specific Shariah contracts to ensure end-to-end compliance with Shariah rulings in the structuring of Islamic financial products and services. The Standards also contain optional practices to guide industry players, particularly in relation to practices" (Bank Negara Malaysia 2018). For example, the Standard for

Tawarruq runs to forty-four pages; only one of these pages is devoted to a theological analysis of the concept, and this is the only page that makes reference to the Quran (Bank Negara Malaysia 2015: 38). The ethnographic interviews reveal that these Shariah Standards are extensively used by Shariah scholars and personnel in their daily work interpreting bank practices, in large part because new products and services require regulatory approval, and regulators' disclosure-based and merit-based evaluations are based on national Shariah standardization.[11]

This standardization has several consequences for the balance of power within the triad, and for altering the trajectory of finance. By providing guidelines of Shariah-compliant business practices and products, investment bankers can cheaply innovate new products by making the case to their own Shariah Committees, and then to their regulator, that an innovation conforms with an existing standard. Standardization also reframes moral debates within Islamic finance from arguing over precedents and first principles to the simpler task of demonstrating whether an innovation is accurately described by one or more existing standards. For both bankers and Shariah experts, standards facilitate financial innovation by acting as components for new innovations, such as when a new *sukuk* structure builds on a combination of *murabahah* and *tawarruq* standards. On the other hand, the perennial risk of standardization is that its ethical categories shield stigmatized behaviors and that such categories impair rather than enhance moral deliberation (DiMaggio 1997; Fourcade et al. 2013).

Standardization has contradictory effects on the control of investment bankers. On one hand, it enhances critics' control of bankers by channeling financial innovations into categories previously judged to be moral. The national standardization by regulatory bodies empowers regulators by requiring that all private parties create financial products out of contracts and principles that the regulators interpret as Shariah-compliant. It also requires that independent or foreign Shariah scholars and experts interpret finance using standardized principles codified by the regulators. Standardization also empowers Shariah scholars and personnel within the bank by creating a "baseline" definition of what constitutes Islamic banking and finance, while permitting Shariah scholars to insist on "stricter" additional requirements as to what is Islamic finance, so long as these additional requirements conform to the national standards.

On the other hand, an unanticipated consequence of standardization is that it empowers bankers vis-à-vis moral critics by deskilling the scholars' interpretive authority and enhancing bankers' capacity to enter into a dialogue with Islamic experts. For example, at an entrepreneur-empowered bank, a Muslim investment banker interpreted the Shariah Committee as being a mere endorser of Shariah opinion, rather than creating its own interpretations, because of the prior standardization and the recycling of previously endorsed financial structures:

> Nowadays, there is not much innovation in Islamic transactions.... Because, like I mentioned, it is nothing new. Because you know, all of us [investment bankers] are quite well-versed in it. We could just, (laughing) we could BE the Islamic scholars, (laughing) because we are the ones who actually come out with the innovation, in consultation with the Shariah adviser. So we don't have to reinvent the wheel. We've been using the same structure over and over again.... That's why we don't need a Shariah officer, or Shariah desk, or Shariah unit in the [financial engineering department]. Because we ourselves—I think it is the same structure in other banks[12]— because [we] are already quite well-versed with the Islamic structure, [so we] don't really need any specific or educated Islamic desk to come out with the structure.

This banker's laughter was incited by his willingness to voice a sub-versive opinion in which investment bankers' expertise in Islamic finance eclipses those of Shariah experts, who are deskilled into auditors who "quite frankly" are only required for their "endorsement" "because of the [Securities Commission] requirements" (Souleles 2017). At another bank, a Chinese non-Muslim investment banker emphasized how he and his team—although lacking Shariah expertise—are able to contest the Shariah decisions of Shariah experts: "Of course there is always a healthy debate if there is any pushback from the Shariah [experts].... Then we'd question [them] and we'd debate [them]. Why was it acceptable in the past but not this time around? So, I wouldn't say they have sole authority in terms of what can or cannot be done from a Shariah perspective."

Here, there is no embarrassed laughter—merely a perspective (grounded in a larger conversation) that Islamic finance is not solely determined by the expertise of Shariah scholars, but also by the non-Muslim investment bankers' interpretations of previously endorsed structures and of Shariah standards.

Quality of Auditing

Another structural problem in Islamic financial institutions is that the Shariah Committee can be insulated and isolated; their voices heard but unheeded. One Shariah scholar with whom I spoke, who was employed by a conventional legal firm rather than an Islamic financial institution, pro-vided a vivid image of a struggle I encountered in every investment bank in my study: "These Shariah Committees are like boxes in one corner, over here making these pronouncements. But [does the firm] implement them? Do[es it] even understand them?" A final factor determining the degree to which Shariah scholars exercise control over investment bankers is the quality of Shariah-auditing within the firm.

Any large organization—including the national and transnational investment banks in which I conducted my research—needs to extend managerial control across space and time. In the US and UK conventional finance industry, white-collar crime and unethical behavior is well known and widespread (Labaton Sucharow LLP 2015). Banks' control over white-collar crime is often observed to fail, as employees stand to make enormous gains if they can circumvent standard operating procedures, risk-based constraints, and accompanying audit procedures (Economist Intelligence Unit 2013; Harrington 2016; Oka and Kuijt 2014). Many of the controls used in the conventional financial sector—and their weaknesses—are identical in Islamic banks, either because the Islamic institution is a subsidiary of a conventional financial institution, or because Islamic financial institutions replicate perceived best practices from their conventional peer competitors.

In conventional finance, corporate compliance with internal control processes and national corporate governance regulations is accomplished in two ways. The first is through external auditors (independent third parties) who are paid to ensure that all information published in the corporation's annual report is a "true and fair" account of the corporation's financial position. For public listed corporations in countries with relatively strong corporate governance regulations, as in Malaysia (World Economic Forum 2017: 191–92), the report of the external auditor is made available to shareholders and generally also to the public. External auditors are insulated from management; they are hired by shareholders at the annual general meeting and may be subject to mandatory rotation requirements. The second method involves internal auditors employed by the firm, who are only permitted to report to internal parties such as the Chief Executive Officer and the firm's Audit Committee. These internal auditors have a broader mandate to support management by identifying risks and ensuring compliance to internal control processes (Islamic Finance Council UK (UKIFC) and International Shari'ah Research Academy for Islamic Finance (ISRA) 2016: 8). "Internal auditors are inherently impaired in providing impartial information due to the nature of their appointment and line of reporting" (UKIFC and ISRA 9).

In Islamic finance, neither of the two multilateral standard-setting bodies requires Islamic financial institutions to have external auditors for Shariah-compliance (i.e., the Accounting and Auditing Organization for Islamic Financial Institutions [AAOIFI] and the Islamic Financial Services Board [IFSB]). During the period of fieldwork, this was not a requirement in Malaysia (UKIFC and ISRA 29), and none of the banks in which I interviewed required the use of external Shariah auditors, at least not for *sukuk*. Since Islamic financial products and instruments in Malaysia must undergo a Shariah-compliance check by the national regulator (i.e., the Central Bank or the Securities Commission), many interviewees interpreted this as a third-party external audit. "It should be noted, however, that the results of [a regulator's] audit are in normal circumstances not communicated publicly" (UKIFC and ISRA 29). Consequently, there is no impartial information publicly available in Malaysia to assure the public that Islamic financial institutions are meeting their own standards of Shariah-compliance.

In almost every bank in which I interviewed, informants spoke plainly about the challenge of hiring and holding on to employees for internal Shariah audits, and about the intellectual and organizational challenges involved in conducting high quality internal audits. Numerous Shariah scholars did not know the organizational outcome of their Shariah Committee deliberations and were well aware of the challenges in implementing Shariah Committee decisions throughout the organization, particularly across all retail branches. During the period of fieldwork, Shariah-compliance was not a sham; internal Shariah auditors, lower management, or public complaints did identify non-compliance and bring such matters to the Shariah Committee, Shariah Department, Audit Committee, or CEO. However, Shariah scholars' control of bank products and processes is inherently weakened by the absence of third-party auditors—in a way analogous to risk-based controls in conventional financial institutions, and in contrast to third-party auditing of financial statements in publicly listed corporations in countries with strong corporate governance regulations. Shariah experts' control of investment bankers ultimately depends on the degree to which Shariah Committee decisions are implemented throughout the bank.

Conclusion: Implications for Altering the Trajectory of Finance

This chapter has argued that the Shariah experts employed in Islamic investment banks, as well as the Shariah experts appointed as independent "scholars" on Shariah Committees, are able to limit the scope of conventional finance and alter its trajectory. These experts exercise agency and can routinely prevent the financing of economic activities that they deem noncompliant with the Shariah. Moreover, by being positioned within Islamic investment banks, they are in a position to learn about, critically appraise, and make moral judgments inside of the financial innovation pipeline. This affords them a position of genuine power, given the rapid pace of restructuring that is characteristic of financial services. However, I have also documented lapses of control, tensions in the balance of power between the Shariah Committees and the Shariah Departments, and strategies whereby investment bankers attempt to evade their Islamic critics. The key site of contestation is in small-group social interactions deep in the bureaucratic structures of investment banks that are themselves embedded in long financial-service commodity chains.

The case of Islamic banking and finance may be generalizable to other moralized markets. The success or failure of a moralized firm to escape the isomorphic pressures of the conventional industry in which it competes (DiMaggio and Powell 1983) depends on the balance of power between the parties I have identified as entrepreneurs, moral critics, and bureaucratic ethicists (c.f. Fligstein 1987). Based on the case of Islamic investment banking in Malaysia, I have identified five factors that shape this balance of power: (1) the manipulation of time, (2) agenda-setting power, (3) entrepreneurs' strategic ability of where to position critics within the firm and within the commodity chain, (4) the quality of auditing within the firm, and (5) ethical standardization. Very powerful isomorphic social forces pressure Islamic financial institutions to create financial instruments and services that closely resemble those of the conventional financial industry (Pitluck 2016). Although the end products of Islamic and conventional finance may be superficially similar, the contractual machinery is distinctive (Pitluck 2013). My informants interpret it as theologically superior, if not morally superior. The institutionalization of critics within Islamic investment banks in Malaysia demonstrates that it is possible—albeit an ongoing challenge—to alter the trajectory of capitalism.

Acknowledgments

The field research was sponsored by Budapesti Közép-Európai Egyetem Alapítvány (CEU BPF). The views expressed in this chapter are those of the author and do not necessarily reflect the views of the Foundation. I am indebted to Robert W. Hefner, Lynette Spillman, and Alya Guseva for their close and insightful critiques of previous drafts. In addition to the meeting in Halle, this research has benefited from feedback at the Association of Asian Studies and the American Anthropological Association in 2015, the University of Notre Dame Culture Workshop in 2016, the Society for the Advancement of Socio-Economics in 2019, and the Sociology Colloquium at the University of Illinois in Champaign-Urbana in 2020.

Aaron Z. Pitluck is an Associate Professor of Sociology at Illinois State University and current President (2018–2022) of the International Sociological Association's Research Committee on Economy & Society (ISA RC02). He has recently served as Guest Editor (with Fabio Mattioli and Daniel Souleles) for a special issue of *Economic Anthropology* devoted to financialization (2018, vol. 5, no. 2).

Notes

1. Analogous to amoral, I define "areligious" as "not within the sphere of religion; not to be characterized as either religious or irreligious or nonreligious."
2. According to the 2013 RAM League Tables, the banks in which I interviewed created approximately 86 percent of the *sukuk* issued that year and at least 85 percent of the *sukuk* funds raised. The 2012 RAM League Table is less detailed; but among the top five firms by market share, my informants' firms produced at least 60 percent of *sukuk* issued in 2012 and at least 52 percent by value.
3. Space constraints prohibit a full analysis of the influence of upstream and downstream parties. For rare analyses of the influence of clients on professional investor's behavior, see Pitluck (2008) and Arjalies et al. (2017).
4. In the 2017–18 index, the World Economic Forum ranks Malaysia as the fifteenth highest country for Accountability of Private Institutions, a widely used measure of corporate governance, based on five indexes (ethical behavior of firms, strength of auditing & reporting standards, efficacy of corporate boards, protection of minority shareholders' interests, and strength of investor protection).
5. Islamic banks are licensed under the Islamic Financial Services Act 2013, which supersedes the Islamic Banking Act 1983.
6. Alkhamees (2013) observes that national regulations requiring Islamic financial institutions to have Shariah Supervisory Boards (Shariah Committees) are rare. Exceptions include Malaysia, Jordan, Kuwait, Lebanon, Pakistan, and the United Arab Emirates (Alkhamees 2013: 139).
7. The others are Bahrain, Bangladesh, Brunei, Indonesia, Malaysia, Nigeria, Oman, Pakistan, Qatar, Sudan, and the United Arab Emirates. An additional three countries—the Maldives, the Philippines, and Syria—do not have a centralized Shariah committee, but have legislated national Shariah Governance Regulations for Islamic financial institutions (Islamic Finance Council UK (UKIFC) and International Shari'ah Research Academy for Islamic Finance (ISRA) 2016: 7; Rusni Hassan et al. 2016).
8. All names are pseudonyms, and all interviewees are given male genders to ensure anonymity. Unfortunately, this obscures gender dynamics in the industry. For a penetrating analysis of gender in Malaysia's Islamic economy, see Sloane-White (2017).
9. Pakistan attempted a similar restriction on Shariah scholars, but ultimately abandoned the restriction due to a shortage of qualified advisors. Kuwait has no

restriction on the number of financial institutions that a Shariah scholar may sit on; but to mitigate conflicts of interest, the scholar may not sit on the bank's board of directors, nor hold more than 5 percent of the bank's capital (Rusni et al 2013: 63).

10. This perception of the Shariah scholar was corroborated in the ethnographic descriptions of daily work that I conducted with the Head of the Shariah Department at the same bank.

11. For example, *sukuk* (like bonds) must typically be reviewed by the Securities Commission before it is issued. This includes a review by Shariah experts within the Securities Commission. Similarly, the Securities Commission's *Guidelines on Sukuk* specifies that every *sukuk* created in Malaysia must use one or more of fourteen approved Shariah principles (distinct from but overlapping with those mentioned in the main text). Otherwise, the investment bank must first seek a ruling from the Securities Commission's Shariah Advisory Council permitting an alternative Shariah principle (Securities Commission Malaysia 2014). The time-constraint created by this additional approval is viewed by investment bankers as costly, except in the unusual case of time insensitive clients.

12. As argued in the main text, and in contrast to this interlocutor's perceptions, the internal organizational structure varies between critic-, entrepreneur-, and bureaucrat-empowered banks.

References

Abbott, Andrew. 1988. *The System of Professions: An Essay on the Division of Expert Labor.* Chicago: University of Chicago Press.

Abend, Gabriel. 2014. *The Moral Background: An Inquiry into the History of Business Ethics.* Princeton: Princeton University Press.

Alkhamees, Ahmad. 2013. "The Impact of Shari'ah Governance Practices on Shari'ah Compliance in Contemporary Islamic Finance." *Journal of Banking Regulation* 14 (April 2013): 134–63. doi:10.1057/jbr.2012.12.

al-Qaradawi, Yusuf. 2001. *The Lawful and the Prohibited in Islam.* Translated by K. al-Hilbawi and M. S. Siddiqi. Cairo: al-Falah Foundation for Translation, Publication & Distribution.

Ariff, Mohamed, ed. 2017. *Islamic Finance in Malaysia: Growth and Development.* Kuala Lumpur: Pearson Malaysia Sdn Bhd.

Arjalies, Diane-Laure, Philip Grant, Iain Hardie, Donald MacKenzie, and Ekaterina Svetlova. 2017. *Chains of Finance: How Investment Management Is Shaped.* New York: Oxford University Press.

Bank Negara Malaysia. 2011. *Shariah Governance Framework for Islamic Financial Institutions.* Kuala Lumpur: Bank Negara Malaysia.

———. 2015. *Tawarruq.* Kuala Lumpur: Bank Negara Malaysia.

———. 2018. "Shariah Standards and Operational Requirement." Kuala Lumpur: Shariah Advisory Council, Bank Negara Malaysia. Accessed 3 February 2020. https://www.sacbnm.org/?page_id=3318.

Callon, Michel. 1998. *The Laws of the Markets*. Malden, MA: Blackwell Publishers/The Sociological Review.

de Goede, Marieke. 2005. *Virtue, Fortune and Faith: A Genealogy of Finance*. Minneapolis: University of Minnesota Press.

DiMaggio, Paul. 1997. "Culture and Cognition." *Annual Review of Sociology* 23: 263–87.

DiMaggio, Paul, and Walter W. Powell. 1983. "The Iron Cage Revisited: Institutional Isomorphism and Collective Rationality in Organizational Fields." *American Sociological Review* 48, no. 2: 147–60.

Economist Intelligence Unit. 2013. "A Crisis of Culture: Valuing Ethics and Knowledge in Financial Services." London: The Economist Intelligence Unit.

Eisenbach, Thomas, Andrew Haughwout, Beverly Hirtle, Anna Kovner, David Lucca, and Matthew Plosser. 2015. "Supervising Large, Complex Financial Institutions: What Do Supervisors Do?" *Federal Reserve Bank of New York Staff Reports* (729).

El-Gamal, Mahmoud A. 2006. *Islamic Finance: Law, Economics, and Practice*. Cambridge, UK: Cambridge University Press.

Fligstein, Neil. 1987. "The Intraorganizational Power Struggle: Rise of Finance Personnel to Top Leadership in Large Corporations, 1919–1979." *American Sociological Review* 52, no. 1: 44–58.

Fourcade, Marion, and Kieran Healy. 2007. "Moral Views of Market Society." *Annual Review of Sociology* 33: 285–311.

Fourcade, Marion, Philippe Steiner, Wolfgang Streeck, and Cornelia Woll. 2013. "Moral Categories in the Financial Crisis." *Socio-Economic Review* 11, no. 3: 601–27. doi: 10.1093/ser/mwt012.

Godechot, Olivier. 2008. "What Do Heads of Dealing Rooms Do? The Social Capital of Internal Entrepreneurs." *The Sociological Review* 56, s. 1: 145–61.

Gomez, Edmund Terence, and K. S. Jomo. 1999. *Malaysia's Political Economy: Politics, Patronage and Profits*. Cambridge, UK: Cambridge University Press.

Hardie, Iain, and Donald MacKenzie. 2014. "The Lemon-Squeezing Problem: Analytical and Computational Limitations in Collateralized Debt Obligation Evaluation." *Competition & Change* 18, no. 5: 383–401.

Harrington, Brooke. 2016. "Social Structure, Power and Financial Fraud." In *The Global Financial Crisis and Its Aftermath: Hidden Factors in the Meltdown*, edited by T. Malliaris, L. Shaw, and H. Shefrin, 340–55. New York: Oxford University Press.

Ho, Karen. 2009. *Liquidated: An Ethnography of Wall Street*. Durham: Duke University Press.

Hopkins, Terrance, and Immanuel Wallerstein. 1986. "Commodity Chains in the World-Economy Prior to 1800." *Review* (Fernand Braudel Center) 10, no. 1: 157–70.

Islamic Finance Council UK (UKIFC) and International Shari'ah Research Academy for Islamic Finance (ISRA). 2016. "External Shari'ah Audit Report." In *UKIFC & ISRA Joint Thought Leadership*. Kuala Lumpur: ISRA.

Knorr Cetina, Karin. 1999. *Epistemic Cultures: How the Sciences Make Knowledge*. Cambridge, MA: Harvard University Press.

Knorr Cetina, Karin, and Urs Bruegger. 2002. "Global Microstructures: The Virtual Societies of Financial Markets." *American Journal of Sociology* 107, no. 4: 905–50.

Labaton Sucharow LLP. 2015. "The Street, the Bull and the Crisis: A Survey of the US & UK Financial Services Industry." New York: Labaton Sucharow, LLP.

Lai, Jikon. 2014. "Industrial Policy and Islamic Finance." *New Political Economy* 20, no. 2: 178–98.

Lépinay, Vincent-Antonin. 2007. "Decoding Finance: Articulation and Liquidity around a Trading Room." In *Do Economists Make Markets? On the Performativity of Economics*, edited by D. MacKenzie, F. Muniesa, and L. Siu, 87–127. Princeton: Princeton University Press.

———. 2011. *Codes of Finance: Engineering Derivatives in a Global Bank*. Princeton: Princeton University Press.

MacKenzie, Donald. 2011. "The Credit Crisis as a Problem in the Sociology of Knowledge." *American Journal of Sociology* 116, no. 6: 1778–841.

Maurer, Bill. 2005. *Mutual Life, Limited: Islamic Banking, Alternative Currencies, Lateral Reason*. Princeton: Princeton University Press.

Muniesa, Fabian, Dominique Chabert, Marceline Ducrocq-Grondin, and Susan V. Scott. 2011. "Back-Office Intricacy: The Description of Financial Objects in an Investment Bank." *Industrial and Corporate Change* 20, no. 4: 1189–213. doi: 10.1093/icc/dtr020.

Nesvetailova, Anastasia. 2014. "Innovations, Fragility and Complexity: Understanding the Power of Finance." *Government and Opposition* 49 (Special Issue 03): 542–68. doi: 10.1017/gov.2014.12.

Oka, Rahul, and Ian Kuijt. 2014. "Introducing an Inquiry into the Social Economies of Greed and Excess." *Economic Anthropology* 1, no. 1: 1–16. doi: 10.1002/sea2.12000.

Pitluck, Aaron Z. 2008. "Moral Behavior in Stock Markets: Islamic Finance and Socially Responsible Investment." In *Economics and Morality: Anthropological Approaches*, Society for Economic Anthropology (SEA) Monographs, edited by K. E. Browne and B. L. Milgram, 233–55. Lanham, MD: AltaMira Press, Rowman & Littlefield Publishers.

———. 2013. "Islamic Banking and Finance: Alternative or Façade?" In *The Oxford Handbook of the Sociology of Finance*, edited by K. Knorr Cetina and A. Preda, 431–49. Oxford: Oxford University Press.

———. 2016. "The Convergence Paradox of Islamic Finance: A Sociological Reinterpretation, with Insights for Proponents of Social Finance." In *Routledge Handbook of Social and Sustainable Finance*, edited by O. Lehner, 364–80. Basingstoke: Routledge.

Pitluck, Aaron Z., and Shikshya Adhikari. 2018. "Islamic Finance in the Global North: Secular Incubators, Elementary Accommodation and Strategic Negligence." In *Handbook of Contemporary Islam and Muslim Lives*, edited by M. Woodward and R. Lukens-Bull, 28. Cham: Springer.

Pitluck, Aaron Z., Fabio Mattioli, and Daniel Souleles. 2018. "Finance Beyond Function: Three Causal Explanations for Financialization." *Economic Anthropology* 5, no. 2: 157–71.

Preda, Alex. 2002. "Financial Knowledge, Documents, and the Structures of Financial Activities." *Journal of Contemporary Ethnography* 31, no. 2: 207–39.

Rethel, Lena. 2010. "Financialisation and the Malaysian Political Economy." *Globalizations* 7, no. 4: 489–506.

Rudnyckyj, Daromir. 2017. "Debating Form, Consuming Substance: Halal Authenticity in Malaysian Islamic Finance." *Practical Matters* Spring 1 (2017).

———. 2019. *Beyond Debt: Islamic Experiments in Global Finance.* Chicago: University of Chicago Press.

Rusni Hassan, Nurdianawati Irwani Abdullah, Aznan Hassan, Agus Triyanta, Uzaimah Ibrahim, Mohd. Faud Md. Sawari, and Akhtarzite Abd. Aziz. 2013. "A Comparative Analysis of Shari'ah Governance in Islamic Banking Institutions across Jurisdictions." *International Shari'ah Research Academy for Islamic Finance* 50: 1–63.

Securities Commission Malaysia. 2014. *Guidelines on Sukuk.* Kuala Lumpur: Suruhanjaya Sekuriti.

Sloane-White, Patricia. 2017. *Corporate Islam: Sharia and the Modern Workplace.* Cambridge, UK: Cambridge University Press.

Souleles, Daniel. 2017. "Don't Mix Paxil, Viagra, and Xanax: What Financiers' Jokes Say About Inequality." *Economic Anthropology* 4, no. 1: 107–19.

Vogel, Frank E., and Samuel L. Hayes. 1998. *Islamic Law and Finance: Religion, Risk, and Return.* Boston: Kluwer Law International.

Warde, Ibrahim. 2010. *Islamic Finance in the Global Economy.* Edinburgh: Edinburgh University Press.

World Economic Forum. 2017. *The Global Competitiveness Report 2017–2018.* Geneva: World Economic Forum.

5

Financialization and Reproduction in Baku, Azerbaijan

Tristam Barrett

> Where marriage establishes a conjugal fund (as in dowry systems) the wedding ceremonial will be more elaborate than where it does not.
> —Jack Goody, *Production and Reproduction*

> You can cut an Azerbaijani's pension and they'll keep silent. You can cut their salary and they'll keep silent. You can step on their rights and they'll keep silent. But don't give the right amount of money at their wedding and they'll come at you with a knife.
> —An informant makes the same point

How does financialization impact household reproduction in a petro-state? Research into financial sector development in Azerbaijan has been done by various multilateral organizations (e.g., Conrad 2012; ADB 2014; IBRD 2016) as part of efforts to develop the country's financial sector and enhance financial inclusion. Other more critical studies have highlighted the dangers of the booming credit market that has been enabled by financial reforms since 2012. These have raised red flags over an overheated and poorly regulated financial sector with loan penetration over capacity and high levels of over- and cross-indebtedness, especially in the capital Baku (Pytkowska and Spannuth 2012; Rozas 2016). Building on such research, this chapter combines quantitative and qualitative methods to investigate how finance is implicated in household reproduction in Baku in the context of Azerbaijan's oil-fuelled, post-Soviet, political economy.

The banking crisis that hit Baku following the 2015 oil-price crash provides an opportunity to understand a banking system that was built up during the preceding decade of oil-based political economic development. Despite the country's double-digit GDP growth between 2000 and 2008, many households in Baku experienced economic insecurity as a post-Soviet *nomenklatura*-style political and economic elite entrenched itself at the head of a largely oligopolistic market economy.[1] The funneling of oil monies into elite hands was accompanied by the withdrawal of many forms of state social assistance and the corruption of social services, essential for the maintenance and reproduction of households, which should theoretically be free at the point of use (e.g., Rzayeva 2013; Safiyev 2013b). Many families financed their consumption through borrowing, thus contributing to a booming market in personal loans. The 2015 oil price crash burst this bubble. It precipitated a double-dip devaluation of the currency, the closure of almost a third of the country's banks, and a doubling of the value of dollar-denominated loans held by a large segment of the population (Barrett, forthcoming).[2] My research investigated household use of financial instruments following this crisis in order to understand how households reproduce in the context of Azerbaijan's ongoing political economic transformation and the role played by financial instruments in these reproduction efforts.[3]

A household survey conducted in September 2017 showed that while almost four-fifths of households in Baku made use of financial instruments, they displayed income-related differences in how they used finance and what they used it for.[4] Poorer households made more use of informal borrowing, while richer households made significantly more use of insurance. There were no differences in rates of formal borrowing, although lower income households were more indebted, obtained credit on worse terms, and were more exposed to dollar-lending, which was cheaper than manat-lending before the devaluations. While the most common reason for incurring formal debts was building or renovating housing (a key element of the reproduction model), lower income households also tended to use debt to meet everyday domestic reproduction expenses. As I discuss below, the lack of income-based differentiation in the formal lending market provides a first hint of obstacles to formal financialization, which make it easier for all households to meet their borrowing needs through informal channels.

In addition to supporting the everyday reproduction of households, the survey also found a strong correlation between lifecycle events—events that mark key stages in the production, reproduction, and dissolution of households—and financialization. Households that had experienced lifecycle events displayed significantly higher rates of both formal and informal borrowing, yet this was not the case with borrowing from social networks. To the surprise of anyone who knows Azerbaijan, it would seem that Bakuvians finance their lifecycle events through formal and informal borrowing rather than borrowing from people they know. This discrepancy calls for an examination of social practices, which are difficult to capture in a quantitative survey (see Leach 1967), and can be explained by taking into account the particular ritual ways in which money is given for these lifecycle events.

This chapter uses qualitative analysis of the political economic context and social practices around finance to shed light on how financialization has unfolded in Baku. Despite the extensive use of financial instruments, examination of the social relations around finance finds that they are shaped not so much by an inexorable, universal capitalist logic as by (1) the efforts of the local bureaucratic oligarchy to manage financialization in its own interests, and (2) the attempts of the local population to domesticate (Stenning et al. 2010) finance according to its needs and concerns.

Autarkic Financialization

As with other sites of peripheral financialization (Mikuš, this volume; Rodik and Žitko 2015), Baku has seen a dramatic financialization of households: rapid extension of foreign-currency–denominated lending, transfer of attendant currency and interest-rate risks to customers, and little accompanying development of the regulatory framework within which this has taken place, including the system for debt settlement and insolvency. Yet financialization in Baku is a product, not of entanglement in the financial chains of global neoliberalism (Sokol 2017) but rather of a divergence common to many post-Soviet states where international capital failed to find such favorable conditions for investment as in Eastern Europe (King 2002). It has thus unfolded differently. Whereas in Croatia a foreign-dominated banking sector extensively penetrated the domestic market, in Azerbaijan, financialization occurred within a state-led economy at the service of a bureaucratic oligarchy. Outside of the oil sector, the political elite has largely insulated the national market from foreign investment and competition (Barrett 2015: 33 et passim). Banking is no exception. The state has limited foreign participation in the banking sector, leaving no entirely foreign-owned banks in the country and only six majority foreign-owned banks, accounting for less than 10 percent of sector assets (Conrad 2012: 5).[5]

There are a number of reasons for this protectionism, all of which are to do with maintaining the status quo and protecting the *political* economy. Banking in Azerbaijan developed especially to service the needs of the local elite. Oligarchs would have their own bank as part of their holding company in order to provide banking services to their own businesses and employees (salaries, loans, bank cards, and so forth) and to facilitate the transfer of the owner's wealth overseas. Foreign participation in the banking sector would jeopardize domestic banks by poaching the skilled labor force, compel local banks to change their business models through a better market offering, and threaten current present murky arrangements for the allocation of capital. It would force a marketization of the economy that bureaucratic elites invested in a state-corporate political economic model cannot countenance (Oleinik 2011). An additional, if often overlooked, factor is that foreign participation in the banking sector—as in the rest of the economy—would undermine state efforts to maintain an ideologically crucial sense of national sovereignty (Abushov 2019) and to manage global integration on their own terms (for systematic articulations of this state concept and worldview, see Mehdiyev 2008, 2015, 2017).

As it stands, the limited foreign presence in the market has a number of effects on financialization. Banking represents some 95 percent of financial sector assets. Subsectors such as capital markets and asset management in Azerbaijan are virtually nonexistent, with the exception of boutique firms like AzFinansİnvest, which manages the money of the prominent Heydarov family and senior officers of their Gilan network of companies, or Pasha Investments, a private equity fund cum family office owned by the Paşayev family (one of the biggest economic actors in the country, not only in the banking sector). This company struggles on both supply and demand sides, against the reluctance of Azerbaijani businessmen to abandon the family business model and sell equity in firms, and against the scarcity of buyers for the equity it purchases. A key reason for the weakness of the nonbank financial sector and the limited involvement of banks in equity-based, rather than simple securitized debt-based (*"lombard"*) investment is the long-term horizons implied in such financialization. To buy equity implies having confidence in the economic fundamentals and growth of a company over a time horizon of fifteen to twenty years, whereas in Azerbaijan, with little certainty in a company's future or fundamentals, three years counts as long-term. This means that as one senior banker told me, "Businessmen operate for short-term quick returns, like gambling." I shall return to other peculiarities of banks' behavior in relation to the domestic consumer lending market below.

In the privatizations of the early 1990s, over 250 banks were founded in Azerbaijan, with many engaging in the highly volatile foreign exchange markets that at that time promised instant riches. This was gradually consolidated to some forty-four banks by 2015. Many of these were oligarch-owned, boutique banks, managing the enormous flows of oil—and embezzled—money since the oil boom took off in 2006, and laundering or channeling the proceeds abroad.[6] These boutique banks were described to me as *bank parniki*, literally "greenhouse banks," which thrive only so long as there is a constant flow of gas to heat them. The entwinement of banking with the oil sector as opposed to global finance reflects the enormous importance of oil to Azerbaijan's economy more generally; oil rents alone accounted for 20.5 percent of GDP in 2016 (The World Bank 2019). It also meant that while Azerbaijan's financial sector was relatively unaffected by the 2008 global financial crisis, it was thrown into tumult by the oil price crisis of late 2015. Nevertheless, one crucial factor had changed in the intervening period to make the sector even more vulnerable to financial shocks: banks had entered extensively into the consumer lending market.

Consumer lending began in 2003 when the multilaterally funded Access Bank began to offer prudential microcredits to small businesses. The market expanded at a rapid pace following financial reforms in 2011 (ADB 2014: 1) and was spearheaded by the efforts of major banks, Bank of Baku and Unibank, to develop business models based on retail lending. The high number of banks in this sector created enormous competition for custom, and led to the development of a dollar-lending market at lower rates of interest than manat lending, with weak credit risk assessment procedures, massive cross-selling, and indiscriminate marketing of credit cards. As one informant put it, "It was like a disease. Everybody got credit, not for investment but for consumption." Near the height of the consumer lending boom, in August 2014, 6.62 billion manats in consumer loans had been granted to 3.5 million recipients—almost 80 percent of the employed population (Salmanov 2014).

The interbank lending market being limited, banks tended to borrow internationally to finance their lending activities. While the oil-fuelled economy grew and the manat was pegged to a basket of foreign currencies, banks remained unexposed to currency risk and funded their domestic lending through lower interest rates on foreign capital. But the precipitous drop in oil price in 2015 to below $40 a barrel—from over $100 a few months earlier—led to a spiraling currency and fiscal crisis. Despite costly central bank attempts to shore up the exchange rate,[7] the manat lost half its value against the dollar in two devaluations. Debtors with dollar-denominated loans found the actual value of their loans had doubled and went into default. Banks faced liquidity crises as their local assets—consumer loans and unsecured preferential loans to "politically exposed persons"—proved insufficient to meet their foreign-currency denominated liabilities and new capitalization requirements.[8] Sixteen banks lost their licenses (although some reentered the market as nonbank financial institutions). The country's largest bank, the state-owned International Bank of Azerbaijan (IBA) filed for bankruptcy protection, and a financial oversight authority [Maliyyə Bazarlarına Nəzarət Palatası] was established to regulate the market and manage the liquidation of banks. When I began my field research in Baku, the economy was in deep recession, the third-biggest lender had just collapsed, and banks were scrambling to recover loans from debtors who were now unable to repay them (see Barrett, forthcoming, for discussion of this loan crisis).

The Domestication of Finance

Finance is a means of relating money and time (Collins et al. 2009). It enables past and present income to offset future needs (savings, insurance, pensions), expected future income to offset present needs (credit, lending, savings clubs, mortgages), or household and personal assets to provide urgent liquidity (such as in pawning or secured lending). It can be either formal (with official providers and regulated by law) or informal (by tacit or explicit agreement with individuals).

Authors have developed a number of ways to conceptualize financialization at different scales. Some see it as a structural transformation (Fernandez and Aalbers 2016) resulting from the accelerating accumulation of global finance where "incomes deriving from financial markets contribute disproportionately to GDP growth" (Polanyi Levitt 2013: 187; Lapavitsas 2013). Others see financialization in the penetration of shareholder logic into firm behavior, or the deeper penetration of financial calculi into everyday life and social reproduction (Martin 2002; Palomera 2014; Weiss 2016; Lazarus 2017; for an overview, see Van der Zwan 2014). The kind of household financialization I am examining here—the extension of the financial sector into the consumer market and the increasing use of financial instruments by households—may be understood simply as financial inclusion (or *"bancarisation,"* Lazarus 2017), but I think it is important to examine it as an instance of financialization, without succumbing to the idea that financialization necessarily produces fundamental changes in subjectivities, performativities, or governmentalities (Martin 2002; Aalbers 2008; Davis 2009). As Pellandini-Simányi and colleagues have demonstrated, this hard version of the "financialization thesis" is in practice not always tenable. She sees instead a "domestication" of finance, in which financial instruments are "appropriated to existing relationships, temporal structures and rationalities that guide everyday life" (Pellandini-Simányi et al. 2015: 21).[9] It is nevertheless worthwhile to consider that as a transformation of the economic landscape, financialization does entangle households in new sets of relationships with implications for their everyday household economies and reproduction efforts.

Recent work has demonstrated the importance of households in social reproduction. Financialized households have been conceptualized as "shock absorbers" for economic risk (Bryan et al. 2009), and indebted households are seen as playing a crucial role in sustaining debt-driven growth in conditions of "privatized-Keynesianism" (Crouch 2009). Households are exploitable in this fashion because their bottom line is that they must attempt to secure the reproduction of the family over time and according to culturally patterned norms and status expectations. This includes the everyday management of households—provisioning to meet consumption needs (Carrier and Heyman 1997; Narotzky 2005) using a variety of assets, such as income, housing, food, and care (Stenning et al. 2010: 2–3)—as well as efforts to reproduce family structure through the generations.

But efforts to reproduce family structure are most dramatically instantiated in lifecycle events, especially those pertaining to the formation of new households. In Azerbaijan, these aspects of social reproduction are highly ritualized and may entail large expenditures for associated ceremonies and purchases. The proper performance of these lifecycle events is important for maintaining respectability, and families devote significant resources to ensuring their success. These events are therefore an important lens through which to examine social reproduction. I therefore concentrate specifically on the ways in which finance is domesticated at the service of these reproduction efforts. In the remainder of this chapter, I analyze the use of finance in lifecycle events and within social networks to reveal how financialization is entangled in the social relations that support household reproduction. Ultimately, I argue, this leads to a domestication of finance, which limits the extension of the market logic to household financial behavior.

Marriage, Azeri-style

Azerbaijan exemplifies the Eurasian pattern of reproduction described by Jack Goody (1969; 1979: 19 et passim), with dowry payment, monogamy, in-marriage of various sorts, and control of marriage partners (especially women) all oriented toward the tight control of property. Many aspects of reproduction are highly ritualized and may entail large expenditures for associated ceremonies and purchases.

Events at different stages of the lifecycle include those associated with birth (including payments to medical staff for the birth of a child [*muştuluq*, a gift for happy news] or for care, rituals around the birth and forty days after, and the giving of milk money); rites of passage, notably, the *sünnet toyu* male circumcision ceremony, but also feasts marking departure for military service; and death (including the funeral, for which *kefen pulu* [money for the funeral shroud] may be saved, and commemorative gatherings held during the forty days after someone's death [*yas*], the anniversary of a death [*il*], and the *qara bayram*, the first feast day after the death of a loved one). But marriages are the most important of these. They involve elaborate preparations and the gifting of *xonçalar* (decorated baskets of gifts, including bridal outfits, lingerie, sweets, perfumes, and so forth), from the first *tanışlıq* or *elçilik* (meeting of the two prospective families) to *heri* (expression of intent to marry), *nişan* (engagement), *xınayaxdı* (the bride's hen-party), and all of the feast days that may occur between engagement and marriage (8 March, the spring festival *Novruz Bayramı, Qurban Bayramı* [Eid al-Adha], New Year, etc.).

Weddings are hugely important indicators of social status (Yalçın-Heckmann 2001). But attitudes to them can vary: some are inordinately proud of the expenses they have gone to, while others are careful not to stretch their new affines' meager resources, and still others go far beyond their means to hold onto a certain identity as a respectable family, despite impoverished circumstances. The costs of weddings are the object of much popular discussion and social media comment. In what I assume to be a tongue-in-cheek endeavor, an economist I met had calculated that Azeri weddings amounted to between 3.1 and 4.7 percent of GDP in 2008–2009.

Ultimately, the main responsibility for seeing their offspring through to adult life and the creation of a new home in marriage falls on the parents, who may incur significant debts in this process. Although there are voluntary matches, matchmaking is still common, and the finding of a suitable partner is often the responsibility of the parents (particularly mothers, but also aunts) of potential spouses. Marriage is ideally neolocal or patrilocal (the youngest son would traditionally retain the family home; widowed mothers would tend to move in with a son's family). There are three main expenses incurred by families around weddings. These are the purchase or renovation of a home by the groom's side to receive the *gelin* [bride, literally "incomer"], the preparation of a dowry of household goods [*cehiz*] by the bride's family (which the bride brings into her new home), and the wedding itself. Friends and relatives may make contributions to all stages of the marriage process, but it is rarely the case in Baku that these contributions will provide a significant financial support to the costs of setting up the new household.

Families make use of debt for both renovation of the home and purchase of *cehiz*, although the practices around this have changed. While ideally a new house or apartment would be built or purchased, the most common variant I witnessed was that newlyweds would move in with the husband's family and the home (or rooms in the home) would be renovated for them. It is likely that the preponderance of formal debt in relation to housing improvements is strongly related to this reproduction model. A *cehiz* is normally estimated in the number of rooms it fills—for instance, "enough for two rooms"—and includes the furniture as well as soft furnishings necessary to make a house a home. Even if the bride is moving into the home of her prospective husband's parents, a *cehiz* will be provided and the old furniture will be disposed of somehow. One older informant recalls collecting her daughter's *cehiz* since she was five years old. Another spent five years to assemble a *cehiz* worth 4,000 manats, and even made trips to Riga to find cheaper goods. Nowadays, people are more likely to meet these expenses through credit instruments.

Of the clients of an agency set up to represent and protect debtors in Baku, half of those who had debts of 15–20,000 manats had taken out loans to buy a *cehiz*. Nonpayment of these debts is particularly difficult to bear, because of the potential shame involved in having the *cehiz* repossessed by bailiffs. A local company that produces furniture for the low-income market established a finance arm to provide "interest-free" credits for *cehiz* goods (the interest was factored into the price). Considering the widespread debt crisis, a financial assessor whom I interviewed was amazed to find that this company had no nonperforming loans on its books. When families do get into trouble, they will draw on social networks to pay the *cehiz* off. As one informant recounts:

> My daughter-in-law's family bought a *cehiz* for 10,000 manats. This filled three rooms. We gave the old furniture to my older son, who had a large apartment to be filled. They got the credit in dollars during the devaluation and they were taken to court because of the debt, so I helped them out. What could I do? I couldn't leave them in that situation; they had bought everything for my son's house, so I had to help. They eventually returned all the money, a hundred manats at a time, and gave me an extra hundred on top at the end.

This points to the way in which debts enter into the social logic of reproduction, producing both new ways of meeting social obligations and new dependencies on the formal sector that households may mediate through their social networks. But weddings themselves also provide opportunities to mobilize finance through social networks.

Attending weddings is an important aspect of social participation in Azeri society. A small wedding may bring together some 250 guests, whereas larger weddings will commonly have 500 and even 700 in attendance. In my survey, 153 households reported spending amounts of between 50 and 2,000 manats in the previous year to attend lifecycle events (M = 305.68 AZN, SD = 285.33 AZN). Unless one is a close relative or friend of the family, it would be typical to give from 50 to 100 manats at a wedding. This implies that many of these households had attended multiple weddings in the past year, which is usual among families in good socioeconomic standing.[10]

Weddings tend to be funded by the guests themselves, with guests putting down at least enough money to cover the cost of their meal (50 manats is the generally accepted minimum in Baku) and more, depending on one's means and relationship to the newlywed couple. The larger one's social network, the more guests one can call upon to attend. One informant, the head of an institute at a local university, had 500 guests at her wedding, with "200 from my side, because my grandfather has many friends and he went to all of his friends' children's and grandchildren's weddings. About three to four tables were occupied by his friends. Another three tables were occupied by my father's football mates." Monetary gifts are noted in a book that is kept throughout one's life as a register of how much was given by whom, and how much should be given should one be invited to a wedding of that person's family. Azər explains that when he married in 2010, he invited 150 guests:

> The poorest one gave 20 manats, but I invited him there because I wanted him to be present. The deputy chairman of ―――― gave 300 manats, a colonel of police 200 manats, a deputy [to the parliament] 200 manats. If I had been called to the police colonel's son's wedding, I would have put in 100 manats, but I wasn't called, so that was lucky!

Azər himself gave $100 at a friend's wedding, and following the devaluation joked that this was going to be a lot of manats when it came to his [still infant] son's wedding.

Weddings, then, are a form of socially institutionalized life-long savings and credit association; or as a friend observed, "they are a big insurance institution, you pay in your monthly premiums and you hope to get your pay-out at the end!"[11] With the intense commercialization of these events nowadays, though, the monies received tend to go to the immediate cost of the wedding hall, musicians, decorations, photographers, and so forth, rather than helping the young couple start life in their new home. The couple will generally end up with a small surplus that can be spent on a honeymoon, or more likely to repay debts incurred in the run-up to the wedding.

Financialization through Social Networks

This description of how social networks are involved in meeting lifecycle-event costs opens the question of how else social networks might be enrolled into seemingly financialized relations. One puzzle that emerged in the survey is why formal borrowing didn't vary with income, even if these loans were used for different purposes. This could relate to the evolution of the lending market, from initially indiscriminate mass-selling (see Guseva 2008) to a total hemorrhaging of lending following the crisis. In the immediate aftermath, banks would only lend with security, essentially entering the pawn-broking market; and only in 2017 did they begin to restart other lending operations. But it may also point to systematic barriers to formal lending, which makes it easier to meet borrowing needs through informal channels. This is anecdotally confirmed by the lack of data points on mortgages in my survey, reasons for which were uncovered during qualitative data collection. As I argue below, this has led to an "informalization" of formal lending.

Despite a decade-long construction boom in Baku (Grant 2014), the presence of a state-backed mortgage fund [*İpoteka Fondu*] mandated to provide loans at 8 percent interest through high-street banks, and the strong imperative to obtain new housing upon marriage, my survey found only one case of households using mortgages. Subsequent discussion with mortgage holders—identified from my own social network in follow-up research—revealed two points of interest.

First, the criteria for mortgages are difficult to meet. Not only are they restricted to those with officially declared incomes of a certain amount (an impossible requirement considering that actual salaries are rarely declared by the employer, but rather paid in cash), but even if one meets this stipulation, mortgages can only be taken out on properties that have an official deed of title [*çıxarış*]. Here again, the market meets the informality of Azerbaijan's political economy.[12] Könül twice obtained approval, valid for forty-five days, for a mortgage. But she could not buy an apartment because she was unable to find one with a *çıxarış* in the given time. Given this restriction, people may seek to patchwork-fund new housing through bank loans (despite interest rates of at least double the mortgage rate) and loans from friends and family.

Second, in an effort to ensure fair play, people seek to obtain mortgages through contacts rather than on an anonymous market. One informant explained, "I managed to get the 8 percent rate because I had a friend working at the bank, so they gave me neither better nor worse, but exactly what they were supposed to." Another told me, "I had a *vəzifəli adam* [highly placed person] make a call on my behalf, otherwise I would have got a higher rate"; and yet another got her mortgage from a particular bank "because I had a *dayday* [figurative, uncle] there." This care to enter into formal financial arrangements only through contacts may be well justified. Even though the Central Bank lent money to banks at 6 percent to be re-lent at an 8 percent rate, it was not uncommon to obtain a mortgage with 10 percent annual interest. Even worse, one informant obtained a mortgage in

2012 and was fleeced by the agent: the loan was officially for 50,000 manats but he only received 45,000 manats, with 5,000 manats being taken as a cut. He nevertheless had to pay interest over the whole of the mortgage on the officially stated principal. This preference for accessing formal finance through informal networks also applies to bank lending. In most cases, people I talked to claimed to have gone to such-and-such a person at such-and-such a bank because they knew him personally, or knew someone who knew him. This demonstrates that even when entering into formal financial relations, people still use informal connections as a way of guaranteeing trust. The formal is therefore in some sense treated as an extension of the informal, and social relations are used as a way of ensuring fair play in a situation of little trust in the formal financial system.[13]

The density of social relations involved in procuring loans from banks affects how formal debt is treated. First, debts are intimate, not necessarily market, transactions. As discussed elsewhere (Barrett, forthcoming), although illegal, banks have applied pressure to nonpayers by disclosing their debts to family, friends, and employers.[14] Second, the intimacy of relations between bank and debtor—produced by the informal ties connecting the bank agent to the borrower—inhibits the development of secondary financialization, such as a secondary market in debt-based assets. Debt-collection agencies (and courts) work directly with and for banks to pursue debts, but banks do not sell on even nonperforming loans for fear that they would provoke the outrage of customers, who would feel that they had violated a relationship of, albeit fragile, trust. Selling on debt would rupture the tight network of connections that brought them into contract in the first place. In this way, as one midlevel banker in charge of market innovation put it, "it's the very density of social ties that makes Azerbaijan antibusiness"; or in a reversal of the Polanyian formulation, the substance of society has not been subordinated to the laws of the market (Polanyi 2001: 71), but the market has rather been subordinated to society—that is to say, domesticated. Not that this has made banks any less violent in their attempts to reclaim unpaid consumer debts!

Balancing Spheres of Financialization

If even the formal financial sector shows informal characteristics—both in how it is accessed, and in how it is constrained by social expectations—it is worth considering how households balance their formal and informal financial commitments, and what factors affect their preference of one over another. Should the financial system simply be considered as an extension of the existing informal system for obtaining finance? If this is the case, then finance has most certainly been domesticated, rather than producing financialized subjectivities. This hypothesis is borne out by the way in which people use their social networks to obtain finance. One informant, for instance, along with four others, had taken out a loan on behalf of his friend in order for him to obtain the starting capital for a business. Another is now on a credit blacklist because his cousin took out a loan for a car in his name and failed to pay it. When he next needed a loan, he took it out in his mother's name. Other examples abound of debtors taking out loans for, or transferring loans from financial institutions to, other parties in informal networks, and retaining formal responsibility for the ultimate payment of the loan.

Informants would also seek to pay down unfavorable loans by soliciting other forms of credit, either on more favorable—or simply more flexible—terms than those offered by banks or from social networks. For instance, two informants detailed how they used moneylenders or *lotoreya* (a form of rotating savings club) to pay down bank loans.[15]

Nəriman's family had a fairly large income of around 2,000 manats, pooled from his father's pension, his mother's work as a teacher and tutor [*repetitor*], and his and his brother's salary contributions. In addition to their living costs, this money was being used to pay off a 7,000 manat credit taken out the previous year to pay for his father's medical costs and for the renovation of their house. Over the year, they had only managed to pay down the principal to 6,700 manats. Nəriman's mother also plays *lotoreya* among her relatives and close friends. She pays between 400 and 500 manats each month, and will get between 2,000 and 3,000 manats when it is her "turn." She will use this to pay down the bank debt in tranches, rather than lose money to interest payments. This is preferable because there is no interest on *lotoreya*, although people may pay their contributions late because those who play are close friends and relatives. "Otherwise," he says, "you're just working for the banks."

Sənan works for a state media company and lives with his mother, who runs a business importing goods from Turkey (his father lives in Russia, importing flour). Until the end of 2017, they had credits totaling some 90,000 manats with five banks, but they have closed these credits and consolidated them by taking out loans totaling 25,000 manats from two moneylenders [*selemçilər*, "*selem*" means "interest"]. They previously made payments on interest alone of 4,000 manats per month over the course of five years; but now they pay a little over 2,000 manats to the *selemçilər*, and his mother plays the extra 2,000–2,500 manats into three *lotoreya* groups. These are large amounts, so they can get 20,000 manats at a time and thereby pay down the principal. Of the interest payments to the *selemçilər*, Sənan says: "We simply throw this money away, but it is better than with a bank, because the *selemçi* accepts that you can delay payment for a few days whereas a bank will charge you fines, so you're always anxious." Because they work in trade, and must give and receive goods on credit, they require this flexibility. Additionally, the banks took securities of gold and personal belongings, which the *selemçilər* did not demand.

Rəşad, a professional economist, did things the other way around, translating *selemçi* debt into formal debt. His family's babysitter had paid interest on a 6,000-manat debt for three years. She had paid this sum twice over in interest and still not reduced the principal. So Rəşad visited the *selemçi* and negotiated (ultimately with the threat of reporting him for illegal banking operations) to accept a final payment of 2,000 manats. They then went to a microfinance organization to arrange a loan to pay this off.

The above examples show how people may resort to informal or formal spheres in order to obtain finance on terms acceptable to them. The high interest rates and administrative inflexibility of banks has encouraged people to resort to nonformal financial instruments either to pay down these debts or to obtain them on more manageable terms. Additionally, the paralysis in the bank lending market since the devaluation and banking crisis has led many to resort to the nontraditional financial system—loan sharks, pawnbrokers, and payday lenders, for instance—because they do not have access to the formal financial system. These private debts are growing in importance relative to bank loans. As a consequence, I heard of some egregious abuse occurring as *selemçilər* also played between formal and informal spheres, and used the intimate aspects of the present system to their advantage.[16]

Conclusion

In the above, I have shown how financialization is tied up with the reproduction efforts and social networks of Bakuvian households. Although households use financial instruments differently according to their income, households generally indebt themselves in order to meet the costs of social reproduction (as measured through lifecycle events). Lifecycle events were the strongest predictor of financialization. While quantitative analysis of social networks did not reveal large differences in financial behavior, qualitative analysis revealed that social networks are highly implicated in financing lifecycle events, and that households not only use informal ties to obtain financial services from agents at formal financial institutions, but also that they mobilize credit money through their social networks (taking out loans in other people's names, or transferring loans), and furthermore they transfer debts between formal and informal spheres to manage them better on their terms. Rather than engendering new subjectivities among Bakuvians, finance has instead been largely domesticated into the social relations, values, and expectations of householders.

Considering the specific way in which Baku's financial sector has developed, with banks operating at the service of the bureaucratic oligarchy, the market largely insulated from foreign competition, and the binding of bankers and creditors into intimate relationships, it is possible to see that the financial system has been domesticated both by the interests of state elites and in the everyday economies (Humphrey 2002) of those who use it. This doesn't by any means imply that these relations are free of logics of accumulation and exploitation common to financialization elsewhere, but rather that the particular forms of exploitation are modulated by the political economic context and the social practices of those subject to it.

One important methodological point to emerge from this research is the difficulty of examining the functioning of social networks using quantitative indicators. As Edmund Leach wrote in an apologia for the anthropological method, "there is a wide range of sociological phenomena which are intrinsically inaccessible to statistical investigation of any kind," especially those pertaining to the definition of and attribution of "interrelationships existing between different units" (1967: 77, 87). Instead, the specific relational operation of social networks and their role in both formal and informal dimensions of financialization should be reconstructed through analysis of the ways in which finance is used in practice and integrated into preexisting sets of social relations. Further studies of financialization, especially those looking to promote or interrogate "financial inclusion" in line with the present-day development orthodoxy, must attend to these relationships and the practices that mobilize and ultimately domesticate finance.

Acknowledgments

Thanks to Patrick Heady, Lale Yalçın-Heckmann, and Sylvia Terpe at the Max Planck Institute for Social Anthropology; and to Kamil Ələsgərov and Fuad Kazimov in Baku for their generous advice and comments at various stages of this research. Thanks also to Vüsalə Əlibəyli and İlkin İskəndərov for invaluable field assistance.

Tristam Barrett is a social anthropologist with regional and thematic expertise on issues of economic transformation in post-Soviet Eurasia. The research reported here builds on his doctoral research (Cambridge, 2016) into Baku's broader post-Soviet social transformation. He has also investigated water resources, food security, and climate change adaptation in Kazakhstan (with Dr. Giuseppe Feola), and sustainable water resource management in Georgia.

Notes

1. This pattern is common in the post-Soviet space, even where mineral wealth has not permitted such dramatic state centralization as in Azerbaijan. For accounts of Russia, see Oleinik (2011), Kononenko and Moshes (2011), and Dawisha (2014). For Kyrgyzstan, see Engvall (2016), and for Central Asia more broadly, see Cooley and Heathershaw (2017). On the broader implications of this authoritarian turn, see Diamond, Plattner, and Walker (2016).
2. *Note on exchange rates:* Before February 2015, the Azerbaijani New Manat (AZN) was fixed against a currency basket at a rate of 1 USD: 0.78 AZN. At the time of my survey (September 2017), the country had moved to a floating exchange rate, and after spiking at 1 USD: 1.91 AZN in January 2017, had stabilized at 1 USD: 1.7 AZN.
3. Initial fieldwork for this project was conducted between October 2016 and March 2017. I conducted a household survey in September 2017 and follow-up interviews in autumn 2018. The household survey (n = 300) comprised households drawn from three socioeconomically and geographically representative neighborhoods of Baku using systematic random sampling. I deliberately did not target particularly rich neighborhoods because of reported low response rates (Ersado 2006). The survey was administered by four experienced, locally recruited interviewers who spoke both Azeri and Russian. I trained the interviewers and invited them to give comment on the survey in advance of administering it. I conducted follow-up interviews (n = 30) with households that had held weddings in the previous five years. These interviews were intended to cover participants of the survey who had consented to participate in this phase of the research, but it proved nigh impossible to obtain such interviews. I therefore conducted interviews in the same buildings or yards, with appropriate households being identified by neighbors or from the distinctive decorations on the doors of newlywed households. I additionally conducted several interviews with bankers, pawnbrokers, lenders, and other actors, and engaged in extensive participant research, including helping a friend with his marriage and subsequent divorce. Further details on the methodology and findings of this survey will be reported in future publications.
4. Financial instruments were categorized in a number of ways: formal vs. informal and by order of complexity, ranging from primary financialization (covering basic lending) to secondary financialization (use of longer-term instruments such as mortgages and insurance) and still more complex tertiary financialization (comprising stocks, shares, and other money market instruments). The survey covered the following financial instruments: bank credit, credit from a loan company, credit from a pawnbroker, credit/store cards, hire purchase [*kreditli lizinq*], mortgage, insurance, money-market instruments, loan from a money-lender, employer loan, individual and other loans, inter-household borrowing and lending, credit at

shop/market, rotating savings and credit association [*lotoreya*], money-guarding for others, having money guarded by others, rent arrears, wage advance, and wage arrears.

5. This is not to deny that Azerbaijan's elite is as highly integrated into other aspects of global finance as the elites of the Central Asian states described by Cooley and Heathershaw (2017).

6. Opportunities for embezzlement are rife in Azerbaijan, either through misdirection of state funds or through an extensive repertoire of corruption, bribery, and misuse of public office. Oil revenues are directed into the sovereign wealth fund, SOFAZ, and from there disbursed to ministries through the state budget. This provides opportunity for heads of ministries to grant inflated contracts to family-or crony-owned companies; such as those granted by former Transport Minister Ziya Məmmədov to the Garant and Bağlan holding companies (Fatullayeva 2013). SOCAR, the state oil company, is reported to operate in a similar way (Altstadt 2017). The extent of bank involvement in money laundering has been demonstrated by the Azerbaijan Laundromat, which has now been folded into the wider Danske Bank scandal. Foreshadowing of these scandals was already evident in interviews in 2016, with disgruntled bank workers detailing the way in which vast sums of cash were picked up at the airport or money siphoned to banks in the Baltic states through opaque lending arrangements.

7. The Central Bank spent $11.2 billion (almost three quarters of its foreign currency reserves) between December 2014 and February 2016 in an attempt to avoid devaluation.

8. The liquidation committee for Bank Standard found that 60 percent of the bank's loan portfolio comprised uncollateralized lending to related parties. A postcollapse audit of Standard Bank's assets by KPMG showed that 90 percent of the portfolio consisted of bad loans. This is ironic, because KPMG was in charge of audit before the bank's collapse and should have identified these irregularities (author interview with Əkrəm Həsənov, head of the liquidation committee, October 2018).

9. This argument about domestication echoes research on socialist and postsocialist societies that has shown how daily practice "domesticates" political economies and disrupts the calculus of top-down policies (see Creed 1998; Humphrey 2002; Stenning et al. 2010).

10. People in prominent positions may find their diaries fully booked with invitations to weddings.

11. It should be noted that, as with all financial products, there is risk involved in these delayed exchanges. As one friend told me, "Often someone who invited you to their weddings or their children's wedding disappears or has the cheek not to turn up to *your* wedding when you call them. This usually happens when a long time has passed since the first wedding." It is, of course, also possible that a guest may not turn up to the wedding and not send money to compensate the cost, but such behavior is a source of censure.

12. I was informed that issuing a deed on a new building requires it to be signed off by the Ministry of Emergency Situations, which in turn requires a large unofficial payment to be made.

13. My survey results show only 6.4 percent of respondents would choose to save spare money in a bank, with 86 percent preferring to save it at home in cash. This is supported anecdotally by the behavior of pensioners in Baku. Pensions are administered through the state bank IBA, and it is common each month for them to withdraw the total amount of the pension rather than leave it in the bank. Asked why, a friend's mother answered with surprise: "Why *would* you keep it there?!"

14. Debtors have also been arrested and imprisoned for nonpayment of debts, although this breaks the European Declaration of Human Rights, to which Azerbaijan is a signatory. Having exhausted the options for redress within the Azerbaijani court system, these cases have been brought to the European Court of Human Rights (see Barrett, forthcoming).

15. In *lotoreya*, a group of (usually ten) participants contribute to a pot, which is taken out periodically by a different member in rotation. People refer to this as a "game" or a "community" in which they participate. From my survey, the most common use for money from *lotoreya* was for the repair of a house; followed by education, lifecycle events, daily expenses, purchase of expensive items (a sofa, washing machine, gold), and travel; and finally, dentist, purchase of a house, repayment of a debt, and to have a cash reserve. Travel appears for the first time here, indicating that for a few households *lotoreya* may imply a degree of discretionary spending, a treat, rather than being uniquely earmarked for reproduction expenses. But in the vast majority of cases, it seems to be a way of meeting slightly bigger-ticket household reproduction expenses. As one interviewee put it: "My sister plays *lotereya* and my mother used to play. It is for specific purchases, or if somebody needs to cover a child's school expenses."

16. In one case, a *selemçi* hooked up with his brother at IBA, which administers the payments to staff of the state oil company SOCAR. He arranged loans to be paid off with employees' salary cards, which were taken from the employees. These cards were, in effect, stolen and the income removed from the accounts each month. When employees complained to the bank and tried to get their cards stopped, they were met by the brother, who prevented this and covered up things at the bank. Eventually, the case made the news and the brother was sacked from IBA, but no case has been brought against them. To the contrary, the brothers have filed over one hundred suits *against* debtors, and even won one of them (author interview with Əkrəm Həsənov, October 2018).

References

Aalbers, Manuel B. 2008. "The Financialization of Home and the Mortgage Market Crisis." *Competition and Change* 12, no. 2: 148–66.

Abushov, Kavus. 2019. "Russian foreign policy towards the Nagorno-Karabakh conflict: prudent geopolitics, incapacity or identity?" *East European Politics* 35, no. 1: 72–92.

ADB (Asian Development Bank). 2014. *Republic of Azerbaijan: Microfinance Sector Development. Technical Assistance Report.* Mandaluyong City, Philippines: Asian Development Bank.

Altstadt, Audrey L. 2017. *Frustrated Democracy in Post-Soviet Azerbaijan*. New York: Columbia University Press.

Barrett, Tristam. 2015. "Political Economy and Social Transformation in Baku, Azerbaijan." PhD dissertation, University of Cambridge.

———. Forthcoming. "'Your Debts Are Our Problem': The Politicization of Debt in Azerbaijan." *Focaal: Journal of Global and Historical Anthropology*.

Bryan, Dick, Randy Martin, and Mike Rafferty. 2009. "Financialization and Marx: Giving Labor and Capital a Financial Makeover." *Review of Radical Political Economics* 41, no. 4: 458–72.

Carrier, James G., and Joshua M. Heyman. 1997. "Consumption and Political Economy." *The Journal of the Royal Anthropological Institute* 3, no. 2: 355–73.

Cooley, Alexander, and John Heathershaw. 2017. *Dictators Without Borders: Power and Money in Central Asia*. New Haven: Yale University Press.

Collins, Daryl, Jonathan Morduch, Orlanda Ruthven, and Stuart Rutherford. 2009. *Portfolios of the Poor: How the World's Poor Live on $2 a Day*. Princeton: Princeton University Press.

Conrad, Jurgen F. 2012. "Azerbaijan: Financial Sector Assessment." ADB Central and West Asia Working Paper Series, No. 3. Mandaluyong City, Philippines: Asian Development Bank.

Creed, Gerald. W. 1998. *Domesticating Revolution: From Socialist Reform to Ambivalent Transition in a Bulgarian Village*. University Park: Pennsylvania State University Press.

Crouch, Colin. 2009. "Privatised Keynesianism: An Unacknowledged Policy Regime." *The British Journal of Politics and International Relations* 11, no. 3: 382–99.

Davis, Gerald F. 2009. *Managed by the Markets: How Finance Reshaped America*. Oxford: Oxford University Press.

Dawisha, Karen. 2014. *Putin's Kleptocracy: Who Owns Russia?* New York: Simon and Schuster.

Diamond, Larry, Marc F. Plattner, and Christopher Walker, eds. 2016. *Authoritarianism Goes Global: The Challenge to Democracy*. Baltimore: Johns Hopkins University Press.

Engvall, Johann. 2016. *The State as Investment Market: Kyrgyzstan in Comparative Perspective*. Pittsburgh: University of Pittsburgh Press.

Ersado, Lire. 2006. "Azerbaijan's Household Survey Data: Explaining Why Inequality Is So Low." *Policy Research Working Paper* No. 4009. Washington, DC: World Bank.

Fatullayeva, Nushabe. 2013. "Azerbaijan: Insider Deals Thrive in Ministry. Organized Crime and Corruption Reporting Project, 3 April 2013." Accessed 13 February 2019. https://www.occrp.org/en/investigations/1907-azerbaijan-insider-deals-thrive-in-ministry.

Fernandez, Rodrigo, and Manuel B. Aalbers. 2016. "Financialization and Housing: Between Globalization and Varieties of Capitalism." *Competition and Change* 20, no. 2: 71–88.

Goody, Jack. 1969. "Inheritance, Property and Marriage in Africa and Eurasia." *Sociology* 3: 55–76.

———. 1979. *Production and Reproduction: A Comparative Study of the Domestic Domain.* Cambridge, UK: Cambridge University Press.

Grant, Bruce. 2014. "The Edifice Complex: Architecture and the Political Life of Surplus in the New Baku." *Public Culture* 26, no. 3: 501–28.

Guseva, Anya. 2008. *Into the Red: The Birth of the Credit Card Market in Postcommunist Russia.* Stanford: Stanford University Press.

Humphrey, Caroline. 2002. *The Unmaking of Soviet Life: Everyday Economies after Socialism.* Ithaca: Cornell University Press.

IBRD (International Bank for Reconstruction and Development). 2016. *Enhancing Financial Capability and Inclusion in Azerbaijan: A Demand-side Assessment.* Washington, DC: World Bank Group.

King, Lawrence P. 2002. "Postcommunist Divergence: A Comparative Analysis of the Transition to Capitalism in Poland and Russia." *Studies in Comparative International Development* 37, no. 3: 3–34.

Kononenko, Vadim, and Arkady Moshes, eds. 2011. *Russia as a Network State: What Works in Russia When State Institutions Do Not?* Houndmills: Palgrave Macmillan.

Lapavitsas, Costas. 2013. *Profiting without Producing: How Finance Exploits Us All.* London: Verso.

Lazarus, Jeanne. 2017. "About the Universality of a Concept: Is There a Financialization of Daily Life in France?" *Civitas—Revista de Ciências Sociais* 17, no. 1: 26–42.

Leach, Edmund R. 1967. "An Anthropologist's Reflections on a Social Survey." In *Anthropologists in the Field*, edited by Deuwe G. Jongmans and Peter C. W. Gutkind, 75–88. New York: Humanities Press.

Martin, Randy. 2002. *The Financialization of Daily Life.* Philadelphia: Temple University Press.

Mehdiyev, Ramiz. 2008. *Modernləşmə xətti yenə də gündəlikdədir / Agenda Remains Unchangeable: Course towards modernisation.* Baku: Şərq-Qərb Nəşriyyat Evi.

———. 2015. *İkili standartların dünya nizami və müasir Azərbaycan* [*Double standards of the world order and contemporary Azerbaijan*]. Baku: Şərq-Qərb Nəşriyyat Evi.

———. 2017. *Nastsional'naya ideya Azerbajdzhana v epokhu global'nykh transformatsij* [*The national idea of Azerbaijan in an epoch of global transformations*]. Baku: Politicheskaya Entsiklopediya.

Narotzky, Susana. 2005. "Provisioning." In *A Handbook of Economic Anthropology*, edited by James G. Carrier, 78–93. Cheltenham: Edward Elgar.

Oleinik, Anton N. 2011. *Market as a Weapon: The Socio-Economic Machinery of Dominance in Russia.* New Brunswick: Transaction Publishers.

Palomera, Jaime. 2014. "How Did Finance Capital Infiltrate the World of the Urban Poor? Homeownership and Social Fragmentation in a Spanish Neighborhood." *International Journal of Urban and Regional Research* 38, no. 1: 218–35.

Pellandini-Simányi, Léna, Ferenc Hammer, and Zsuzsanna Vargha. 2015. "The Financialization of Everyday Life or the Domestication of Finance?" *Cultural Studies* 29, no. 5–6: 733–59.

Polanyi, Karl. 2001 [1944]. *The Great Transformation: The Economic and Social Origins of Our Times.* Boston: Beacon Press.

Polanyi Levitt, Kari. 2013. *From the Great Transformation to the Great Financialization: On Karl Polanyi and Other Essays.* London: Zed Books.

Pytkowska, Justyna, and Sylvia Spannuth. 2012. *The Risk of Over-indebtedness of Microcredit Clients in Azerbaijan: Results from a Comprehensive Field Study.* Frankfurt: Finance in Motion / European Fund for Southeast Europe.

Rodik, Petra, and Mislav Žitko. 2015. "Financialization, Household Debt and New Vulnerabilities in Post-Socialist Societies." In *Financialisation and Financial Crisis in South-Eastern European Countries,* edited by Dubravko Radošević and Vladimir Cvijanović, 49–70. Frankfurt am Main: Peter Lang.

Rozas, Daniel. 2016. *MIMOSA Microfinance Index of Market Outreach and Saturation Report—Azerbaijan.* April 2016.

Rzayeva, Sara. 2013. "Oil and Healthcare in Post-Soviet Azerbaijan." *European Journal of Sociology* 54, no. 1: 33–63.

Safiyev, Rail. 2013a. Azerbaijan: A Dictatorship Built on Capitalist Economy. *Caucasus Analytical Digest* 50, no. 3: 7–10.

———. 2013b. "Informality in a Neopatrimonial State: Azerbaijan." In *Informality in Eastern Europe: Structures, Political Cultures and Social Practices,* edited by Christian Giordano and Nicolas Hayoz, 433–50. Bern: Peter Lang.

Salmanov, Hüquq [Salmanov, Khiugug]. 2014. "Azerbaidzhantsi—raby kreditov, 7 August 2014." Accessed 14 September 2015. Minival.az. Link no longer available, but the article was reproduced and commented upon in Disput.Az Forum: https://www.disput.az/topic/679578--азербайджанцы-рабы-кредитов-в-других-странах-разве-иначе/.

Sokol, Martin. 2017. "Financialisation, Financial Chains and Uneven Geographical Development: Towards a Research Agenda." *Research in International Business and Finance* 39: 678–85.

Stenning, Alison, Adrian Smith, Alena Rochovská, and Dariusz Świątek. 2010. *Domesticating Neoliberalism: Spaces of Economic Practice and Social Reproduction in Post-Socialist Cities.* Oxford: Wiley-Blackwell.

The World Bank, World Development Indicators. 2019. "Total Natural Resources Rents (percent of GDP) [Data file]." Accessed 13 February 2019. https://data.worldbank.org/indicator/NY.GDP.TOTL.RT.ZS.

Van der Zwan, Natascha. 2014. "Making Sense of Financialization." *Socio-Economic Review* 12, no. 1: 99–129.

Weiss, Hadas. 2016. "Contesting the Value of Household Property." *Dialectical Anthropology* 40, no. 3: 287–303.

Yalçın-Heckmann, Lale. 2001. "The Political Economy of an Azeri Wedding." Working Paper No. 28. Halle/Saale: Max Planck Institute for Social Anthropology.

6

Financialization and the Norwegian State

Constraints, Contestations, and Custodial Finance in the World's Largest Sovereign Wealth Fund

Knut Christian Myhre

The Norwegian Government Pension Fund Global (GPFG) commonly ranks as the world's largest sovereign wealth fund, valued at just below 8,500 billion Norwegian kroner—or a little in excess of one trillion US dollars.[1] Its capital is invested in the shares of more than 9,100 companies in seventy-two countries, and in government-related and corporate bonds issued by more than 1,262 entities in fifty-four countries. GPFG owns on average 1.4 percent of all listed stocks in the world, and 2.4 percent of the publicly traded shares in Europe. It is the continent's largest shareholder and a significant securities investor. In addition, the fund holds an expanding real estate portfolio that centers on office, retail, and logistics properties in select markets and locations, and prepares for investments in unlisted infrastructure for renewable energy.

In its own words, "The fund is invested in most markets, countries and currencies to achieve broad exposure to global economic growth."[2] In line with this, the fund has explored the notion of "universal owner" or "universal ownership" to characterize itself and its activities (Krohn Gjessing and Syse 2007; NBIM 2006). A universal owner is a well-diversified investor with a global reach for whom overall market risk dominates other risks due to its large number of holdings (Krohn Gjessing and Syse 2007: 436). The notion hints at how the fund forms part of a process of financialization, understood as "the increasing role of financial motives, financial markets, financial actors and financial institutions in the operation of the domestic and international economies" (Epstein 2005: 3). It is underscored by the role GPFG plays in Norwegian society, where its expected real returns cover the annual fiscal budget deficit. In 2017, this transfer amounted to

259.5 billion, for a total budget of nearly 1,302 billion kroner. On par with the year before, the fund covered 20 percent of all state commitments and activities, thus playing a key role in social reproduction.[3]

As a noun of action derived from a verb, "financialization" captures both a state and process endured by nations, corporations, and households in the past thirty to forty years that scholars commonly explain in terms of neoliberalism. Financialization refers both to structural changes in the political economy and to the development of tools and practices that extend the role and significance of financial markets (Davis and Kim 2015). Like "economization," it affords a view of how concepts, models, devices, and practices move and combine to constitute economies and realities of particular kinds (Çalışkan and Callon 2009, 2010). However, financialization also creates new possibilities for reflexivity, critique, and dreams that the movements and extensions of such technologies enable and create (Miyazaki 2013; Riles 2011). Recent scholarship has furthermore explored how ideas and practices, like hope and value, emerge in the interstices between economic theories or models and people's lives and experiences (Narotzky and Besnier 2014; Appel 2017).

In what follows, I draw inspiration from these approaches to explore a condition that notions like universal ownership, financialization, and economization often elide. The condition is the fact that GPFG operates through specific constraints, which constitute it as an investment vehicle of a specific kind. This condition is not particular to GPFG, but applies to all investors who operate according to comparable constraints. Chief among these is the investor's liquidity requirements: the need for cash to cover costs or investments of other kinds.[4] Equally significant is the time-horizon of such needs, which determines the investor's capacity to accept risk. Other constraints may include tax considerations, legal and regulatory aspects, or other circumstances restricting the ability to deploy capital.

The fact that all investors operate according to some constraints means that one can describe the character of the former through the latter. Accordingly, this chapter tells the story of the creation and development of the Norwegian sovereign wealth fund through shifts in its constraints. Relying on the legal, regulatory, and policy documents that established and developed the fund, I explore how the evolving constraints changed the money involved from short-term revenues to long-term financial capital, gradually affording a diversified portfolio of assets. This process changed the relationship between the Norwegian state and international financial markets, which gave rise to political contestations, as it turned the Norwegian state from a debtor to a creditor state. I also show how GPFG embeds in constitutional processes, and is subject to democratic deliberations and bureaucratic procedures that impose their own, rather different constraints. The result is that GPFG involves a custodial finance, where it has a duty of care to act with the Norwegian public in mind, and serves to meet a multitude of social commitments.

The account thus illuminates the financialization of the Norwegian state while pushing against the idea that financialization inevitably involves the reduction of constraints—and especially those of democratic control. I do not dispute that "The freedom of capital to flow everywhere has subordinated politics to markets for decades" (Hart 2018: 54), but wish to nuance such claims by showing that this does not apply straightforwardly to the world's largest sovereign wealth fund. Furthermore, attention to GPFG as an investment vehicle may expand the anthropological literature on finance, where debt takes precedence over credit (Elyachar 2012; Graeber 2011; Han 2012; James 2015). Relatedly, other social scientists investigate how banks create money through lending, and how this played a significant role in the recent financial crisis. The topic is especially amenable to social studies, as it is widely agreed that "money and the rate of interest are both *social constructs*: social relationships and social arrangements based primarily and ultimately on trust" (Pettifor 2017: 18—emphasis in original). While credit is recognized alongside debt as an "inseparable dyadic unit" (Peebles 2010: 226), this perspective commonly yields to a focus on liabilities and privileges, and the destabilizing and destructive role of lending. Hence, Philip Goodchild argues, "An economy based on debt is characterized by radical uncertainty and insecurity" (2016: 278).

Recent scholarship relatedly addresses the austerity policies that emerged in response to the sovereign debt crisis in Europe, yet have historical antecedents elsewhere in the world. According to Laura Bear, state debt is a complex mechanism that "brings citizens, state and the market into a network of interconnected obligations" (2015: 9; cf. Rakopoulos 2018). Public debt and austerity evoke society as a whole and its constitutive relations. Nevertheless, a bias toward debt at the expense of credit leads one to overlook how *all* nations and corporations are both lenders and borrowers simultaneously, as they take out loans, issue bonds, or offer shares to raise capital, yet extend credit in different forms to partners, clients, and citizens. Similarly, citizens take on debt through loans, mortgages, credit cards, or consumer credit, yet provide credit through their bank accounts, pension contributions, or bond- or shareholding. Attending to investments and their constraints is a way to correct a one-sided emphasis on debt and thereby deepen the understanding of finance as a *relation*, where money mediates between different actors. Attending to the GPFG and its constraints and contestations can thus illuminate how all citizens of modern states entangle in finance.

Creating a Fund

Norway's sovereign wealth fund was established by law in 1990 as the Government Petroleum Fund (Statens petroleumsfond) with the purpose "to underpin long-term considerations regarding the use of the petroleum revenues."[5] These revenues accrue mainly from taxes levied on the production of oil and gas, and the income and dividends generated by the state's involvement in this activity. The idea of a fund to manage these revenues was first mooted in 1983 by a public commission that enquired into the economic and social effects of the petroleum industry, and its future governance and development (NOU 1983). The commission argued that the petroleum resources must be utilized to the benefit of society as a whole, yet warned of their possible effects on the structure and demand of the nonoil-related economy. Specifically, the commission warned of possible shifts in industrial production and employment as the oil-sector attracted skilled labor and drove up costs and wages. It moreover warned of likely regional imbalances and macroeconomic fluctuations deriving from an unstable oil price and shifting rates of petroleum production.

These warnings rested on the concept of "Dutch disease," which was coined by *The Economist* in 1977 to describe the experience and effects of foreign currency influx resulting from the Netherlands' exports of natural gas (see Callum 2014). The notion became central to theorizing the "resource curse" with reference to other petroleum economies (Appel 2017; Mitchell 2009). While the commission did not mention this notion, it took the gas fields of Groningen as a point of departure for assessing Norwegian petroleum production (NOU 1983: 16). It moreover surmised, "It appears to be broad political agreement that the Norwegian economy should be based on a diversity of business that still needs to be developed," and conjectured, "It seems to be a widespread desire that the petroleum industry ought to provide a basis for the delivery of goods and services from Norwegian business" (NOU 1983: 93). To reconcile these potentially conflicting concerns, the commission recommended a fund to separate the earning of the revenues from their use, and thus control the incursions of foreign capital and buffer the economy against their fluctuations.

The legislative history argued that the petroleum revenues differed significantly from other state income due to their uncertainty, particular origin, and peculiar effects.[6] Nevertheless, the law mandated that these funds should be managed by the Ministry of Finance on behalf of the state, like its other revenues. Since their use was decisive, the law moreover stipulated that the funds could only transfer to the fiscal budget by parliament—Stortinget. Through an alteration of the budgetary process, it aimed to improve the governance of fiscal policy by requiring two separate parliamentary resolutions: the first to approve budgetary expenses, and the second to transfer means from the fund to finance them. In this way, the petroleum revenues were lifted out of the budget and into the fund before parliament allocated means in reverse to cover the budget deficit.

The law was, however, contested by parties at both ends of the political spectrum. The right-wing Progress Party (Fremskrittspartiet) supported saving the increased revenues, but wanted the resulting reserves earmarked for future pension payments. They moreover proposed a limit enshrined in the constitution on the amounts transferrable from the fund to the budget for ordinary expenses. Meanwhile, the Socialist Left Party (Sosialistisk Venstreparti) was concerned that the fund would serve as an instrument of saving at the expense of public welfare spending. Rather than routing revenues first into a fund and only then to the fiscal budget, they proposed transferring funds in the other direction through parliamentary process. The fund would then consist of the surplus available after budgetary expenditures rather than all the revenues from which means would transfer to cover budget shortfalls; one would thus spend the revenues and save a fraction rather than save the revenues and spend a fraction.

Gaining Capital

Economic downturn and high unemployment in the early 1990s ensured that all petroleum revenues went to cover state running costs. Senior official Svein Gjedrem (2011: 37) points out that the fund therefore initially only involved a bookkeeping exercise, whereby the revenues entered as income, but transferred in their entirety to cover expenditure. However, the prospect of a surplus in 1995 precipitated a return to the original intentions. Amid concerns that higher costs and salaries would hurt Norwegian industries that compete internationally, it was argued that the "solidarity alternative" involving a political consensus concerning wage policies required restricting domestic use of the revenues, and that the fund therefore should invest the forecasted surplus abroad.[7]

Moreover, the budget surplus would manifest as an increased kroner deposit in the central bank—Norges Bank. The fund was therefore established as a separate account in Norges Bank, where its counterpart would be foreign assets held on the bank's balance sheet.[8] While the law mandated that the ministry manage the fund, the new guidelines devolved its operational management to the central bank. Gjedrem (2011: 39) claims that the reason for this was Norges Bank's experience in managing the foreign currency reserves, which already buffered those variations in the petroleum revenues that stemmed from fluctuations in currency exchange rates. Moreover, the statutes of Norges Bank, which already served as the bank of the state and enjoyed a solid reputation based on its long history, subjected it to democratic insight and control. International investments would furthermore not prejudice its conduct of monetary policy, so earlier provisions for a separate institution to manage the fund were dropped.

Despite these arguments, political misgivings remained. Representatives of the rural and agrarian Centre Party (Senterpartiet) argued that the additional responsibilities would create confusion regarding the different roles of Norges Bank. Meanwhile, the revolutionary Red Electoral Alliance (Rød Valgallianse) surmised that foreign investments by the fund would benefit the owners of capital, rather than the public.[9] Its representative feared that, "Hard saving domestically thus shall finance imperialistic investments abroad."[10] At the other extreme, representatives of the Conservative Party (Høyre) and an independent libertarian defector from the Progress Party argued that all increased revenues should be invested abroad to meet future welfare commitments. They argued: "This goal entails that the fund should be redefined from being an 'oil-fund' to becoming a 'support-fund for the National Insurance Scheme.'"[11] The governing Labour Party (Arbeiderpartiet) wanted the bulk of increased revenue to be placed internationally, but did not want them earmarked, "since this breaks with the principle that the fiscal budget should be considered holistically."[12] This echoed an earlier Conservative government position that fund transfers should not be tied to particular objectives, and was consistent with legislative history that such transfers required macroeconomic and fiscal policy justifications.

The initial public commission referenced a broad political consensus to maintain a moderate rate of petroleum extraction. While one attempted to control this through grants of concession, the spending of the petroleum revenues was subject to a different fiscal policy process (Bjerkholt, Offerdal, and Strøm 1985: 192). Nevertheless, some parties endeavored to consider the two together. Concerned that even foreign investment would raise domestic inflation, the Centre Party for instance advocated "resource saving" over "financial saving."[13] They moreover held that a resulting smaller fund could invest domestically to boost economic growth and improve infrastructure. Similarly, the Socialist Left recommended reduced extraction for environmental reasons and advocated investments in other forms of wealth than just finance capital. This would moreover render Norway less oil dependent, while the revenues should serve to secure full employment, fair distribution, and stable welfare provisions. The Liberal Party (Venstre) and the Christian Democrats (Kristelig Folkeparti) also wanted to store a share of the petroleum reserves for future generations, but simultaneously recognized the rationale for investing the bulk of revenues abroad, albeit for different reason. The Liberals wanted investments linked to existing welfare commitments, while the Christian Democrats emphasized sustainable and international economic development, and the need for an "energy fund" to develop alternative sources for the benefit of future generations.

These considerations show that the fund emerged from a political consensus concerning the need to restrain the use of the petroleum revenues and buffer the economy from their fluctuations. The legislative history accordingly argued: "The fiscal policy governance problem pertaining to the petroleum revenues consists in *restricting* their use for the purchase of goods and services."[14] Despite this broad consensus, there was widespread dissent concerning how and where to impose which constraints. Since the fund separated the earning of the revenues from their use, it allowed some to emphasize restrictions on extraction, and others to advocate constraints on public expenditure. At the same time, some favored international financial ventures, and others argued for domestic spending and investments in other wealth objects. Similarly, some preferred to sequester funds for particular purposes, where others preferred their inclusion in the fiscal budget. Some emphasized fiscal constraints entailed by existing and future welfare commitments, while others stressed those arising from the fiscal policy process and macroeconomic concerns. Multiple constraints were thus at play, and the political debate revolved around which to prioritize and for what purpose.

Becoming an Investor

The issue of constraints gained concretization when the budget for 1996 forecasted a large surplus. When the first deposit to the fund occurred in May 1996, the ministry set new guidelines in the form of a *forskrift*: a legally binding regulation that stipulates the rights and duties of particular parties. The *forskrift* specified that the fund's investments were to be limited to bonds, bills, and other instruments issued or guaranteed by national governments or international organizations with high credit ratings. It also specified that the vast bulk of funds were to be invested in European currencies, with only minor fractions allocated to US and Canadian Dollars and Japanese Yen. In case of need for an imminent withdrawal, Norges Bank advised ensuring minimal fluctuations in the value of the fund. It therefore recommended currency investments in line with monetary policy, but in bonds with even shorter rates of maturity, or debt instruments that were imminently due to be repaid. However, the ministry downplayed this risk and instead emphasized maintaining the international purchasing power of the fund. Allocations between currencies should therefore be made on the basis of import-weights, or the size and significance of imports from the countries concerned for the Norwegian economy, while longer rates of maturity should secure returns for the fund. This was in line with the government's view that security of the fund was more important than its liquidity.

The *forskrift* for the fund was nevertheless quickly revisited. The reason was a new prognosis that the fund would become much larger than previously assumed, and that impending withdrawals were increasingly unlikely. As a result, the time-horizon of the fund extended significantly, which required a reassessment of its investment opportunities. In April 1997, less than a year after the first deposit to the fund, Norges Bank recommended drastic changes in where and how it could invest. In its advice to the ministry, the bank invoked portfolio theory to argue that a strategy for managing the relationship between risk and return required investments across multiple asset-classes, markets, and securities.[15] It pointed out that equities historically have outperformed bonds and that a portfolio consisting of many such assets would reduce the risk of fluctuations in their value, increase the likelihood of higher returns, and delink the fund from fluctuations in the oil-price. Despite their short- and medium-term uncertainty, investment in equities would thus serve to stabilize the combined national wealth. The extended time-horizon, moreover, meant that the international purchasing power of the fund would be a question of geographical distribution and diversification of investments, rather than import-weights. On this basis, the bank advised an equity share of at least 30 percent, and recommended investments in a range of securities across a multiplicity of sectors, markets, and currencies. Accordingly, the fund should hold only minor stakes and invest a larger share outside Europe. It also proposed restricted recourse to financial derivatives, but with a strict limit on the "tracking error," or the deviation between the expected returns of the fund and those of a recognized market index.

The new advice from Norges Bank reveals how emphasis shifted from a concern for maintaining the value of the fund to its expected returns. Accordingly, the petroleum revenues shifted from being means to cover running costs to become financial assets or capital—understood as money one can use to make more money (Muniesa et al 2017: 12). Where earlier stress on maintaining purchasing power rendered the fund a saving device, the new emphasis on returns transformed it into an investment vehicle. The chief concern accordingly shifted from Dutch disease to portfolio theory, and from a concept and theory of resource economics to others concerning financial economics. Pioneered by Harry Markowitz (1952), portfolio theory enables investors to assemble multiple assets with the aim of maximizing expected returns within a determined level of risk by considering the return and risk of each asset in relation to others, and thus the portfolio as a whole. Its chief concern is the relationship between risk and return, and its management through diversification, or the allocation of investments among a variety of assets. On this basis, it was moreover argued that the fund would turn petroleum extraction into a form of reallocation that could benefit others beyond the present. Already two years before, Stortinget had argued: "The petroleum revenues are based on the extraction and sale of a non-renewable resource. Through the petroleum fund, it is possible to build an alternative fortune that can provide returns in a longer run and from which coming generations may benefit."[16] Similarly, Norges Bank claimed: "The petroleum fund can be considered as wealth reallocated from oil and gas to foreign assets."[17] The fund was thus conceived of as a mechanism for converting mineral wealth in the ground into financial assets abroad with a view to their expected returns. This accorded with the idea that the petroleum revenues are not income in the usual sense, but involve the extraction and reduction of a limited natural resource. By reallocating this wealth, the fund ensures its benefit for society as a whole, which now would extend even beyond those who happened to extract and sell it.

Again, politicians varied in their responses to this advice. The Socialist Left and Red Electoral Alliance objected to what they perceived as a proposal that the state should behave like a large international "equity speculator" (*aksjespekulant*). Their representatives protested the failure to consider how this could affect working environments and labor rights in corporations around the world. Their claim regarding speculation overlooks how portfolio theory meets Benjamin Graham's definition of an investment operation as "one which, upon thorough analysis promises safety of principal and an adequate return" (1973: 1). Graham contrasts this precisely with speculation, which rather would apply to the proposals to save petroleum in the ground with a view to gain from higher yet uncertain prices in the future. Meanwhile, the Centre Party warned of foreign policy consequences if Norway were to become a large international investor concerned only with returns. In particular, they worried about democratic governance: "This may in sum have neo-colonial features and may occasion reactions in those countries that become even poorer due to Norwegian dividend demands … . Great returns are usually found in politically unstable countries or countries with immature democratic processes or a failure to comply with human rights."[18]

Unsurprisingly, Labour supported its own government's view that the fund should be able to invest up to 50 percent of its capital in international equities, but only as financial and not strategic investments. The Conservatives and the lone libertarian also endorsed the new proposal, emphasizing their opposition to any provisions other than the pursuit of maximum return within acceptable limits of risk. They thus underscored the key concepts of portfolio theory. By contrast, the Christian Democrats and Liberals proposed restricting equity investments to 30 percent of the fund's value, with priority given to corporations complementing Norwegian export industries. The latter idea accorded with a 1984 Labour proposal for the fund to support the development of Norwegian business and industry through strategic acquisitions of large international corporations (Bakken Øvald 2018: 33). This proposal gained support from both the Confederation of Trade Unions and the Confederation of Norwegian Enterprise, and was consistent with the aforementioned consensus that the Norwegian economy should continue to develop a diversity of business. Both the Christian Democrats and Socialist Left also called for investment restrictions or ethical guidelines to ensure that GPFG did not invest in companies in breach of human rights or environmental standards; guidelines they claimed were common among private investment funds.

In October 1997, the ministry issued a new *forskrift* resting on further advice from Norges Bank and deepening the role of portfolio theory. The *forskrift* provided a range for an equity share with a defined target of 40 percent and declared twenty-one countries eligible for investments. The scope for allocation between different regions and currencies weighted for both their gross domestic products and their significance for Norwegian imports. The ministry was required to tailor a reference portfolio for the fund from established indices to reflect the strategic choices for the fund and serve as a yardstick for its management. Meanwhile, a limit on relative volatility, or the expected variance between the return of the fund and the reference portfolio, would act as a limit on and means for governing its risk. The new *forskrift* took effect in January 1998. At the same time, the central bank established Norges Bank Investment Management (NBIM) as a separate division to manage the fund. NBIM made the first equity investments within three weeks, and by May, the fund was invested in more than two thousand companies, after converting 40 percent of its bond portfolio to equities in what it later called "one of the largest injections of capital into the global equity markets of its time" (NBIM 2007: 74).

By the end of 1998, the fund hence engaged extensively in international equity markets as an effect of the extended time-horizon that followed from the restriction on the use of the petroleum revenues in the Norwegian economy. It was this constraint that turned the revenues into financial capital and a diversified portfolio of assets. It furthermore changed the relationship between Norges Bank and international financial markets, where the bank now invested in equities, as well as managing the government debt and foreign currency reserves. The constraint on spending turned Norway into a creditor state, and thus provided additional connections to international financial markets. By being barred from strategic investments, the fund moreover enabled the state to invest without concern for the capital needs of specific corporations, and it allowed corporations to pursue finance capital without regard for the state's investment needs (Gjedrem 2011: 37). In other words, the fund separated the choices of the state and those of the corporations, and enabled the financial markets to mediate between them. The former can thereby pursue the highest possible return within accepted levels of risk, and the latter can seek the best possible financing for its operations. As such, the fund makes the state an investor, and ensures the existence and operation of capital markets as an intermediary between lenders and borrowers or savers and investors. In this way, the fund expanded the role and significance of financial motives, markets, actors, and institutions for both the state and the domestic economy, and thus contributed to their financialization.

It is crucial to note that this mode of financialization is circumscribed by policy advice and political decisions. It is policy and politics that define the tax regime and make the petroleum revenues state assets, and that determine the fund's investment strategy. The early strategy, moreover, included and excluded countries in the investment universe based on multiple criteria, such as the size of gross domestic products and their significance for Norwegian imports. Norges Bank furthermore advised: "The Petroleum Fund shall only invest in countries with well-functioning financial markets and satisfactory securities legislation."[19] The fund's ability to invest is therefore an effect of multiple economic, legal, and technical concerns. In addition, the initial *forskrift* stipulated that the fund could not own more than 1 percent of a given company's stock, and that it should not exercise the attendant ownership rights unless required for securing its financial interests. It prioritized financial investments to gain the benefits of diversification, while rejecting strategic investments that would expose the fund to other kinds of risk. The fund therefore supported the diversity and development of Norwegian business and economy only by sequestering the petroleum revenues and controlling their effects. It follows from this that the fund's ability to invest was constituted by hybrid concerns and diverse constraints. Meanwhile, its actual investments were the result of the return and risk of each asset in relation to the others, and the portfolio as a whole. In a manner that speaks to anthropological concerns, the fund is an effect of multiple relations that give form to its portfolios and shape Norway as a creditor state (cf. Myhre 2013).

Constitutional Processes

These relationships continued to change shape in the ensuing decades, as the ministry revised the *forskrift* for the fund. These changes occurred as part of Stortinget's fiscal budgetary process, and always involved the advice of Norges Bank. Accordingly, NBIM's website makes twenty years of correspondence publicly available, where Norges Bank consults the ministry on a variety of issues. Since 2007, these consultations form part of a separate government white paper that the ministry tables to parliament every spring. The white paper is subject to a public hearing by the standing committee on finance and economic affairs, and then a debate and vote in Stortinget. For important decisions, proposals are subject to public consultations, and the ministry appoints on occasion public commissions and expert committees. On this basis, Stortinget has gradually expanded investment opportunities to include corporate bonds, unguaranteed government bills, unlisted real estate, and unlisted infrastructure for renewable energy. They moreover increased the equity share to 60 percent in 2007 and 70 percent in 2017, and raised the ownership limit from 1 percent to 10 percent of a company's shares. They also opened for investments in emerging markets, and included small- and medium-sized companies in the benchmark index.

All these changes resulted from the rapid accumulation of capital in the fund. In fact, the ability to constrain the use of petroleum revenues by means of the fund enabled their earning without concern for their effects on the national economy. Norway could therefore capitalize on high oil-prices in the new millennium to double the value of the production, despite a reduction in volume (Noreng 2018: 56–57). Large inflows of capital ensured that market downturns did little to affect the size of the fund. Thus, the bursting of the dot-com bubble had a negligible effect, and the fund even grew between 2007 and 2008 despite the onset of the international financial crisis.

However, the increased size jeopardized the fund's character as a diversified financial investor and unsettled the relationship between its risk and return. Size meant that the fund would become a big actor in relation to the markets, and a large owner of the corporations in which it invests. To maintain its character and constraint on risk, the growth meant it was necessary to diversify investments further. Yet while some restrictions were relaxed, others were reinforced, and new ones imposed. In 2004, parliament, for instance, adopted ethical guidelines for the observation and exclusion of companies from the fund due to their products or conduct.[20] After the financial crisis, NBIM moreover took steps to curtail its use of derivatives, and subprime bonds were removed from its reference index. Most importantly, the ministry reduced the tracking error or expected relative volatility from 1.5 percent to its current 1.25 percent. This means that the scope of deviation from the benchmark index has narrowed in the past twenty years to ensure largely passive management of the fund. The ministry still defines this index by modifying commercial alternatives to reflect and operationalize decisions by Stortinget on the strategic allocation between equities and bonds, the weighting of countries and regions, and other restrictions on the investment universe. NBIM's management is, in other words, constrained by an index that also emerges as a hybrid effect of parliamentary decisions, bureaucratic considerations, and commercial efforts to gauge the market.

It follows from this that politicians and bureaucrats make the most important decisions regarding the fund, and not the asset managers at NBIM. The fund is therefore chiefly managed by acts of law, regulations, and white papers, and not financial ratios, yield curves, or discounted cash flow models. Accordingly, the fund and its management embed in constitutional processes that involve democratic deliberations, bureaucratic procedures, and expert advice, which include public hearings, commissions, committees, and consultations. The fund is therefore also constrained by the parliamentary system and its politics. Despite earlier political opposition to the fund and its investments, a practice has developed where parliament only approves proposals that receive unanimous support from the standing committee and accord with the recommendations of the white paper. The fund has hence joined defense, foreign, and petroleum policies as another domain of Norwegian politics governed by broad consensus. Nevertheless, smaller parties make minority proposals around which consensus may form in the future to shape the fund in new ways. Such proposals may either constrain the fund, as the ethical guidelines that were initially advanced by the Socialist Left and later adopted by Stortinget. Alternatively, they may open the fund up for new investment opportunities, as those planned in unlisted infrastructure for renewable energy that parliament approved in 2018, after being proposed by the Liberals and Socialist Left the previous year. In either case, consensus is contrived through the white paper process, which musters and combines arguments of different kinds, and subjects these to a multitude of perspectives and considerations. In this way, the fund is subject to revision and refinement, which result in legal and regulatory amendments that sediment in its governing documents and render GPFG a work in progress.

Custodial Finance

In late 2005, parliament passed a new law that replaced the Government Petroleum Fund with the Government Pension Fund Global, and the National Insurance Scheme Fund with the Government Pension Fund Norway. At first glance, this appears to be a fulfillment of earlier Conservative and Progress Party pleas to earmark the fund for future pension payments. However, GPFG does not have pension liabilities. Instead, the law states: "The capital of the Government Pension Fund may only be used for transfers to the central government budget pursuant to a resolution by Stortinget."[21] Meanwhile, a 2001 fiscal spending rule stipulates that parliament should limit such transfers to the fund's expected real return, currently estimated at 3 percent of its market value. By constraining transfers in this way, the spending rule transforms GPFG from a buffer fund into a return fund. The rule serves as a means to sustain the capital of the fund and further extend its time-horizon. Accordingly, NBIM states: "We work to safeguard and build financial wealth for future generations."[22] When parliament debated the white paper for 2018, a Socialist Left representative moreover argued: "Properly managed, the fund can contribute to welfare and investments for many generations ahead, and those who live in Norway in a century from now will hopefully also enjoy the benefits of this enormous fund. We must assume the perspective of eternity when we consider the optimal way of managing the fund."[23]

The spending rule constrains the size of the budget deficit that GPFG may serve to cover, and thus underlines its role as a fiscal policy tool fully integrated in the parliamentary process. It is in this way that the fund covers a significant portion of all state expenditure and public services. On this basis, one might argue that Norway has become a rentier state that derives its revenues from the rents of the petroleum resources and the financial investments they enable. Undoubtedly, Norway has earned and retained great wealth by means of the fund. Yet conceiving of Norway as a rentier state misconstrues the character of GPFG and its operation in the national economy. The chief purpose of the fund remains to sequester the petroleum revenues and control their effects in order to enable the diversity and development of the Norwegian economy. The ministry therefore conceives of the fund as an integral part of the national wealth that includes so-called human capital, and exceeds public finance and the state capacity for taxation. As the fund provides for a variety of business and waged employment, it in fact affords labor as the most significant form of wealth, and tax receipts as the dominant form of public finance. Accordingly, the ministry estimates that human capital makes up 75 percent of national wealth, while finance capital—where GPFG makes up the bulk—is less than 10 percent, and the remaining petroleum resources less than 3 percent.[24] Similarly, the fund may cover a significant 20 percent of the fiscal budget, but this still means that tax receipts and other revenues make up the remaining 80 percent. Moreover, these conditions only obtain because the fund keeps the petroleum revenues and their financial return at bay. Paradoxically, one may therefore argue that the fund impedes the role of these rents, and thus counteracts the rentier character of the Norwegian state.

It is moreover significant that all citizens retain an equal claim to the state expenditure and public services to which GPFG contributes. The fund therefore does not benefit any segment of the population more than the budget at large, as it would if earmarked for particular purposes. For instance, public pension claims depend on labor contributions, and therefore benefit those with long employment histories and high salaries. Similarly, selective investments to improve economic growth or develop infrastructure would favor particular sectors or regions, while investments in knowledge capital would benefit those involved in education, science, and technology. Instead, the fund covers a flat rate of all state expenditure, as approved by elected politicians. GPFG thus embeds in all policies and lives in Norway, and these in turn embed in international financial markets. It means that the fund conducts a custodial finance, where it has a duty of care to act with the Norwegian public in mind, and serves to meet a multitude of social commitments. Moreover, the purpose of these commitments is not to make a profit or provide a return, but to create welfare for the public. They are therefore subject to other concerns than those that govern commercial or financial activities. Like state debt, the fund is rather "a mechanism that mediates between ethical, political and economic relationships" (Bear 2015: 9). The management objective is to achieve the highest possible return within acceptable limits of risk; but the fund does not require the political processes or people's lives to which it contributes to accord with financial motives. The public of Norway entangles with financialization through the fund, but only at a remove in line with the idea the NBIM acts with them in mind. Relatedly, NBIM (2007: 74) points out that its own most striking aspect is that, "It is a publicly owned organization within a central bank, but is, in every respect, run on commercial lines like a private-sector operation." Its name reflects this hybrid character, as it combines the Norwegian title of a public institution with the English term for a profit-making activity in financial markets. Through parliament, the public determines the enabling conditions for the fund, which in turn provides enabling conditions for politics, policies, and everyday lives in Norway. Accordingly, the fund is intimate to life and politics, yet does not determine their shapes or trajectories. Paraphrasing Bear et al. (2015), the fund affords "our varied pursuits of being and becoming particular kinds of people, families, or communities." While the fund converts mineral wealth into a financial fortune, parliament and the populace convert its expected return into a multitude of political processes and life-projects through budget allocations and the uses to which people put them.

Conclusion

This chapter shows how the world's largest sovereign wealth fund emerged from the economic and political exigencies of the Norwegian state and Norwegian society. In particular, the fund materialized from a political consensus over the need to constrain the expenditure of petroleum revenues in order to prevent Dutch disease. In turn, the expansion of the fund changed the money involved from short-term revenues to long-term financial capital, and gradually afforded a diversified portfolio of investments. In the process, the Norwegian state changed from a debtor to a creditor state. Nevertheless, its investments are subject to temporal, geographical, and product- and conduct-based constraints through which GPFG operates. Most importantly, the chapter shows that increasing financialization in this case does not contradict democratic control. Rather, the fund is embedded in constitutional processes and its operation is shaped by democratic deliberations and bureaucratic procedures. In combination, these constraints forge the fund's connections to international financial markets and shape it into an investment vehicle of a particular kind. As such, they constitute the relationships and character of the creditor state. It recalls how financial markets historically emerged from parliamentary restraints on executive power (North and Weingast 1989), yet foregrounds the constitutive role constraints play for investments, and the deeply embedded relationship between finance and politics (cf. Carruthers 1993).

The chapter moreover shows how the fund's development occasioned a shift from resource economics, where the concern is Dutch disease, to financial economics and portfolio theory, where the concern is the relationship between risk and return. Erling Matsen, one-time professor of economics and current deputy governor of Norges Bank, underscored this in a recent speech regarding GPFG with an explicit reference to Harry Markowitz—the father of portfolio theory.[25] Moreover, two financial economists recently concluded: "The creation and management of the oil-fund has by and large been a phenomenal success. When oil and gas reserves were discovered on the continental shelf, the national wealth not only increased, but also became more risky. To reduce the risk, theoretical economic principles were put into practice and a process begun to reallocate wealth from oil and gas reserves to a global portfolio of equities and bonds."[26] The application of financial theory accentuates financialization; yet the role of the fund in Norwegian society entails a custodial finance that embeds in democratic politics and constitutional processes, and in turn embeds in people's lives.

Acknowledgments

I am grateful to Stephen Gudeman and Richard Robbins for their encouraging suggestions. I furthermore thank those who responded to an early version of this chapter and, finally, Douglas Holmes for regular conversations on this and related topics. This chapter forms part of the research project *Forms of Ethics, Shapes of Finance: Ethnographic Explorations of the Limits of Contemporary Capital*, funded by the Research Council of Norway (grant number 259495).

Knut Christian Myhre is a Senior Researcher in the Museum of Cultural History at the University of Oslo, where he currently leads the project *Forms of Ethics, Shapes of Finance: Ethnographic Explorations of the Limits of Contemporary Capital*. His extensive experience in Tanzania has generated numerous publications, including *Returning Life: Language, Life Force, and History in Kilimanjaro* (Berghahn Books, 2018).

Notes

1. https://www.nbim.no/. Accessed 8 October 2018.
2. https://www.nbim.no/en/the-fund/about-the-fund/. Accessed 8 October 2018.
3. https://www.statsbudsjettet.no/Upload/Statsbudsjett_2017/dokumenter/pdf/R-0650%20E_Budget%202017.pdf. Accessed 18 February 2019.
4. https://www.investopedia.com/exam-guide/cfa-level-1/portfolio-management/return-objectives-investment-constraints.asp. Accessed 11 October 2018.
5. "Lov om Statens petroleumsfond" (LOV-1990-06-22-36). All translations from Norwegian are by the author.
6. Ot.prp. nr. 29 1989-90. *Om lov om Statens petroleumsfond*, 5.
7. St.meld. nr. 2 1994-95. *Revidert nasjonalbudsjett* 1995. The solidarity alternative emerged from a public commission tasked by a centrist coalition government to devise a strategy for enhancing employment. The policy became a central tenet of subsequent long-term programs by various Labour governments.
8. St.meld. nr. 2 1994-95. *Revidert nasjonalbudsjett* 1995, 70.
9. B.innst.S. nr. IV 1994-95. *Innstilling fra finanskomiteen om Revidert nasjonalbudsjett for 1995*, 42–43.
10. B.innst.S. nr. IV 1994-95. *Innstilling fra finanskomiteen om Revidert nasjonalbudsjett for 1995*, 138.
11. B.innst.S. nr. IV 1994-95. *Innstilling fra finanskomiteen om Revidert nasjonalbudsjett for 1995*, 38.
12. B.innst.S. nr. IV 1994-95. *Innstilling fra finanskomiteen om Revidert nasjonalbudsjett for 1995*, 38.

13. Centre Party representatives argued that this would both increase the oil price and help meet goals for reduced carbon emissions, presumably stemming from the UN Framework Convention on Climate Change developed during the 1992 Earth Summit.

14. Ot.prp. nr. 29 1989-90. *Om lov om Statens petroleumsfond*, 8—emphasis in original.

15. St.meld. nr. 2 1996-97. *Revidert nasjonalbudsjett* 1997, 155.

16. St.meld. nr. 2 1994-95. *Revidert nasjonalbudsjett* 1995, 68.

17. St.meld. nr. 2 1996-97. *Revidert nasjonalbudsjett* 1997, 155.

18. B.innst.S. nr. IV 1996-97. *Innstilling fra finanskomiteen om Revidert nasjonalbudsjett for 1997*, 43.

19. St.meld. nr. 1 1997-98. *Nasjonalbudsjettet* 1998, 202.

20. The list of such products has expanded from inhumane weapons and ammunition to include tobacco and coal. Conduct refers to aggravated or systematic human rights abuses, serious violation of the rights of individuals in situations of war or conflict, severe environmental damage, gross corruption, or other violations of fundamental ethical norms. St.meld. nr. 2 2003-04. *Revidert nasjonalbudsjett* 2004, 53.

21. Lov om Statens pensjonsfond (LOV-2005-12-21-123).

22. https://www.nbim.no/. Accessed 14 February 2019.

23. https://www.stortinget.no/no/Saker-og-publikasjoner/Publikasjoner/Referater/Stortinget/2017-2018/refs-201718-06-11/?m=7#132802-1-5. Accessed 14 February 2019.

24. St.meld. nr. 26 2016-2017. *Forvaltningen av Statens pensjonsfond i* 2016, 111.

25. Matsen paraphrased Markowitz's Nobel Lecture by arguing: "An important insight from finance theory is that the expected return of an investment is not determined by its risk in isolation, but the contribution of that investment to the systematic risk of a portfolio." He moreover attributed Markowitz as saying: "Diversification is the only free lunch in finance" (Norges Bank 2018: 4–5). Egil Matsen, "Forvaltning og risiko. Foredrag av visesentralbanksjef Egil Matsen på et seminar i regi av Norges Bank," 29 November 2018. https://www.norges-bank.no/aktuelt/nyheter-og-hendelser/Foredrag-og-taler/2018/2018-11-29-matsen/.

26. Thore Johnsen og Espen Henriksen, "Å skille klinten fra hveten," 6 September 2018, https://www.dn.no/innlegg/oljefondet/oljeaksjer/energi/a-skille-klinten-fra-hveten/2-1-413905.

References

Appel, Hannah. 2017. "Toward an Ethnography of the National Economy." *Cultural Anthropology* 32, no. 2: 294–322.

Bakken Øvald, Camilla. 2018. *Drømmefondet*. Oslo: Forlaget Manifest.

Bear, Laura. 2015. *Navigating Austerity: Currents of Debt along a South Asian River*. Stanford: Stanford University Press.

Bear, Laura, Karen Ho, Anna Lowenhaupt Tsing, and Sylvia Yanagisako. 2015. "Gens: A Feminist Manifesto for the Study of Capitalism." *Society for Cultural Anthropology*.

30 March. Accessed 14 February 2020. https://culanth.org/fieldsights/gens-a-feminist-manifesto-for-the-study-of-capitalism.

Bjerkholt, Olav, Erik Offerdal, and Steinar Strøm, eds. 1985. *Olje og gass i norsk økonomi.* Oslo: Universitetsforlaget.

Çalışkan, Koray, and Michel Callon. 2009. "Economization, Part 1: Shifting Attention from the Economy towards Processes of Economization." *Economy and Society* 38, no. 3: 369–98.

Çalışkan, Koray, and Michel Callon. 2010. Economization, Part 2: A Research Programme for the Study of Markets." *Economy and Society* 39, no. 1: 1–32.

Callum, W. 2014. "*The Economist* Explains What Dutch Disease Is and Why It's Bad." *The Economist.* 5 November. https://www.economist.com/the-economist-explains/2014/11/05/what-dutch-disease-is-and-why-its-bad.

Carruthers, Bruce G. 1993. *City of Capital: Politics and Markets in the English Financial Revolution.* Princeton: Princeton University Press.

Davis, G. F., and S. Kim. 2015. "Financialization of the Economy." *Annual Review of Sociology* 41: 203–21.

Elyachar, Julia. 2012. "The Passions of Credit and the Dangers of Debt." *Society for Cultural Anthropology.* 15 May. https://culanth.org/fieldsights/the-passions-of-credit-and-the-dangers-of-debt.

Epstein, Gerald A. 2005. *Financialization and the World Economy.* Cheltenham: Elgar.

Gjedrem, Svein. 2011. "Statens pensjonsfound utland: Bakgrunn og noen utviklingstrekk." In *Finansråd i utfordrende tider,* edited by N. Bjerkedal, H. Heggenes, R. Malkenes, K. Moum, M. Skancke, and S. B. Sæther, 34–43. Oslo: Finansdepartementet.

Goodchild, Philip. 2012. "What Is Wrong with the Global Financial System?" *Journal of Interdisciplinary Economics* 24, no. 1: 7–28.

———. 2016. "Debt, Finance and Social Justice: The Enduring Significance of William Temple." *Journal of Beliefs and Values* 37, no. 3: 273–81.

Graeber, David. 2011. *Debt: The First 5000 Years.* New York: Melville House.

Graham, Benjamin. 1973. *The Intelligent Investor: A Book of Practical Counsel.* New York: Harper and Row.

Han, Clara. 2012. *Life in Debt: Times of Care and Violence in Neoliberal Chile.* Berkeley: University of California Press.

Hart, Keith. 2018. "After 2008: Market Fundamentalism at the Crossroads." *Cultural Anthropology* 33, no. 4: 536–46.

James, Deborah. 2015. *Money from Nothing: Indebtedness and Aspiration in South Africa.* Stanford: Stanford University Press.

Krohn Gjessing, Ola Peter., and Henrik Syse. 2007. "Norwegian Petroleum Wealth and Universal Ownership." *Corporate Governance* 15, no. 3: 427–37.

Markowitz, Harry. 1952. "Portfolio Selection." *The Journal of Finance* 7, no. 1: 77–91.

———. 1992. "Foundations of Portfolio Theory." In *Nobel Lectures, Economics*, edited by K. G. Mäler, 279–87. Singapore: World Scientific Publishing Company.

Mitchell, Timothy. 2009. "Carbon Democracy." *Economy and Society* 38, no. 3: 399–432.

Miyazaki, Hirokazu. 2013. *Arbitraging Japan: Dreams of Capitalism at the End of Finance.* Berkeley: University of California Press.

Muniesa, Fabian, Liliana Doganova, Horacio Ortiz, Álvaro Pina-Stranger, Florence Paterson, Alaric Bourgoin, Véra Ehrenstein, Pierre-André Juven, David Pontille, Başak Saraç-Lesavre, and Guillaume Yon. 2017. *Capitalization: A Cultural Guide.* Paris: Presses des mines.

Myhre, Knut Christian. 2013. "Cutting and Connecting: 'Afrinesian' Perspectives on Networks, Relationality, and Exchange." *Social Analysis* 57, no. 3: 1–24.

Narotzky, Susana, and Niko Besnier. 2014. "Crisis, Value, and Hope: Rethinking the Economy." *Current Anthropology* 55, no. S9: S4–S16.

NBIM 2006. *Annual Report 2006.*

NBIM 2007. *Annual Report 2007.*

Noreng, Øystein 2018. *Oljeboblen.* Oslo: Gyldendal.

North, Douglass C., and Barry R. Weingast. 1989. "Constitutions and Commitment: The Evolution of Institutions Governing Public Choice in Seventeenth-Century England." *Journal of Economic History* 49, no. 4: 803–32.

NOU. 1983. *Petroleumsvirksomhetens framtid: Det framtidige omfanget av petroleumsvirksomheten på norsk sokkel.* Oslo: Universitetsforlaget.

Peebles, Gustav. 2010. "The Anthropology of Credit and Debt." *Annual Review of Anthropology* 39: 225–40.

Pettifor, Ann. 2017. *The Production of Money: How to Break the Power of Bankers.* London: Verso.

Rakopoulos, Theodoros., ed. 2018. *The Global Life of Austerity: Comparing beyond Europe.* Oxford: Berghahn Books.

Riles, Annelise. 2011. *Collateral Knowledge: Legal Reasoning in the Global Financial Markets.* Chicago: University of Chicago Press.

Weiss, Hadas. 2018. "Reclaiming Meillassoux for the Age of Financialization." *Focaal* 82: 109–17.

7

Capital's Fidelity

Financialization in the German Social Market Economy

Hadas Weiss

A group of teachers gathered in the north German town of Kiel to discuss how to instruct pupils on financial matters pending their first bank accounts. The first speaker to address the teachers mentioned that German law obliges banks to open an account for anyone who seeks it, rich or poor. Yes, even for registered asylum seekers. Asking them to guess why, he confirmed a teacher's proposition that being able to transact financially is a form of integration, while banking, "like water from a tap or electricity from an outlet," cannot be withheld from anyone. The rest of the seminar was taken up by moderated exercises on financial rights and obligations. The last speaker projected slides documenting the implementation of this program at a Saarland school. She grew sheepish when she arrived at the poster that the pupils had prepared at its conclusion sporting the headline: The Bank Is There For You!

"It looks like an ad," she conceded. "Something went wrong."

"Maybe we should spend more time on rights," suggested a teacher.

"What did you expect the pupils to conclude?" wondered another.

Upon which a third teacher quipped: "Capitalist exploitation!"

I want to linger on this scenario, which recurred throughout my 2016–2017 fieldwork on financial advice in Germany, in which finance was introduced as a pillar of the social market economy, even as it underscored its limitations. It stands out against more common scenarios of finance as a vehicle of neoliberalism and globalization, serving to replace public provisioning with private risk management: sidelining employment in favor of capital formation and inflation curbing, binding people's savings to global firms as external investors acquire the resources of one's own community, and effacing the social foundations of the wealth from which the revenues are extracted. Describing these processes, Randy Martin (2002) identified financialization with a waning belief in capital's fidelity.

Bearing witness to current developments, anthropologists have written about financialization's intrusive and socially destructive effects, wreaking havoc on local economies through transnational agencies like the International Monetary Fund and the World Bank. They describe it transforming institutions and households, which either try to resist it (Bear 2015; Elyachar 2005; Shipton 2010 or adapt by becoming calculating and entrepreneurial (Appadurai 2016; Gershon 2011; Miyazaki 2013; Zaloom 2016). The focus on populations contending with finance in its socially corrosive instantiation has, in some cases, generated an image of financialization undermining more authentic and moral forms of economic regulation (Ho 2015).

In Germany, however, financialization proceeds along a different path. An economic powerhouse constructed upon an export-based growth model, Germany self-identifies as a social market economy in which public provisioning and market mechanisms go hand in hand. A component of the social market, finance is expected to follow the same logic. This logic can be spotted, among other institutions, in Germany's public pay-as-you-go pension system, in which the premiums of current workers fund the annuities of retirees at a level that corresponds to their wages while working. It includes a redistributive component (having been modernized in the late 1950s to allow the elderly to gain from Germany's rapid economic growth, and including a "solidarity" transfer from West to East Germany), at the same time as it incentivizes the pursuit of gainful employment by consolidating differences in workers' social status through the preservation of their living standards upon retirement.

This system of providing for old age (*Altersvorsorge)* is now said to be buckling under the weight of demographic pressures and under zero-bound interest-rates, which are eroding the value of household savings. A growing number of citizens without full-time employment, as well as many others struggling economically, are threatened with poverty at old age (*Altersarmut).* As a result of one common countermeasure, Germany has the most pronounced increase, in global comparison, of employment into old age (Börsch-Supan and Coile 2018).

Financialization enters Germany not to replace the public pension system but to make it more sustainable. Citizens who have a regular income are encouraged to supplement it through financial instruments and products. This would increase the amount of circulating capital for financial markets, while reducing the pressure on the public system. Finance is represented to the German public, in other words, not as an economic policy designed to overturn existing priorities, but as a utility that remains subordinate to the same priorities. Financial advisors and other intermediaries see themselves accordingly as providing a public service. It is precisely capital's fidelity, in the sense of its being harnessed for the accomplishment of social welfare as well as individual status protection, which is invoked in the financialization of Germany's households.

My aim in this chapter is to show how financialization is introduced into a social market economy by emphasizing the continuities of this brand of capitalism, particularly in safeguarding the population's welfare while allowing its members to maintain their relative status. Financial instruments promise to help people provide for their households by exercising the independence and responsibility they hold dear. But assigning finance such a role has unintended consequences. The emphasis on continuities with what German capitalism does well also brings some of its shortcomings to the fore, specifically its inequalities and the agency it undermines. In light of these failings, the role of the state in maintaining the welfare of the population is held up for scrutiny. I will develop this argument by briefly explaining how German capitalism works, and then by describing how finance is incorporated into it.

German Capitalism

A couple of months after the teachers' training in Kiel, I attended another in Nuremberg. There, we pored over worksheets that modeled the economy as represented pedagogically. An inner circle depicted households purchasing goods and services provided by firms that reward households with work. An outer circle depicted banks investing deposited savings in firms, which in turn supply more goods, services, and work to households. The government was absent from this and other models put forth, as were rent/revenue extracting property and financial assets. The model portrayed a closed national economy whose institutional mediation of work and savings empowered workers and savers to provide for themselves.

A critical observer might have pointed out that, in its narrow focus on the wealth distributed by wages, the model also neglected exploitation, as workers contribute more value to the production of this wealth than the value represented in their paychecks. Likewise missing was inequality, as some get miserable pay for backbreaking work while others get handsome pay for little work; and precariousness, as permanent, full-time employment becomes scarce and irregular.

Capitalist economies have developed systems of public provisioning that extend beyond the mediation of work, firms, and banks to address such inadequacies. In Germany, this has been a tenet of the social market economy—the term used to describe a competitive economy free of cartels and trusts, whose efficiency is also meant to produce the best social outcomes. Socially, this model has been associated with Germany's industry-wide structures of negotiation between capital and labor (Plumpe 2016). Ideationally, it has been associated with ordoliberalism: an economic school that assigns the state the role of preventing monopolies, limiting speculation, and coordinating workers' education and training to meet market demand. Institutionally, it has been associated with responsibilization, as put forth by Michel Foucault (2008) and elaborated by Nikolas Rose (1989): the creation of interlocking freedoms, constraints, and incentives, which encourage the citizenry to regenerate industry by working and consuming, and to accomplish security by acting prudently.

Responsibilization is also an expressed goal of financial literacy campaigns. Their initiators explain that, with the deregulation of markets and growing complexity of financial products, informed participants must attend privately to their needs through financial instruments, and so refrain from drawing on the public purse (OECD 2015; OECD 2016; Survey on Financial Literacy 2007). This behavior is deemed particularly urgent among the aging populations of Europe, where it would ease demographic pressures on pension systems (Batsaikhan and Demertzis 2018). Critics of these campaigns likewise consider them a means of promoting responsibilization in the sense of legitimizing cutbacks on public goods and services (Delanty 2014; Finlayson 2009; Langley 2007; Willis 2008; Wolf 2018).

In Germany the valorization of personal responsibility has a far longer history (Boyer 2005), while calls for a strict savings regimen have sounded for well over a century under the banner of "German virtue" (Weiss 2018b). What is now a core of Germany's public discourse has grown out of a unique set of historical circumstances. In the late nineteenth century, Germany was under geopolitical pressure to catch up with already industrialized countries like Britain. The German state had to underwrite the risk of investment in industrialization, whose scale would have been too large for the capacity of any individual entrepreneur. In playing this role over decades, it has adopted a more directive position in the economy than is typical of liberal states. One way in which it filled this role has been to suppress consumption and encourage saving among the population. This was intended to build up pools of capital for investment in large-scale industrial development. The strategy persisted after World War II, with the goal of lowering German labor costs so as to recover Germany's export markets and make them globally competitive (Blyth 2013: 134-35).

The coupling of responsibilization with the state's management of its citizens' savings is nowhere more apparent than in the pension system. The German model thereof is often traced back to Chancellor Otto von Bismarck, who had established a scheme of social insurance in the 1880s. It fortified status positions by pegging pensions and other benefits to the height of wages and contributions. Designed to incentivize the competitive pursuit of employment, a variant of this system is now implemented among a broad working population with a wide range of salaries. But just as in the late nineteenth century, Germany is again in a position of having to catch up with states whose pension reforms prioritize the deepening and broadening of financial markets over the protection of their working populations. Germany started on this path in the early 2000s with measures like the Riester reform, which promoted privately funded pensions. It continued down the same path a decade later by intensifying the risks borne by employees in occupation pensions, and by facilitating the growth of auto-enrollment pension schemes (Wiß 2019)

Observing an economy through the lens of pensions and other forms of provisioning helps connect fragmented domains under a single rubric. Provisioning encompasses the social relations that make goods and services available, the institutions that regulate their flow, and the historical forces that shape them (Narotzky 2005). The interconnectedness of provisioning arrangements foregrounds the inequalities that plague them. In Germany, as elsewhere, this foregrounding accounts for the diminishing readiness of the haves to support the have-nots through their taxes and premiums (Mau 2014; Streeck 2017). Inequalities also make critics fault social security systems for being patronizing, exclusionary, and unjust; for amplifying family pressures on wage earners and on recipients of public assistance; and for encouraging dependency and disinclination to work (Ferguson 2015; Frazer and Gordon 1994; Han 2012; James 2015; Offe 1984).

In other countries, critiques of this kind have prepared the ground for the curtailment of public provisioning in favor of liberalized insurance systems, which François Ewald (1991) has famously characterized as substituting charity for a principle of justice. Risks to households have come to be represented as sources of profit, to be embraced and managed rather than avoided (O'Malley 2004). Yet, Germany has so far held most of these forces at bay. It has been able to do so by exporting financialization to the Eurozone and other economies. German banks lend their capital surpluses to these countries, while their populations are also major consumers of German industrial products whose value is fortified by the Euro.[1] Germany's exported variant of financialization (Fuller 2016) allows its domestic growth to continue hinging upon industrial export rather than debt financing and asset-price inflation at home. Most of its firms are not publicly traded, reducing the exigency of quick profits to provide "shareholder value." Germany's major banks are public, as are large parts of its pension system, healthcare, education, and professional training. It has relatively low rates of homeownership, thus curbing a key source of household debt elsewhere in the world. And its household savings are typically placed in bank deposits rather than equity (Detzer 2019; Fischer 2014; Haves, Vitols, and Wilke 2014; Mertens 2017).

Germany's insistence on public provisioning also means that its economic policies are relatively visible and contestable. As the opening vignette indicates, even capitalism (or, more accurately, what are deemed its excesses) can be named and negotiated in Germany (Fischer 2014: 93). The inclination to do so is intensifying with changes to the European social and economic landscape, including stepped up competition, unemployment, deindustrialization, immigration, welfare retrenchment, and social schisms. In Germany, organized labor is weakening while contingent and poorly paid jobs are on the rise, as are poverty rates and social disaffection. Since the early 2000s, the unpopular "Hartz IV" workfare regime toughened the conditions for claiming welfare and unemployment benefits. Part of the subsequent malaise is directed against immigrants and against the major political parties, whose hegemony is eroding. The social market economy faces scrutiny by those whose needs are not being met. This is the context in which financialization gathers steam in German society.

The global financial market, which grows by locating unused financial resources and placing them in circulation, has been eying Germany's surpluses and household savings for a while now. Banks and firms can profit through sales and fees from intensified financial activity. The German government, in turn, can expand public reserves by getting citizens to draw on private resources, while consumer organizations are committed to helping consumers make the best use of the opportunities available to them. Actors with distinct agendas have a stake, then, in finance playing a greater role in the daily lives of German households; hence the proliferation of financial education and advice.

The initiatives I examined included media reports and informational websites along with courses, seminars, and one-on-one consultancies on financial matters. They are offered year-round and countrywide by banks and advice firms, consumer organizations, corporations, and federal government administrations—providers that traverse geographical and political divides. The seminars and consultancies take place in schools, employment agencies, training programs, workplaces, churches, old-age homes, event halls, adult education colleges, and community colleges. Most are free of charge, while consultancies charge a modest hourly rate. They refrain from advertising specific products and are financed publicly or through donations by firms that present this as their corporate social responsibility.[2] Above all, they are framed as a public service. This framing shapes the messages they deliver, adjusted to what consumers and their representatives have grown to expect of German capitalism.

Finance as Utility

My interest in financial education initiatives has provoked expressions of distaste by the very Germans at whom this advice was directed. "I don't know anything about finance," was the standard response I received when explaining my research project, mostly followed by "and I don't care." "People of my generation resent the call to invest our money, save independently for a pension, or buy a house," explained a woman of around fifty. When I asked her why, she replied: "We already work and save. We need to take care of our children and will have to care for our parents. We have nothing to spare." Those who attended finance seminars were no different. Audiences challenged what they heard, demanding nonfinancial alternatives to the products mentioned. Despite the oft-repeated threat of poverty at old age, people I spoke with in and outside these seminars directed their retirement concerns at how the government was running the pension system, rather than setting off individually on a race for higher returns. Their greater worry, in the words of one near-retiree, was "that the whole system come crashing down and then we'll all be in trouble."

Advisors expressed similar misgivings. Many complained between meetings or after seminars that it was no fun trying to help people save for their retirements, since there was little they could actually do. The one-on-one consultancies I observed were drab: consultants named instruments that offered marginally higher returns while warning about risks, and their recommendations were received with matching tepidness. When I pointed this out to an official coordinating them, he explained that people do not like being told that what they had counted on in the past is no longer secure. Rather than insisting, however, they tell clients to not worry too much and to simply call them if they have a specific concern.

Antipathy toward finance appeared to issue from a deep-running commitment to and insistence upon a social market economy, where prudent spending and saving would be rewarded with security. Sharing this commitment, financial advisors pitched their messages about finance, not as a means of self-enrichment for the risk-taker, but rather as utility for everyman: something to help consumers buy things now they would pay for later, and save for the future. They would stress continuities with familiar situations and popular values, which the right financial strategies would

merely be updating. In almost every seminar on provisioning for retirement, audiences would grumble about the riskiness of the products on
offer. Speakers would take the time to explain that life itself is risky, that
because of inflation and insufficient insurance coverage, sitting back and
doing nothing is also risky, that they are merely suggesting ways to manage
risks better, and that properly chosen, diversified, and managed, financial
products are actually quite safe.

Advisors intimated that personal finance and the health of the national
economy go hand in hand. German politicians liken the state budget to a
family budget (both denoted by the German word *Haushalt)*, representing
German society as family-like in its common fate. Just as parents ought
not burden their children with their own debts, current workers should
refrain from burdening future ones with excessive pension claims (Offe
2015: 95–96). Advisors conflated people's responsibility toward their children with the notion that it is up to everyone to ensure that the pension
system remains intact so that workers will ultimately get the same benefits as retirees today. An advisor around my age made this point when I
interviewed him, by likening the next generation of workers to slaves that,
if nothing changes, we would be forcing to work for us. Others enjoined
audiences to practice responsibility by supplementing their claims on the
public system with private investments.

Audiences would likewise bring up the national economy. When the
speaker at a seminar in Zellingen warned that overspending leads to
over-indebtedness, a participant interrupted to mention Germany's
zero-deficit policy as another reason for why people fall into debt.

"It used to be that you bought something and had it your whole life,"
added another participant in agreement: "Now you always have to buy the
new model. If politicians really wanted sustainability, they'd tell manufacturers not to build things that expire so quickly."

"It's a reflection of our economy," chimed in a third. "It always has to
grow. It used to grow by 2, 3 percent a year. Now if it grows by 0.2 percent,
the media presents this as a catastrophe. But how can an economy always
be growing?"

Such grievances gave voice to people's sense of having a stake in the way
their economy was run. In a comparative ethnography of consumption
and trade, Edward Fischer (2014) asserted as much by observing shop-
pers in Hannover who were willing to pay more for products they deemed
ethical. He made sense of their choices in terms of Germany's social-market
arrangements underpinning a sense of stake holding—citizens deeming
their self-interests to be bound up with national interests. To the extent
that they identify with their political-economic orders, and that these
orders respond to their moral demands, he concluded, Germans consider

their personal goals furthered by their selective willingness to sacrifice for the greater good.

German central banking likewise invokes the mutual implication of self-interest with the common good when communicating with the public, according to Douglas Holmes. The Bundesbank strives to maintain price stability consistent with the growth potential of the national economy. Its officials issue guidelines for the expansion and contraction of employment, and they oppose wage- and price-setting attempts that threaten the soundness of the currency. They cultivate trust in these measures through "a broader story about the German state and its ability to manage the future by aligning its citizens' expectations with national interests" (Holmes 2014: 65).

The greater good and national interests were, in fact, perennial themes in the seminars I observed. Participants demanded to know the social and ecological impacts of financial products, while speakers referenced ethical products among those on offer. Some seminars included discussions of the environment and sustainability. Advice on investment in corporate stock, even when endorsing global diversification, would single out national enterprises like Volkswagen, Siemens, Bayer, and Lufthansa. At an event in Hamburg for residents approaching retirement, the speaker mentioned Turkish, Czech, and Italian banks in the city that offered higher interest rates on savings deposits. But she warned that if the economies of those countries fail, the savings might disappear, unlike those in German banks, which are insured and backed by a more stable economy. Seminars on investment compared Germany favorably to post-crisis USA or Greece, whose populations were supposedly punished for the profligacy Germans avoid.

Savings rates in Germany have traditionally been high despite public provisioning (Bundesbank Monthly Report 2013). My older informants rehearsed the values of independence and thrift as cornerstones of their upbringing. The importance they placed on saving privately, matched with an aversion toward debt and conspicuous consumption, expressed an unwavering belief in taking personal responsibility over their fortunes (Weiss 2019).[3] Advisors would recommend real estate and stock funds along these lines. They instructed clients to reach sober conclusions about what to buy and how to budget for it. They promoted investment strategies as ways of saving better. They recast dependence on market fluctuations beyond anyone's control as means of attaining financial independence. They deemed the right kind of debt (primarily mortgage, but also student debt) to be no debt at all but rather a means of building reserves, and the self-imposition of a saving discipline through regular repayment where one might otherwise spend frivolously.

Advisors made much of finance's usefulness for the family unit. Since tending to multigenerational needs calls for long-term planning, a family could be matched with stock funds, which take a long time to realize their value. Advisors invoked parental responsibilities in recommending that parents give children allowances and teach them how to manage their money. They instructed parents to open long-term stock-based savings accounts for each child, and spoke of homeownership as providing the family with stability. This property, they added, could form a nice inheritance. At a seminar on inheritance, the advisor spoke about expressing resentment or love by cutting relatives out of the will or by specifying who would inherit one's piano or stamp collection. This seminar took place in the small East German town of Fürstenwalde, where the attending octogenarians could scarcely have owned much more. But it was the principle that counted: family sentiments would be manifested through financial transfers.

Family also loomed large in one-on-one consultancies. Advisors would catch clients off guard by inquiring about what they stood to inherit from their still-living parents. People trying to save for their retirement found out that anything could serve this purpose. Beyond inheritance, advisors would ask about their pension credit points but also about possibilities for acquiring private insurance policies, equity, and real estate. I recall one consultancy interrupted by a call from daycare telling the client that her son was sick. The advisor waved away her apology, pointing out that her children were also her old age provision.

The ideal, however, was financial independence from one's children, as well as from one's husband.[4] At a seminar in Göttingen for professional women, the speaker decried the situation whereby women, abusing problematic allowances in the pension system, curtailed their work after marriage or childbirth to rely on their husband's pension. When some women voiced concern over the size of their expected pensions, the speaker responded by expounding on the merits of stock funds. Her message was that women who can invest should do so, as this was the true spirit behind the social market economy. Resting on the pillars of independence, status, and responsibility, this form of capitalism incorporated finance almost seamlessly. It did so by framing finance as a utility—operating to fulfill one's duty to one's family as well as enabling one's independence therefrom.

Coming Apart at the Seams

Not everyone at whom financial advice was directed was doing well. Postwar West Germany reconstructed its economic power to achieve high standards of living and democratic freedoms—ideals that were to extend eastward following Reunification (Siegrist 2002). Rising levels of consumption have given some credibility to that promise (Carter 1997), but many were left out. Anthropologists studying East Germany after reunification found mass unemployment and discontent (Berdahl 2005; Jancius 2006; Rudd 2006), while ethnographies elsewhere in Germany document enduring exclusions based on race, class, and religion (Amrute 2016; McGill 2017; Partridge 2012; Shoshan 2016). With poverty and disaffection on the rise, populations unempowered by consumption challenge the supposed inclusivity of Germany's wealth (Berdahl 2005; Ringel 2018).

Treating finance as a utility of the social market economy makes it easier for Germans to identify its seam lines and reject it from the standpoint of the tenets it fails to uphold. Waiting for a seminar on real estate financing in Chemnitz to begin, I struck up a conversation with the woman sitting beside me. She and her husband had inherited a small piece of land, and they were thinking of building a house on it. Showing me the plot on Google Maps, she spoke excitedly about the freedom her family would enjoy with all the space of a private home. But when the seminar began and the costs dawned on her, she wavered. The speaker encouraged her to think about the house as a retirement saving and bequest. Mortgage repayments could be covered by renting the place out, while ground tax could be saved if future grandchildren inherit the house. "We're just looking for a place to live in," she countered his first suggestion, and scoffed at the notion of investing in something whose value would only be realized after she's dead. When I asked her after the seminar about giving up the dream of freedom, she was resigned. In continuing to live in their cheap rental, she said, her family would at least be free of debt.

Rejecting finance in this way chains those unable to benefit from it to their disadvantages. They are encouraged, moreover, to perceive their situation through the perspective of finance. East Germans experienced reunification as a form of economic shock therapy; but they were also swayed by the rhetoric of generous inclusion. Anthropologist Ursula Dalinghaus (2017) collected life histories from East and West Germans some twenty years later. She analyzes these interviews against a backdrop in which labor in East Germany is still remunerated at lower rates than labor in the West. Nevertheless, she demonstrates, people from both Former East and Former West pay greater attention to the money that goes into paying East Germans' pensions, and therefore share a view of the West having sacrificed more.

It is here that financialization diverges most markedly from the principles of the social market economy. Systems of public provisioning place the state under the spotlight, turning its policies into matters of political contention. So, for example, the fact that much of the support for East Germans since 1990 has been funneled through social insurance funds has heightened Germans' awareness of the contributions they pay into it. That unemployment remains higher and wages lower in the East similarly magnifies the political and economic costs of integration.

But for finance, there is no East vs. West, just as there are no immigrants vs. nonimmigrants, Catholics vs. Protestants, or any other of the political groupings that could spark political unrest. Instead, finance targets individuals. It classifies these individuals according to their consumer powers. Variables like background, income, age, gender, and so forth are taken into account only to the extent that they affect present and future consumption. Financial products prefigure distinct fortunes ranging from revenue-generation and wealth building for the rich to the protection of minimal subsistence for the poor. People who use these tailored products ideally benefit from them as individuals, not as members of a distinct ethnic, regional, or other group. Collectively, this cannot but reproduce and even exacerbate existing inequalities. But in effacing the structural foundations of these inequalities, finance deprives the populations subjected to them from recognizing their foundations and demanding political redress.

Finance seminars and consultancies are therefore thoroughly depoliticized. Some private consultants charge a hefty fee for managing high-paying clients' money to make it grow. While consultancies of this kind were not the focus of my study, I did interview a couple of private consultants. They explained that they analyze their clients' personal lives, and elicit their risk preferences and liquidity constraints, to fit them with appropriate products; not unlike a family doctor, as one consultant described himself. In stock-market events I attended in both (East German) Dresden and (West German) Mannheim, slogans such as "dividends are the new interest rates" were to awaken choice audiences' interest in stock, while the products on offer emphasized the extraction of shareholder value. At the other end of the social spectrum, church alliances run debt-support centers, helping weak populations all across Germany to manage overwhelming debts. Teaching proper consumption habits rather than moneymaking strategies, much of their advice is an injunction toward debt repayment (c.f. Davy 2017 for the UK).

Everyone between these extremes is served by organizations that see themselves as providing a public service for anyone who needs it. Two of Germany's largest providers of financial advice are the countrywide education service of the Sparkasse bank, active for over half a century now, and the consumer rights organization Verbraucherzentrale, with independent branches in each of Germany's federal states. Their advice varies according to the needs of distinct populations and new consumer demands.

Changes in their offerings reflect changes in society, the administrator of the Sparkasse service told me. One of their oldest seminars is on how to balance a household budget. Its contents have altered over the years to include new things on which people spend money, but the need for this skill is constant. In contrast, a new seminar has been designed on how to save for retirement, prompted by fear that the benefits from the public system will not suffice. The key is not merely to address changing circumstances, the administrator added, but to serve everyone.

Sparkasse seminars I attended in different social settings have, indeed, differed to serve respective populations, even when their titles were identical. For example, a seminar called "Young and Fit in Money Matters," picked up from the annual brochure for relatively affluent families vacationing in Bavaria, discussed consumption pressures by children and wealth-building strategies, while a seminar by the same name for the long-term unemployed in the East German town of Seelow dealt with how best to use regular bank deposits.

The outreach of each Verbraucherzentrale likewise differs according to the concerns of the populations they serve. Seminars on real estate financing and inheritance are more common in parts of Germany where property ownership is the rule rather than the exception. There are also many hit-or-miss attempts to identify specific areas of interests. I was the only person to show up at a seminar in Leipzig for young adults entering the job market (*Berufsstarter*). When I asked the speaker why she thought this was so, she speculated that youngsters moving to the city for their studies leave to find jobs in cities with better employment opportunities. Once burnt, I hesitated before traveling to Hamburg to attend a seminar with the same name; but on this occasion, some forty young professionals showed up, posing pointed questions about what to do with the money they envisioned making.

Recommendations on saving for retirement through stock funds, mixed (stock and bond) funds, and index funds addressed people everywhere whose savings were large enough and incomes regular enough to lock some of them up for decades and accept the risk of illiquidity. For the less privileged, advice fell back on work and social security. These differences were sometimes predesigned with specific populations in mind. Otherwise, seminars and consultancies were open to the general public and advertised on the Internet with an explanation about their content, under the assumption that there would be self-selection among those choosing to attend them.

Advisors caution the less privileged against the risks of financial investment. They either point them out plainly or imply them by rehearsing the importance of social security. They do so primarily when advising the self-employed, whose participation in many of these arrangements is voluntary. In one consultancy, a self-employed therapist was eager to save for retirement, but she and her husband did not have much. Their parents were no longer around to help, and they inherited only a summerhouse of meager value on the Baltic Sea. The bank would not help finance the purchase of a home because neither had a steady income. The rent on their Berlin apartment was low, but the consultant doubted it would remain low. "Don't forget the house on the Baltic Sea," the woman joked as the advisor ran out of ideas. He replied sternly: "That's a wild card. Inflation is a wild card. Your rent is a wild card. Your children are a wild card. You don't know how expensive things will be thirty years from now." He concluded with an exasperated: "Is there any possibility for you to find steady employment?"

At a seminar in Fulda for single mothers, the speaker praised the pension system for the benefits it affords such women and urged them to avail themselves of their rights while shouldering their responsibilities. She told them, as parable, about her widowed Bavarian aunts. Tante Hildegard never worked while her husband had invested his business earnings. Their value didn't grow, and Tante Hildegard is now struggling. Tanta Greta married an alcoholic who only worked sporadically, so she had to work too, and paid into the pension system. Well, guess who gives Tante Hildegard two-dozen eggs each month? None other than Tante Greta, who is so proud of the money she earned for retirement. "As soon as you manage it, go out, get a job, and pay your pension," the adviser concluded. "Work is the most important thing. You won't get anything from the finance market."

Against the backdrop of zero-bound interest rates and pressures on the pension system, financialization was framed as offering some a chance to complement what they expected to get from social security, while others would be partly protected from it through the same arrangements. Advisors approached consumers as having unequal horizons. Where some stood to gain by embracing risk, others were simply at-risk and in need of protection. Where some could save better by investing, others had to tighten their belts. And where some could use debt as a wealth-building strategy, others were in danger of becoming over-indebted.

But even those steered toward finance received no guarantees. Germany's social market economy projects high living standards and protections for responsible workers and savers. Soliciting citizens' trust on the basis of this conceit, it also stands accountable for its failures. Exclusions and deficiencies make it come apart at the seams. These predicaments turn into grounds for political challenges, social unrest, and renegotiation of the terms of the social market economy. Global finance affords no such recourse. Financialization's individualizing, depoliticizing, and responsibilizing tendencies leave its terms to be validated by individuals' own moneymaking capacities. It is therefore unsurprising that Germans of all classes would be loath to embrace it.

The advisors I observed performed their public charge in good faith. They enlightened savers about financial instruments that would help complement their pensions, and warned vulnerable populations against the pitfalls of finance while informing them about their rights and protections. Consumers could either place their stakes in global finance while making their peace with its deficiencies, or they could entrust their resources to national banks that offered no interest, and to a pension system under threat. All advisors could really do, then, was to show which of the alternatives available to them would be the lesser of the two evils. In their commitment to a social market economy in which finance features as a utility, they were unwittingly raising awareness of the deficiencies of capitalism itself.

Conclusion

Germans unhappy with changes in their financial landscape recoil from implicitly affirming these changes by learning to adjust to this new reality. They are also averse to letting their politicians off the hook by taking charge of something that social market arrangements were to manage for them. Financial advisors try to allay these concerns by associating finance with the resonant values of independence, responsibility, thrift, and stake holding. They approach finance as a utility through which various populations can spend and save in order to accomplish their preexisting aims according to their preexisting values. Anchoring finance in Germany's social market economy accentuates, however, the exclusions and inequalities of German capitalism, its failure to bring about universal wellbeing and security, and the limited agency it offers those subject to it.

Most studies of financialization focus on either fully financialized economies, or on the vulnerable populations of countries upon which finance encroaches from without. They draw scholarly attention toward finance's corrosive intrusion upon earlier forms of regulation that are often construed as more moral. The dearth of attention to processes of financialization in a social market economy like Germany's occludes, however, the enduring ambitions to which capitalism itself gives rise, as well as the shortcomings it fails to resolve. There are advantages in tracing the extent to which financialization reproduces capitalism's own logic. This is particularly true for Germany, where the tenants of a social market economy provide the orientation and rhetorical justification for incipient financialization. Capital's fidelity is the terrain upon which its appeals are made and contested. These responses expose some of the subterranean contradictions of capitalism that, though long running and deeply entrenched, are now bubbling to the surface in new forms.

Hadas Weiss is a Fellow at the Madrid Institute for Advanced Study. She studies social aspects of capitalism and financialization in Israel, Germany, and Spain. Her publications include *We Have Never Been Middle Class: How Social Mobility Misleads Us* (Verso, 2019).

Notes

1. Germany's financial sector encouraged its banks to broaden securitization and participation in global markets. Financial liberalization of the Eurozone created a new marketplace for German financial institutions, which increased the risk of crisis as current accounts diverged between core states like Germany and peripheral ones (Eichacker 2015).
2. I explain elsewhere that it is precisely this position of financial advisors that makes their interactions with clients the perfect setting in which to observe the relation between financial markets and households (Weiss 2018a).
3. The promotion of thrift and degradation of debt is put to political use in Germany's relations with Eurozone peripheries: its politicians frame debt relief as a policy that might prevent debtors from assuming the virtue of self-sufficiency (Offe 2015: 97).
4. Such was not always the case in West Germany, where in previous decades it was common for young mothers to exit the job market due to inadequate childcare and other considerations (Galambos and Walper 1997).

References

Amrute, Sareeta. 2016. *Encoding Race, Encoding Class.* Durham: Duke University Press.

Appadurai, Arjun. 2016. *Banking on Words: The Failure of Language in the Age of Derivative Finance.* Chicago: University of Chicago Press.

Batsaikhan, Uuriintuya, and Maria Demertzis. 2018. "Financial Literacy and Inclusive Growth in the European Union." *Policy Contribution* 8: 1–18.

Bear, Laura. 2015. *Navigating Austerity: Currents of Debt along a South Asian River.* Stanford: Stanford University Press.

Berdahl, Daphne. 2005. "The Spirit of Capitalism and the Boundaries of Citizenship in Post-Wall Germany." *Comparative Studies in Society and History* 47, no. 2: 235–51.

Blyth, Mark. 2013. *Austerity: The History of a Dangerous Idea.* New York: Oxford University Press.

Börsch-Supan, Axel H., and Courtney Coile. 2018. *Social Security Programs and Retirement Around the World.* Working Paper 25280. National Bureau of Economic Research. Accessed 14 February 2020. http://www.nber.org/papers/w25280.

Boyer, Dominic. 2005. *Spirit and System: Media, Intellectuals, and the Dialectic in Modern German Culture*. Chicago: University of Chicago Press.

Bundesbank Monthly Report. 2013. *Household Wealth and Finances in Germany: Result of the Bundesbank Survey*. 23 June.

Carter, Erica. 1997. *How German Is She? Postwar West German Reconstruction and the Consuming Woman*. Ann Arbor: University of Michigan Press.

Dalinghaus, Ursula M. 2017. "Between Memorialization and Monetary Revaluation: The 1990 Currency Union as a Site of Post-Unification Memory Work." In *Money in the German Speaking Lands*, edited by Mary Lindemann and Jared Poley, 383–402. New York: Berghahn Books.

Davy, Ryan. 2017. "Polluter Pays? Understanding Austerity through Debt Advice in the UK." *Anthropology Today* 33, no. 5: 8–11.

Delanty, Gerard. 2014. "Introduction: Perspectives on Crisis and Critique in Europe Today." *European Journal of Social Theory* 17: 207–18.

Detzer, Daniel. 2019. "Financialization Made in Germany: A Review." Working Paper, no. 122/2019. Berlin School of Economics and Law, Institute for International and Political Economy Berlin. Berlin.

Eichacker, Nina. 2015. "German Financialization, the Global Financial Crisis, and the Eurozone Crisis." Working Paper 404. Political Economy Research Institute.

Elyachar, Julia. 2005. *Markets of Dispossession: NGO's, Economic Development, and the State in Cairo*. Durham: Duke University Press.

Ewald, François. 1991. "Insurance and Risk." In *The Foucault Effect*, edited by Graham Burchell, Collin Gordon, and Peter Millar, 197–210. London: Harvester Wheatsheaf.

Ferguson, James. 2015. *Give a Man a Fish: Reflections of the New Politics of Distribution*. Durham: Duke University Press.

Finlayson, Alan. 2009. "Financialisation, Financial Literacy and Asset-Based Welfare." *The British Journal of Politics and International Relations* 11: 400–21.

Fischer, Edward T. 2014. *The Good Life: Aspiration, Dignity, and the Anthropology of Wellbeing*. Stanford: Stanford University Press.

Foucault, Michel. 2008. *The Birth of Biopolitics*, edited by Michel Senellart. Translated by Graham Burchell. New York: Palgrave Macmillan.

Fraser, Nancy, and Linda Gordon. 1994. "A Genealogy of Dependency: Tracing a Keyword of the US Welfare State." *Signs* 19, no. 2: 309–36.

Fuller, Gregory. 2016. *The Great Debt Transformation: Households, Financialization, and Policy Responses*. New York: Palgrave Macmillan.

Galambos, Nancy L., and Sabine Walper. 1997. "Employed Mothers in Germany." In *Families of Employed Mothers: An International Perspective*, edited by Judith Frankel, 35–62. New York: Garlend Publishing.

Gershon, Ilana. 2011. "Neoliberal Agency." *Current Anthropology* 52, no. 4: 537–55.

Han, Clara. 2012. *Life in Debt: Times of Care and Violence in Neoliberal Chile*. Berkeley: University of California Press.

Hart, Keith, and Horacio Oritz. 2014. "The Anthropology of Money and Finance: Between Ethnography and World History." *Annual Review of Anthropology* 43: 465–82.

Haves, Jakob, Sigurt Vitols, and Peter Wilke. 2014. "Financialization and Ownership Change: Challenges for the German Model of Labor Relations." In *Financialization, New Investment Funds, and Labour: An International Comparison*, edited by Howard Gospel, Andrew Pendleton, and Sigurt Vitols, 148–75. Oxford: Oxford University Press.

Ho, Karen. 2015. "Finance, Anthropology of." In *International Encyclopedia of the Social and Behavioral Sciences*. 2nd ed., vol. 9, 171–76. New York: Elsevier.

Holmes, Douglas R. 2014. *Economy of Words: Communicative Imperatives in Central Banks*. Chicago: University of Chicago Press.

James, Deborah. 2015. *Money for Nothing: Indebtedness and Aspiration in South Africa*. Stanford: Stanford University Press.

Jancius, Angela. 2006. "Unemployment, Deindustrialization, and 'Community Economy' in Eastern Germany." *Ethnos* 71, no. 2: 213–32.

Langley, Paul. 2007. "Uncertain Subjects of Anglo-American Financialization." *Cultural Critique* 65: 67–91.

Martin, Randy. 2002. *Financialization of Everyday Life*. Philadelphia: Temple University Press.

Mau, Steffen. 2014. *Inequality, Marketization and the Majority Class: Why did the European Middle Classes Accept Neoliberalism?* New York: Palgrave Macmillan.

McGill, Kenneth. 2017. "'Tangled Up in These Conceptualities': Sanction, Protest and Ideology in Berlin, Germany." *American Anthropologist* 119, no. 4: 603–13.

Mertens, Daniel. 2017. "Putting 'Merchants of Debt' in Their Place: The Political Economy of Retail Banking and Credit-Based Financialisation in Germany." *New Political Economy* 22, no. 1: 12–30.

Miyazaki, Hirokazu. 2013. *Arbitraging Japan: Dreams of Capitalism at the End of Finance*. Berkeley: University of California Press.

Narotzky, Susana. 2005. "Provisioning." In *A Handbook of Economic Anthropology*, edited by James G. Carrier, 78–93. Northhampton, MA: Edward Elgar:

OECD. 2015. "National Strategies for Financial Education: OECD/INFE Policy Handbook." Paris: OECD Publishing.

OECD. 2016. "Core Competencies Framework on Financial Literacy for Adults." Paris: OECD Publishing.

Offe, Claus. 1984. *Contradictions of the Welfare State*. Cambridge, MA: MIT Press.

———. 2015. *Europe Entrapped*. Malden, MA: Polity Press.

O'Malley, Patrick. 2004. *Risk, Uncertainty and Government*. London: Routledge.

Papon, Kerstin. 2016. "Die Deutschen sparen wieder mehr." *Frankfurter Allgemeine*. 14 October.

Partridge, Damani J. 2012. *Hypersexuality and Headscarves: Race, Sex and Citizenship in the New Germany*. Bloomington: Indiana University Press.

Plumpe, Werner. 2016. *German Economic and Business History in the 19th and 20th Centuries*. New York: Palgrave Macmillan.

Ringel, Felix. 2018. *Back to the Postindustrial Future: An Ethnography of Germany's Fastest Shrinking City*. Oxford: Berghahn Books.

Rose, Nikolas. 1989. *Governing the Soul: The Shaping of the Private Self*. 2nd ed. London: Free Association Books.

Rudd, Elizabeth. 2006. "Gendering Unemployment in Postsocialist Germany: 'What I Do Is Work, Even If It's Not Paid.'" *Ethnos* 71, no. 2: 191–212.

Shipton, Parker. 2010. *Credit between Cultures: Farmers, Financiers, and Misunderstanding in Africa*. New Haven: Yale University Press.

Shoshan, Nitzan. 2016. *The Management of Hate: Nation, Affect, and the Governance of Right-Wing Extremism in Germany*. Princeton: Princeton University Press.

Siegrist, Hannes. 2002. "From Divergence to Convergence: The Divided German Middle Class, 1945–2000." In *Social Contracts Under Stress: The Middle Classes of America, Europe and Japan at the Turn of the Century*, edited by Oliver Zunz, Leonard Schoppa, and Nobuhiro Hiwatari, 21–46. New York: Russell Sage Foundation.

Streeck, Wolfgang. 2017. *Buying Time: The Delayed Crisis of Democratic Capitalism*. 2nd ed. London: Verso.

Survey of Financial Literacy Schemes in the EU27. 2007. *VT Markt/2006/26H—Final Report*.

Weiss, Hadas. 2018a. "Popfinance: From the Economic Man to the Swabian Housewife." *Hau: Journal of Ethnographic Theory* 8, no. 3: 455–66.

———. 2018b. "Virtue out of Necessity: An Exhibition on Saving in Germany." *Reflections*. Accessed 14 February 2020. http://www.carmah.berlin/reflections/.

———. 2019. "Lifecycle Planning and Responsibility: Prospection and Retrospection in Germany." *Ethnos* 84, no. 5: 789–805.

Willis, Lauren E. 2008. "Against Financial Literacy Education." *Iowa Law Review* 94, no. 1: 197–285.

Wiß, Tobias. 2019. "Reinforcement of Pension Financialization as a Response to Financial Crises in Germany, the Netherlands and the United Kingdom." *Journal of European Public Policy* 26, no 4: 501–20.

Wolf, Marcus. 2018. "Ain't Misbehaving: Behavioral Economics and the Making of Financial Literacy." *Economic Sociology* 19, no. 2: 10–18.

Zaloom, Caitlin. 2016. "The Evangelical Financial Ethic: Doubled Forms and the Search for God in the Economic World." *American Ethnologist* 43, no. 2: 325–38.

8

Redistribution and Indebtedness

A Tale of Two Settings

Deborah James

This chapter builds a comparative picture of the interrelation of redistribution and financialized debt in two different national contexts. It does so not by adding to the already voluminous literature written from a neo-Marxist or anarchic anticapitalist perspective, nor by endorsing the position of free-market fundamentalists, but by exploring a kind of middle ground between them. This is the arena where a "mixed economy," long prevalent in the funding and administering of welfare (Cunningham 1998), has become even more dominant in recent times; where we find a "pluralist hybrid of market, non-market (e.g., redistribution by the welfare state) and non-monetary (based on reciprocity) forms of economy" (Alexander 2010). Animated by the work of authors who have explored the "ethics of care" (Fraser 2014; Lawson 2007), and the complex ways in which these inform the "new public good" (Bear and Mathur 2015), I seek to challenge deterministic accounts of the ways in which financialized capitalism is experienced by those on its margins. These suggest, *inter alia*, that capitalism in its newest form ceaselessly seeks out new zones for profit (Lapavitsas 2013), now including those at the bottom of the pyramid; that capitalist accumulation is further facilitated in this process (Harvey 2003); and that democratic/civil options have dissolved as subjects and are reconfigured in the form of a new and more insidious type of *homo economicus* (Brown 2015).

My account takes two very different settings, one from the global North (austerity Britain) and the other from the global South (post-democracy South Africa), and illustrates both commonalities and contrasts between them. Both have seen a complex mix of expanding financialization and increased borrowing with (actual, in the UK case, or imminent, in the South African one) government austerity, and the retreat of the kind of state regulation that formerly curbed the fees and interest rates creditors were able to charge. Those at the bottom of the pile—be they the poor or unemployed, low-paid workers, or formerly middle-class people migrating to work abroad and now on "zero hours" contracts—have been brought into the ambit of, or "enfolded within," formal financialized arrangements (Kar 2018, this volume; Meagher 2018; Soederberg 2014). In the terms used by Gustav Peebles (2010), they are not so much beneficiaries of its good side ("credit"), as victims of its most rapacious aspects ("debt"). Such accounts point to the fact that the shrinking of the welfare state in northern settings and its new instantiation via the provision of cash transfers in southern ones seem to lead inexorably—albeit in different ways as documented below—to an increase in borrowing: what Soederberg calls "debtfare" (2014). Against this backdrop, I demonstrate the often-counterintuitive ways in which financialized capitalism, even as some of its logics and agents plunge people further into debt, also provides funds to ensure that welfare arrangements are not erased altogether. I attend to the ways in which borrowers/welfare recipients—and those who provide them with advice—battle to secure the welfare that is due to them, and to the emerging folk models of fiscal behavior or "householding" that emerge in the course of such interactions.

One might query the validity of such an exercise. Surely the global spread of financialized techniques and the making of money "from nothing" (James 2015) or "from money" (Harvey 2003) involve transnational corporations, use standardized technologies of extraction, and must have a uniformly deleterious (and broadly homogenizing) effect worldwide? It is not my intention to present an idealized image of forms of support that transcend the stark realities of capitalist exploitation, nor to flatly deny the claims of scholars in a neo-Marxist/Foucauldian tradition who are inclined to see activist/adviser/volunteers as doing the state's work for it by providing momentary redress and protection against the worst effects of capitalism or austerity (see Koch and James, forthcoming). Rather, my account is motivated by a recognition that activities at the boundaries of formal processes, even if these are initiated or funded by commercial companies, can mitigate and counter what would otherwise be the exclusion of poorer people (Kirwan, McDermont, and Clarke 2016); and by ideas about "care ethics" that move us "beyond critique and toward the construction of new forms of relationships, institutions, and action that enhance mutuality and well-being" (Lawson 2007).

Central to this chapter is a focus on agencies and activists who embrace a normative view of bureaucratic techniques. Often outside of but entangled with state purview, they deploy these techniques to protect welfare benefits that are under threat. They thus try to ensure fairness of redistribution. The "new orienting values" they embrace are equated by Bear and Mathur with the "new public good": a slippery and often contradictory-sounding phenomenon that combines the unlikely bedfellows of "fiscal discipline, marketization, consensus, transparency and decentralization … [which] are associated with the market ethics of the economist's public good and are linked to new technical mechanisms of accountability. But their resonances as an ethos, a lived persona, a contested referent or frustrating impossible goal cannot be captured in their social reality by economists' models or the analysis of audit techniques alone" (2015). The "new orienting values" of bureaucracy that these activists hold dear are thus entangled with "market ethics" rather than opposed to them.

Redistribution and financialization can and do intersect; although on the face of it, they may seem incompatible: one embodies social values; the other is planted in and arises from the world of impersonal contracts. Many anthropologists, and famously Polanyi, have seen redistribution as a quintessentially nonmarket, premarket, or antimarket process (see Hann and Hart 2009). Economists, although preoccupied (especially in the early years of the modern neoclassical discipline) with the formal logic of how income and wages are determined, and how and whether redistribution might factor in these processes, are ultimately left to conclude that redistribution is a matter of exogenous ethics (or philosophies of justice) rather than being an intrinsic part of the calculus of economic growth (Sandmo 2015). Similarly, theorists like Jon Elster point to the way that "redistributive policies … are intended to compensate people for various sorts of bad luck, arising mainly in the market" (Elster 1991: 273). Putting it more strongly, Göran Therborn (2012b: 587) writes of how "redistribution and recompensation are powerful tools," arising largely out of the struggles of the labor movement, through which "remedial action" can be undertaken to counter the egregious inequalities that arise out of the unequal distribution of income and wealth. The usual assumption is that such "tools" have to be applied by society and/or the state in order to curb the worst excesses of capitalist exploitation and free trade. Feminist philosopher Nancy Fraser, offering a reinterpretation of Polanyi's ideas on "fictitious commodities," similarly shows how the forces of the market, which may promote growth but which lead to exploitation and inequality, are deemed to be incompatible with those of the state and society (2014: 547). As Hann and Hart put it "the leading capitalist societies at one stage all signed up for Hegel's (1821) idea that states should try to contain the inequality and ameliorate the social misery generated by markets" (2009: 2). From these underpinnings, in postwar Europe, was the welfare state born.

However, Polanyi's morally loaded binary between market (or contract) and benevolent nonmarket (variously construed as "society," "state," or "mutuality") is too simple (Gudeman 2010). For one thing, as Nancy Fraser points out, it obscures relations of power and domination. To entrust the upholding of communal, family, or welfarist values to unpaid and non-commodified care regimes may mean devaluing female activities, whereas paying for that work by bringing it into the realm of contract (the labor market) may serve emancipatory goals (2014: 550).

All this is to say that provisioning and welfare can no longer be assumed to exist beyond the world of the financial, nor do they depend solely on state- or society-driven initiatives. Anthropologist Erik Bähre, writing about post-democracy South Africa, argues for an "important complication" of the redistribution concept: "When diverse institutions are infused by redistribution, it becomes difficult to distinguish redistribution from other forms of economic integration." Rather, it is "entangled with and a part of" both "the state (social grants and development aid)" and "markets (commercial insurances)" (2011: 375). It is well documented that, since the 1980s, voluntary sector activities and market-oriented arrangements have modified and mediated state-driven initiatives (Alexander 2010). But Bähre is making a more provocative claim: he argues that the sudden and swift inclusion of black South Africans as potential clients for insurance companies enables them to engage with impersonal and "large-scale" institutions for economic reallocation and thus escape from onerous forms of neighbor- or kin-based reciprocity. It is these "large-scale" arrangements that Bähre sees as the central characteristic of redistribution. Those who readily embrace it are people—such as upwardly mobile members of the new middle class in South Africa—who seek to escape the more personalized sharing, lending, and helping that typified life under apartheid.

Bähre's interest in "complicating" the redistribution concept points us toward a zone where market and nonmarket dynamics interpenetrate. But his insistence on large-scale processes is somewhat misleading. Faced with the dissolution, privatization, and insidious undermining of state-based welfare provision, I show in what follows that it is precisely through per-sonalized and piecemeal relationships between debtors and their activist/advisers—positioned between market, state, and society yet not fully aligned with any of these—that redistribution must now be largely pursued. It is in the course of interactions between debtfare recipients and what Elster calls "second-order decision makers" (Elster 1991) that some of the worst effects of financialized capitalism are challenged and countered.

"Mixed Economies" of Welfare

In the 1990s and 2000s, as financialized capitalism was consolidated worldwide, more and more relatively poor people became dependent on readily available loans to supplement state welfare. Yet it is too simple to argue that "welfare" became "debtfare" (Soederberg 2014) or that former welfare beneficiaries have been transformed into repayers of debt (Adkins 2017). The involvement of market (and specifically financial) actors in redistribution is more complex.

In the UK, much debt advice is funded by creditors. Following the onset of austerity measures adopted by the Coalition and Conservative Governments in the 2010s, the gap between incomes and expenditures has grown incrementally, forcing many people to borrow in order to pay rent and other crucial expenses (Davey 2017, this volume; Patrick 2017: 70–73). The average UK household debt (including mortgages) was £58,540 in June 2018, and people owed nearly £1.6 trillion, up from £1.55tn the previous year.[1] Parallel to the sharp upturn in private debt, the withdrawal of state funding to the advice sector has led to a situation in which debt advice, introduced in the 1980s alongside the expansion of consumer credit and formerly deriving from general taxation, is now privately funded on the basis of "fair share" contributions from creditors and a bank levy on the basis of a "polluter pays" principle (Davey 2017: 8–9). This is an industry-specific levy, channeled toward offsetting the harms produced by that industry. Davey describes the system as "self-defeating," since it encourages people "to re-engage with credit markets" and thus "serves the interests of the financial industry"; "it taxes the agencies that lend to poorer people at high rates of interest in order to give those same people advice that is increasingly redundant" (Davey 2017). The cases discussed here, however, show that debt advisors' interventions do not simply function to ensure that debtors repay what they owe to the financial institutions that fund their operations. When advising their poorer clients whose loans are predominantly unsecured ones, they typically encourage clients to weigh up repaying the banks with repaying other creditors that may have more importance. A rising number of clients struggle with so-called "priority debts," especially rent arrears owed to landlords and council tax owed to the local state, "whose non-repayment would produce the greatest consequences, from the presence of bailiffs through to the loss of one's home and imprisonment" (Kirwan 2018). Advisers thus often act in view of logics that are guided by imperatives other than those of the mainstream lenders that pay them.

In South Africa, the funding of initiatives that combat debt problems, relatively miniscule to start with, has expanded thanks to the initiatives of companies, private individuals, and churches. The sharp rise in indebtedness here resulted from expectations of prosperity following democratization in a climate of economic liberalization. What followed was a situation of "explosive lending, intensive credit surveillance and ongoing reluctance from the large banks to offer services to the rural poor" (Breckenridge 2019; see James 2015). Following a sharp rise in the provision and uptake of unsecured, high interest loans in the early 1990s (Ardington et al. 2004), by 2014, the World Bank noted that 86 percent of South Africans had taken out a loan, more than double the global average of 40 percent. Around half of these borrowers were at least three months behind on debt payments, and the debt-to-income ratio stood at 86.4 percent (James 2019: 218). What these stark figures do not reveal is the extremely low level of consumer protection, which has enabled the collection of debt from the wages of employees via poorly regulated or—increasingly—forged "garnishee" orders,[2] and more recently, by biometric means, in the shape of deductions from social welfare payments made to poor people.

Advice services to deal with these problems have never been more than patchy. Although free, independently funded advice from trained lawyers was (and remains) available in some university law clinics, and was provided in certain areas by human- and consumer-rights organization The Black Sash and its regional associates, "debt counseling" was typically construed as an income-generating activity and outsourced to often poorly prepared entrepreneurs (James 2015: 62, 71, 94; Schraten 2014: 11). As donations to consumer rights charities by overseas church-based organizations have dwindled, companies, foundations, and private individuals have had to shoulder more of the burden, usually in partnerships with community-based organizations in specific neighborhoods. In the absence of more comprehensive and concrete "on-the-ground" advice, "cause-lawyering" efforts (Sarat and Sheingold 1998) have concentrated on high-profile court cases with the aim of establishing legal precedents or modifying legislation. Besides helping to provide funding for both advice and legal costs, certain companies have branches or subsidiaries that aim to curb the worst activities of lenders—in the courts and elsewhere. Given that a "cowboy capitalist" extractivist ethic has prevailed in the country for over a century (see Van Onselen 2017), this includes countering the activities of those who often *masquerade* as helpful advisers/helpers but are often, in fact, intent on making profit from the poor.[3] Taking the form of a kind of Corporate Social Responsibility, those who act to curb such profiteering—in particular a firm called Summit Financial Partners—do so partly at the behest of, and paid for by, employers. Running scared in the wake of events like the Marikana trade union protest, where miners demanding higher pay turned out to be forfeiting most of their wages to high-interest lenders via automatic deductions (Alexander et al. 2012; James and Rajak 2014), many employers wish to ensure that their workers have a sustainable form of life.

In sum, then, the involvement of financial actors in both settings is not confined to the provision of loans, but extends to funding and even initiating the work—principally by challenging wrongdoing by moneylenders—which makes it possible to resist such demands. The activists and advisors draw on funds from the "mixed economy" on which the charitable/welfare sector has long relied. They see their job as exercising surveillance over the activities of state actors, while also constraining the worst ravages of commercial creditors. They try to persuade welfare/debtfare beneficiaries to follow appropriate courses of action in the interests of living a sustainable life. Making sure that trickles of funds continue to reach poor people, they have become the ultimate redistributors in settings where, because of austerity measures in the UK and the depredations of predatory lending in South Africa, other instruments of redistribution have been severely weakened.

Mastering Bureaucracy between State and Market

To illustrate how this works in practice, let us explore the two settings in more detail. In both the UK and the South African cases, literature on the psychosocial aspects of debt helps us conceptualize both the way that financialization is "domesticated" (Deville and Seigworth 2015) and the way its domestication is, in turn, dislodged. In the UK case, debtors have become accustomed to "living in default"; "market attachments" (Deville 2015) often make them unable to envisage ever living outside of it. The strength of these attachments and ties is intensified via banking algorithms that make it possible for "monies of all sorts to routinely live in and through our lives" and for the relationships between creditors and debtors to "become deeper, more profound, more granular, more personal" (Tiessen 2015). Here, debt advisors' work must focus on "disrupting" these attachments (Kirwan 2018), using a set of bureaucratic tools to counter the strong emotions involved in order to help clients distinguish those which ought—in their own best interests—to be given priority, or where they can be dodged or even cancelled through a variety of bankruptcy procedures.

In the complex amalgam of commercial borrowings and what is owed to the state that makes up a beneficiary's "debtfare" portfolio in the UK, debt advice involves interacting with a range of companies and institutions on a client's behalf. In one case, Elaine, a domestic cleaner, consulted Aaminah, an officer in a London debt advice office, after receiving a letter from a credit card company that had taken out a court order requiring her to pay

£50 monthly to settle her debt. She also owed her internet provider £48, and had a debt with Provident and one with Shop Direct that had been sold on to a debt-collection company (see Mikus, this volume). Aaminah, after sifting through documents, noting income, budgets, and owings, reassured Elaine that, compared to other clients, her total debt of less than £2,000 was not as big as it seemed. Seeking a way to tackle each of its separate components (see Kirwan 2016: 467), Aaminah wrote a note requesting that the court order for the credit card debt be lessened (or "varied"), wrote a letter asking the court to excuse Elaine from paying fees, and sent a written request to her other creditors for a stay of six months to give Elaine some time. She also outlined the possibility, in the long-term, of applying for a Debt Relief Order[4] to write off the debt.

Working part-time, Elaine took pride in earning her own living; but she relied, besides her wage and the money she had borrowed to supplement it, on various systems of state support. In a mosaic of benefits that had waxed and waned over the years, she was receiving child tax credits and working tax credits, and was waiting to hear the outcome of her application for housing benefit to help pay her rent. Aaminah worked out that Elaine had two so-called "priority debts" that were more important than the ones she owes to the commercial sector: seven weeks' rent arrears amounting to £850 and council tax—charged for various municipal services—of £70, for which the council had sent her a letter instructing her to settle the backlog within two working days. To avoid a visit from the bailiffs and to remain in her flat, Elaine understood that she had no option but to pay these "priority debts." Aaminah sent an email to the council to ask them to delay taking action and, given the expectation of a positive decision concerning housing benefit, to set up a regular payment in order to clear the arrears.

Compared with the "economies of default" investigated by Deville and his collaborators in the UK, in the South African case, debtors tend to be more aware of the need to juggle and prioritize debts, even without formal debt advice. Possibly due in part to the lack of such advice, they may be shrewdly pragmatic rather than "attached" to their debts or seized by a psychic desire for "things." Akhona, a domestic cleaner like Elaine, was similarly reliant on a mixture of commercial loans and state welfare. "Sometimes I only get paid R1,800 [about 98GBP] a month,"[5] she was reported as saying. "And it's not enough because transport is expensive and I have to buy household things, and support other family members." Supplementing her wage as a part-time worker were a monthly child-support grant from SASSA (the state welfare agency) of R640 and a regular monthly loan of R200 from a company called Moneyline. This was a subsidiary of Net1/Cash Paymaster Services, the company to which the state had outsourced the delivery of these welfare or "social" grants in the early 2000s. Akhona needed this loan in order to pay her weekly transport bill to get to work.[6] Much like the shack-dwellers documented by Ariel Wilkis in Buenos Aires, one of whom told him "we don't have savings but we do have debt" (2018), Akhona had factored in borrowing as an essential element in the household budget rather than an accidental aberration. Such canny matter-of-factness has also been documented by anthropologist Fiona Ross (2010). Being poor involves managing a series of conflicting debts and often necessitates taking short-term decisions, themselves subject to scrutiny and criticism from relatives and neighbors, which might need to be immediately reassessed and altered. This leads to a patchy and fragmented experience of time and monetary value. A quandary over allocating funds involved both trust in providence and careful deliberation for a woman called Sandra, who owed money both for her son's school fees and to complete her installments on a cupboard that she paid a "lay-bye" to secure (if she failed to honor the agreement by a certain date, she would forfeit both the cupboard and the payments already made). She decided to use the money set aside for school fees to pay off the cupboard, presuming later to be able to rely on a relative's help for the fees or "pay them off over the year." The choice was between education (for which others might be pressured into paying) or respectability and social propriety (the costs of which would have to be borne by the household). In this case, the choice paid off. A well-wisher gave money for the school fees, while owning the cupboard enhanced her status (Ross 2010: 131).

In other cases, however, social grant recipients are unable to parse and weigh up their debts, because their interweaving makes them difficult to disentangle and conceptualize as separate "pieces of money" or as distinct amounts (Wilkis 2017). Technologies of biometric registration have brought the millions of South Africans who are grant recipients within the ambit of the banking system (cf. Kar, this volume). Banking algorithms achieve their goals through sheer automation. Until it was relieved of its state contract in October 2018, the provider company, Net1, had turned social welfare into debt collateral through financial transactions that were virtually immune to human intervention (see Lavinas 2018 for a similar case in Brazil). While South Africa, like the UK, uses automated credit transfers to deliver welfare (see Datta 2012: 32–36, 66; see also Kar, this volume), their respective approaches to banking and to client privacy are very different. South Africa's Net1 had not only been furnishing regular payments to pensioners, parents (mostly mothers) of children, and disabled people, it also had been offering them loans and selling them products—via its complex web of subsidiaries and using agents paid on commission—for which it was deducting payments from the grant at the end of the month.[7] People were coming in "with tears in their eyes.... With regard to the unauthorized deductions on their SASSA grant, you realize these people feel disempowered.... We had one woman here that was in tears about the fact that she felt so abused by the system and she had no recourse," I was told by Mareesa Kreuser, a team member at Summit Financial Partners. Debt advisers, activists, paralegals, and financial sector companies, such as the one for which she works, have been engaged in a common (though not always united) endeavor to counter the "machinic" extractivism (Lazzarato 2012) facilitated by the algorithms used in the lending sector.

Householding and Clawing Back Funds

Advisers in both the UK and South Africa help clients list and conceptualize their incomings and outgoings. They aim to prevent clients from getting caught up in arrangements that will make their money trickle away, and to help them reclaim that money once taken. They take action to combat aggressive—sometimes illegal—actions of creditors, both in market and state arenas. What is already a pitifully small amount of money must not be allowed to dwindle further because of extortionate interest (now increasingly reconfigured as "charges") or councils reclaiming erroneous payouts. In both cases, there is a sense of the need to "put a finger in the dyke" to ensure that money does not escape. The way the advisers accomplish this, in both settings, follows the original principles of Aristotle's *oekonomia*, as echoed more recently in the school subject that used to be known as "home economics" or "domestic science." *Oekonomia* implies perpetuating self-sufficiency through careful household budgeting rather than engaging in risky trade through market transactions (Hann and Hart 2009: 11).

In the London debt advice office, Aaminah's telephone calls and letters were aimed not only at forestalling and deflecting the demands of Elaine's creditors but also at making sure she received all the benefits to which she was entitled, so that at some point these might enable a more viable household economy. In the course of "sorting out" Elaine's finances, Aaminah drew up a Common Financial Statement, a spreadsheet that balanced her income on one side against her debt on the other (see James and Kirwan 2019).[8] A key (and little-known outside the sector) aspect of such an adviser's work, and one that further blurs lines between state and market, is the way she helps clients withstand demands for repayment made by the state (Davey 2017: 9; Kirwan 2018). In a case similar to that of Elaine, Yusuf, an advisor at the North London Muslim Community Centre, helped an elderly client faced with an "overpayments" demand. Where welfare recipients like him owe a substantial sum to the council for benefits allegedly overpaid, these are reclaimed or deducted from future benefits. This situation results from the piecemeal administering of a "mosaic" of funds by diverse agencies (Forbess and James 2014). They include "tax benefits" introduced by the Labor Government—though punitive changes from 2010 onward have restricted such payments—as a means of encouraging people to enter the labor market, and serving a moderate but important redistributive function in favor of the poorest households (Hills 2015: 2, 226). Yusuf's client produced a letter from the council reclaiming £16,000 allegedly overpaid for housing benefit and council tax. Yusuf phoned the council to ask for an explanation and was told, "we have checked with HMRC—he has two jobs, one for a security firm.... We are using good systems.... We have to do what it says on the screen." Yusuf discovered that although it appeared as though the client was working for two companies, he was employed by only one—that had changed its name. Earning less than the tax office claimed, the client was thus entitled to both sets of benefits after all. Lodging such challenges is time consuming and requires the specialist knowledge and connections of the advisor. "I normally give a client one hour," Yusuf said. Although success is far from certain, there is a sense that the ends of justice have been served when they do work out.

Like many "globally redistributive policies" that are "designed centrally, at the level of the national government" (Elster 1991: 273), clawing back money in this way requires the intervention of what Elster calls "second-order decision makers" in order to ensure that "local justice" is delivered. What the state gives in the name of redistribution it may take away in the name of equity or combating so-called benefits fraud. These demands may need to be resisted in turn: errors can result when misspent funds are collected, and yet further intervention is needed to set matters right. Where enquiries reveal that the overpayment demands are justified, however, such clients are obliged to honor their obligations to noncommercial creditors such as the council, or face a visit from the bailiff.

Like other intermediaries charged with delivering "local justice" (Elster 1991), with administering "care" to combat egregious market forces (Lawson 2007), or with safeguarding the "public good" (Bear and Mathur 2015), Yusuf and Aaminah were committed to mastering bureaucratic techniques of allocation and to implementing these in line with the redistributive spirit that is presumed to have animated their original design, no matter how much these may have been diverted or interrupted by subsequent austerity measures (Elster 1991: 274). Where Elster's account of "second-order decision makers" is chiefly concerned with state employees at local level, advisers like Yusuf and Aaminah work outside the ambit of the state to correct the errors made by its functionaries. While Elster contrasts the benefits and costs of using "discretion" and "impersonal mechanisms" respectively, these advisers do not consider themselves to be using personalized criteria to overturn the use of "mechanical formulae" (1991: 288).

Rather, they take pride in carrying out and adhering to—and holding their equivalents in the state bureaucracy to account to implement—the strictly fair arrangements that bureaucracy *ought to* embody.

In South Africa, Mareesa and other activist/advisers are equally keen to lay out all debts in logical array, establish which need to be repaid with greatest urgency, and resist those that are mistaken or unjust. But it is more difficult to "claw back" resources in the South African case for several reasons. First, although the impetus for commercial companies to tempt customers into taking out further loans and making further purchases differs little in the two cases, debtors in South Africa face particular problems because of the way repayments are secured. A beneficiary/client can be vulnerable to complex processes of deduction, especially one with a less deliberate budgeting strategy than Akhona, the domestic cleaner mentioned earlier who was borrowing from Moneyline to fund her monthly transport. Until 2018, when Net1 lost the tender to deliver grants, grant holders were able to swap their welfare benefits ("SASSA") card for an alternative card known as "Easypay Everywhere," also administered by Net1, and to apply for further loans to different moneylenders, for which further deductions were made. The proliferation of debts is potentially confusing, especially where—because of biometrically facilitated automation and the lack of a paper trail—little or no volition was left to the debtor. Although Easypay functioned as a bank account, few of its "clients" had postal or email addresses. In cases where team members from Summit or activist organizations like The Black Sash have sought to offer advice or help a beneficiary work out what she owed to whom, getting hold of "bank statements" was challenging, if not impossible.

Even once procured, these statements are often incomprehensible, because debts are difficult to disentangle. Until October 2018, some beneficiaries had two payment streams or "accounts"—the original "SASSA" card and the new "EasyPay" card. In one case I noted at a meeting, many of the deductions for airtime (telephone credit) had been moved from SASSA to Easypay, but other loans and the funeral cover payments still remained with SASSA; in another, each of these two accounts was linked to a separate mobile number. When attempts were made to seek recourse, company representatives were reluctant to speak to anyone but the "actual beneficiary." "Actual beneficiaries," however, rarely had enough airtime to be able to stay on the telephone for the amount of time that it might take to get through the "security questions" and challenge the details of the account—and in any case, they often felt intimidated, embarrassed, and unconfident when speaking English. Advisers also expressed dismay on their clients' behalf that, despite all these transactions and loans taking place in a highly formalized payment space, errors were frequent, often amounting to fraud (practiced both by "street level" agents and at the level of high-tech deductions). Most worrisome among the latter was the tendency to treat beneficiaries' payment streams as if they were current accounts with overdraft facilities. To comply with regulations in the National Payment System, a debit order ought only to be activated once there is money in an account. If there is none, the debit order ought to be refused. It should not be possible, while repaying a specific creditor, to go into a negative balance: to do so would contravene the law that prevents favoring certain lenders over others. Despite corporate denials that this was happening, the IT system seemed to allow a kind of parallel payments arrangement to exist.[9] These technical complexities compounded the stark facts of the situation: Net1 was, in effect, using grant beneficiaries' ignorance to turn a profit.

Advisers in South Africa's charity and business sectors attempting to "claw back" funds from lenders often use the metaphor of piracy and plunder to describe the ransacking of grant holders' monies. Unlike their UK equivalents, they are not able to challenge overpayments demands or to help clients put the brake on repayments. Since financial automation means that such repayment has *already occurred*, the advisor must set out, instead, to reclaim what has been "stolen." "The bank account is almost a place for looting ... for pushing through as many different [loans] as possible," said an officer from the human rights charity sector. She celebrated the fact that, after much effort, she and her colleagues had helped a client "to get some of the money back, a cash refund."

"Pillage" was the term used by the CEO of Summit Financial Partners, Clark Gardner, to describe the situation. Lenders of all sorts, he said, follow

> an unwritten rule to chase market share.... . [I]f I don't take your wallet, your full wallet, someone else is going to take it. If you can afford R100 a month on debt installments, I want to take that full 100. Because if I take 80, someone else is going to take the other 20. That is putting my loan at risk. And no one is policing that. So I can do whatever I want.... . [T]he lack of enforcement has ... created a reckless lending environment. If you don't play that game you're going to lose.

This CEO has taken it upon himself, in the absence of activity by the state regulator (the NCR),[10] to hire private investigators and pursue moneylenders through civil court cases. Working in one particular case on behalf of borrowers who were waged employees rather than simply grant beneficiaries (the two categories often overlap), his company was taking a firm of attorneys to court for continuing—long after lenders themselves had been repaid for their loans—to chase debtors in order to get "collection fees." Describing the *modus operandi* of this firm, Gardner told me how it gives you R500 [and] collects R11,000. And we said, "How do you go from R500 to R11,000?" The High Court said to the NCR, "You've got to investigate these guys—you've got to find out what's going on." We promised the NCR 40,000 cases to investigate. But they've not done a thing. So we've spent our own money and gone to the courts.... How is this possible when [the relevant legislation] says that you can never charge more fees than the capital outstanding on default?

As one of Summit's team members explained it to me:

It's open to interpretation of what "collection costs" mean. We're saying, "include legal costs and collection costs." Because otherwise you're going to have this unending amount of litigation fee, or collection fee, that people are going to end up paying back forever. The way the payments work is you first pay your collection costs, then you pay your legal fees, then you pay interest, then only you pay capital. So these people end up never paying off capital.

The court case brought by Summit was aimed at clarifying how much a lender may legitimately recoup from a borrower (the National Credit Act stipulates that a lender may never "charge more fees than the capital outstanding on default"), as well as seeking recompense for the borrowers. At the time of writing, after the judge had dismissed the application without hearing its merits, Summit was lodging an appeal.[11]

These South African officers, paralegals, and corporate employers/ employees, like those who advise on debt in the UK, are motivated by a sense of the need to get the bureaucracy right, which they accomplish by unpicking the interwoven strands of debt in order to clarify which are serious or legitimate owings and which are not, and to highlight cases of fraud. For human rights charity The Black Sash, their opposition to what they call "grants grab" is underpinned by a strong tradition of rights activism accompanied by a "cause-lawyering" ethic. For Summit, a similar motivation exists but is combined with an impetus that comes, in part, from two major mining employers that have employed the company to act on their behalf in order to protect their employees. Summit's Clark Gardner believes it ought to be possible to secure a "fair capitalist" system. In both cases, their efforts are focused not on preventing over-hasty or ill-considered repayment (as in the UK), but on retrieving illicitly looted funds so as to restore a client's bank balance to what it should be. Insisting that the money be reimbursed, both aim to redress what they evocatively describe as "plunder."

Informed by their notions of what *ought* to be, activists and paralegals in South Africa thus attempt to challenge the behavior of lenders. They also try to shape and reconfigure their advisees' responses to the depredations of these lenders with the aim of creating a more humane way to live with debt. In the UK case, countering the contradictory emotions of attachment and shame, advisers use bureaucratic tools in order to help the client parcel up and classify the various types of owing, showing why some of these ought to be given more priority than others. In South Africa, these activist/advisers are infused with a stronger conviction that the poor are being robbed. For them, it is less a matter of persuading people of their own best interests and nudging them to behave in certain ways, than of standing alongside them, shoulder-to-shoulder, against rapacious creditors. Given that the promise of post-apartheid democracy was one in which welfare—and a sense of dignity—would be newly delivered to those dispossessed by apartheid, there is a strong moral sense that what is being stolen are these newly delivered aspects of citizenship—hence the prevalence of metaphors that invoke looting and grabbing. For the activists, the central guiding concept is one in which there is a pot of money that ought to be available to the poor in its entirety. Although that pot of money may need to be divided into appropriately targeted portions or piles (in a budgeting exercise), no part of it should find its way into the coffers of large financial firms. There is a feeling of outrage that this should even be possible. It is this sense of indignation that underpins their notion of budgeting or householding.

Tax and Services—the Other Side of Redistribution

Differences between the two modes of indebtedness and debt advice outlined above are, of course, shaped by a range of other factors, including those more usually associated with redistribution. Beyond welfare and grant payments, these include the way that taxes are levied to pay for those aspects of welfare—like healthcare and education—known as "benefits in kind" (Hills 2015: 63). The differences between the two countries discussed in this chapter are too many and too complex to cover in any detail, but contrasts between their broader welfare regimes and relative levels of formalization are worthy of a brief consideration.

Although social scientists, challenging the drawing of any simplistic dichotomy between "formal" and "informal" economies (Guyer 2004), point out that the informal economy has now "taken over the world" (Hart 2015), there is still some value in contrasting a highly regulated and bureaucratized economy with one that is far less so. Factors that eventually led to the post 2010 austerity regime in the UK, following in the wake during the *trente glorieuses* of the establishment of a robust welfare state based on relatively effective taxation, contrast markedly to those at play in societies like South Africa, where there has been greater reliance on informal, often "unpaid" or unregistered, forms of work, welfare, and taxation (Bolt 2012;

Cichello, Fields, and Leibbrandt 2005; Gibbs 2018; Hull and James 2012; Neves and Du Toit 2012).

As we saw earlier in the case of Elaine's "priority debts" in the UK case, the provision of secure accommodation, the services that accompany it, and the way revenue payments and taxes are recouped for these are all crucial when considering how wealth is reallocated in that country. Under the austerity regime, local councils there have started to pursue debtors with greater vigor than do commercial creditors (Kirwan 2018). As central government has cut their budgets, they are left with little option but to pursue repayment by those in arrears—even though, in a spirit of "enlightened self-interest," some of them simultaneously fund advice services to help these same people (Forbess and James 2017). In contrast, for low-paid workers and/or grant recipients in South Africa, although many do owe money for rent, utilities, or municipal/council services, these kinds of obligations constitute a lower percentage of the overall debt burden. Recent democratization twinned with corruption scandals have, in the South African case, made the state both more circumspect about extending the revenue base beyond the "middle classes" and somewhat more reluctant to press for the effective repayment of bills owed to the state or its adjuncts for rent, utilities, and the like. Toward the end of apartheid (and subsequently), there was a long struggle over such payments, with rent and service boycotts eventually countered, in more planned and formal areas, by state implementation of prepaid electricity and water meters (Von Schnitzler 2016). In more recent times, with the electricity supply commission billions of rands in debt, local municipalities have started offering rebates to indigent residents or giving them the opportunity to repay in small amounts, extending institutional reach while recognizing widespread inability. This again signals the hesitation about going after debts to the state.[12] Increasing numbers, however, have taken up residence in informal settlements further from their places of employment, where rental and utility costs are relatively low in relation to transport costs. For someone like Akhona, it was to cover the cost of traveling to work in privately owned taxis rather than to pay rent, taxes, or bills to the state that she took out the monthly loan of R200 from commercial creditor Moneyline.

In South Africa, the provision of housing and accompanying services is skewed by the coexistence of a thriving real-estate market in the cities, on the one hand, with informal rights (often under so-called "communal" tenure) in some peri-urban and rural areas, on the other. The battle over payments to the state—in a zone where "tax," "rent," and "service payments" become difficult to distinguish from "debt"—is still being fought. In the case of the UK, that battle (at least in relation to housing) was lost long ago. In the more formalized economy of the latter, the option to drive down housing costs or get out of paying council tax by living in the kind of low-cost "squatter" accommodation in which many South African grant holders reside is, of course, virtually nonexistent. The stock of state-provided housing, which once provided an alternative, is also rapidly shrinking. There was a moment in the heyday of the UK's welfare state when social housing, generally affordable if one received housing benefit, was available to those who relied on welfare for part or all of their livelihood. In a context where housing itself—even in the low-cost sector—is being rapidly financialized (Aalbers 2017), the diminished supply of this accommodation makes welfare beneficiaries increasingly reliant on private landlords, many of whom are reluctant to accept tenants who depend on benefits, or are ready to seek eviction when their tenants default.[13]

Asymmetries in the way local taxes and payments are levied—or avoided—thus fill out the picture of contrasting forms of debt advice/activism I have painted above. If Elaine was more vulnerable to having the local state demand payment (sourced from her welfare benefits alongside her meager income) for services, and/or to eviction by her private landlord, Akhona's primary threat was from private companies who were deducting funds, similarly derived from a mix of state grants and her wage, directly from her bank account. In the first case, we are witnessing the undoing of a welfare state through a regime of enforced austerity; in the second, we are seeing its flimsy low-cost construction using the medium of cash transfers.[14] In both cases, the work of activist/advisers is key to preventing the collapse of redistributive processes.

Conclusion

This chapter has contrasted two models of budgetary logic developed by debt activist/advisers. Working within a hybrid "mixed economy" of welfare, partly funded by financial companies as well as other sources, they operate at a relatively micro level rather than via "large-scale" arrangements (Bähre 2011). In settings where the hegemonic powers of capitalism seem to be operating unchecked, and where more ambitious reinstantiations of the welfare state or more radical reconfigurations of lending regimes seem destined to run into the sand, these agents facilitate redistribution by helping their clients or by pooling their knowledge to provide evidence for court cases in order to push back against unjust demands.

In both settings, advisers are motivated by a wish to promote sustainable householding. In the UK, austerity policies mean that government agencies are withdrawing what was previously, in the heyday of the welfare state, publicly funded and seen as a right. People are encouraged to turn to increasingly fragile casual (or "zero hours" contract) employment rather than relying on benefits, while also being pushed to practice frugality and to "economize." Advisers, as "second order decision makers" in Jon Elster's sense, both enforce but also contrive to undermine these agendas. Here, "householding" means maximizing income from dwindling sources, and challenging repayment obligations. In South Africa, a recent democratic transition—combined with financial liberalization and accompanied by growing unemployment—has encouraged a borrowing boom. Despite the difficulty of reversing a long-standing tendency to extractivism, now in heavily financialized form, partly private/corporate initiatives have stepped in where the state refuses to go, functioning to curb the otherwise untrammeled activities of lenders. Here, "householding" means seeking to reclaim appropriated funds while tirelessly working to challenge, in court, those who ransack pay packets and bank accounts.

To say that an "ethics of care" (Lawson 2007) is central to the work that advisers do is not, of course, to celebrate unmitigated success. Care can direct the distribution of resources, but it can also misallocate them, as I have shown in a 2020 article co-written with Insa Koch: "In debt advice, where the state, the market and charity are locked in an uneasy embrace, payments take on different moral meanings: they may be viewed as owed to the state so as to balance the fiscus and contribute to the common good, or owed to financial creditors where they accrue as immoral profit" (Koch and James 2020). While it is true, as shown in this chapter, that "financial corporations, in recognition of the negative way they are perceived, have started to subsidize advice and are newly endowed with moral agency," it is equally true that the (re-)emergence of paternalistic forms of charity (through faith-based, unpaid advice work) indicate a neo-Victorian remoralization of poverty (ibid.).

The ambivalence surrounding advisers' work relates to their positioning in a space where boundaries blur between redistributive welfare, wages, debt, and financialized capitalism. But, although their work is situated where the state neither provides adequate benefits nor adequately regulates the depredations of those lenders whose loaned money is an essential part of "debtfare," such blurring should not necessarily be seen as yet one further stage in the onward march of financialized capitalism in its most egregious form. Nor is it an outcome of what Graeber calls "the iron law of liberalism" in which "the government itself" has become "the main mechanism for the extraction of corporate profits" (2015: 24). Instead, the advice officers and decision-makers presented in this chapter have a normative view of bureaucratic procedure, which guides their use of formalized techniques to enact change beyond the orbit of state, market, and society, although linked to all three. As with second-order decision makers elsewhere, "the appeal of rule-bound bureaucracy lies in the desire to constrain arbitrary ... power" (Weinberg 2017: 1101). Advisers help clients "bureaucratize their lives," not (or not only) in the spirit of complying with repayment demands but of challenging them, reversing the flow of money those demands enable, and buttressing and even recreating a sphere—however contradictory—of what Bear and Mathur (2015) call the "new public good."

Acknowledgments

This chapter of *Financialization*, edited by Chris Hann and Don Kalb is available open access under a CC BY-NC-ND 4.0 license, thanks to the support of the Economic and Social Research Council of the UK (ESRC Grant ES/M003825/1 'An ethnography of advice: between market, society and the declining welfare state'), the Leverhulme Trust (ECF-2016-518), and the LSE Anthropology's RIIF fund. Thanks to all the advisers who helped with the research and the clients who were willing to have me sit in (names have been changed in the interests of confidentiality). Grateful acknowledgments to Harry Walker, Mathijs Pelkmans, Maxim Bolt, and Patrick Pearson for a close reading of the paper. Thanks also to Re: work, IGK Arbeit und Lebenslauf in globalgeschichtlicher Perspektive, Humboldt-Universität zu Berlin, and Stellenbosch Institute for Advanced Study, Wallenberg Research Centre, at Stellenbosch University, South Africa, for providing restful but stimulating environments for thinking through and writing this chapter.

Deborah James is Professor of Anthropology at LSE and a Fellow of the British Academy. She has done fieldwork in South and Southern Africa, and more recently in the UK. Recent work includes *Money from Nothing: Indebtedness and Aspiration in South Africa* (Stanford University Press, 2015).

Notes

1. Lora Jones, "Household Debt: How Much Do We Owe?" BBC News, 6 September 2018, https://www.bbc.co.uk/news/business-45343236. Accessed 14 January 2020.
2. If a creditor is owed money and presents an employer with a garnishee order, the employer is obliged to enable that creditor to take a portion of the debtor's monthly pay before the employee receives it. The monthly earnings of miners, other migrant wageworkers, and workers and salary earners more generally have

been the principle targets of lenders using these repayment technologies with ever-increasing frequency, causing great concern to these industries at higher levels. The accumulation of multiple debts, paid back to a series of creditors in rapid succession as soon as payday arrives, means that many earners have little left to live on (James 2019: 225; James and Rajak 2014: 455–56).

3. Ciaran Ryan, "Confessions of a Debt Counsellor," Moneyweb, 19 July 2018, https://www.moneyweb.co.za/mymoney/moneyweb-financial-planning/confessions-of-a-debt-counsellor-turned-whistleblower/. Accessed 14 January 2020.
4. The maximum debt level for a Debt Relief Order is £20,000 (Kirwan 2018).
5. The exchange rate was about 18ZAR = 1GBP.
6. Pharie Sefali, "Money Lender Targets Social Grant Beneficiaries," GroundUp, 21 July 2015. https://www.groundup.org.za/article/money-lender-targets-social-grant-beneficiaries_3140/. Accessed 14 January 2020.
7. Erin Torkelson, "Deductions from Social Grants: How It All Works," GroundUp, 3 March 2017, https://www.groundup.org.za/article/deductions-social-grants-how-it-works/. Accessed 14 January 2020. Erin Torkelson, "Sophia's Choice: Farm Worker Has to Decide Which of Her Children to Feed," GroundUp, 15 March 2017, https://www.groundup.org.za/article/sophias-choice-farm-worker-has-decide-which-her-children-feed. Accessed 14 January 2020.
8. The Common Financial Statement, http://www.cfs.moneyadvicetrust.org (accessed 14 January 2020), is an Excel-based budget sheet that represented "a uniform approach to … financial statements … to encourage consistent responses from creditors" and enable "a fair resolution." It has been replaced by the Standard Financial Statement (Money Advice Service 2018).
9. Discussion with officers of The Black Sash, team members of Summit Financial Partners, Geoff Budlender, Erin Torkelson, 15th February 2018. Following a public outcry, the outcome of a Constitutional Court case saw the contract for awarding social grants withdrawn from Net1 and awarded to the Post Office (Breckenridge 2019). Some of these anomalies might have been remedied since, but my interlocutors in 2018 were skeptical.
10. The National Credit Regulator was established by the National Credit Act of 2005. Described by The Wall Street Journal as a "consumer advocate that is charged with registering lenders," it has not had the political or economic clout to do much more than register lenders and produce reports on debt levels (James 2015: 30).
11. Carin Smith, "How Some Attorneys Turn R500 Debt into R10,000," fin24, 20 July 2016, https://www.fin24.com/Money/Debt/how-some-attorneys-can-turn-r500-debt-into-r10-000-20160720. Accessed 14 January 2020. Although the firm of attorneys indicated its willingness to settle if that meant abiding by the Act in future, it was unwilling to "pay back all of that money" already extracted from unsuspecting borrowers.
12. Maxim Bolt, personal communication; Joburg, "Expanded Social Package Rebates," https://www.joburg.org.za/services_/Pages/City%20Services/Rebates/Expanded-Social-Package-Rebates.aspx. Accessed 14 January 2020.
13. Given that councils to a certain extent retain responsibility to ensure that residents do not suffer eviction or become homeless, many have begun to buy housing

stock in more affordable places far away from London, where they rehouse evicted tenants. Matt Wilde, "Our Immoral Housing Policy Is Set Up to Punish the Poor," *The Guardian*, 26 September 2016, https://www.theguardian.com/commentis free/2016/sep/26/immoral-housing-policy-punish-poor-councils-poverty-peo ple-losing-homes. Accessed 14 January 2020.

14. Dar Es Salaam and Dakar, "How Africa Is Creating Welfare States: Africa Is Stitching Together Social Safety-Nets Even Though It Is Still Poor," *The Economist*, 21 February 2019, https://www.economist.com/middle-east-and-africa/2019/02/23/how-africa-is-creating-welfare-states. Accessed 14 January 2020.

References

Adkins, Lisa. 2017. "Speculative Futures in the Time of Debt." *The Sociological Review* 65, no. 3: 448–62.

Aalbers, Manuel B. 2017. *The Financialisation of Housing: A Political Economy Approach.* London: Routledge.

Alexander, Catherine. 2010. "Third Sector." In *The Human Economy, A Citizens' Guide*, edited by Keith Hart, Jean-Louis Laville, and Antonio David Cattani. Cambridge, UK: Polity Press.

Alexander, Peter, Thapelo Lekgowa, Botsang Mmope, Luke Sinwell, and Bongani Xezwi. 2012. *Marikana: A View from the Mountain and a Case to Answer.* Johannesburg: Jacana Media.

Ardington, Cally, David Lam, Murray Leibbrandt, and James Levinsohn. 2004. "Savings, Insurance and Debt over the Post-Apartheid Period: A Review of Recent Research." *South African Journal of Economics* 72, no. 3: 604–40.

Bähre, Erik. 2011. "Liberation and Redistribution: Social Grants, Commercial Insurance, and Religious Riches in South Africa." *Comparative Studies in Society and History* 53, no. 2: 371–92.

Bear, Laura, and Nayanika Mathur. 2015. "Remaking the Public Good: For a New Anthropology of Bureaucracy." *The Cambridge Journal of Social Anthropology* (Spring 2015).

Bolt, Maxim. 2012. "Waged Entrepreneurs, Policed Informality: Work, the Regulation of Space and the Economy of the Zimbabwean-South African Border." *Africa: Journal of the International African Institute* 82, no. 1: 111–130.

Breckenridge, Keith. 2019. "The Global Ambitions of the Biometric Anti-Bank: Net1, Lockin and the Technologies of African Financialization." *International Review of Applied Economics* 33, no. 1: 93–118.

Brown, Wendy. 2015. *Undoing the Demos: Neoliberalism's Stealth Revolution.* Boston: MIT Press.

Cichello, P., G. S. Fields, and M. Leibbrandt. 2005. "Earnings and Employment Dynamics for Africans in Post-Apartheid South Africa: A Panel Study of KwaZulu-Natal." *Journal of African Economies* 14, no. 2: 143–90.

Cunningham, Hugh. 1998. "Introduction." In *Charity, Philanthropy and Reform, from the 1690s to 1850*, edited by Hugh Cunningham and Joanna Innes. London: MacMillan.

Datta, Kavita. 2012. *Migrants and Their Money: Surviving Financial Exclusion*. Bristol: Policy Press.

Davey, Ryan. 2017. "'Polluter Pays?' Understanding Austerity through Debt Advice in the UK." *Anthropology Today* 33, no. 5: 8–11.

De l'Estoile, Benoit. 2016. "Is 'the Economy' Really Real?" Unpublished paper presented at workshop on The Real Economy, Rio.

Deville, Joe. 2015. *Lived Economies of Default: Consumer Credit, Debt Collection and the Capture of Affect*. London: Routledge.

Deville, Joe, and Gregory J. Seigworth. 2015. "Everyday Debt and Credit." *Cultural Studies* 29, no. 5–6: 615–29.

Elster, Jon. 1991. "Local Justice: How Institutions Allocate Scarce Goods and Necessary Burdens." *European Economic Review* 35, no. 2–3: 273–91.

Forbess, Alice, and Deborah James. 2014. "Acts of Assistance: Navigating the Interstices of the State with the Help of UK Non-profit Legal advisers." *Social Analysis* 58, no. 3: 73–89.

———. 2017. "Innovation and Patchwork Partnerships: Advice Services in Austere Times." *Oñati Socio-legal Series* [online] 7, no. 7. http://ssrn.com/abstract=3056205.

Fraser, Nancy. 2014. "Can Society Be Commodities All the Way Down? Post-Polanyian Reflections on Capitalist Crisis." *Economy and Society* 43, no. 4: 541–558.

Freund, Bill. 2010. "The Social Context of African Economic Growth 1960–2008." In *The Political economy of Africa*, edited by Vishnu Padayachee. London: Routledge.

Gibbs, Timothy. 2018. "The Rise and Fall of Peasant Taxation in South Africa, from Rhodes to Mandela & Mbeki." Unpublished seminar paper, UCL African Studies Research Centre.

Graeber, David. 2015. *Utopia of Rules: On Technology, Stupidity, and the Secret Joys of Bureaucracy*. New York: Melville House.

Gregory, Chris. 2009. "Whatever Happened to Householding?" In *Market and Society: The Great Transformation Today*, edited by Chris Hann and Keith Hart, 133–59. Cambridge, UK: Cambridge University Press.

Gudeman, Stephen. 2010. "A Cosmopolitan Anthropology?" In *Culture Wars: Context, Models, and Anthropologists' Accounts*, edited by Deborah James, Christina Toren, and Evelyn Plaice. New York: Berghahn Books.

Guyer, Jane. 2004. *Marginal Gains: Monetary Transactions in Atlantic Africa*. Chicago: Chicago University Press.

Hann, Chris, and Keith Hart. 2009. "Introduction—Learning from Polanyi." In *Market and Society: The Great Transformation Today*, ed. Chris Hann and Keith Hart. Cambridge, UK: Cambridge University Press.

Hart, Keith. 2015. "How the Informal Economy Took over the World." In *Informal Market Worlds Reader: The Architecture of Economic Pressure*, edited by P. Moertenboeck, H. Mooshammer, T, Cruz, and F. Forman, 33–44. Amsterdam: NAI010 Publishers.

Harvey, David. 2003. *The New Imperialism*. Oxford: Oxford University Press.

Hills, John. 2015. *Good Times, Bad Times: The Welfare Myth of Them and Us*. Bristol: Policy Press.

Hull, Elizabeth, and Deborah James. 2012. "Introduction: Local Economies and Citizen Expectations in South Africa." *Journal of the International African Institute* 82, no. 1: 1–19.

James, Deborah. 2015. *Money from Nothing: Aspiration and Indebtedness in South Africa.* Palo Alto: Stanford University Press.

———. 2019. "Indebtedness and Aspiration in South Africa." In *Poverty and Inequality: Diagnosis, Prognosis and Responses*, edited by Crain Soudien, Ingrid Woolard, and Vasu Reddy. Cape Town: HSRC Press.

James, Deborah, and Samuel Kirwan. 2019. "'Sorting Out Income': Transnational Householding and Austerity Britain." *Social Anthropology.* 11 April. https://doi.org/10.1111/1469-8676.12619.

James, Deborah, and Insa Koch. Forthcoming. "Economies of Advice." *Oxford Research Encyclopedia of Anthropology*

James, Deborah, and Dinah Rajak. 2014. "Credit Apartheid, Migrants, Mines and Money." *African Studies* 73, no. 3: 455–76.

Kar, Sohini. 2018. *Financializing Poverty: Labor and Risk in Indian Microfinance.* Palo Alto: Stanford University Press.

Kirwan, Samuel. 2016. "The UK Citizens Advice Service and the Plurality of Actors and Practices That Shape 'Legal Consciousness.'" *The Journal of Legal Pluralism and Unofficial Law* 48, no. 3: 461–75.

———. 2018. "On 'Those Who Shout the Loudest': Debt Advice and the Work of Disrupting Attachments." *Geoforum* 98: 318–326.

Kirwan, Samuel, Morag McDermont, and John Clarke. 2016. "Imagining and Practising Citizenship in Austere Times: The Work of Citizens Advice." *Citizenship Studies* 20, no. 6–7: 764–78.

Koch, Insa, and Deborah James. 2020. "The State of the Welfare State: Advice, Governance and Care in Settings of Austerity." *Ethnos.* doi: https://www.tandfonline.com/doi/full/10.1080/00141844.2019.1688371.

Krige, D. 2014. "Letting Money Work for Us: Self-Organization and Financialisation from below in an All-Male Savings Club in Soweto." In *People, Money and Power in the Economic Crisis*, edited by K. Hart and J. Sharp. New York: Berghahn Books.

Krippner, G. 2005. "The Financialization of the American Economy." *Socio-Economic Review* 3: 173–208.

Lapavitsas, Costas. 2011. "Theorizing Financialization." *Work, Employment and Society* 25, no. 4: 611–26.

———. 2013. "The Financialization of Capitalism: 'Profiting without Producing.'" *City* 17, no. 6: 792–805.

Lavinas, Lena. 2013. "Twenty-first Century Welfare." *New Left Review* 84: 5–40.

———. 2018. "The Collateralization of Social Policy under Financialized Capitalism." *Development and Change* 49, no. 2: 502–17.

Lawson, Victoria. 2007. "Geographies of Care and Responsibility 2007." *Annals of the Association of American Geographers* 97: 1–11.

Lazzarato, M. 2012. *The Making of the Indebted Man: An Essay on the Neoliberal Condition.* Cambridge, MA: MIT Press.

Meagher, Kate. 2018. "Cannibalizing the Informal Economy: Frugal Innovation and Economic Inclusion in Africa." *European Journal of Development Research* 30, no. 1: 17–33.

Money Advice Trust. n.d. "CFS: The Common Financial Statement." http://www.cfs. moneyadvicetrust.org.

Neves, David, and Andries Du Toit. 2012. "Money and Sociality in South Africa's Informal Economy." *Africa* 82, no. 1: 129–46.

Patrick, Ruth. 2017. *For Whose Benefit? The Everyday Realities of Welfare Reform.* Bristol: Policy Press.

Peebles, Gustav. 2010. "The Anthropology of Credit and Debt." *Annual Review of Anthropology* 39: 225–40.

Ross, Fiona. 2010. *Raw Life, New Hope.* Cape Town: UCT Press.

Sandmo, Agnar. 2015. "The Principal Problem in Political Economy: Income Distribution in the History of Economic Thought." *Handbook of Income Distribution* 2, no. a: 3–65.

Sarat, Austin, and Stuart Sheingold. 1998. *Cause Lawyering: Political Commitments and Professional Responsibilities.* New York: Oxford University Press.

Schraten Jürgen. 2014. "The Transformation of the South African Credit Market." *Transformation* 85: 1–20.

Soederberg, Susan. 2014. *Debtfare States and the Poverty Industry: Money, Discipline and the Surplus Population.* London: Routledge.

Therborn, Göran. 2012a. "Class in the 20th Century." *New Left Review* 28: 5–29.

———. 2012b. "The Killing Fields of Inequality." *International Journal of Health Services* 42: 579–89.

Tiessen, Matthew. 2015. "The Appetites of App-Based Finance." *Cultural Studies* 29, no. 5/6: 869–86.

Van Onselen, Charles. 2017. *The Cowboy Capitalist: John Hays Hammond, the American West and the Jameson Raid.* Cape Town: Jonathan Ball.

Von Schnitzler, Antina. 2016. *Democracy's Infrastructure: Techno-Politics and Protest after Apartheid.* Princeton: Princeton University Press.

Weinberg, Jonathan. 2017. "Bureaucracy as Violence." *Michigan Law Review* 115, no. 6: 1097–116.

Wilkis, Ariel. 2017. *The Moral Power of Money: Morality and Economy in the Life of the Poor.* Stanford: Stanford University Press.

———. 2018. "From Violence to Solidarity: Credit and Debt Experience in Argentine's Lower Classes during the Last Decade." Paper presented at GRECO conference, Onati.

9

Retail Finance and the Moral Dimension of Class

Debt Advice on an English Housing Estate

R YAN D AVEY

Financializing processes at both personal- and state-debt levels have raised questions for anthropologists about how class is changing. Eschewing the tenet that extraction and exploitation depend ultimately on surplus labor in production, Kalb argues that recent political-economic transformations in Euro-America have left "surplus populations ... whose lives are not centered on the wage relationship" (2015: 18–19). Indeed, some have claimed that the extraction of rents in debt relations has displaced the exploitation of productive labor as the "center of gravity" of class-based economic extraction today (Graeber 2014: 76). Investigations of class formation in various relations of economic extraction, including tenancy and credit-debt, therefore supplement the classic Marxian impulse to define class solely in relation to the means of production (Friedman 2015: 192; Kalb 2015: 26; Narotzky 2015).

Financialization is also linked to an observed reliance of capital accumulation on dispossession and violent coercion (Carbonella and Kasmir 2015; Elyachar 2005; Harvey 2005; Mollona 2009). Graeber writes: "The role of the state in making corporate profits possible has undergone a fundamental change. It no longer merely preserves the infrastructure and property relations that make indirect extraction through the wage possible; the coercive mechanisms of the state—the legal system, the threat of courts, bailiffs, prisons, and police—play a direct role in the extraction itself" (2014: 76). This turn to coercion contrasts with what Mollona calls the "hegemonic" form of capitalism that prevailed in twentieth-century Britain, which was based more on consent than coercion, and achieved through welfare rights and trade unionism (2009: 20). Indeed, financial debt confers legitimacy over the right to extract via violent means (Roitman 2005: 6). In the UK, with personal debts, such as credit cards and mortgages, payments from debtor to creditor are secured by the threat of legally sanctioned dispossessions, such as bailiffs seizing household goods or evicting people from their homes (Deville 2015).

The significance of the reliance of financial accumulation on state coercion for class goes beyond how it facilitates the extraction of wealth, however. Building on the above studies, this chapter explores the ways in which consumer debt has a complex effect on the inequalities in ascribed moral worth that constitute what I call "the moral dimension" of class. To understand class in terms of these inequalities in ascribed moral value, I draw on research into class stigma and the notion of the "underclass." Following Thatcher's assault on public housing, manufacturing, and trade unions, the "chav" stereotype demonized a section of the working class that allegedly has no aspiration, thus justifying rampant inequality and expressing the belief "that everyone should become middle class" (Jones 2012: 138). Imogen Tyler (2013) describes this as a process of "abjectification" through which stereotypes of scrounging teenage mums, benefits cheats, and "sink estates" discursively produce an "underclass" of people who collectively embody negative value. This denigration can be interpreted through the Bourdieusian lens of Beverley Skeggs (2003, 2015), who argues that class is formed through unequal exchanges of moral value.

The correspondence, or not, of a denigrated "underclass" to a shared economic condition and social formation is a matter of debate (including on the left). Ray Pahl argued that "the declining centrality of employment … as the basis for social and political consciousness" (1984: 335) in postindustrial Britain transformed the old division between the middle and working classes into a cleavage between an expanded "middle mass" and a residual "underclass." Others disagree. As Lydia Morris (1993, 2002) writes, most definitions of the "underclass" stress exclusion from mainstream society and a rejection of its values and norms—primarily, through dependency on welfare over a desire to work. But, she says, it is far from certain that a shared economic condition of unemployment implies internal social cohesion and shared subcultural values, and vice versa. Leo Howe similarly showed that class-based stigma can divide the very communities it targets. In 1980s Northern Ireland, a notional divide between the "deserving" poor—those out of work for no fault of their own and so deserving of welfare benefits—and their "undeserving" counterparts, who allegedly chose not to work, compelled the individual members of neighborhoods with high unemployment to strenuously distance themselves from their neighbors (Howe 1990).

As this indicates, debates about class stigma and "the underclass" have tended to revolve around unemployment and welfare, but debt and financialization are equally pertinent to the class transformations that have taken place.[1] The hegemonic decline of the United States and western Europe and the consequent declining profitability of production there led not only to wage stagnation and mass unemployment but also to "a shift from industrial to financial dominance in the accumulation process" (Friedman 2015: 186). In the case I present, the debts generated by this shift to financial dominance were a focal point for moral pronouncements about profligacy and irresponsibility, which fed into a broader discourse on the existence of a supposed "underclass."

I argue that financialization has directly influenced processes of class stigmatization in contemporary Britain. Specifically, the shift to financialized accumulation affects a new organization of legitimate coercion, which, first, reshapes processes of class-based denigration and, second, incites in those who are vulnerable to enforcement an ambivalence toward their debts. Financialization thus influences the reproduction of class inequality not just in terms of economic extraction, but also through its complex effects on inequalities in ascribed moral worth and worthlessness (Kalb 2013: 6). Thus, I add a consideration of the moral or jural aspects of debt to recent advances in understanding the implications for social class on the reliance of contemporary accumulation on financial rent-taking.

I start from the basic observation that, in the UK, consumer debt consolidates ascriptions of fault to people living on low and precarious incomes. This contributes to a broader structure of class-based denigration. Through close ethnographic engagement in this field of interpellation—observing both sites where negative evaluations arise and the lives of those evaluated—I highlight the complex and unpredictable effects of the fault that often attaches to debt. Further, I draw attention to the crucial role of debt and its associated institutions, including debt advice, in the discursive attempt to produce an "underclass" outside mainstream society. I show that over-indebted people living on low and precarious incomes often fluctuate between avowing and disregarding the notional obligation to repay. This implies the existence of many people who confound the imagined boundary between an aspiring middle class and an abjected "underclass."

I focus on debt advice as a site where moral evaluations around debt crystallize, especially for debtors who at some point have disregarded their debts. These evaluations are usually insinuated rather than expressed. Numerous scholars have shown how debt advice can ameliorate the problems of those struggling to repay financial and nonfinancial debts. Advice can mitigate the tendency of retail finance to extract wealth from those at the bottom, "by persuading creditors to accept reduced payments or hold off on their demands, and by separating debts into discrete strands or channels of payment so that they can be managed, contested or even written off" (James 2020: 2). In a similar spirit, Kirwan writes that debt advice can disrupt the power of creditors "to seek to reform and reconstruct the behavior of debtors," for instance by giving clients greater confidence in dealing with creditors (2019: 7). Such points are well taken. Yet in focusing on whether debt advice counteracts or colludes with financial accumulation, and on the personal views of advisers, the moral evaluations that quietly infuse the bureaucratic forms and procedures of debt advice are sometimes overlooked.

In studying the tentative formation of an "underclass" in Britain, through debt, the chapter is, in a sense, about class formation. But this is not in Thompson's sense of class formation as a teleological process of collective self-making, where "some men [*sic*], as a result of common experiences (inherited or shared), feel and articulate the identity of their interests as between themselves, and as against other men whose interests are different from (and usually opposed to) theirs" (Thompson 1991: 9). While Thompson stressed the formation of imagined commonalities, I am interested in class formations in the plural, which implies engaging with imagined and practiced divisions. This plural concept of class formations is perhaps a more pliable and neutral one, which does not preempt the question of whether the collectivities that form are necessarily progressive.

Fieldwork on a so-called "deprived" housing estate (or housing project) in a city in the south of England, around half of whose five thousand residents live in social housing, provided the ethnographic material for this chapter. I call the housing estate Woldham. My fieldwork also included participant observation at a debt advice charity also based on the estate. In what follows, I outline how an expansion of consumer credit in the UK impacted the livelihoods of the residents of Woldham, many of whom must borrow in order to subsist. Exploring the implications of financialization on the moral dimension of class, I then describe how debt advice in Woldham was a site for the ascription of legal fault to those who were struggling to keep on top of debt repayments and bills, informed by a classed logic that made a virtue of upward mobility. Those who borrow in order to subsist, and subsequently struggle to manage their repayments, occupy a grey area between arrears and default. They waver radically in their commitment to the general moral rule that if a debt is legally valid then it is also morally binding. Relating this to theories of class in Britain, I argue that this interstitial position prevents the formation of an abjected "underclass."

Consumer Debt in the UK

Credit has long been a key element in the livelihoods of the British working classes, notably those with low incomes and no property. Until the 1980s, unsecured loans from banks were generally reserved for the better-off. In their absence, working-class borrowers turned to mail order companies, doorstep moneylenders, and hire purchase. New forms of consumer credit were exported from the United States to Europe in the 1950s (Deville 2015: 81). The UK was enthusiastic in embracing them, and its consumer credit market is today the largest in Europe (Deeming, Collard, and Hayes 2011: 9). In the 1980s, the UK's financial services expanded, increasing the total outstanding personal debt from £10 billion in 1980 to £53 billion in 1993 (Leyshon and Thrift 1995). The Thatcher government lifted many of the existing controls on retail lending (Deville 2015: 82). The financial services market contracted with the early 1990s financial crisis, grew dynamically from the late 1990s to the late 2000s, and then contracted again in the wake of defaults caused by the 2008 crisis (Finney and Davies 2011; Kempson et al. 2000; Leyshon and Thrift 1995).

On the Woldham housing estate in 2012–13, the common economic predicament of many residents was that wage labor was unreliable as a sole means of subsistence. Many worked, many were unemployed, and many moved in and out of casual work. But almost all relied for some or all of their income on claiming welfare benefits, consumer borrowing, undeclared cash-in-hand work, and/or petty criminality. As a result, residents took out credit not with aspirations for upward mobility, but for essential purchases, or immediate comestibles—from electricity to children's birthday presents. The debtors I knew told me their recourse to consumer credit was essential to their livelihood; yet as a result, they struggled in their efforts to be punctual with repayment. Many were in arrears and liable to be taken to court at any time. This exposed them to a small but almost inescapable risk of debts being enforced, for instance by bailiffs confiscating household goods or ultimately evicting them from their homes. For many, this interstitial position between arrears and default was an ordinary condition of life.

I was a volunteer in the debt advice service on the Woldham estate in 2012–13. I give the service the pseudonym "Beacon Advice." The advisers at Beacon Advice were generally lower middle class: independent of welfare benefits, and owners of cars. Their full-time salaries were under £20,000. One adviser was a Navy veteran who after the Falklands war had worked for a commercial bank in their mortgage lending department. Some advisers owned their homes, with one adviser living with her parents following a divorce. There was a spatial and social separation between advisers and their clients, since none of the advisers lived on the Woldham estate, nor did any of them ever mention having friends or family who lived there. Clients could "self-refer" to the advice service by telephoning the office, or—what was more common at Beacon Advice given that it was funded specifically to assist "hard-to-reach" groups—they could be referred by some public- or voluntary-sector professional already working with them, such as a social worker, a support worker, a housing association worker, or a Royal British Legion employee.

When I started my placement at Beacon Advice, I initially imagined that the advice process would involve a client approaching the service with a list of debts, uncertain about what course of action to take. I soon learned that the bulk of the work lay in actually compiling that list of debts, after which the rest followed relatively straightforwardly. With clients often confused about how much money they owed and to whom, the advisers saw their job as disentangling and enumerating their debts. One of the key interventions advisers made to this end was to press upon clients the full scope of the category "debt," so as to include rent arrears, water bill arrears, mobile phone bill arrears, overpayments of welfare benefits, and hire purchase agreements.

This process of forming knowledge about debts, as quantities of owed money, was a political one, for it often relied on invoking the coercion of the law. One of the advisers told me:

> When you're told about the council tax debt and so on, you then want to ignore it. You're in denial, like: "It's my wife's, not mine." They will be completely unreceptive while they're in denial. The only way out of that is to shock them. Tell them what the implications are. For example, one client had several debts and disputed her debt to her landlords. But they were quite right, so I said: "How long do you think it'd take them to evict you?" Then she realized.

Advisers would routinely say that bailiffs "can," "may," or "are entitled to" use coercive force. By invoking legally enforceable consequences in neutral-sounding language, debt advice thus functioned to legitimize legal violence and insinuate the debtor's legal fault.

While sympathetic to their clients' difficulties, and while the advice sector as a whole encompasses a wide variety of political positions, the advisers at Beacon Advice generally favored individualistic explanations of why debt problems occurred. Macroeconomic considerations, such as a scarcity of local job opportunities, were not denied, but seemed to be, for the advisers, rather "academic" considerations, of little practical relevance to their work. The Beacon Advice advisers acknowledged the impacts of social policy, such as austerity cuts to welfare benefits, though most of them felt these cuts were necessary both fiscally and to counteract so-called welfare dependency. Individual behavioral traits were their most common explanation for debt problems: failings of character such as profligacy, idleness, dishonesty, and welfare dependency. One of the advisers, called Bernie, often drew on superficial observations and stereotypes of Woldham residents to understand the debt problems of his clients, even though the latter lived all over the city. One day, he said: "You don't get many energy arrears [in this job], because most people in this area are on key-meters." In the next breath, he said: "The vast majority of our people don't have the ability to get a job. Instead, you get cash-in-hand work, cheap tobacco, drugs, [stolen] goods falling off the back of a wagon. The vast majority of houses you go into as an adviser have one thing in common: their TV. The size is even above my means. They've all got them."

Wider discourses also informed how the advisers understood their clients: the folk devil of the scrounger, embodying welfare dependency and deceitfulness, as well as notions of profligacy, based on stereotypes about excessive spending or wantonly evading repayment. An adviser called Tom said people "these days" did not wait to buy things until they could afford them, whereas he and his wife had "lived with near to nothing until [they] saved up enough to purchase a sofa." He said people "lack[ed] the skills," such as "financial literacy," to manage their financial affairs properly through budgeting, saving, or economizing. And he attributed his clients' spending habits to widespread impulses to "keep up with the Joneses" (maintaining standing with one's neighbors by consuming similar goods) or to "have the latest thing," both of which Tom considered problematic. In contrast, the people I met who lived on the Woldham estate generally said that credit had become a vital means of subsistence. As one man said during an eighteen-month spell of unemployment: "Benefits and loans are the only things you can rely on these days." While this contrast circulated in discourse around Woldham and its debt advice service, such oppositions between debts of necessity and debts of prestige, appetite, excess, or frivolity are best seen as cultural facts to be described ethnographically rather than reproduced analytically. Indeed, as anthropologists, we can question the idea that maintaining social esteem is extraneous to subsistence.

Along similar lines, the advisers at Beacon Advice distinguished between what they called "credit for investment," such as a mortgage on a house or car finance for a car for work, and, on the other hand, "credit for consumption," such as a holiday, a hire-purchase television, or a car for leisure. While they deemed using credit for investment "sustainable" and respectable, they saw taking out credit for consumption as "unsustainable" and indicative of profligacy. The advisers' distinction between borrowing "for consumption" (being bad) and borrowing "for investment" (being good) implied an ethical valorization on their part of upward social mobility, because they positively evaluated borrowing practices that helped someone get richer. Almost by definition, the advisers viewed those who needed the advice center's help (because they had fallen into arrears) either as having borrowed "for consumption"—and thus been irresponsible—or as having borrowed "for investment" but been unsuccessful in the entrepreneurial project they were pursuing. Otherwise, the advisers believed, the client would not need their help.

The advisers never told their clients to their face that their borrowing and livelihood practices were irresponsible or failures. But there was no need to say it out loud. The same ethical valorization of upward mobility was also embedded within the bureaucratic documentary forms of the advice service—in particular, one template document known as the "Common Financial Statement." The Common Financial Statement was a document to which the entire UK debt advice sector and the retail finance industry had agreed as a standardized means for advisers to calculate offers of repayment, which lenders were then meant to accept.[2] On the Common Financial Statement, financial debts were divided into mortgages and "other debts," meaning all unsecured consumer debts (such as credit cards, personal loans, and overdrafts).

What counted as a debt on the Common Financial Statement subtly differed between mortgages and unsecured consumer debts. An amount owed on a mortgage was not counted as a debt at all. Only the mortgage *arrears* (i.e., missed payments) were stated on the form and thus counted as a debt. But with the unsecured consumer debts, the entire "balance outstanding" (rather than the arrears) was stated on the form and thus counted as the debt. On the Common Financial Statement, the word "debt," therefore, meant *either* arrears on a bill or mortgage *or* the balance of an unsecured consumer debt. Not counting mortgages as debts in their own right evinces a very specific ethical mindset about which kinds of debt matter (High 2012). On the Common Financial Statement, an amount you had borrowed without owning property mattered as a debt, and was (as I outline below) considered problematic. But debts relating to property-ownership (namely, mortgages) did not matter as debts in themselves, nor were they considered problematic. Only the arrears on such debts (i.e., missed payments on a mortgage) mattered as a debt and were seen as a problem. This reaffirms property ownership as a virtue, because mortgage arrears pose a risk of someone losing their property.

The advisers followed procedures that rendered this highly specific definition of "debt"—the balances outstanding on unsecured credit instruments and missed payments on a mortgage or bill—as problems to be eliminated. This was due to a bureaucratic sleight of hand. Being in arrears (and not simply owing money) was the precondition for becoming a debt advice client or "case" in the first place. Consider a counterexample. A man visited the advice service because he had been unable to pay his credit card bill in full one month, as he always tried to do. He was not in arrears, strictly speaking, because he had still paid the minimum amount. The advisers sent him home, telling him he did not have a problem with which they could help him.

The indebted people whom the advice service *could* take on as clients, meanwhile, were those who were already in arrears. But as soon as they had been accepted as new clients, the definition of "the problem" to be remedied subtly changed to include not just arrears, but all balances outstanding on unsecured credit instruments. Clients had to sign an agreement at the start of their case saying they promised not to take out any further credit, not even "emergency" credit facilities such as using an overdraft. (If an adviser found out the client had used an overdraft or credit card or the like, they were obliged to close the case.) The "debt solutions" that advisers tried subsequently to arrange sought to purge clients' unsecured consumer debts entirely, either through insolvency or by steady repayment until cleared (Davey 2019a).

It made little difference that the advisers often told their clients they would help the clients to get their debts "back under control," meaning to reduce the arrears and prevent enforcement. Nor did it make much difference that the advisers joked privately about the decades, even centuries, it would take some clients to fully clear their debts through the repayments the advisers negotiated. By defining "debt" to include all balances outstanding on unsecured credit instruments and promoting an aim to purge unsecured debts by prohibiting any further use of credit, the advice service implied that having borrowed money at all was the source of the problem for those having problems with repayment.

This may appear common sense. But it rests on a false equation between, on the one hand, debtors asking for help to clear their arrears and prevent enforcement and, on the other, the advice service promoting a goal of purging unsecured debts. Like a doctor telling someone who is sick to change their diet, debt advisers do not simply provide a "sticking plaster" for the problem, but attempt to address its putative source. The identified problem is the inability to pay and the consequent risk of enforcement. The identified source of the problem harks back to the borrower's decision to take out money in the first place. But the problem (the difficulty repaying) is not reducible to this initial decision to borrow. It also includes multiple pressures on people's finances, including cuts to public welfare, stagnated wages, increased rents and cost of living, a decline in manufacturing in the UK, and the dependency of the UK economy's growth on debt-financed consumption. Lenders charging interest, generally in proportion with the estimated risk of a borrower defaulting, also adds to problems repaying. Finally, that people often borrow money under compromised economic circumstances (i.e., less than freely) undermines the idea of weaning yourself off credit as a solution. By treating debtors in isolation from lending practices and structural inequalities, the advice service's false equation meant that owing money was considered benign for those who had not fallen on hard times, but problematic for those who had.

Some would say that identifying debt—in the sense of money owed—as a problem does not necessarily entail moralization. It is true that debt advisers explicitly framed their work as a technical, nonjudgmental matter of solving problems of legal liability. But, as the over-indebted people I met were only too aware, legal obligations are not always easily separable from moral obligations when it comes to debt. Indeed, for the many who attempted to detach themselves from a sense of moral duty to repay despite the compulsions of the law, this took an existential effort involving careful techniques of spatial distancing, attentional discipline, and subversive humor (Davey 2019a, 2019b). So while Kirwan's claim that "the debt advice process disrupts the framing of debt as an issue of personal morality" (2019: 7) holds for spoken interactions between advisers and clients, it overlooks the moral evaluations of debt that are engrained into the bureaucratic forms and technical knowledge of advice work. As Good (1994) writes for medicine, so too for debt advice: remedial practices often have obscured moral characteristics.

In these ways, professional debt advice crystallized moral evaluations where the question of whether a given borrowing practice was problematic or not depended on whether it was associated with property ownership or upward mobility or not. Debts were considered problematic if they did not advance a person's class position. Granted, the advisers or clients did not speak much about class. Since the early 1990s until around the Brexit referendum, the language of "class" fell out of favor in British public life (Jones 2012). Instead of talking about class, politicians and public services increasingly promoted "aspiration"—meaning getting ahead in life, home-ownership, and economic self-sufficiency through work—"as some kind of panacea for inequality with pledges to 'combat ... intergenerational cycles of poverty' by 'raising the aspirations' of working-class families" (Allen 2014: 2). At the same time, they increasingly claimed the existence of a "classless" social structure comprising a separation between those who espouse a virtue of upward mobility and those who reject it. For instance, Tony Blair declared "We're all middle class now," except for "an underclass of people ... with no shared purpose" (cited in Tyler 2013). Likewise, in Woldham, housing officers and community workers repeatedly complained that local residents were "apathetic" because they were not (apparently) striving for a better life outside the housing estate.

This norm for aspiration in an unequal society all too easily individualizes the onus for economic disadvantage. At Beacon Advice, the discrepant moral status of mortgages and unsecured credit debts, and the assumption that those in arrears had borrowed erroneously, happened to reinforce (not necessarily by intention) the normativity of aspirations for upward mobility. In doing so, it fed into an ideologically imposed social division between an expanded middle class and an apathetic underclass.

Social Divisions in Woldham

The class-inflected moral evaluations that circulated within the advice service resonated with wider social divisions on the Woldham estate. These social divisions extend beyond financialization; and by outlining them now, I highlight how the expansion of consumer credit contributed to a wider societal denigration of a notional "underclass." One social hierarchy on the estate was between two groups wrongly imagined to be totally separate: the people who contribute taxes, and the people who claim benefits and as such drain public resources (Hills 2017). One resident, a widower and Navy veteran who now worked as a nurse and owned his home, referred to benefit claimants as "dole scum." He said, when asked for his view about the area: "I hate it. I wish the Germans would come back and bomb the place.[3] People round here will take all the benefits they can get their hands on." He told me he thought there would be a revolution following the riots of 2011. "But it's not going to be a revolution of people against the police or anything like that. It's going to be us—the people working for a living—against people like the people round here who want to take everything they can get their hands on [i.e., benefit claimants]." Echoing the notion that claiming benefits meant wrongful dependency on public funds, a bumper sticker on a car parked around the corner read: "Work harder—those on benefits depend on you!"

A second hierarchy was based on housing tenure, divided between homeowners, private renters, and council tenants. A woman who had moved with her partner and four children into a newly built council house told me: "The only thing I don't like [about the new location] is that some of the houses are private or homeowners, and when something happens, it's like they look down at us, because they know we're council. But there's no difference between us; it's just that we're council, so we don't pay."

Of course, the ideology of work-shy scroungers was not always swallowed whole. A self-employed homeowner I knew in Woldham criticized some of his neighbors' snobbery: "Some people think all council tenants are benefits scroungers, but the vast majority of council tenants I know work hard." Others were more ambivalent. Many benefit claimants justified their own situation but often reproduced the stigmatization of welfare dependency when speaking in more general terms (cf. Howe 1990). One woman initially accepted the narrative that welfare provision encouraged laziness: "Everybody always waits for it to be given to them on a plate. Britain's like that now." However, in recounting her own difficulties finding work and the unaffordability of childcare, she went on to praise the support she received as a single parent, because: "Not everyone's got family and friends who'll run after you." This ambivalence was especially marked among those claiming sickness and disability benefits—one resident claimed that most of the incapacity benefit claimants on his street were faking their medical conditions, despite his own strife with medical assessors that had callously dismissed his health needs.

The morality of debt repayment figured prominently in these social divisions. One morning, I noticed four sofas and several sofa cushions strewn on the grass around footpaths and roads of the estate. Further along, a man wearing a housing association logo on his overalls was picking up more bits of discarded sofa. I asked why they had appeared. "What it is," he said, "there'll have been some advert—DFS [a furniture company] or something like that—saying buy now [on credit] and pay nothing for a year. So everyone will have gone and bought one, and then in a year's time, they'll move out so they can't get them [i.e., so that the sofa company could not trace them to recover the debt]. Some people ain't got no conscience or morals like that." Throwing out old items of furniture made space for the new purchases in the buyers' homes. The housing association caretaker inferred from this that the furniture had been bought with a deliberate aim of evading repayment. But whether the people who had bought new sofas were planning on not paying for them was surely uncertain. The caretaker's conclusions thus show a readiness to ascribe negative moral value on the basis of barely apparent debt refusal. Another resident to whom I recounted the episode put it more plainly: "They're living on the never-never. Evil bastards."

Stereotypes of amoral debtors coalesced with stereotypes of welfare "scroungers" and council tenants on the estate in the imagined figure of a discrete group of residents set apart from mainstream society by rejecting its supposed values. The fact that the content of this stigma now included not only allegations of welfare dependency and scrounging but also profligacy, wanton debt evasion, and "poor financial literacy" shows (*pace* Howe 1990) that by 2012, financialization was directly informing the discursive constitution of this imagined "underclass." In reality, there was no strict separation between people who fully accepted norms around debt and others who fully rejected those norms. Most residents' feelings were more mixed, as I show now.

Debtors' Ambivalence about Having to Pay

Many of the debt advice clients I interviewed spoke about their personal debt crises—which always involved fears of imminent legal enforcement—as a turning point in their lives. They said these crisis moments had incited them not only to attach a moral value to the obligation to repay, but also to learn self-restraint in spending, to defer gratification, and generally to "be more responsible." One woman said, "I've learned my lesson. I'm more mature now." In contrast, a few of the debtors I met informally, as neighbors, forthrightly *dis*avowed the obligation to repay their debts. In other words, they rejected the dominant morality of debt. One young man advised several of his neighbors to pay only a pound a month toward their water bills, because apparently the regional water company rarely took such customers to court. He told several people, complaining about extortionate regional water rates: "[T]he water company can't disconnect you if you don't pay your bills. I got letters from them saying they were gonna take me to court, and they never did. I've not paid for years; I have thousands unpaid, and they've not done anything." Another resident told me how he had fleeced all the loan companies in the city: "I've had Provident [a doorstep lender], you name it. You can do them all and get loads off them." I asked: "But don't you run out of companies who will lend to you eventually?" "No," he explained. "You get them all out on the same day. Two hundred pounds from one; two hundred from another. Then, when I move up to Preston, I can do all the ones up there." All this shows that while a legally enforceable debt is always a legal obligation, it is not always also a moral obligation in Englund's sense of an "existential compulsion" (Englund: 2008).

Rather than fully accepting or rejecting the dominant morality of repayment, the debtors I met had a varying relation to it. At times, they avowed an obligation to pay particular debts; and at other times, they disavowed such an obligation. They resisted ascriptions of fault, and yet their economic circumstances meant they could not always afford to be fully compliant debtors. Most debt advice clients turned to the service after losing hope of avoiding enforcement. In one debt advice appointment I attended, the client showed her adviser a letter mentioning court costs. She said: "That's what made me think, 'Oh god, we've gotta sort this out.' It says they're gonna send someone 'round in the evening. So I've not opened the door." She eventually admitted: "I stopped opening them. I just put them away. Sometimes it keeps me up at night thinking about it. I don't sleep properly." The woman had disregarded her creditors' repayment demands and, upon the threat of a debt collector visiting her home, then swung round to earnestly assuming an obligation to pay. The threat of imminent enforcement had induced this change with this and many other clients.

To understand how and why so many debtors fluctuate in their commitment to dominant moral standards around debt repayment, it bears taking seriously how, on the basis of their firsthand experiences, debt advice clients define the category "debt." As I described above, debt advisers followed a definition of the word "debt" as owing money on an unsecured instrument or being in arrears on a bill or mortgage. But clients' usage of the word "debt" connoted intractability and moral failure. Let me unpack this. When clients used the word "debt," in phrases such as "I'm in debt," they often meant their repayment obligations were intractable. As one man told me: "My sisters are all right. They're not in debt. Well, when you say 'debt,' everyone's in debt; but it's when you've got it so you can't manage." For him, owing money was not particularly problematic in itself. Nor was falling behind with repayments. Rather, coming to see oneself as being "in debt" meant feeling one could no longer cope. Being "in debt" in this sense almost always involved a realization of individual fault, thus implying a moral quality to debt. Clients commonly told me about "admitting to yourself you're in debt." One said: "It's a sort of realization of you doing something wrong." Another said: "I should've learned when I was younger. My dad got into fifteen grand of debt and tried to commit suicide over it. I've learned my lesson [now], and I've learned it the hard way." By recognizing a debt as such, then, clients bought into the idea that they were individually responsible for their economic circumstances insofar as these circumstances affected their ability to pay.

When clients did avow an obligation to pay their debts, they tended to characterize their debts as worrisome and stressful. Many anticipated worst-case scenarios of legal action. One woman said: "In extreme circumstances, I could've lost my daughter. One of the bailiffs was telling me failure to pay would result in me going to prison." Many clients told me their debt worries induced sleep problems, or physical or mental illness, and several said they had contemplated suicide. It appeared that the threshold between avowing and disavowing a moral obligation to pay a particular debt was porous and often unstable. Clients demonstrated this in the way they moved back and forth between ignoring and confronting their debts. One described this process as involuntary, like a reflex action: "To work out how much you owe each person—you just can't. It just seems insurmountable. It's so much that your brain just switches."

While this may give an impression of debtors refusing to pay for as long as they can before finally facing the music when enforcement threatens, in fact, this was generally a back-and-forth movement. Not only were "drop out" rates high among the clients of Beacon Advice, with clients disengaging once the adviser had written to creditors to ask them to stop threatening legal action, but also the debt advisers were fond of telling me of their many recalcitrant clients who, barely months after the adviser found a "debt solution" such as a repayment or insolvency arrangement, were once again ignoring any putative obligation to pay.

All this implies that the act of disregarding or disavowing debts for which lenders are demanding repayment is both cognitively and politically complex. While few clients explicitly advocated debt refusal, nearly all said they had at some stage "buried their heads in the sand," hoping their debts would go away. "You just wish it will all go away, but it doesn't," said one client. Even where they disregarded their debts only involuntarily and fleetingly, nevertheless, in doing so, they dispensed with the moral "should" of the debt obligation. Such debtors at once refused to take onto their shoulders a moral obligation to pay more than they could afford,[4] more than their health or sanity could bear, or more than they considered reasonable. They effectively renounced legally authorized determinations of how much was owed and to whom, and thereby challenged a jural framework for ascribing individual fault.

Woldham residents I met informally as neighbors were reluctant to seek official advice for their debts. At the start of my fieldwork on the estate, I met two individuals who told me about insurmountable debts totaling multiple thousands. In both cases, I encouraged them to seek the help of the local debt advice service. Both tactfully declined. One said that receiving debt advice would impact his credit score, and thus obstruct his future access to credit. This was a valid concern, as certain debt solutions (such as insolvency and debt management plans) reduce credit scores.[5] The other said he did not want advisers to know he was doing undeclared cash-in-hand work while also claiming unemployment benefits, because he felt that debt advisers would report this to the Job Centre, leading to penalties such as a loss in income. The same applied to informally earned income—such as trading unlicensed tobacco, or drugs, or stolen goods. As one man said, "You never tell them everything." When I asked the debt advisers about this, they said an adviser would never report any illegality to the authorities, but that they would be forced to tell the client that they would not be able to continue the service. Other residents correctly expected that the advice service would insist that it was necessary to honor any legally valid debt, but the resident themselves deemed that some of their debts were exploitative and did not deserve to be repaid. In sum, economic circumstances where wage labor was insufficient as a means of subsistence ampli-fied the disciplinary and potentially punitive dimensions of debt advice, and led some debtors to question whether it was really morally necessary to comply with their creditors' demands.

My portrayal of debt advice differs from those who stress its benign effects (James 2020; Kirwan 2019). This derives in part from my interac-tions with indebted residents outside of the institutional context of the debt advice center. Debt advice, of course, very often helps people by negotiating lower repayments with creditors or eliminating some debts altogether. This may lessen the extractive function of retail finance. Still, in the eyes of those I got to know outside the advice center, the punitive, intrusive dimension was hard to ignore. Those who have never needed to see a debt adviser may consider the process of writing down your entire income and expenditure quite reasonable (as did I). But many who need such support cannot afford the luxury of having all of their sub-sistence practices wholly compliant with laws and regulations. Not only do they consider (not always correctly) that advice may carry a danger of making their difficulties worse, but they also keenly (and correctly) perceive a moral judgment upon them of having erred in their pursuit of a livelihood.

Conclusion: Implications for Class Formations

Financialization effects a new organization of legitimate coercion, which both contributes to the class-based denigration of the nonupwardly mobile and incites in those who are vulnerable to enforcement an ambivalent rela-tion to dominant (i.e., enforceable) moral standards around repayment. In addition, then, to those who have detailed how financialization transforms the economic basis of class inequality through new modes of accumulation (Adkins 2017; Kalb 2015; Narotzky 2015), I have tried in this chapter to show that the reliance of contemporary accumulation on financial rent-taking has a direct effect on the moral dimension of class. This is because, as a mode of accumulation, the reliance of consumer debt on legal coer-cion shapes inequalities in ascribed moral worth. Since all the expropria-tions consumer debt engenders (including evictions) are legally mediated, they all carry an authoritative ascription of fault. Debt advice consolidates ascriptions of fault to nonupwardly mobile, propertyless debtors for their economic circumstances. This is a consequence not of malicious intent among debt advisers, but of the fact that professional advice upholds the law and so implies that legally valid repayment obligations carry moral weight. Through insinuations of legal fault and/or profligacy, it treats such debtors as if they belong to an inferior class of person. It thus contributes to a wider structure of class-based denigration, wherein moral worth and worthlessness become euphemisms for class difference. This forms part of what Imogen Tyler (2013) describes as the discursive production of an "underclass" of people who collectively embody negative value. While writers on the "underclass" have focused on unemployment and welfare dependency, I have shown that an "underclass" was tentatively being formed on the Woldham estate through claims that some debtors had somehow erred in discharging their responsibilities as debtors.

My point in examining the moral dimension of class is not to suggest that this is somehow more important than its economic dimension. The point is to note that shifts in production and accumulation that affect the reproduction of economic inequality also have far-reaching and unpredictable effects on human ethical life and social relations that may, in turn, reinforce, amplify, or undermine those inequalities. In Woldham, certain principles of working-class respectability had become aligned with a wider valorization of upward social mobility, involving economic self-sufficiency through work and the ownership of property. This could be seen in the social divisions on the estate, between homeowners and renters, and between those who claimed welfare benefits and those who did not. The expansion of financial debt fed into this, since it provided a new channel for ascribing fault or inferiority to nonupwardly mobile, propertyless people.

In the face of this ascription of fault, debtors in Woldham responded in manifold, complex ways. Negative judgments around debt fed into local social divisions, similar to those observed by Leo Howe in 1980s Northern Ireland, but now with reference to debt as well as welfare. In both my case and Howe's, the targets of class-based contempt lacked the social means to build a collective riposte to a denigrating dominant morality. Instead, Woldham residents sought to resist ascriptions of fault as far as their wallets and their health would allow. But as a result, many debtors in Woldham fluctuated in their commitment to the morality of repayment. Every debt advice client who had put off turning to the advice service had sought, for a time, to detach themselves from any compulsion to repay.

This suggests there is a substantial population who waver in their commitment to dominant moral standards around debt repayment. They generally struggle to distance themselves from stereotypes of an underclass—as with the example I gave of benefit claimants justifying their own claim yet diagnosing "scrounging" among others, or (as I suggest is equally pertinent to the discursive constitution of an "underclass" today) with the many cases of over-indebted people who strive to disregard their debts and the judgments those debts convey. Yet their success in distancing themselves from such stereotypes can never be assured, since their economic circumstances mean they cannot guarantee that they will be able to avoid all legal enforcement. While there are, of course, many who reject outright the injunction to pursue upward mobility, there are many more whose position is more ambivalent. Their ambivalence expresses an impulse for a better life with serious misgivings about the available terms by which "better" is defined: primarily, individual enrichment. While writers such as Tyler have observed the formation, through discourse, of an abject "underclass," my research shows a less predictable consequence of this tentative class formation: the emergence of a vast grey area occupied by those who waver in their commitment to dominant moral standards and seemingly fluctuate between two imposed class categories: the aspiring members of a dominant moral community, on the one hand, and an abject "underclass," on the other. The existence of so many people who fluctuate between avowing and disavowing the obligation to comply with their creditors' demands prevents the formation in reality of the imagined "underclass."

Acknowledgments

This research was funded by the William Wyse Fund, the Cambridge Political Economy Society Trust, and the Economic and Social Research Council of the UK (Grant ES/M003825/1).

Ryan Davey is a social anthropologist who obtained his PhD from Cambridge University in 2016. He specializes in debt, class, and subjectivity, and is currently Vice-Chancellor's Fellow at the University of Bristol.

Notes

1. While beyond the scope of this chapter, a body of work connects financialization to class polarization wherein a cosmopolitan elite pits itself against a subproletarianized and, crucially, indigenized working class. Kalb and Halmai argue that in many settings, "the erstwhile 'Fordist' working-classes are unmade … into a new ethnicized 'folk,' and the lower tiers are turned … into racialized classes dangereuses" (2011: 7).
2. The Common Financial Statement was a standard budget format agreed between the Money Advice Trust, the British Banking Association, and the Finance and Leading Association. It has since been replaced by another form, called the Standard Financial Statement.
3. The city in which Woldham is located was among the worst damaged in the UK by bombing during World War II.

4. The people I met varied in what expenditure they would forego first when short of money, but to make a few general observations: debt advisers reported that debtors were often keen to keep repaying doorstep lenders even if they were not repaying bank loans or cards; parents often expressed anxieties about not being able to provide presents for children at Christmas and birthdays (and sometimes took out loans to this end); "priority" debts with immediate legal consequences (such as rent arrears or council tax arrears) were usually repaid before unsecured consumer credit debts; people who smoked might cut down their tobacco consumption; in general, many residents told me they socialized and relaxed at home, for instance watching TV or playing video games, as a more economical alternative to going out to pubs, restaurants, or the cinema; and holidays were rare.
5. See, for instance, https://www.experian.co.uk/consumer/guides/debt-management-plan.html. Accessed 4 February 2020.

References

Adkins, Lisa. 2017. "Speculative Futures in the Time of Debt." *The Sociological Review* 65, no. 3: 448–62.

Allen, Kim. 2014. "'Blair's Children': Young Women as 'Aspirational Subjects' in the Psychic Landscape of Class." *The Sociological Review* 62, no. 4: 760–79.

Carbonella, August, and Sharryn Kasmir. 2015. "Dispossession, Disorganization and the Anthropology of Labor." In *Anthropologies of Class: Power, Practice and Inequality*, edited by Don Kalb and John G. Carrier, 41–52. Cambridge, UK: Cambridge University Press.

Cruikshank, Barbara. 1999. *The Will to Empower: Democratic Citizens and Other Subjects*. Ithaca: Cornell University Press.

Davey, Ryan. 2019a. "Suspensory Indebtedness: Time, Morality and Power Asymmetry in Experiences of Consumer Debt." *Economy and Society* 48, no. 4: 532–53.

———. 2019b. "*Mise En Scène*: The Make-Believe Space of Over-Indebted Optimism." *Geoforum* 98 (January): 327–34.

Deeming, Chris, Sharon Collard, and David Hayes. 2011. *Affordable Credit: Lessons from Overseas. A Report Prepared for Consumer Focus by the Personal Finance Research Centre (PFRC)*. Bristol: University of Bristol.

Deville, Joe. 2015. *Lived Economies of Default: Consumer Credit, Debt Collection and the Capture of Affect*. Abingdon: Routledge.

Elyachar, Julia. 2005. *Markets of Dispossession: NGOs, Economic Development, and the State in Cairo*. Durham: Duke University Press.

Englund, Harri. 2008. "Extreme Poverty and Existential Obligations: Beyond Morality in the Anthropology of Africa?" *Social Analysis* 52: 33–50.

Finney, Andrea, and Sara Davies. 2011. *Facing the Squeeze 2011: A Qualitative Study of Household Finances and Access to Credit*. Bristol: Personal Finance Research Centre, University of Bristol.

Friedman, Jonathan. 2015. "Global Systemic Crisis, Class, and Its Representations." In *Anthropologies of Class: Power, Practice and Inequality*, edited by Don Kalb and John G. Carrier, 183–99. Cambridge, UK: Cambridge University Press.

Good, Byron. 1994. *Medicine, Rationality and Experience: An Anthropological Perspective*. Cambridge, UK: Cambridge University Press.

Graeber, David. 2014. "Anthropology and the Rise of the Professional-Managerial Class." *HAU: Journal of Ethnographic Theory* 4: 73–88.

Harvey, David. 2005. *The New Imperialism*. Oxford: Oxford University Press.

High, Holly. 2012. "Re-Reading the Potlatch in a Time of Crisis: Debt and the Distinctions That Matter." *Social Anthropology* 20: 363–79.

Hills, John. 2017. *Good Times, Bad times: The Welfare Myth of Them and Us*. Bristol: Policy Press.

Howe, Leo. 1990. *Being Unemployed in Northern Ireland: An Ethnographic Study*. Cambridge, UK: Cambridge University Press.

James, Deborah. 2020. "Owing Everyone: Debt Advice in the UK's Time of Austerity." *Ethnos*.

Jones, Owen. 2012. *Chavs: The Demonization of the Working Class*. London: Verso.

Kalb, Don. 2013. "Regimes of Value and Worthlessness: Two Stories I Know, Plus a Marxian Reflection." *Max Planck Institute for Social Anthropology Working Papers* 147.

———. 2015. "Introduction: Class and the New Anthropological Holism." In *Anthropologies of Class: Power, Practice and Inequality*, edited by Don Kalb and John G. Carrier, 1–27. Cambridge, UK: Cambridge University Press.

Kalb, Don, and Gábor Halmai. 2011. *Headlines of Nation, Subtexts of Class: Working-Class Populism and the Return of the Repressed in Neoliberal Europe*. New York: Berghahn Books.

Kempson, Elaine, Claire Whyley, John Caskey, and Sharon Collard. 2000. *In or Out? Financial Exclusion: A Literature and Research Review*. (Consumer Research Series). London: Financial Services Authority.

Kirwan, Samuel. 2019. "On 'Those Who Shout the Loudest': Debt Advice and the Work of Disrupting Attachments." *Geoforum* 98: 318–26.

Leyshon, Andrew, and Nigel Thrift. 1995. "Geographies of Financial Exclusion: Financial Abandonment in Britain and the United States." *Transactions of the Institute of British Geographers* 20, no. 3: 312–41.

Mollona, Massimiliano. 2009. *Made in Sheffield: An Ethnography of Industrial Work and Politics*. New York: Berghahn Books.

Morris, Lyida. 1993. "Is There a British Underclass?" *International Journal of Urban and Regional Research* 17, no. 3: 404–12.

———. 2002. *Dangerous Classes: The Underclass and Social Citizenship*. 2nd ed. London: Routledge.

Narotzky, Susana. 2015. "The Organic Intellectual and the Production of Class in Spain." In *Anthropologies of Class: Power, Practice and Inequality*, edited by Don Kalb and John G. Carrier, 53–71. Cambridge, UK: Cambridge University Press.

Pahl, Ray. 1984. *Divisions of Labour*. Oxford: Wiley-Blackwell.

Roitman, Janet. L. 2005. *Fiscal Disobedience: An Anthropology of Economic Regulation in Central Africa*. Princeton: Princeton University Press.

Skeggs, Beverley. 2003. *Class, Self, Culture*. London: Routledge.

———. 2015. "Introduction: Stratification or Exploitation, Domination, Dispossession and Devaluation?" *The Sociological Review* 63: 205–22.

Thompson, Edward P. 1991. *The Making of the English Working Class*. New ed. London: Penguin.

Tyler, Imogen. 2013. *Revolting Subjects: Social Abjection and Resistance in Neoliberal Britain*. London: Zed Books Ltd.

10

Making Debt Work

Devising and Debating Debt Collection in Croatia

Marek Mikuš

In March 2017, I accompanied Tea, my informant[1] in her early forties, to her bank branch in central Zagreb. She had already taken me to three appointments with her young "personal banker" Maja, the purpose of which was to negotiate a lower interest rate on the mortgage she was repaying with her husband, Denis. Maja told Tea a modest cut was possible; but because she had had repayment issues earlier, the bank demanded an additional instrument of repayment insurance. To meet this condition, Tea wanted to enroll into a pension fund as well as a housing savings scheme. However, when Maja turned to her computer, she found that Tea's current account had been "blocked" (*blokiran*) by Fina, a state-owned company. This was part of a procedure known formally as "enforcement over monetary assets."[2] In essence, current and future deposits on the person's bank accounts are seized for repayment of her mature liabilities. Tea was shocked—she was not aware of having any unpaid debts. Maja commented with her usual resigned cynicism: "That's what you get in the Republic of Croatia."

Tea and I walked over immediately to Fina's nearby headquarters. In a large hall with dozens of counters for "clients," we learned that Tea's original unpaid debt was 335 Croatian *kuna* (ca. €45) for five months of garbage collection services in 2014. However, her present liability was nearly 2,000 *kuna* (€270), about a quarter of her net wage. It included default interest, the fees of the public notary and the law office that conducted the proceedings, Fina's fees, and 25 percent VAT. The enforcement decision had been issued in mid-2015, but the law firm had waited nearly two years before asking Fina to execute it, allowing the interest to accumulate. We learned all this only after I had paid a fee for the printing of four pages of documentation and another fee for the payment of that fee, which made us laugh bitterly. Angry and frustrated, Tea suggested going for a shot of *rakija* although it was only 11 a.m. As we sipped the brandy, she told me that 2014 had been an especially tough period: she was changing jobs, and Denis had taken a big salary cut. At the time, Denis had been responsible for paying such bills. She believed he did but could not prove it. She preferred not to tell him anything so he would not get a heart attack. She was particularly angry about the high extra costs and the fact that nobody had told them about the debt earlier.

Tea's story illustrates several key features of Croatia's unique and controversial system of debt collection, which took its present form in the early 2010s. Previously, as Fina's legal expert told me, creditors had had to obtain a preliminary court enforcement decision and then try to access the debtor's bank accounts. Since banks were not legally bound to provide information in a timely manner, the procedure was basically defunct. This changed dramatically with amendments of enforcement laws from 2010 to 2012 (Menđušić Škugor 2018; Tafra 2015). Fina's direct predecessor in socialist Yugoslavia, the Social Accounting Service (Služba društvenog knjigovodstva, SDK), had a monopoly on domestic payments processing that Fina retained until 2002 (Tafra 2015: 46). It maintains an up-to-date registry of Croatian bank accounts, which enables it to execute enforcement across all accounts of any given individual within hours and to prevent evasion by transferring the account to another bank. Debtors are allowed to keep three quarters (before 2017, only two thirds) of their income, or two thirds of average net salary if their income is above average, by opening a Fina-authorized "protected account." After this enforcement mechanism was introduced, the number of "blocked" people went from about 34,000 in late 2011 to 320,000 by the end of 2017 (Fina 2012: 3, 2018b: 1). This amounted to 8 percent of Croatia's entire population (4.2 million). By November 2018, Fina has accepted 9.2 million requests for monetary assets enforcement, of which about three quarters were against natural persons (Fina 2018a). More than three quarters of all enforcement proceedings are executed through Fina (Menđušić Škugor 2018: 58).

Despite, or perhaps rather because of, Fina's apparent efficiency, citizens, activists, experts, media, and politicians increasingly criticize the Croatian debt collection system as one that privileges the interests of creditors and collection actors, entraps debtors in long-term over-indebtedness, and harms the national economy. There is no limit on the proportion of accumulated default interest and enforcement costs to the principal and, until recently, the duration of enforcement.[3] Limits on fees charged by collection actors are rather generous so that fees can inflate the total cost of enforcement significantly, especially in the case of small debts such as Tea's. Many debtors claim they learned about their debts only when their accounts were already blocked (Boban Valečić 2018; Tafra 2015: 46). In the last few years, an additional layer of controversy has emerged over the rapidly expanding activities of private, mostly foreign-owned debt collection companies. In short, debt collection in Croatia has become an issue of increasing practical and analytical significance, as it has elsewhere (see below). However, despite growing interest in debt, scholars have so far paid little attention to debt collection.

In this chapter, I draw on the Croatian case to analyze debt collection as a dynamic frontier of the financialization of households and social reproduction. It shores up financialization by making debt work when it would otherwise fail; but, as I shall show, manifold obstacles and challenges set in train a reembedding of debt in moral and political frameworks. The discussion is organized as follows. In the following section, I review the anthropological literature on credit/debt to identify debt collection as an "absent presence" and specify the relevance of the present study for this scholarship. The third section draws on the work of Joe Deville (2015) to unpack practices of debt collection in the United Kingdom in order to set up a comparative point of reference for the Croatian case. The fourth section analyses recent struggles over Croatian enforcement laws to identify key demands and initiatives for enforcement reform. In the final substantive section, I turn to the activities of private, mostly foreign-owned debt collection agencies.

Debt Collection: An Absent Presence in the Anthropology of Credit/Debt

Anthropology boasts a long history of reflection on credit/debt, in which an essay by Marcel Mauss ([1925] 2016) holds pride of place. What people in many societies refer to as a "gift" works in fact much like a credit/debt relationship, establishing ties of obligation and hierarchy alongside those of reciprocity and solidarity. Mauss's work is a good example of the anthropological tendency to "seek out the flow of credit/debt in modalities outside the standard market for such instruments" (Peebles 2010: 228)—in other words, modalities not oriented (only) to self-interested utility-maximization (High 2012). In this vein, anthropologists have investigated nonmainstream and/or non-Western, more or less "informal" forms of credit/debt (Durst 2015; Gregory 1997; Guérin, Morvant-Roux, and Villarreal 2014; James 2015; Mattioli 2018; Pedersen 2017), as well as Islamic finance (Maurer 2005, 2006; Pitluck, this volume). They have also documented the expansion of market-oriented lending in agricultural and pastoral societies (Shipton

2009, 2011; Sneath 2012), including ostensibly emancipatory and proentrepreneurial microcredit in the Global South (Elyachar 2005; Guérin 2014; Karim 2008; Moodie 2008). In recent years, doubtless related to the global crisis that began in 2007, anthropologists have joined other scholars in investigating "mainstream" (i.e., formal) lending to households (Halawa 2015; Han 2012; James 2012, 2014, 2015; Palomera 2014; Sabaté 2016; Suarez 2017; Weiss 2014; Barrett, Buier, and Kofti, this volume). The formal/informal boundary should not be reified; ethnography shows how the two types of practices often overlap or mimic each other in practice (Durst 2015; James 2015: 5–7; Mattioli 2018; Mikuš 2019; Suarez 2017: 267, 269). In this chapter, the focus is thus on formal lending in the sense of legal formalization (through legally effective contracts and property rights) that the discussed debt collection practices require; but precisely what this legality entails may be disputed and uncertain.

Increasing anthropological interest in debt is a reflection of its importance in contemporary life. Numerous scholars have addressed the crises of public debt and subsequent austerity policies (Bear 2015; Herzfeld 2011; Rakopoulous 2018; Song 2009; Theodossopoulos 2013). Debt is becoming a "total social fact" promising explanations of all kinds of social relationships (Graeber 2011; High 2012: 364; Lazzarato 2012: 32). The expansion of household debt is one aspect of this totality. It has been driven by financial deregulation, welfare cuts, changing business models of banks, and stagnating real wages (dos Santos 2009; Fuller 2016; Soederberg 2014). The concept of financialization, understood as a transformation of capitalist societies under the increasing dominance of finance (van der Zwan 2014: 99–100; Kalb, this volume), is another way to grasp this totality.

While some anthropologists have turned conventional (often moralistic) discourse about debt upside down by arguing that debt can be "productive" for debtors (Peebles 2010: 227; Roitman 2005: 73–99), in this chapter, I focus on the more obvious productivity of debt for lenders. Through the provision of credit to households, holders of loanable capital extract profits (interest and fees) from their income. Beyond this direct exploitation, debt exposes individuals and households to the vagaries of financial markets and financialized housing markets (through adjustable interest rates, exchange rates, housing prices), subjects them to financial discipline (through repayment schedules) and calculation (through credit scoring and risk-based pricing), and increases their vulnerability to economic cycles (Beggs, Bryan, and Rafferty 2014; Bryan, Martin, and Rafferty 2009; Değirmencioğlu and Walker 2015; LeBaron 2014; Roberts 2016; Soedeberg 2014; Buier and Kofti, this volume). At the same time, the emergence of predictably financialized subjects cannot be taken for granted, as ethnographic studies document people's efforts to "domesticate" debt for agendas of well-being and social mobility (Guérin 2014; Guérin, Morvant-Roux, and Villarreal 2014; Han 2012: 31–38; James 2015).

Overall, anthropologists and other scholars researching household debt have paid surprisingly little attention to what happens when debtors stop repaying—when debt becomes "nonperforming" and its productivity for capital is disrupted (Deville 2015: xiii–xv; but cf. Elyachar 2005: 199–200; Kar 2013; James 2015: 73–76, 113; Davey, James, and Kofti, this volume). Peebles's review of the anthropology of credit/debt makes virtually no reference to nonrepayment, default, and debt collection, apart from a brief discussion of corporate bankruptcy (Peebles 2010: 229). Yet debt collection plays an important, albeit mostly implicit, role in several key themes in the anthropology of credit/debt—it is a kind of absent presence. As has frequently been noted, debt establishes materially effective links between past, present, and future (Halawa 2015; James 2015: 15, 219; Peebles 2010: 227). The necessity for credit money to "return to its place of origin for redemption" (Harvey [1982] 2006: 46) describes the very essence of credit as a financial device and social relationship (Christophers 2011: 1078–79). But what if the debtor defaults? Expectations of repayment presuppose an effective mechanism of debt collection. The same is true when anthropologists emphasize how power relationships determine who has to repay debt (despite the hegemonic moral notion of debt as "something that must be paid back") (Graeber 2011: 1–17; High 2012: 364). If debt tends to be associated with hierarchy and its refusal with freedom and sovereignty (Peebles 2010: 230), it is precisely because, by entering into a credit/debt relationship, the debtor submits to a future possibility of being *forced* to repay. Whether this succeeds will depend, inter alia, on available means of debt enforcement. Finally, debt collection is an absent presence also in the sense of being the obvious contemporary locus of the association of debt with violence, which anthropologists discussed so far in historical contexts of slavery and debtors' prisons (Graeber 2009, 2011, 2012; Peebles 2012, 2013; on today's debtor prisons, see LeBaron and Roberts 2012; Roberts 2014; Wamsley 2019). In summary, debt collection is a crucial mechanism and stage in the unfolding of many credit/debt relationships: the point at which coercion is used to "rematerialize the temporal bond" (Peebles 2010: 227) previously established between the parties, with a range of possible outcomes. It deserves more explicit and sustained attention than it has received to date.

Devices and Politics of Debt Collection

Literature on personal over-indebtedness and bankruptcy (Micklitz and Domurath 2015; Niemi, Ramsay, and Whitford 2009), though informative, tends to focus on laws and formal procedures rather than the actual processes of debt collection. Relevant work in radical political economy focuses on institutions and analysis of aggregate data (LeBaron and Roberts 2012; Roberts 2014; Wamsley 2019). Against this backdrop, Joe Deville (2015) offered welcome insights into the practices and experiences of unsecured debt collection in the United Kingdom. Aiming to transcend morally charged binaries about defaulted debtors (as either victims or irresponsible spendthrifts) and debt collectors (as either bullies or guardians of payment discipline), he engages instead with the actual workings of debt collection. Unlike Deville (2015: 16–17, n. 1), I did not conduct observation in collection firms (however brief in Deville's own case) or listen to recordings of collection calls. Such methods were not feasible in Croatia. Private collection firms release very little data about their activities, preferring to rely on glitzy websites and promotional materials. Some of their employees were taken aback even by very basic questions about their work and preferred to change the subject. My data set therefore consists of interviews and informal interactions with four current or former employees of debt collection agencies, two employees of banks' internal collection departments, six debtors who experienced debt collection, and ten professionals/experts (lawyers, bankers, employees of Fina and companies providing credit and debt restructuring services to overindebted people), as well as publicly available data, media and online contents (including accounts of debt collection experiences and photos of collection letters), and promotional materials.

Deville situates his work within the tradition of "social studies of finance" (SSF) inspired by Latourian actor-network theory (ANT). He is therefore particularly interested in (market) "devices" (see Muniesa, Millo, and Callon 2007), such as collection letters and phone calls, and their work of "economization" (i.e., enabling and stimulating market-oriented, calculative engagements) (Çalışkan and Callon 2009, 2010; Callon 1998). Collection devices are market devices par excellence since they make "optimal use of the anticipatory landscape of default as *a space for the generation of calculative attention*" (Deville 2015: 60, emphasis in original). However, Deville goes beyond the conventional SSF framework in two key respects. First, he emphasizes how collection devices are developed for the purposes of the "capture of affect." Debtors are led to feel fear and anxiety about the possible legal consequences of nonrepayment, which collectors invoke to threaten while deliberately leaving them opaque (Deville 2015: 115–19). Market devices are not "just concerned with the making of markets"; they also elicit engagement outside "economic" registers (Deville 2015: 10). Second, Deville attends to the politics of debt collection, which is laudable in itself in view of the tendency of SSF to neglect the dimension of power

(Mirowski and Nik-Khan 2007). He emphasizes the unequal capacities of debtors and collectors to format "the anticipatory landscape of default" (Deville 2015: 112–42). The strategically constructed distinction between consumer lending and debt collection, in particular the threatening representation of collection firms as not sharing the scruples of original creditors, helps to "amplify calculative opacity" (Deville 2015: 143–67).

However, due to a combination of his theoretical commitments and the empirical context in the UK, Deville (2015: 46) still takes collection relationships to be fundamentally market relationships of "producers" and "consumers/customers." Their interactional emergence is described as a way of making visible how "relations we might identify as broadly capitalist come into being" and as preferable to "abstractions" such as capitalism and neoliberalism that obscure those processes (Deville 2015: 172–73). But Deville himself recognizes that interactions are often "formatted" by pre-existing structures beyond the market. For example, we learn that British collection firms prefer noncoercive methods of initiating repayment since their activities are more regulated and enforcement through the court is less effective than in the United States (Deville 2015: 114). Similarly, my analysis of the Croatian case will demonstrate that the effectiveness and immediacy of the threat of coercion depends to a significant extent on the evolved institutional context, and in particular on the forms in which state law enables a range of actors to use coercion to collect debts (see also Roberts 2014).

"Enforcement Has Become Business": Debating Enforcement, Envisaging Alternatives

Since 2010–2012, Fina has played a key role in enforcement where monetary assets (and later real estate) are concerned. Creditors or their lawyers can trigger enforcement by serving Fina with either "private documents" (for example debentures signed by debtors) or, as in Tea's case, "enforcement decisions" issued by public notaries on the basis of private documents, invoices, business books, or other "authentic documents" (Fina n.d.). This system was presented as a fix for the ineffectiveness of the previous court-based mechanism, which had generated a huge backlog and been noted as an issue during Croatia's EU integration process (CJEU 2016: 3–5; EC 2010: 2–8). The "externalization of certain judicial functions to Fina" (Menđušić Škugor 2018: 58) became part of a broader dejudicialization of enforcement, as a result of which enforcement proceedings routinely bypass the courts.[4] The enforcement reforms were made shortly after the climax of Croatia's household debt boom, which took a semiperipheral form similar to other Eastern and Southern European countries in the 2000s. Croatian banks, following their near-total foreign takeover around 2000, imported large amounts of capital borrowed from their Western European mothers or in interbank money markets and lent them out at higher interest rates in Croatia. As in other similar settings, monetary policies maintaining high interest rates and overvalued exchange rates supported a (semi) peripheral pattern of financialization associated with fragile growth, deindustrialization, the deepening of current account and trade deficits, and growing external debt (Becker et al. 2010; Gabor 2010; López and Rodríguez 2011; Radošević and Cvijanović 2015; Rodrigues, Santos, and Teles 2016). Much of the household lending took high-risk and predatory forms, including foreign exchange loans, loans with interest rates that creditors could adjust at will, poor credit checks, and various illegal practices (Bohle 2014, 2018; Burton 2017; Mikuš 2019; Rodik and Žitko 2015). After Croatia had sunk into protracted economic stagnation in 2008, the share of nonperforming loans (NPLs) in total bank loans to households rose from 4 percent in 2008 to a peak of more than 12 percent in 2015 (CNB 2011: 23, 2017: 22, 14). Croatia posts one of the highest rates of arrears on utility bills in the EU (Eurostat 2019b), and its share of arrears on "hire purchase installments or other loan payments" is well above the average (Eurostat 2019a).

The enforcement reforms did not improve the above indicators in the years after their passing; the improvement that has occurred more recently (since 2015) is probably attributable rather to the resumption of economic growth.[5] The government nevertheless expressed its satisfaction with the "expedience and efficiency" of the new system (Republic of Croatia 2013: 67). While most individual politicians were more wary, Justice Minister Dražen Bošnjaković was quoted as saying, "Croatia has the best enforcement law in the world" (Šimatović 2018: 5). Although the Enforcement Law and the Enforcement over Monetary Assets Law were amended on numerous occasions, the fundamentals did not change. Changes in the ruling political party did not make a difference either—while the right-wing Croatian Democratic Union (HDZ) led the governments in 2009–2011 and from 2016 onward, the coalition ruling in 2012–2015 was led by the center-left Social Democratic Party (SDP).

Fina itself was a vocal advocate of the enforcement system in which it played such a central role. Its legal adviser, Verica, told me that the current legislation was "definitely effective." Fina's infrastructures such as the Unified Accounts Registry made enforcement proceedings more feasible and fast. The "neutrality" and "inevitability" of enforcement were guaranteed by the fact that Fina was required only to verify the formal requirements of enforcement applications, not their substantive validity—that is, whether they were based on actual legal claims. The legality of enforcement could only be challenged in court when enforcement was already ongoing or even completed and the fees of Fina and other parties duly charged. While citizens criticize precisely these features, Verica characterized them as essential for speed and impartiality (including the prevention of corruption). Fina (2016) also pointed out that its fees, unlike those of notaries and lawyers, were fixed. They were not a percentage of the claim to be pursued "in order to make greatest possible profit at the expense of those subjected to enforcement." Fina claimed that it kept costs low for everybody—yet its charges often seemed extortionate, such as the equivalent of 2€ (or 6€ for companies) for printing one page of documentation (Wiesner 2018b).

Negative views of the enforcement system were widespread in Croatian society. To begin with, enforcement was high on the agenda of various civic associations and social movements dealing with household debt, some of which became junior parliamentary or extraparliamentary parties (Mikuš 2019). The association known as Blocked Ones (Blokirani) has demanded a "deblocking" of those currently subjected to enforcement and the passing of a new law that would make enforcement once again the responsibility of the courts (Jutarnji.hr 2018; Novak 2017). The organization achieved considerable media visibility, though other debt activists have criticized it for its PR-based modus operandi and undeveloped organizational structures.

Another political actor dealing with enforcement issues is Human Shield (Živi zid, literally "Living Wall"), an up-and-coming parliamentary party. "Eviction obstructions" typically involve activists (sometimes with additional supporters) physically resisting the eviction of the former owners of a home who had been subjected to enforcement. The inherent drama of such events, promoted on social media, stimulated media and public interest. HS leaders use strong rhetoric about "modern-age slavery" and "enforcement mafia" to criticize the enforcement system in general (Hina 2018).

In March 2017, I attended a street protest organized by the extraparliamentary party Free Croatia, set up by former HS members, and an informal group of debtors of Raiffeisen credit-savings cooperatives from Austria, many of whom faced home repossessions (Mikuš 2019: 302–6). The protest took place on one of the best-known squares in central Zagreb under the title *Get Out and Get Rid of Imposed Debts!* It was followed by a series of protests at the same spot at the same time of day over seven consecutive days. While turnout was modest, the event was later described as the launch of the "Enforcement Uprising," an ongoing online and protest-based campaign (Ovršni ustanak n.d.). The event began with a speech by the Free Croatia leader, Danijel Galović, in which he connected the recent wave of emigration from Croatia to debt-enforcement issues. Rejecting the usual explanations in terms of poverty and unemployment as "liberal capitalist swinery" (*liberalno-kapitalističke svinjarije*), he argued that emigration was the real purpose of the "cannibalistic Enforcement Law," with the ultimate goal of justifying the import of cheap migrant labor to Croatia. Other Free Croatia members and their allies attributed suicides and demographic decline to the pernicious enforcement system. They called for a new Enforcement Law that would be "humane" and "tailored for the people."[6]

Critics accuse Fina of abusing its legal monopoly over particular services to charge excessive fees and of being more concerned with profit than the social implications of its activities, though one would expect otherwise from a state-owned company (Tafra 2015; Wiesner 2018b). The influence of political elites over the company has given rise to conspiracy theories. For example, it is sometimes asserted that its "true" owners are (the wives of) well-known politicians. Similar arguments are made about what one newspaper headline described as the "chain of parasites" (Šimatović 2018) in enforcement proceedings, namely lawyers and public notaries. It is widely held that their enforcement business is often part of clientelistic relationships in which large companies and banks favor leading law firms by "giving them" the bulk of their enforcement agenda and the lawyers then have to "return the favor" somehow. A notorious example is Hanžeković & Partners, a leading Croatian law firm that conducts tens of thousands of enforcement proceedings against natural persons. The claim-holders include major public sector organizations such as HRT, the state TV, and, as in the case of proceedings against Tea described at the beginning of this chapter, Zagrebački holding, a large service-providing company owned by the City of Zagreb. The controversial head of the law firm, late Marijan Hanžeković, also owned Hanza Media, a leading media corporation. Some of my interlocutors hinted that his ownership of influential Croatian media enabled him to repay his substantial enforcement commissions through positive coverage of his clients.

This self-serving and potentially clientelistic nature of the enforcement system is increasingly seen as a matter of fact. In a 2018 televised interview, Renata Duka, formerly Assistant Justice Minister and a member of working groups that drafted several amendments of the Enforcement Law from 2013 to 2016, noted that "enforcement has become a business" and that the making of the legislation was captured by "interest groups" (Duka 2018). In her view, the fees of law firms and notaries and the powers of notaries to initiate extrajudicial enforcement were particularly problematic. One consequence of this bitter ongoing debate is that an alternative concept of enforcement has become familiar and popular with the Croatian public—one in which it is not an unrestrained "business" but instead a low-cost, regulated public service. People do not contest the institution of enforcement *per se*; debates unfold over more specific issues, such as the ratio of additional costs to actual debts, the legitimacy of the roles played by particular actors, and the (lack of) transparency of the entire system. The repossession of owner-occupied real estate is perceived as a moral dilemma in its own right. Here, activists and politicians have campaigned to raise the minimum value of claims on the basis of which such property can be repossessed, and to ensure that this occurs only in legally clear-cut cases, as a last resort, and without selling the repossessed real estate for excessively low prices. Overall, despite their sometimes-technical character, the proposals debated in recent years imply potentially far-reaching changes in debt collection, defined in reference to narrowly "economic" as well as moral considerations. But pragmatic responses by governments so far have stopped short of scrapping the technique of blockades, and there has been no modification of the central role of Fina, which policymakers continue to see as the key to the "expedience and efficiency" of the enforcement system.

"A Very Polite Terrorizing": The Rise of Debt Collection Agencies

During the same years in which it became increasingly politicized, Croatia's debt collection system underwent significant changes based on market-based and profit-oriented agency: the vertiginous expansion of specialized private debt collection agencies. Several such companies, known formally as "claims collection agencies" (*agencije za naplatu potraživanja*), were formed in the 1990s. However, the biggest players entered the market more recently. EOS Matrix Ltd., part of the German EOS Group posting 138m *kuna* revenues in 2016, was established in 2008. B2 Kapital Ltd., part of the Norwegian B2Holding with 262m *kuna* revenues in 2016, was founded in 2013. Competitors seem to be significantly smaller, though some newcomers have expanded rapidly (Lider 2017). There are now about fifteen to twenty collection agencies, most of them foreign-owned. According to my industry interlocutors, the two largest companies had 150–200 employees at the time of my fieldwork. The main departments, at least in the largest companies, are colloquially known to insiders as "collection" (or "operations"), "skiptracing," "legal," and "acquisitions." Collection departments tend to be the largest. At least in one of the largest companies in which I was allowed a peek inside, it resembled a standard open-space call center.

The expansion of the biggest players is closely linked to the recent increase in banks' sales of bad loans. Telecom companies were the first to sell claims on natural persons, while banks hesitated to do so. According to my interlocutors, companies such as telecoms and utilities sell off portfolios consisting of large numbers of small claims, while bank NPL portfolios contain larger claims on average and are themselves larger than other portfolios. While banks sold only about 53m *kuna* worth (gross) of NPLs in 2011, a huge jump to 5.9bn *kuna* occurred in 2012. Smaller but still significant volumes were sold in 2013 and 2014. Growth then resumed, and a new peak of 8.1bn NPLs was reached in 2017.

The media tended to present the activities of these agencies in a highly negative manner. The standard term *utjerivači dugova* (literally "debt enforcers") might sound neutral, but it has pejorative connotations and would perhaps be more accurately translated as "extortionists." Collection industry representatives were highly critical of this label, which they dismissed as tendentious and sensationalist media coverage. In some online blogs and articles, even more aggressive phrases such as "legal usurers" (*legalni kamatari*) are used (Blokirani n.d.). Human Shield MPs described the agencies' practices as "daily terror" and "human rights abuses," and proposed a draft Law on Protection of Debtors in Special Cases of Claims Transfers (Sinčić 2017). They further accused the agencies of breaking legal rules on limitation and called for restrictions on personal data transfers in debt purchase transactions (Bunjac 2017).

The agencies are most often criticized for persistent and intrusive attempts to make contact with the debtor by telephone. One "victim" told the media that he had been called up to eleven times a day (Gregorović 2016). Another practice is skiptracing: calls are made to the debtor's neighbors and/or relatives in an effort to determine their place of residence and/ or extract contact details. It is alleged that this results in unwanted disclosures of personal financial issues. Collection agency representatives, for their part, insist that their agents do not disclose the subject of their communication with the debtor to other persons. They do, however, mention the name of the company. In particularly dramatic narratives, it is claimed that, after being called by an agency, the debtor landed in an emergency department or suffered depression, high blood pressure, ulcers, weight loss, and other health problems (Kramarić 2016a, 2016b).

Self-representations and the justifications proffered by industry representatives often seem like a mirror image of the negative coverage. Compared to Deville's UK collection firms, their Croatian counterparts seem to find it necessary to soften rather than to maintain/amplify their public representation as ruthless and unscrupulous. For example, managers admit that their agents call debtors persistently, but argue that this is an indispensable aspect of their work. By doing so, agencies in fact "help" debtors, since when the latter are finally contacted and agree to resume repayment, they avoid further accumulation of default interest and enforcement costs (see also Gregorović 2016). Staff also stress that they do not charge debtors any additional fees: they merely demand the repayment of principal and default interest. Managers position themselves as actors who make the system cheaper for debtors, as opposed to those profiting from enforcement—Fina, lawyers, and notaries. This argument is based on the distinction between enforcement and voluntary repayment (see below). In an interview, the EOS Matrix director further insisted that they do not buy debts for water or electricity, only those for loans and telecom services (Wiesner 2018a), thereby making a moral claim that implies classifying the former as primary needs and the latter as optional, perhaps even luxurious. She stressed the agency's individualized approach and claimed, "We are accommodating toward welfare cases (*socijalni slučajevi*) and overindebted citizens as far as we can, if they document their status." In practice, this means agencies accept small repayment installments "temporarily," or they postpone suing the debtor. Those who can repay more steadily or even in a single payment are eligible to receive various benefits and sometimes previously initiated legal proceedings are suspended as a reward. The agencies brand their agents "collection advisers" or "financial advisers" and portray their work as counseling people on how to deal sensibly with their debts. Their promotional publications talk about "amicable solutions" (EOS Group 2017: 25) and highlight the industry's supposed systemic role of ensuring liquidity and payment discipline, thus functioning as an "engine of the economy" (EOS Group 2017: 19). An additional mode of justifying industry activities as a kind of neocolonial *mission civilisatrice* derives from the fact that most of these agencies in Croatia and other postsocialist European countries have foreign owners. It is well established that debt collection groups owned by capital from Western Europe or richer Eastern European countries expand to poorer Eastern European countries. Some have a near-exclusive focus on the region.[7]

However, the actual practices of these agencies often do not correspond to their rosy self-promotion. As some debtors told me, agents' calls may be extremely persistent, and they do not necessarily cease when the debtor has given objective reasons for not being able to repay. The objective of semiautomatized, IT-assisted recurrent calls (called "dialing" by the agencies) is to make debtors recognize their debts and start voluntary repayment. Small installments are encouraged and accepted in the beginning, but they are only temporary. After half a year or so, the agency will apply psychological pressure on the debtor to increase the rate of repayment. Agencies also try to stimulate voluntary repayment by promising that when the debtor has repaid the entire principal, they will write off all the interest.[8]

In addition to phone calls, agencies also send letters to debtors, mostly standard mail but occasionally also emails or even Facebook messages. I was able to see several types of such letters. They included cession notices, which the acquirer of a debt is legally obliged to send the debtor upon acquisition. Such notices inform the debtor that the ownership of the claim has changed, who the new owner is, and how much the total claim is (sometimes but not always broken down to principal, default interest, and fees). They further demand repayment in a one-off payment, sometimes without quoting a deadline and sometimes specifying it simply as "NOW." Another type of letter makes an offer of a big "discount" (20 to 50 percent of the total debt) if the debtor repays in a single payment within a short period of time. Finally, there are final notice warnings before enforcement is initiated, which often include a prefilled check for a cash payment at the post office. These letters or checks often include payment deadlines very shortly after or even before the letter is received, presumably to increase the sense of urgency. The letters are generally quite formal and dry. There is less experimentation with format, colors, fonts, or more emotional phrasing than Deville (2015: 143–64) described in the British context, with the partial exception of "discount offers." As in the British case, however, threats and attempts to capture forms of affect such as fear and anxiety are explicit in the final notice letters, some of which specify that if the enforcement over monetary assets is unsuccessful, the claimholder will attempt to enforce over the debtor's real estate and movable property. Interviewed debtors who received such letters were later often afraid to open correspondence.

One of the most important contradictions between how the agencies seek to present themselves and their actual practices concerns their use of legal coercion. While agency representatives emphasize how they see enforcement against debtors as the measure of last resort, in interviews, they admitted that if enforcement had been initiated by the previous claimholder before they bought the claim, they seldom stopped it and instead let it continue while attempting to convince the debtor to make additional voluntary repayment. If there is no voluntary repayment at all, or if it is considered to be insufficient, the agency will initiate enforcement eventually, at least when it makes sense economically. A low-level manager in one of the biggest companies told me that enforcement proceedings are periodically initiated against entire "segments of clients," for example those who have made no repayment in the past two years. Resorting to Croatia's highly procreditor and often-brutal enforcement system is thus a very real threat in the supposedly "amicable" dealings between agencies and clients. This institutional background to their practices is crucial; yet it would be easily overlooked with an SSF-type approach focusing on devices, even one that pays attention to the use of affect.

Croatia has no laws regulating the work of these agencies. They all emphasize that they have their internal codes of conduct and also observe the rules of the European industry association FENCA. But compliance is nonenforceable and subject to no external supervision. In spite of rhetoric concerning professional and ethical training, a former skiptracing agent told me that training and supervision were minimal and limited almost exclusively to instrumental aspects of the work. This interlocutor resigned after a particularly disturbing call with a mentally unstable debtor who threatened to kill herself and her small children. He had previously witnessed various practices he found morally objectionable, such as agents trying to convince debtors to start repaying through manipulative statements such as, "Do you want your kids not to have money for lunch?" Skiptracing agents are commonly casual student workers on short-term contracts who earn about €3 an hour.

Nevertheless, debtors are not entirely powerless either. They commonly ignore phone calls from the agencies and resort to blocking strategies or changing their phone numbers. Long lists of numbers used by the agencies have been posted on online forums. Many debtors believe (inaccurately) that it is advisable not to repay anything because this would constitute an "admission" of the debt. This is connected to a belief that one does not need to repay to the agency, because they have no written agreement with them, only with the original claimholder (in fact, cession of claims based on consumer loans became unambiguously legal in 2013). A more drastic strategy of debt evasion is to move abroad. Skiptracing is supposed to extend to such debtors, but this does not always succeed. Even when it does, the requisite international legal arrangements may not be in place. I was also told by agency workers that some debtors attempt to negotiate a substantial write-off by arguing that the agency had bought the claim at a large discount, and that therefore the debt does not have its original value any more.

Concluding Remarks

I have argued that institutions and practices of debt collection deserve much more attention than they have so far received in scholarship on credit/debt and financialization in anthropology and beyond. Debt collection is a stage in the life cycle of many credit/debt relationships; it is the site at which "bad" debts are "fixed." As such, it is the major site of power dynamics and violence that anthropologists associate with credit/debt in the abstract but have not yet systematically explored in all its concrete forms. Beyond individual credit/debt relationships, an effective debt collection system is also crucial for the reproduction of the market-based credit system. However, while I started from a conceptualization of debt collection that emphasized this functional aspect, the analysis showed that debt collection is more than this; it is also the terrain on which broader debates and struggles over debt and its social embedding unfold.

The case of Croatia is instructive due to the explicitness and concreteness of the public debate about debt collection. This debate demonstrates the central role of the state in debt collection, in particular through its capacity to set the terms of legitimate coercion. On the one hand, the prerogatives and material infrastructures of the state have been mobilized to create an exceptionally disciplinary and procreditor debt collection system. On the other hand, activists and politicians channel the growing social discontent with this system in a number of ways whose combined effect is to build up pressure on established political elites to make it more equitable and efficient. At the same time, debt collection agencies exploit the dysfunctionalities of the system and a lack of regulation to introduce changes through market-based, profit-oriented innovations. While some of these changes might be an improvement on the status quo, the agencies' practices generate new forms of abuse and suffering which then become objects of contestation and attempts at reregulation.

The Croatian case also points to variations in financialization processes and the social formations in which these are embedded. Like Greece, Croatia experienced a household debt boom driven by capital inflows, leading to major problems after the bust. However, strategies for dealing with bad household loans were rather different. While the Croatian state facilitated extrajudicial enforcement against debtors (and allowed for robust profit-making on these proceedings), Dimitra Kofti (this volume) describes how the Greek state empowered debtors to apply for judicial debt relief.[9] While Croatian banks (with some delay) sold off much of their NPLs to collection agencies, their Greek counterparts resisted the pressures of the European Central Bank to do this, instead keeping NPLs on their books and undertaking the work of collection agencies (such as encouraging modest voluntary repayment) in-house (Streinzer 2018). Speculatively, we might connect this difference to the low rate of foreign bank ownership in Greece. Beyond the different levels of influence over banks, Croatian political elites might be tentatively characterized as generally operating in a more technocratic and elitist mode than their Greek counterparts, with clear continuities with the preceding period of postsocialist privatization, internationalization, and the peripheral financialization of Croatia's political economy. While Greek politicians faced an insurgent public in the setting of a draconian, internationally imposed austerity program, more limited mobilizations in Croatia allowed local leaders to focus on the final steps of EU integration processes. It is revealing that the EU itself authorized the Croatian approach to enforcement reform by defining the backlog of enforcement cases as the main problem to be fixed, rather than the ways in which enforcement takes place. The limited scope of popular resistance has allowed policymakers to let the particularistic interests of collection actors, both public and private, to dominate ongoing reform processes.

Acknowledgments

I undertook revisions of this chapter as a Research Fellow in "Western Banks in Eastern Europe: New Geographies of Financialisation" (GEOFIN), a research project based at Trinity College Dublin and funded by the European Research Council under the European Union's Horizon 2020 program (grant agreement no. 683197). Laura Bear and an anonymous reviewer read various versions of the text and offered helpful comments.

Marek Mikuš received his PhD in Anthropology at the LSE in 2014 and is currently Head of the Emmy Noether Research Group "Peripheral Debt: Money, Risk and Politics in Eastern Europe" at the Max Planck Institute for Social Anthropology. He studies finance (especially household debt), civil society, the state, public policy, and political economy in former Yugoslavia and East-Central Europe. His publications include *Frontiers of Civil Society: Government and Hegemony in Serbia* (Berghahn Books, 2018).

Notes

1. In 2016–17, I undertook five months of fieldwork on household indebtedness in Zagreb, Croatia. I observed activist meetings, banking events, court hearings, protests, evictions, and other relevant situations and conducted more than ninety in-depth interviews with debtors, bankers, activists, regulators, lawyers, experts, and various household lending and debt collection professionals. This chapter is based on a subset of this data as explained below.
2. Involuntary collection of mature claims on both natural and legal persons is known as *ovrha* under Croatian law. An authoritative handbook defined *ovrha* as a "series of legally regulated and functionally coordinated actions of the court, parties and other participants in proceedings aimed at an enforced realization of the claim of the enforcement-seeking party" (Dika 2007: 7). The term is usually translated as "execution" or "enforcement" (also in EU documents). In addition to enforcement over monetary assets, Croatian law also provides for enforcement over immovable (real estate) and movable property. In this chapter, I use the terms "enforcement" to refer to *ovrha* proceedings and "collection" to debt collection practices more broadly, including enforcement as well as "voluntary" repayment.
3. The latter changed with the entry into force of a new Enforcement over Monetary Assets Law in August 2018, according to which enforcement proceedings against

natural persons (with some exceptions) are suspended when the entire liability has not been repaid within the past three years *and* no money has been confiscated from the debtor's accounts toward repayment of the liability in the past six months. However, the creditor may subsequently start new enforcement proceedings for the same liability.

4. Public notaries had been empowered to issue enforcement decisions as early as 2005 (FIIAP 2016: 12). Hungary appears to be the only other European country with a similar role for notaries (Harsági 2011). Another mechanism of enforcement, which bypasses the courts as well as Fina and notaries, is to serve the debtor's employer with a "statement of consent to the garnishment of wages" signed by the debtor (Jakić 2015).

5. Following six years of recession from 2009 to 2014, Croatia's GDP has returned to growth since 2015 (Eurostat 2019d). Consumption expenditure of households copied the dynamics of GDP growth: it was falling from 2009 to 2014 (with the exception of one year) and growing since 2015 (Eurostat 2019c).

6. At the end, Danijel Galović read a list of demands for enforcement reform that brought together the key issues around which the public debate coalesced: the technique of account "blockade"; high costs/fees in enforcement proceedings; the questionable roles of particular actors (Fina, notaries); the dejudicialization of enforcement; and the repossession of homes.

7. For example, the Czech APS Holding has branches exclusively in postsocialist European countries, except those in Cyprus, Greece, and Vietnam. The Netherlands-based Creditexpress Group (whose Croatian subsidiary is CEI Zagreb Ltd.) is only active in postsocialist Europe, while the Slovenian Pro Kolekt group, present in Croatia under that name, is even more narrowly focused on postsocialist South East Europe (former Yugoslavia, Romania, and Bulgaria). The Croatian website of B2Holding latches onto the Norwegian origins of the company and boasts about their "Norwegian model of comprehensive financial services in receivables collection and management" (B2 Kapital n.d.) without explaining what the model actually is. According to the website of CEI Zagreb, the company combines "legal certainty, compliance with agreements and enforcement of agreements [that] have a centuries-long tradition in the countries of Northern Europe" with "professional experience, competence and local knowledge that is unique for the territory of Central and Eastern Europe" (CEI Zagreb n.d.).

8. This typically seems to take the form of a mere verbal agreement. These offers benefit only debtors in relatively better positions, as reflected in their ability to access a substantial sum of money at a short notice.

9. Croatia introduced the institute of personal bankruptcy in 2016, likewise in the form of judicial proceedings. However, it has been so far used by a very small number of people, presumably due to tough requirements imposed on debtors (enforcement over their property, loss of much of their income and financial autonomy, and subjection to a monitoring of their behavior over a period of five years, only after which remaining debts are written off).

References

B2 Kapital. n.d. "Home page." Accessed 16 December 2018. http://b2kapital.hr.

Bear, Laura. 2015. *Navigating Austerity: Currents of Debt along a South Asian River.* Stanford, CA: Stanford University Press.

Becker, Joachim, Johannes Jäger, Bernhard Leubolt, and Rudy Weissenbacher. 2010. "Peripheral Financialization and the Vulnerability to Crisis: A Regulationist Perspective." *Competition & Change* 14, no. 3–4: 225–47.

Beggs, Mike, Dick Bryan, and Michael Rafferty. 2014. "'Shoplifters of the World Unite!' Law and Culture in Financialized Times." *Cultural Studies* 28, no. 5–6: 976–96.

Blokirani. n.d. "Kako dolazi do bogaćenja dioničara ovršnog postupka (B2 Kapital i država)." Accessed 3 October 2019. U.

Boban Valečić, Iva. 2018. "Novi Ovršni zakon bolji, ali ne pomaže građanima u dugotrajnim blokadama." Accessed 3 October 2019. https://www.vecernji.hr/vijesti/novi-ovrsni-zakon-bolji-ali-ne-pomaze-gra-anima-u-dugotrajnim-blokad ama-1261758.

Bohle, Dorothee. 2014. "Post-socialist Housing Meets Transnational Finance: Foreign Banks, Mortgage Lending, and the Privatization of Welfare in Hungary and Estonia." *Review of International Political Economy* 21, no. 4: 913–48.

———. 2018. "Mortgaging Europe's Peripheries." *Studies in Comparative International Development* 53, no. 2: 196–217.

Bryan, Dick, Randy Martin, and Mike Rafferty. 2009. "Financialization and Marx: Giving Labor and Capital a Financial Makeover." *Review of Radical Political Economics* 41, no. 4: 458–72.

Bunjac, Branimir. 2017. "Speech in the Croatian Parliament. 6 April 2017." Accessed 31 August 2018. https://www.youtube.com/watch?v=-UchTVTFEL4.

Burton, Dawn. 2017. "Credit Inclusion and the Home Credit Market in Post-communist Member States of the European Union." *Critical Social Policy* 37, no. 3: 444–63.

Çalışkan, Koray, and Michel Callon. 2009. "Economization, Part 1: Shifting Attention from the Economy towards Processes of Economization." *Economy and Society* 38, no. 3: 369–98.

Çalışkan, Koray, and Michel Callon. 2010. "Economization, Part 2: A Research Programme for the Study of Markets." *Economy and Society* 39, no. 1: 1–32.

Callon, Michel, ed. 1998. *The Laws of the Markets.* Oxford: Blackwell.

CEI Zagreb. n.d. "O nama." Accessed 3 October 2019. https://www.creditexpress.com/cro/o-nama.

Christophers, Brett. 2011. "Follow the Thing: Money." *Environment and Planning D: Society and Space* 29: 1068–84.

CJEU. 2016. "Judgment of the General Court (Second Chamber) of 26 February 2016 in joined cases T-546/13, T-108/14 and T-109/14." Accessed 3 October 2019. https://eur-lex.europa.eu/legal-content/EN/TXT/PDF/?uri=CELEX:62013TJ0546&from=EN.

CNB. 2011. "Banks Bulletin No. 23." Accessed 3 October 2019. https://www.hnb.hr/documents/20182/121579/ebilten-o-bankama-23.pdf.

———. 2016. "Godišnje izvješće 2015." Accessed 3 October 2019. http://www.hnb.hr/documents/20182/1005947/h-gi-2015.pdf.

———. 2017. "Banks Bulletin No. 30." Accessed 3 October 2019. https://www.hnb.hr/documents/20182/2020824/ebilten-o-bankama-30.pdf.

Değirmencioğlu, Serdar M., and Carl Walker, eds. 2015. *Social and Psychological Dimensions of Personal Debt and the Debt Industry*. Basingstoke: Palgrave Macmillan.

Deville, Joe. 2015. *Lived Economies of Default: Consumer Credit, Debt Collection and the Capture of Affect*. Abingdon: Routledge.

Dika, Mihajlo. 2007. *Građansko ovršno pravo: Opće građansko ovršno pravo*. Zagreb: Narodne novine.

Dos Santos, Paulo L. 2009. "On the Content of Banking in Contemporary Capitalism." *Historical Materialism* 17, no. 2: 180–213.

Duka, Renata. 2018. Interview with Renata Duka on the Show *Točka na tjedan*, N1 TV (Croatian channel), broadcast on 14 January.

Durst, Judit. 2015. "Juggling with Debts, Moneylenders and Local Petty Monarchs: Banking the Unbanked in 'Shanty-Villages' in Hungary." *Szociológiai szemle* 25, no. 4: 30–57.

EC. 2010. "IPA 2010 Croatia Project Fiche: HR-2009-01-23-01." Accessed 3 October 2019. https://ec.europa.eu/neighbourhood-enlargement/sites/near/files/pdf/croatia/ipa/2010/01_improvement_of_the_enforcement_system_in_the_republic_of_croatia_track_changes_com_en.pdf.

Elyachar, Julia. 2005. *Markets of Dispossession: NGOs, Economic Development, and the State in Cairo*. Durham: Duke University Press.

EOS Group. 2017. "Insights—the EOS Group in 2016/17." Hamburg: EOS Holding.

Eurostat. 2019a. "Arrears on Hire Purchase Installments or Other Loan Payments—EU-SILC survey." Accessed 3 October 2019. https://ec.europa.eu/eurostat/web/products-datasets/product?code=ilc_mdes08.

———. 2019b. "Arrears on Utility Bills—EU-SILC survey." Accessed 3 October 2019. https://ec.europa.eu/eurostat/en/web/products-datasets/-/ILC_MDES07.

———. 2019c. "GDP and Main Components (output, expenditure and income)." Accessed 3 October 2019. https://appsso.eurostat.ec.europa.eu/nui/show.do?dataset=nama_10_gdp&lang=en.

———. 2019d. "Real GDP Growth Rate—volume." Accessed 3 October 2019. https://ec.europa.eu/eurostat/tgm/table.do?tab=table&init=1&language=en&pcode=tec00115&plugin=1.

FIIAP. 2016. "Mission Report: Improvement of the Enforcement System in the Republic of Croatia." Accessed 3 October 2019. https://pravosudje.gov.hr/UserDocsImages/dokumenti/Projekti/IPA%20komponenta%20I/Final%20Report%20ACTIVITY%201%203%201.pdf.

Fina. 2012. "Informacija o neizvršenim osnovama za plaćanje poslovnih subjekata za prosinac 2011." Accessed 31 August 2018. http://haw.nsk.hr/arhiva/vol-hidra/5485/62168/www.fina.hr/Default.aspx%3Fart%3D9914.html.

———. 2016. "FINA: 'Postupci ovrha kod nas su brzi i učinkoviti.'" Accessed 3 October 2019. https://www.index.hr/vijesti/clanak/fina-postupci-ovrhe-kod-nas-su-brzi-i-ucinkoviti/906189.aspx.

———. 2018a. "Informacija o neizvršenim osnovama za plaćanje poslovnih subjekata i građana za listopad 2018. godine." Accessed 3 October 2019. https://www.fina.hr/-/informacija-o-neizvrsenim-osnovama-za-placanje-poslovnih-subjekata-i-gra-ana-za-listopad-2018-.

———. 2018b. "Pregled blokiranih građana po vjerovnicima i ročnosti—31.12.2017." Accessed 31 August 2018. https://www.fina.hr/-/pregled-blokiranih-gra-ana-po-vjerovnicima-i-rocnosti-31-12-2017-.

———. n.d. "Postupak provođenja ovrhe." Accessed 3 October 2019. https://www.fina.hr/default.aspx?sec=1490.

Fuller, Gregory W. 2016. *The Great Debt Transformation: Households, Financialization, and Policy Responses*. Basingstoke: Palgrave Macmillan.

Gabor, Daniela. 2010. "(De)financialization and Crisis in Eastern Europe." *Competition and Change* 14, no. 3–4: 248–70.

Graeber, David. 2009. "Debt, Violence, and Impersonal Markets: Polanyian Meditations." In *Market and Society: The Great Transformation Today*, edited by Chris Hann and Keith Hart, 106–32. Cambridge, UK: Cambridge University Press.

———. 2011. *Debt: The First 5,000 Years*. New York: Melville House.

———. 2012. "On Social Currencies and Human Economies: Some Notes on the Violence of Equivalence." *Social Anthropology* 20, no. 4: 411–28

Gregorović, Paulo. 2016. "'Žrtva' agencije za naplatu potraživanja: 'Znali su me zvati po jedanaest puta dnevno da platim dug.'" Accessed 3 October 2019. http://www.novilist.hr/Vijesti/Hrvatska/Zrtva-agencije-za-naplatu-potrazivanja-Znali-su-me-zvati-po-jedanaest-puta-dnevno-da-platim-dug.

Gregory, C. A. 1997. *Savage Money: The Anthropology and Politics of Commodity Exchange*. Amsterdam: Harwood Academic Publishers.

Guérin, Isabelle. 2014. "Juggling with Debt, Social Ties, and Values: The Everyday Use of Microcredit in Rural South India." *Current Anthropology* 55, no. S9: S40–S50.

Guérin, Isabelle, Solène Morvant-Roux, and Magdalena Villarreal, eds. 2014. *Microfinance, Debt and Over-indebtedness: Juggling with Money*. Abingdon: Routledge.

Halawa, Mateusz. 2015. "In New Warsaw: Mortgage Credit and the Unfolding of Space and Time." *Cultural Studies* 29, no. 5–6: 707–32.

Han, Clara. 2012. *Life in Debt: Times of Care and Violence in Neoliberal Chile*. Berkeley: University of California Press.

Harsági, Viktória. 2011. "The Notarial Order for Payment Procedure as a Hungarian Peculiarity." *FS Kaissis Revista de Processo*. Accessed 3 October 2019. https://papers.ssrn.com/sol3/papers.cfm?abstract_id=2302284.

Harvey, David. [1982] 2006. *The Limits to Capital*. New and fully updated edition. London: Verso.

Herzfeld, Michael. 2011. "Crisis Attack: Impromptu Ethnography in the Greek Maelstrom." *Anthropology Today* 27, no. 5: 22–26.

High, Holly. 2012. "Re-reading the Potlatch in a Time of Crisis: Debt and the Distinctions that Matter." *Social Anthropology* 20, no. 4: 363–79.

Hina. 2018. "Oporba poduprla SDP-ove dopune Ovršnog zakona, vladajući najavili novi zakon." Accessed 3 October 2019. https://www.vecernji.hr/vijesti/oporba-poduprla-sdp-ove-dopune-ovrsnog-zakona-vladajuci-najavili-novi-zakon-1241477.

Jakić, Ivan. 2015. "Provedba ovrhe na plaći temeljem izjave o zapljeni po pristanku dužnika." Accessed 3 October 2019. http://www.notarius.hr/DailyContent/Topical.aspx?id=21635.

James, Deborah. 2012. "Money-go-round: Personal Economies of Wealth, Aspiration and Indebtedness." *Africa* 82, no. 1: 20–40.

———. 2014. "'Deeper into a Hole?' Borrowing and Lending in South Africa." *Current Anthropology* 55, no. S9: S17–S29.

———. 2015. *Money from Nothing: Indebtedness and Aspiration in South Africa.* Stanford, CA: Stanford University Press.

Jutarnji.hr. 2018. "Predstavnici udruge 'Blokirani' kod predsjednice: 'sustav je postavljen tako da mu nije cilj naplata potraživanja, već iscrpljivanje dužnika.'" Accessed 3 October 2019. https://www.jutarnji.hr/vijesti/hrvatska/predstavnici-udruge-blokirani-kod-predsjednice-sustav-je-postavljen-tako-da-mu-nije-cilj-naplata-potrazivanja-vec-iscrpljivanje-duznika/7105203/.

Kar, Sohini. 2013. "Recovering Debts: Microfinance Loan Officers and the Work of 'Proxy-Creditors' in India." *American Ethnologist* 40, no. 3: 480–93.

Karim, Lamia. 2008. "Demystifying Micro-credit: The Grameen Bank, NGOs, and Neoliberalism in Bangladesh." *Cultural Dynamics* 20, no. 1: 5–29.

Kramarić, Damir. 2016a. "Četvrtina Hrvatske bolesna zbog ovrha! Svi o tome šute, a pitaju se ZAŠTO IZUMIREMO?!" Accessed 3 October 2019. http://promise.hr/cetvrtina-hrvatske-bolesna-zbog-ovrha-svi-o-tome-sute-a-pitaju-se-zasto-izumiremo/.

———. 2016b. "Vojska blokiranih sve je veća, EKSPLODIRAT ĆE NEPRAVDA i više neće moći ovako!" Accessed 3 October 2019. http://promise.hr/vojska-blokiranih-sve-je-veca-eksplodirat-ce-nepravda-i-vise-nece-moci-ovako.

Lazzarato, Maurizio. 2012. *The Making of the Indebted Man: An Essay on the Neoliberal Condition.* Los Angeles: Semiotext(e).

LeBaron, Genevieve. 2014. "Reconceptualizing Debt Bondage: Debt as a Class-Based Form of Labor Discipline." *Critical Sociology* 40, no. 5: 763–80.

LeBaron, Genevieve, and Adrienne Roberts. 2014. "Confining Social Insecurity: Neoliberalism and the Rise of the 21st Century Debtors' Prison." *Politics & Gender* 8: 25–49.

Lider. 2017. "Zaba prodala 3,3 milijarde kuna 'loših' plasmana APS-u." Accessed 3 October 2019. https://lider.media/aktualno/zaba-prodala-3-3-milijarde-kuna-losih-plasmana-aps-u-40961/.

López, Isidro, and Emmanuel Rodríguez. 2011. "The Spanish Model." *New Left Review* 69: 5–29.

Marić, Jagoda. 2018. "Agencije za utjerivanje dugova cvjetaju: Banke im prodale čak 8,1 milijardi kredita. Moraju ih utjerati od građana i poduzeća." Accessed 3 October 2019. http://www.novilist.hr/Vijesti/Hrvatska/Agencije-za-utjerivanje-dugova-cvjetaju-Banke-im-prodale-cak-8-1-milijardi-kredita.-Moraju-ih-utjerati-od-gradana-i-poduzeca.

Mattioli, Fabio. 2018. "Financialization without Liquidity: In-kind Payments, Forced Credit, and Authoritarianism at the Periphery of Europe." *Journal of Royal Anthropological Institute* 24, no. 3: 568–88.

Maurer, Bill. 2005. *Mutual Life, Limited: Islamic Banking, Alternative Currencies, Lateral Reason.* Princeton: Princeton University Press.

———. 2006. *Pious Property: Islamic Mortgages in the United States.* New York: Russell Sage Foundation.

Mauss, Marcel. [1925] 2016. *The Gift.* Chicago: Hau Books.

Menđušić Škugor, Ema. 2018. "Quo vadis, Fina? Teškoće u provedbi agencijske ovrhe." *Zbornik radova Veleučilišta u Šibeniku* 1–2: 57–14.

Micklitz, Hans-W., and Irina Domurath, eds. 2015. *Consumer Debt and Social Exclusion in Europe.* Farnham: Ashgate.

Mikuš, Marek. 2019. "Contesting Household Debt in Croatia: The Double Movement of Financialization and the Fetishism of Money in Eastern European Peripheries." *Dialectical Anthropology* 43, no. 3: 295–315.

Mirowski, Phillip, and Edward Nik-Khan. 2007. "Markets Made Flesh: Performativity, and a Problem in Science Studies, Augmented with Consideration of the FCC Auctions." In *Do Economists Make Markets? On the Performativity of Economics*, edited by Donald MacKenzie, Fabian Muniesa, and Lucia Siu, 190–224. Princeton: Princeton University Press.

Moodie, Megan. 2008. "Enter Microcredit: A New Culture of Women's Empowerment in Rajasthan?" *American Ethnologist* 35, no. 3: 454–65.

Muniesa, Fabian, Yuval Millo, and Michel Callon. 2007. "An Introduction to Market Devices." *Sociological Review* 55, no. 2-suppl.: 1–12.

Niemi, Johanna, Iain Ramsay, and William C. Whitford, eds. 2009. *Consumer Credit, Debt and Bankruptcy: Comparative and International Perspectives.* Oxford: Hart.

Novak, Ivana. 2017. "Ovršni zakon je ozakonjena pljačka političara u Hrvatskoj!" Accessed 3 October 2019. http://www.7dnevno.hr/izdvajanja/izdvojeno/ovrsni-zakon-je-ozakonjena-pljacka-politicara-u-hrvatskoj/.

Ovršni ustanak. n.d. "About." Accessed 3 October 2019. https://www.facebook.com/pg/ovrsni.ustanak/about/?ref=page_internal.

Palomera, Jaime. 2014. "Reciprocity, Commodification, and Poverty in the Era of Financialization." *Current Anthropology* 55, no. S9: S105–S15.

Pedersen, Morten Axel. 2017. "Debt as an Urban Chronotope in Mongolia." *Ethnos* 82, no. 3: 475–91.

Peebles, Gustav. 2010. "The Anthropology of Credit and Debt." *Annual Review of Anthropology* 39: 225–40.

———. 2012. "Whitewashing and Leg-Bailing: On the Spatiality of Debt." *Social Anthropology* 20, no. 4: 429–43.

———. 2013. "Washing away the Sins of Debt: The Nineteenth-Century Eradication of the Debtors' Prison." *Comparative Studies in Society and History* 55, no. 3: 701–24.

Radošević, Dubravko, and Vladimir Cvijanović, eds. 2015. *Financialisation and Financial Crisis in South-Eastern European Countries.* Frankfurt am Main: Peter Lang.

Rakopoulos, Theodoros, ed. 2018. *The Global Life of Austerity: Economic Crises beyond Europe.* New York: Berghahn Books.

Republic of Croatia. 2013. "Economic Programme of Croatia." Accessed 3 October 2019. http://www.mfin.hr/adminmax/docs/2013%20Economic%20Programme%20of%20Croatia.pdf.

Roberts, Adrienne. 2014. "Doing Borrowed Time: The State, the Law and the Coercive Governance of 'Undeserving Debtors.'" *Critical Sociology* 40, no. 5: 669–87.

———. 2016. "Household Debt and the Financialization of Social Reproduction: Theorizing the UK Housing and Hunger Crises." In *Risking Capitalism*, edited by Susanne Soederberg, 135–64. Bingley: Emerald Publishing.

Rodik, Petra, and Mislav Žitko. 2015. "Financialization, Household Debt and New Vulnerabilities in Post-socialist Societies." In *Financialisation and Financial Crisis in South-Eastern European Countries*, edited by Dubravko Radošević and Vladimir Cvijanović, 49–70. Frankfurt am Main: Peter Lang.

Rodrigues, João, Ana C. Santos, and Nuno Teles. 2016. "Semi-peripheral Financialisation: The Case of Portugal." *Review of International Political Economy* 23, no. 3: 480–510.

Roitman, Janet. 2005. *Fiscal Disobedience: An Anthropology of Economic Regulation in Central Africa*. Princeton: Princeton University Press.

Sabaté, Irene. 2016. "The Spanish Mortgage Crisis and the Re-emergence of Moral Economies in Uncertain Times." *History and Anthropology* 27, no. 1: 107–20.

Shipton, Parker MacDonald. 2009. *Mortgaging the Ancestors: Ideologies of Attachment in Africa*. New Haven: Yale University Press.

———. 2011. *Credit between Cultures: Farmers, Financiers, and Misunderstanding in Africa*. New Haven: Yale University Press.

Šimatović, Mislav. 2018. "Ovršni zakon stvorio je lanac parazita koji gura građane u propast." *Večernji list* No. 19598 (1 February): 5.

Sinčić, Ivan Vilibor. 2017. "Speech in the Croatian Parliament." 9 November 2017. Accessed 31 August 2018. https://www.youtube.com/watch?v=Ur3IJf-_QnI.

Sneath, David. 2012. "The 'Age of the Market' and the Regime of Debt: The Role of Credit in the Transformation of Pastoral Mongolia." *Social Anthropology* 20, no. 4: 458–73.

Soederberg, Susanne. 2014. *Debtfare States and the Poverty Industry: Money, Discipline and the Surplus Population*. Abingdon: Routledge.

Song, Jesook. 2009. *South Koreans in the Debt Crisis: The Creation of a Neoliberal Welfare Society*. Durham: Duke University Press.

Streinzer, Andreas. 2018. "Interlocked Dependencies—Households and Paradoxical Embeddedness in Greece." Paper presented in the workshop Households and Peripheral Financialization in Europe, Halle (Saale), 22–23 February 2018.

Suarez, Maka. 2017. "Debt Revolts: Ecuadorian Foreclosed Families at the PAH in Barcelona." *Dialectical Anthropology* 41: 263–77.

Tafra, Lea. 2015. "Postupanje financijske agencije u postupku provedbe ovrhe na novčanim sredstvima." *Pravnik: časopis za pravna i društvena pitanja* 47, no. 95: 45–54.

Theodossopoulos, Dimitrios. 2013. "Infuriated with the Infuriated? Blaming Tactics and Disconent about the Greek Financial Crisis." *Current Anthropology* 54, no. 2: 200–21.

Van der Zwan, Natascha. 2014. "Making Sense of Financialisation." *Socio-Economic Review* 12: 99–129.

Wamsley, Dillon. 2019. "Neoliberalism, Mass Incarceration, and the US Debt–Criminal Justice Complex." *Critical Social Policy* 39, no. 2: 248–67.

Weiss, Hadas. 2014. "Homeownership in Israel: The Social Costs of Middle-Class Debt." *Cultural Anthropology* 29, no. 1: 128–49.

Wiesner, Valentina. 2018a. "Mi ne otkupljujemo dug za vodu ili struju, već naplaćujemo kredite i telekom-usluge." Accessed 3 October 2019. https://www.vecernji.hr/vijesti/mi-ne-otkupljujemo-dug-za-vodu-ili-struju-vec-naplacujemo-kredite-i-telekom-usluge-1222808.

———. 2018b. "Ovršeni: Fini plaćamo više od 30 naknada, oduzmite joj monopol." Accessed 3 October 2019. https://www.vecernji.hr/vijesti/ovrha-fina-naknada-monopol-zakon-1225777.

Z. K. 2018. "Udjel loših bankarskih kredita krajem 2017. smanjen na 11,37 posto." Accessed 3 October 2019. https://www.tportal.hr/biznis/clanak/udjel-losih-bankarskih-kredita-krajem-2017-smanjen-na-11-37-posto-20180302.

11

Financialized Kinship and Challenges for the Greek Oikos

Dimitra Kofti

Since the beginning of the financial crisis in 2009, discussion of public and private debt has been an everyday preoccupation in Greece.[1] Declining income and rising taxation affected both the working class and the middle class. This economic and political turmoil was invoked to legitimize the implementation of austerity measures, leading to the further demise of the welfare state. It also engendered new practices of irregular and informal work, based on a state of exception and emergency (Athanasiou 2012).

This state of emergency resulted in political, media, and scholarly debate about a "humanitarian" crisis. This underlining of "humans" struggling for survival highlighted practices of solidarity (Bakalaki 2015) but tended to neglect inequalities related to gender, class, and ethnicity.[2] Studies of solidarity paid attention to free services in social medical centers (Cabot 2016), community soup kitchens (Kravva 2014; Douzina-Bakalaki 2017), food distribution cooperatives (Rakopoulos 2014), and the politics of solidarity with refugees (Rozakou 2016). Attention to such phenomena has underlined the importance of social relations and support across classes as well as beyond intimate and familial ties. Another body of literature pays attention to often conflictual economic practices in households, families, and family businesses in Greece's shifting economic contexts (Streinzer 2016; Knight 2018; Vetta and Palomera, forthcoming).

This chapter investigates household debt and explores ways in which households participate in multilevel processes of financialization (Van der Zwan 2014). In Thessaloniki, individual indebtedness is experienced and practiced through relations of dependency, support, and conflict within the household and the *oikos*. In portraying the "indebted man," Lazzarato

(2012) connects individual and public debt and shows how pressure is put to individuals to take responsibility. The ethnography in this chapter suggests that individual debt in Thessaloniki is entangled with kinship, household, and intimate relations, and can only be understood as part of these relations. I argue that debt collection practices have implications for collective responsibility and relations of mutual obligation among kin. Research in Thessaloniki was conducted between 2016 and 2018 with individual debtors and their families, with lawyers and judges, bank employees, and with activist groups protesting against confiscations. The first part of the ethnography is based on everyday solidarities and tensions related to debt, and the second part is based on 280 court cases of "over-indebtedness" in which familial and intimate relations are put into a legal and public scrutiny.

Responses to the rapid expansion of private debt in Greece are shaped by a number of factors. First, deepening state dependence on credit and on international financial and political institutions, a consequence of peripheral financialization, has led to intensified austerity and a vicious circle between credit dependency and austerity (Offe 2015). Second, moral accusations of overspending have influenced discussions between state officials, private creditors, and debtors, and political decisions regulating indebtedness. Anthropologists have underlined the intertwinement of moral debates with the economic effects of debt (Peebles 2010). Creditors and debtors in Thessaloniki discuss, negotiate, and even "police" the boundaries of legitimate debt, beyond formal-legal definitions. Debates and ideas about legitimate and illegitimate forms of indebtedness point to class boundaries and to political contestation. Third, the ethnography in this chapter is placed in a context of illiquidity similar to other contexts of peripheral financialization (Mattioli 2018). Although new legal procedures promote the confiscation of property, creditors are not always interested in confiscation in this context of illiquidity and property devaluation. Rather, they need some sort of cash flow.[3] The lack of liquidity was also central in work settings, as salaries and payments were often reduced, delayed, or even cancelled, and small-scale companies often relied on unpaid labor.

Anthropological studies on financialization have underlined the importance of kin and intimate relations in household strategies (James 2015; Palomera 2014; Sabaté 2016). This chapter contributes to these discussions by showing that financialization in Greece relies on processes of deepening informalization of familial and intimate ties. Dependency and exploitation among family members is mostly based on unpaid and invisible (often female) labor, but the growing indebtedness of households since the mid-2000s has added credit to traditional familial relations of dependency. The quality of creditworthiness (πιστοληπτική ικανότητα) has come to challenge longstanding hierarchies of gender and seniority. The ethnography focuses on ways in which intimate ties are employed in both individual loan taking and debt repayment and in court cases of over-indebtedness. Although taking bank loans and negotiating over-indebtedness are legally defined as individual practices, both rely on a wide range of informal collective practices that are enabled and even encouraged by formal institutions. While bank representatives, judges, and lawyers emphasize the moral obligation of the debtors' kin, they situationally shame debtors for their social relations of dependency and emphasize individual responsibility, a dominant idea of neoliberalism and capitalism, including finance capitalism (Martin 2002; Lazzarato 2015). I document the pressures applied by bank representatives, judges, and lawyers involved in cases of indebtedness and the way these play out through the entanglement of collectivity and individuality in debt collection. Individual responsibility turns out to be largely discursive, as debt collection becomes a collective matter for family members and extended social networks of friends. The ethnography highlights the crucial role of kinship in two main ways. On the one hand, the crisis has given rise to new forms of intimate cooperation and exploitation within what I view as the modern *oikos*. On the other, I go on to show how the intertwinement of household, kinship, and housing contributes to macro-level resistance to processes of deepening financialization.

Transformations and Interconnections of the Greek *Oikos*

It was common in the everyday discourses of my interlocutors to hear that family relations were being transformed by Greece's financial crisis. Such statements were accompanied by stories of debt, tax liabilities (and how to avoid them), changing strategies for passing on property, and multigenerational housing arrangements. They underlined how increased taxation[4] along with illiquidity and rising unemployment[5] transformed their lives in multiple ways. Kin relations, household, and housing were at the core of these discussions. Here, I use *oikos* (οίκος) in an expanded sense to encompass three interconnected meanings: the household (νοικοκυριό), the family (οικογένεια), and the housing (κατοικία or οίκος or οικία). Economy (οικονομία), according to Aristotle, is the management of the *oikos*. The strong connections between the household, the family, and the house shape both everyday practices and the wider politics of debt management. In other words, I shall show how practices within the *oikos*, including family and household values, are critical to decision making in the *polis*.

Focusing on the *oikos* does not mean restricting the ethnographic exploration to the family. Rather, the multiple layers of the concept allow for the exploration of other types of relations. Gudeman and Hann (2015: 2) argue that mutuality in relation to house economy is a notion broader than kinship. It includes friends and other associates who are directly involved in the house economy. Reaching to networks beyond close kin in order to access financial products became a common pattern in the decade that followed the crisis. Rising unemployment, closures, and bankruptcies caused problems of cash flow. In the course of the credit-crunch, taking out a small consumption loan to help a friend became a common practice.[6] People who could get bank loans or credit cards did so and gave the amount or the cards to kin or friends who were in greater need, trusting that the informal beneficiary would eventually return the amount to the bank. Even if things sometimes turn sour, the importance of mutuality with nonkin can be as strong as kinship or common residence.

Housing was one of the main preoccupations. Income irregularity impacted those in rented accommodation. Returning to the parental home became a common pattern. The crisis also had an impact on property owners with the imposition of an "emergency tax" in 2011 that soon became permanent, leading to a decline in the proportion of households that owned the property in which they resided.[7] The housing market that had seen strong growth since the 1990s stagnated.[8] Family values and intergenerational relationships were challenged accordingly, as shown in the well-known joke of that period: "Formerly you had to behave to your parents to receive property, but now you have to behave to not receive property." However, the transmission of property to younger generations did not cease. Rather, older generations explored different options. A common practice was to pass on property earlier than initially planned and not through wills, in order to avoid property taxation. Moreover, the first piece of housing property one owns is liable to less tax and protected under "first housing property" (πρώτη κατοικία) regulations.[9] While this makes transmission to the younger generation an advantageous choice for the extended family, elders would still keep some legal control over the property via usufruct rights until their death. It is also common to retain the property while sharing tax liabilities with those who will eventually inherit the property. While strategies of passing property vary according to the amount of property owned, the number of children, and different class backgrounds, intergenerational dependencies are a common denominator.

Syriza, the ruling party in Greece between 2015 and 2019, committed itself to protecting a family's primary housing in the event of debt. In other words, even in cases of inability to repay the debt, the law would, under certain circumstances, protect the family's main housing. Nevertheless, those who cannot repay their housing debt could apply for this protection under a legal procedure, introduced in 2010, that includes court hearings in which the amount of debt, the value of the property, and the level of the family's (in)ability to pay are all publicly aired. This legal procedure is sometimes called Katselis' Law, after the parliamentarian who introduced it. It is also popularly known as the "law for the over-indebted households." The law does not specify the household, only individual debt. However, it is always implemented through the lens of the household. Debtors apply to avoid the confiscation of their "primary housing" and to secure some sort of debt relief.[10] If they own additional pieces of property other than their housing, the court might decide to confiscate part or all of these assets. The negotiation of debt through court hearings differs from Croatia (Mikuš, this volume) or Spain (Palomera 2014: S112), where the debt is not relieved when a debtor's apartment is foreclosed and auctioned.

This protection for "primary housing" is supported by a wide range of political voices.[11] Nevertheless, since the beginning of the economic crisis in 2008, the threat of foreclosures has increased. The only way to guard against this possibility is to be granted the status of "over-indebted" in the household protection scheme. Much of the tension between the Greek governments since 2009 and the "Troika" (EC, IMF, ECB) has turned on this protection.[12] The protection of housing property and the physical assets of small-scale (family-owned) enterprises, commonly described as "property of the people" and "peoples' housing," is supported by a wide range of the political spectrum, fearful of bank interventions and especially of foreign capital. A political movement named "Movement against Foreclosures" has been highly successful due to its ability to draw support from both class-conscious leftist elements and more nationalist, yet class-conscious, right-wing elements.[13] This politically heterogeneous group was critical of the housing protection offered by Katselis' Law, reasoning that this legal procedure could open space for negotiation that might, contrary to stated intentions, lead to housing confiscation. Much of the political debate has been based on discourses about how this law will affect the "people's families" or "the Greek family" while the Syriza government insisted that the state will protect "the peoples' family housing."

Anthropologists of Greece have paid considerable attention to property relations and the importance of inheritance (Friedl 1967; Hirschon 1989; Just 2000; Nitsiakos 1991; Vernier 1991). Passing on property to the next generations was found to be one of the strongest family values. More recent research has pointed out the importance of belonging to a household and a family. Papataxiarchis has argued that "the household" (νοικοκυριό) formed through marriage provides the means for secure and autonomous individuality (2008: 330). He further argues that the strong model of domestic family life cuts across classes in Greece (2008: 331). In her research on reproductive technologies in Athens, Tountasaki confirms the continuing strong valuation of marriage and households (2015). On the other hand, Knight identifies an increasing "desire for disconnectedness, for exiting not only political structure but also kinship structures that have been historically closely linked with a Greek sense of self as particular political subjects" (2018: 40). He draws this conclusion on the basis of a case in which two siblings signed their disinheritance of their father's indebted property. In Thessaloniki, such strategies of disinheritance became common postcrisis, but only when the value of the property was smaller than that of the inheritor's debt. However, the value of being a family member within the household setting did not change significantly. While my interlocutors complained about family dependencies brought about by the recent economic crisis, they did not challenge the core idea of the importance of family and household membership. Rather, this very importance adds to the pressure on household/family members in practices related to debt. Moreover, debt collection by bank and state representatives relies on such relations of mutual obligation. Unlike Knight (2018), who sees indebtedness as disintegrating family ties, I find the consequences of the crisis playing out in the complexities of these attachments, which are based on both solidarity and conflict. There are indeed tectonic changes taking place in the gender- and age-related hierarchies. Older people bemoaned their "inability" to provide for the younger generation as previously envisioned while the young complained that their generation was missing out in comparison with all previous generations. Despite these challenges of previous intergenerational reordering, replete with the kind of tensions described by Knight (2018), younger generations in Thessaloniki are not detached from the older ones, but instead reconfigure their mutual obligations. Those with regular income have to support other extended household members, including elder family members, irrespective of established norms of gender and age and previous expectations of parental support, challenging previous hierarchies within the *oikos*. Despite conflicts and challenges to the previous power relations, family ties seem to remain strong.

Creditworthiness, Gender, and Family

Melina, a thirty-eight-year-old manager at a bakery in Thessaloniki, did not expect to spend her working life in food and retail services. Having studied English literature during a period when her uncle's private foreign language school was still prospering, she had previously expected to work there as an English teacher, or alternatively at a public school. But she only worked there for five years before her uncle's school, located in a working class area of the city, closed down due to diminishing numbers of enrolled students.

In the state sector, there were no openings, only a long waiting list of casually employed teachers to fill the most urgent gaps.

Melina's sixty-two-year-old mother, Eirini, who is a second cousin of the sixty-seven-year-old school owner Yannis, used to work for him as a secretary at the language school since its founding in 1991. She worked long hours, but Yannis documented only those that would enable her to claim unemployment benefits. She was routinely "fired" in the quiet summer months, when she was able to draw a (much lower) payment from the unemployment office. Eirini continued to work without a contract for long periods, which meant that she could not claim any benefits when the school finally closed in 2011. She was still unemployed in 2018 and had no prospect of a pension. Despite her own precarious condition, back then, she was confident that her husband (Melina's father), Kiriakos, who had a career as a restaurant manager at expensive hotels, would be entitled to a pension and that he would support her in the future. Having changed several positions from waiter to manager, Kiriakos decided to set up his own business in the early 2000s. But the luxurious restaurant that he opened in 2004 in the years when consumerism and a sense of prosperity were pervasive closed down in 2009, and he remained heavily indebted. Kiriakos had to repay the loan that had been so easy to obtain and was obliged to start working again as a waiter. Kiriakos and Eirini already had long-term marital tensions, and eventually they divorced in 2012, thereby enabling Eirini to disassociate herself from Kiriakos's debt. This meant giving up their jointly owned flat, which had been bought in 1993 with the substantial support of Eirini's parents. Kiriakos and Eirini sold the flat in 2013, when housing prices were at their lowest, and got 31,000 euros each. Eirini and Melina moved into modest rented accommodation in the vicinity of Melina's married younger brother. Eirini used part of the money from the flat to help her son establish his household, while the greater part went to assist her own elder parents with medical expenses (the health care system did not support their needs). She kept some of the money to meet her own regular expenses. Her capital was soon significantly diminished, and she worried that she would have to rely on her children's support, given that she was not expecting to get a pension. Kiriakos faced mental health problems and was unable to work, but as he was still sixty-two years old, he needed to work for another three years to qualify for a pension. Meanwhile, he was financially supported by his brother, with whom he lived after his divorce.

Melina was very close friends with Georgia, a thirty-seven-year-old waitress who had also studied literature and been unable to find a job in that field. When Georgia married Nikos in 2016, they lacked the resources to purchase household appliances and furniture. Neither was creditworthy for a bank loan. Georgia's father had a debt for which she was a guarantor, and

Nikos had a similar dependency as he had inherited an indebted company from his father, who was applying for housing protection as "over-indebted." Georgia asked Melina to get a bank loan of 3,000 euros that Georgia would repay. Melina did so, trusting her friend to pay the installments. This was an important act of support to Georgia. Melina had to lie to the bank that the loan was for her own needs, rather than for Georgia's. Given that Melina could not rely on familial financial support, she described her act as "risky" but "important" for her friendship. She was eligible for the loan as she could prove she had a stable income of 800 euros per month. The 3,000 euros was a significant amount of money for Melina, as her salary barely covered her own living expenses, and she was anxious to build up some savings in case she or her mother were in need.

A few months after Melina obtained the loan, she was invited to Georgia's flat for dinner, along with other friends. During dinner, Nikos said that he was not happy that the two women were meeting regularly for drinks. Melina departed angrily and did not meet the couple again. Although Georgia and Melina did not communicate with each other, Georgia continued to make the monthly payments to the bank. Melina explained that Nikos viewed her as a moral threat, because she was single and two girlfriends drinking in public would attract male attention. In her opinion, men in Thessaloniki who were financially insecure were also inse-cure with women. Nikos was another "insecure guy" who doubtless felt uneasy because Melina was more stable financially than he was and, there-fore, she could get approval for a bank loan. Melina, expressing a common sentiment, repeated that Nikos had "lost his masculinity."

This story illustrates the shift from cross-generational dependencies and solidarities to intensifying "horizontal" ties to nonmembers of the nuclear family. Neither Georgia nor Nikos was deemed creditworthy by the bank due to their fathers' debts. Melina's father, with whom she had little contact, was also indebted to several banks. His absence was omnipresent though, given that Melina's mother had lost this source of support. Kiriakos did not manage to perform his patriarchal role to support his family. Melina's friends narrate her father's absence as a case of male disempowerment caused by the crisis. They would reason that it was this disempowerment and inability to play the patriarchal role that caused his mental health prob-lems. Melina herself criticized both her father for being "irresponsible" and not a "proper father," and Georgia for obeying Nikos, not contacting her, and not being a "proper friend." Despite the feeling of betrayal, she contin-ued to think that helping her friend with the loan was the right thing to do. Georgia never stopped paying the installment to the bank and eventually, a year after their fight, the two friends slowly resumed meeting with each other again.

Melina was one of the few people in her circle of friends who was deemed "creditworthy" by the bank. Her story highlights common ways in which the abundance of cash and credit in the precrisis period and the shift to a shortage of cash and credit in the postcrisis period have affected familial relations and shaken peoples' plans. Kiriakos relied on credit to make plans and had to face the consequences of the crisis. Georgia and Nikos were implicated in their parents' debt and thus unable to secure credit on their own. Such dependencies and informalities are also discussed and scrutinized in more formal court settings. Judges and bank lawyers, aware of such solidarities, push debtors to repay what they owe by drawing on their familial networks, as I shall demonstrate in the following section.

Family Relations and Moral Values in the Courtroom

The individual debtor seeking debt relief has to prove that her/his household is over-indebted for unforeseen reasons, and that their income is insufficient for subsistence, let alone repayment. It is also necessary to prove that the loan taken was reasonable and above board given the applicant's circumstances at that time. If there was "deceit" (i.e., if the debtor is held to have been aware of his/her inability to repay the loan), then the application is often rejected. The language of deceit underlines the debtor's individual responsibility. Such accusations are not leveled against creditors, although debtors and their lawyers often argue that banks offered loans and credit cards too easily, and without explaining all the details properly (cf. Mikuš 2019 and this volume, on Croatia). According to this reasoning, the loan agreement resulted from the bank's "deceit" rather than the debtor's mere individual responsibility. Judges would sometimes seem to agree with such allegations, but they were careful not to say so officially in court decision documents.

Although the application is for an individual, the entire household is scrutinized. If it is found to be over-indebted, then the main housing property is protected by the law. The court then determines the rate of repayment and the piece(s) of property to be confiscated (if the applicant owns property other than the main housing). Although confiscation of property is a possible outcome, bank lawyers explained to me that, in view of the collapse in real estate prices, given prevailing illiquidity, their main interest was to secure a regular cash flow to the bank.

Since Katselis' Law was passed, one's main housing can be protected if found to be of a "reasonable" size[14] and of a "reasonable" "objective value."[15] Objective property value is estimated by the state, based on standardized per-square-meter prices for every street. Property taxes and other transactions are made on the basis of this value, which in the wake of the crisis exceeded market price considerably. People complain that this is an additional way to collect money to repay the public debt. While prices fell, the market price is implied to be subjective as opposed to the "objective" value, which the court takes into account. Ironically, it is the subjectivity of the market prices that has brought those people before the judge.

The applicant-debtor is generally represented by a lawyer and accompanied by witnesses (kin and friends). Creditors, usually banks or the Greek state, are also represented by private lawyers. An applicant needs to provide evidence of income, expenses and inability to pay loan installments regularly. Applicants must not own a business: entrepreneurs may apply for "business bankruptcy," which does not offer housing protection.[16] The courtroom is open to the public. Other lawyers and witnesses often intervene with sharp comments directed against the banks, laughter directed against applicants perceived to be conspicuous consumers, or support for debtors perceived as victims of the financial market. Parallel to the legal and moral judgment performed by the judge, a moral judgment is also made by citizens. Although the applicants make reference to their individual debts, judges often asked about their kinship relations with a view to determining whether members of the family, including kin outside the household, could help in repaying. However, when applicants happened to mention that they have been supporting their close kin, judges would commonly underline individual values and criticize family dependency as a sign of irresponsibility. The debtors' narratives are necessarily selective and often rather stereotypical, but through them we can identify "common knowledge" concerning values and a wide range of economic practices.

Ioanna Papadopoulou is a forty-two-year-old single mother who works for an outsourcer that provides cleaning services at Thessaloniki University. She lives in a rented flat with her child in a working class neighborhood. After 2010, her wages of 480 euros monthly were not paid regularly. She explains to the judge: "There was a period that my boss would not pay me for four months in a row. Then I decided to get help from the bank. I was going through hard times because I was new in that job. I used to work for a pharmaceutical company before, but I was laid off like many colleagues that period. I got a 600 euro consumer credit once, which now amounts to 5,600 due to its interest rates [19 percent]. I am completely unable to pay this amount. I applied here because the debt grows bigger, and I hope this nightmare would stop." Some unpaid workers who had sought loans to tide them over took out second loans to repay the first and soon became trapped in a vicious circle of debt to multiple banks. The lawyer of Ms. Papadopoulou declared: "We are unable to repay this debt which is based on excessive interest rates. A well-known strategy of the banks. She gets threatening phone calls from debt collector companies. Another well-known bank practice." The audience nodded in support.

The judge asked whether she had parents or siblings who could financially help her raise her child and also to pay off the debt. Ioanna replied that she had no siblings and that her parents could hardly get by themselves on their agrarian pension. In fact, her parents lived with her during the winter, while remaining registered in their village, where they owned a small house and land on which they grew vegetables.[17] They live together in the winter to economize on heating costs and to assist Ioanna raising her son, while she is busy working long hours. Ioanna's ex-husband, Antonis, whom she divorced in 2013, contributed to his son's monthly expenses until 2015, when the electrical appliances chain store where he worked closed down. Although he worked informally as a technician in the construction industry, he did not earn enough to make a living. During the time of the court hearing, he was preparing his documents to migrate to Germany, to work for a Greek company that offered house construction services there. Ioanna preferred not to mention seasonal coresidence with her parents or the fact that nowadays she is again on good terms with her husband, as to do so would raise questions about their potential help. Indeed, although her parents helped her with food provisioning and childcare, they could not do so in monetary terms. Judges would always enquire into the extended family network, including relatives who had migrated abroad but who might still be in a position to contribute to the loan payment.

The lawyer representing the bank urged a rejection of the application: "The applicant owns a car that she could sell and pay the amount to the bank." She replied with anger: "It is a twenty-two-year-old Skoda! If you check its market value, it's less than 300 euros. Nobody would actually buy it. I only keep it in order to drive to work as I do not only clean at the university but I sometimes go to other places where the company offers services. Otherwise, its taxation is indeed an extra burden for me."

The court's decision came a year later. Ioanna Papadopoulou had to pay only a little more than the initial loan of 600 euros. This was a straightforward case that did not evoke much debate in the room. Rather, it elicited a moral consensus that rejected high interest rates and dubious debt collection practices.

The audience, consisting mostly of other applicants queuing for their cases to be heard and their lawyers, reacts differently when the applicant is considered to belong to the category of *lamogio*. *Lamogio* literally means a man who pretends to be a customer or client in order to attract more clients to the business. It has also come to mean people who cheat the economic and political system. Applicants thought to tick the boxes of this characterization attract criticism, laughter and scorn. Such derision is

especially strong when credit cards and loans are used to pay for conspicuous consumption such as luxurious housing and foreign travel. Consider
the case of sixty-seven-year-old Mr. Hatzis, who owes 71,524 euros. This is
made up of two housing loans and a consumption loan. These were taken
out in 2004 through 2006, when loans were readily available. One could
get a housing loan without necessarily buying a house. It could be used to
refurbish the existing home, in which case it functioned as a mortgage. All
three bank representatives urged the judge to reject the application. In case
of rejection, the applicant would have to repay the bank, and if he did not,
confiscation of his property could eventually happen. Although banks are
more interested in regular income flow than in getting any property, this
did not hinder their lawyers from making this argument before the court in
the hope of securing some sort of cash flow back to the bank.

Mr. Hatzis used to work at the state run telecommunication company as
a manager. He lives with his family in Retziki, previously a periurban area
that, after the housing construction boom in the mid-nineties, was developed with middle class housing. One could describe this area as nouveau
rich. However, much of this nouveau wealth was based on housing loans
that could not be paid back postcrisis. Mr. Hatzis was treated in the courtroom as a typical example of the previous era's overspending. He used part
of one housing loan to construct an extra story onto his house to accommodate his daughter and her household. His pension declined from an initial
estimate of 2,150 euros (when he took out his loans), a large sum even
precrisis, to 1,240 euros per month.

Judge: Where did you spend your money?
Mr. Hatzis: I had two heart operations, which cost approximately 15,000.
Judge: Well, this is part of the amount. How about the rest?
Mr. Hatzis: My daughter got married; I had to help her begin her life. I also had to
    pay for the wedding expenses.
Judge: How much did the wedding cost?
Mr. Hatzis: Well, we brought the best musicians! One sees his daughter getting
    married once in a lifetime. And you know, back then, it was the period of spend-
    ing. Who could foresee this coming? So we paid some 8,000 for the party.... You
    know, the whole family, friends, colleagues, all were invited. (By now there was
    scorn and laughter in the room).
Judge: So you paid for a luxurious wedding. How about the rest of the money?
Mr. Hatzis: I helped my son to open his business in 2007. He is an electrician and
    makes installations and automatic systems. Back then there was industry and
    construction. It worked well in the first years; it closed in 2012. Meanwhile, my
    pension was cut.
Judge: 1,250 is quite a lot for a pension. Can't you use some of this to pay off the loan?
Mr. Hatzis: Not really; my wife, who does not get a pension, and I hardly make it with
    this amount. We pay 180 monthly for our medicine. We also cook for the whole

family. Our children work, and we cook for them and the grandchildren. Their income is very low.

Bank lawyer: That's not an excuse before the court! That's not a good excuse for a creditor either! Your children are employed, you get a decent pension, and you keep not paying off your loan. You do not travel to work. Your only needs are medicine and food. You can certainly use some of it for a monthly bank installment. You actually came to the bank, asked for a smaller installment in 2012—we did agree on a lower installment; but soon after that arrangement, you stopped paying this as well.

Mr. Hatzis did not, on the face of it, have a very strong case. The judge sounded quite critical of the choices he had made, and the public gallery seemed to agree. There are two possible outcomes to such an application. If it is accepted, then the standard court sets a monthly repayment that is significantly lower than the initial one, coupled with a reduction of the total amount of the debt. But such applications can be rejected for many reasons, such as "vagueness" in relation to data submitted, or "deceit" related to the applicant's "unrealistic" borrowing plans or consumption choices. Mr. Hatzis applied in order not to have to repay anything while the matter was sub judice. He paid 1,500 euros for the cost of the legal procedure, including the lawyer's fee. This was significantly less than the amount he would have had to pay to the creditors during the same period. However, his application was eventually rejected due to the "vagueness" of the information submitted and his failure to convince the court that he was unable to pay installments to the bank. Although another application was possible, Mr. Hatzis knew that his chances of success were poor.

Mr. Hatzis's story highlights conflicting ideas about gender and seniority. As an old man and a grandfather, he justified his behavior as the provider in his family. He relied on a well-known and morally endorsed fact that families live off pensions and that younger generations depend on this stable source of income during the years of the financial crisis. He also reminded the judge that his actions were consistent with the mores of earlier times, as it was only expected that one should spend large amounts for a daughter's or son's wedding party. However, he was retrospectively criticized for a highly legitimized practice of the recent past. The question hanging in the air was whether the court would enforce a public repudiation of past practices.

The audience and the judge reacted to class difference. Unlike Mrs. Papadopoulou, Mr. Hatzis belonged to the middle class. Contrary to pervasive ideas that "all Greeks are responsible" for the country's debt, or the related "all Greeks are victims," the audience was setting the boundaries of legitimate debt practices. It was acceptable to take out a loan for a family's main housing or for bare survival of the family, including the support of the extended members. For such loans, usually taken by the working class, there is a general consensus that a way should be found to reduce the debt to manageable proportions. However, there was less tolerance for debt relief for loans related to nonessential consumption.

Individuals were held to be responsible for taking financial risks. Financial products were widely considered to be generically fraudulent and hence their purchase an act of irrationality or, almost fraud. A few applicants (less than 5 percent) declared that they had lost money in the stock market. Since this practice is considered as almost tantamount to gambling, it was not a good argument to use at the court. However, Mr. Argiridis, a fifty-six-year-old ex-bank employee himself, elaborated to the court about how he had lost a large amount of his savings on the stock market and thus descended into a vicious circle of debt. He owed 243,000 euros to several banks, and he lived in a house he owned in Panorama, where the wealthier town inhabitants lived. In trying to convince the court, he mentioned how banks and stock market sellers did not warn clients about the risks of the financial products, portraying himself as a victim. He also described how he himself would receive bonuses as a bank employee for convincing people to take out loans. Mr. Argiridis did not manage to convince the court that he himself was a victim of such practices. His story evoked only laughter and scorn in the public gallery.

Despite the differences in the above examples, they have common broader implications. First, informal employment routinely enters into formal-legal deliberations. While informal practices are not new, acknowledgment of them by the judge is new, according to lawyers. Applicants for debt relief can claim that they took out a loan during a prosperous period when they could reasonably expect to be able to pay it back through both formal and informal labor market activity. But such a declaration may arise suspicion concerning current informal income. Judges and lawyers explore whether the applicant has informal income in order to set the monthly installment accordingly. However, they would not delve into further legal aspects of informal employment.

Second, criticism and even shaming of indebted individuals are commonplace. But equally strong moral disapprobation is directed toward the banks, especially where it is known that staff were remunerated with bonuses for aggressively selling financial products without paying due care and attention to the financial situation of their clients. Some applicants spelled this out in their defense. A fifty-five-year-old indebted woman asked the bank's representative: "Why did you offer me another loan? You probably supposed I would be able to pay it back." Ideas and practices about easy and quick money were also shared by bank employees who took out loans that they were unable to pay back.

Another common theme in the courtroom is the strength of family obligations. In legal terms, the household consists of those who live under the same roof; but applicants and judges often invoke the extended family members of several generations to strengthen their points. Family reciprocity is taken for granted by all participants. Applicants need to explain how they make a living if they do not have any income. They do so by referring to the help they get from the family. Judges assume that extended family members (outside the household and the nuclear family) and formal guarantors should be willing to help with repaying loans. They often ask about parents and the amount of their pension, and about the incomes of children. If an applicant's offspring have migrated abroad, the court expects some sort of financial remittance. However, if an applicant claims that she or he cannot get by due to obligations to support the extended family, this argument is often rejected: they should first pay off their own loan and only then help other members of their household and more distant family.

Conclusion: Financialized Kinship

When Melina started communicating with her friend Georgia anew, she underlined how their relationship had been affected by debt within their families: "It would have been a pity for our friendship to end. After all, we were both tired and stressed from all the problems we face in our times. Debt, family problems due to our parents' failing businesses . . . ." Similarly, Eleni said that stress, poverty, and indebtedness had led to tensions with her husband, but she now felt that they could continue together. The stories presented in this chapter illustrate dynamic relations between close kin and friends within the *oikos* that have been challenged by financialization. The ethnography underscores the intertwinement of official individual credit with informal debt among relatives and friends. Despite tensions, common ideas and practices of solidarity and moral obligations persist. Idealized expectations, for example concerning the elders' obligation to support younger generations, are not always realized in practice. Those who are in a position to help indebted kin and friends do so out of moral obligation, irrespectively of seniority. I have shown how this moral obligation not to act as a mere individual is further enforced by official practices. In collecting formally recorded credits to individuals, informal debt relations come into the picture by mobilizing forces within the *oikos*. Although legal regulations and procedures on debt are officially individual, indebted individuals are put under pressure by judges to exhaust all possible familial/household means to honor their obligations. However, it is not permissible to claim that a loan cannot be repaid due to other familial obligations. Debtors find themselves simultaneously in a context of family pressure, obligation, and support, and in a legal context of individual responsibility that further mobilizes the family dependency. The blurred boundaries between moral collective obligation and individual responsibility make navigation between the two hazardous. In several cases, this paradox pushes people to repay their debts and provides a protection and care network for people who need support (such as Melina's father who lives with his brother). Individual debtors cannot default via a legal mechanism. Rather, they are expected to make use of their networks within the *oikos*, which includes coresidents, nuclear family, and extended networks of kin and close friends. As the collection of debt becomes more pressing, familial ties become more important, while relations of gender and seniority are being challenged. Ideas of the indebted individual, which fit well with hegemonic discourses of financial and flexible capitalism, find their way into legal documents but not into the ensuing implementation procedures. Debt collection mechanisms and people's survival strategies vis-à-vis financialization are bound up with complex relations and moralities of mutuality, tension, and conflict within the *oikos*. Contrary to some other interpretations, I have argued that family, friendship, and the extended household ties emerge strengthened through these processes of financialized kinship, where mutual dependence is crucial for managing debt and for getting by.

Acknowledgments

Thanks to Laura Bear, Deborah James, Charlotte Bruckermann, and Theodora Vetta for discussing previous versions of the paper, and to Eirini Tountasaki and Alexandra Bakalaki for sharing ideas.

Dimitra Kofti obtained her PhD from University College, London, in 2012, and is currently Assistant Professor of anthropology at Panteion University of Social and Political Sciences in Athens, Greece. She has conducted research on work, deindustrialization, and flexibilization of labor in Bulgaria, and on debt and financialization in Greece. Her research interests include economic and political anthropology, historical anthropology, and anthropological film.

Notes

1. Private debt, which includes household and non-financial corporations debt has risen significantly since the mid-1990s, from 35.7 percent of GDP in 1995

to 128.1 percent in 2010, after which it fell to 115.3 percent in 2018. Household indebtedness, which is included in the above numbers, includes housing loans, tax and insurance bills, and consumption loans. See https://ec.europa.eu/eurostat/tgm/table.do?tab=table&plugin=1&language=en&pcode=tipspd20 (accessed 22 December 2019).

2. On gender, see Bakalaki 2015. There is no doubt that the feminization of poverty in Greece deepened in these years (Avdela 2011; Karamessini 2014).

3. This reflects the period of my fieldwork from 2016 to 2018. The gradual revaluation of property in urban and touristic areas due to the intensification of short-term rental practices has gradually changed this condition (cf. Morrell, this volume). Compared to 2016, creditors two years later were becoming more interested in property confiscation as opposed to recovering their cash.

4. In 2014, a flat-rate income tax of 22 percent was introduced and the previous threshold of 5,000 euros per year was abolished. Taxation of basic consumer goods rose from 13 percent to 24 percent in 2013. An additional "emergency" property tax per square meter was applied not only to urban housing but also to abandoned parcels of agricultural land.

5. Unemployment has increased significantly, from below 3 percent in 1975 to over 25 percent in 2015, and almost 30 percent in 2018.

6. It is difficult to estimate how common this informal practice has become. During my fieldwork, it was widespread among my interlocutors.

7. From 84.6 percent in 2005 to 73.9 percent in 2017. See https://www.kathimerini.gr/238258/article/oikonomia/ellhnikh-oikonomia/sto-846-to-pososto-idiokatoikhshs-sthn-ellada and https://ec.europa.eu/eurostat/statistics-explained/index.php/Housing_statistics (accessed 24 December 2019).

8. Prices in Thessaloniki fell by 45 percent between 2008 and 2016.

9. According to the Katselis Law of 2013 (discussed further below), the "first housing property" refers to the first housing property acquired by an individual. The "primary housing" (*κύρια κατοικία*) refers to the main residence of a family. While those two categories often coincide, they are legally different.

10. The housing that is protected should not fall into the category of luxurious housing and it should have a maximum market value of 180,000 euros.

11. The Katselis' Law was first introduced in 2010 by the centre-left PASOK government. It was amended in 2013 by the centre-right Nea Demokratia government and continued to be implemented by the leftist Syriza government.

12. European Commission (EC), International Monetary Fund (IMF), and European Central Bank (ECB). The property foreclosures and auctions that have taken place are mostly related to bankrupt companies rather than private households.

13. The way these categories were drawn up was based on intensive political discussion that cannot be outlined here. I refer to this activist group in order to underline the variety of political voices that supported the protection of housing and small-scale family company property.

14. Up to 70 square meters for a couple, with up to 20 square meters extra for each child.

15. Its "objective value" should not exceed a total amount of 200,000 euros. The value of the main housing is estimated with the objective value and not its market price.

While property market prices fell up to 50 percent, the objective value, which is estimated by the state, has remained quite stable. Before 2009, the market value of a property was higher than that of its objective value, which is estimated according to the position of the property, its condition, and its size.

16. For similar cases of business owners, see Vetta (manuscript under review).
17. Until 2007, they also grew tobacco. Tobacco production was an important agricultural activity in North Greece from the 1960s, though it gradually lost significance after 1992 when subsidies were cut. It almost ceased after 2006, following a change in EU regulations.

References

Athanasiou, Athena. 2012. *I Krisi os Katastasi Ektaktis Anagkis* (The Crisis as "State of Emergency"). Athens: Savvalas. (In Greek)

Avdela, Efi. 2011. "To filo stin (se) Krisi i ti Simvainei stis 'Ginaikes' se Halepous Kairous?" ("Gender in [the] 'Crisis': What Happens to 'Women' in Hard Times?") *Sighrona Themata (Contemporary Issues)* 115: 17–26. (In Greek)

Bakalaki, A. 2015. "Crisis, Gender, Time." *Allegra-Lab*. Accessed 9 August 2019. https://allegralaboratory.net/crisis-gender-time/.

Cabot, Heath. 2016. "'Contagious' Solidarity: Reconfiguring Care and Citizenship in Greece's Social Clinics." *Social Anthropology* 24, no. 2: 152–66.

Douzina-Bakalaki, Phaedra. 2017. "Volunteering Mothers: Engaging the Crisis in a Soup Kitchen of Northern Greece." *Anthropology Matters* 17, no. 1: 1–24.

Friedl, Ernestine. 1967. *Vasilika: A Village in Modern Greece*. New York: Holt, Rinehart and Winston.

Gudeman, Steve, and Chris Hann. 2015. "Introduction: Self-Sufficiency as Reality and Myth." In *Oikos and Market: Explorations in Self-Sufficiency after Socialism*, edited by Steve Gudeman and Chris Hann. New York: Berghahn Books, 1–23.

Hirschon, Renée. 1989. *Heirs of the Greek Catastrophe: The Social Life of Asia Minor Refugees in Piraeus*. Oxford: Clarendon.

James, Deborah. 2015. *Money from Nothing: Indebtedness and Aspiration in South Africa*. Stanford, CA: Stanford University Press.

Just, Roger. 2000. *A Greek Island Cosmos: Kinship & Community on Meganisi*. Melton, UK: James Currey.

Karamessini, Maria. 2014. "Structural Crisis and Adjustment in Greece: Social Regression and the Challenge to Gender Equality." In *Women and Austerity: The Economic Crisis and the Future of Gender Equality*, edited by Maria Karamessini and Jill Rubery, 165–84. London: Routledge.

Knight, Daniel. 2018. "The Desire for Disinheritance in Austerity Greece." *Focaal* 80: 30–42.

Kravva, Vasiliki. 2014. "Politicizing Hospitality: The Emergency Food Assistance Landscape in Thessaloniki." *Hospitality & Society* 4, no. 3: 249–74.

Lazzarato, Maurizio. 2012. *The Making of the Indebted Man: An Essay on the Neoliberal Condition*. Cambridge, MA: Semiotexte.

Lazzarato, Maurizio. 2015. *Governing by Debt*. Cambridge, MA: Semiotexte.

Martin, Randy. 2002. *Financialization of Everyday Life*. Philadelphia: Temple University Press.

Mattioli, Fabio. 2018. "Financialization without Liquidity: In-kind Payments, Forced Credit, and Authoritarianism at the Periphery of Europe." *JRAI* 24: 1–21.

Mikuš, Marek. 2019. "Contesting Household Debt in Croatia: The Double Movement of Financialization and the Fetishism of Money in Easter Europe Peripheries." *Dialectical Anthropology* 43, no. 3: 295–315.

Nitsiakos, Vassilis. 1991. *Paradosiakes Koinonikes Domes* (Traditional Social Structures). Athens: Odusseus. (In Greek)

Offe, Claus. 2015. *Europe Entrapped*. Cambridge, UK: Polity.

Palomera, Jaime. 2014. "Reciprocity, Commodification, and Poverty in the Era of Financialization." *Current Anthropology* 55, no. S9: S105–S15.

Papataxiarchis, Evthymios. 2008. "Oikiakes Anataraxeis: Diaforopoiisi tou 'Noikokuriou' kai Politismiki Pollaplotita" (Domestic turbulences: Differentiation of the "household" and cultural multiplicity). In *Kosmoi tis oikiakis ergasias: Fulo, Metanasteusi kai Politismikoi Metashimatismoi stin Athina tou Proimou 20ou aiona* (Worlds of domestic labor: Gender, migration and cultural transformations in Athens in the early 20th century), edited by Evthymios Papataxiarchis, 329–46. Athina: Alexandreia. (In Greek)

———. 2013. "Shaping Modern Times in the Greek Family: A Comparative View of Gender and Kinship Transformations after 1974." In *State, Economy, Society (19th–20th Centuries): Essays in Honor of Emeritus Professor George Dertilis*, edited by Ada. Dialla and Niki Maroniti, 217–44. Athens: Metaihmio.

Peebles, Gustav. 2010. "The Anthropology of Credit and Debt." *Annual Review of Anthropology* 39: 225–40.

Rakopoulos, Theodoros. 2014. "Resonance of Solidarity: Meanings of a Local Concept in Anti-Austerity Greece." *Journal of Modern Greek Studies* 32, no. 2: 313–37.

Rozakou, Katerina. 2016. "Socialities of Solidarity: Revisiting the Gift Taboo in Times of Crises." *Social Anthropology* 24, no. 2: 185–99.

Sabaté, Irene. 2016. "The Spanish Mortgage Crisis and the Re-emergence of Moral Economies in Uncertain Times." *History and Anthropology* 27, no. 1: 107–20.

Streinzer, Andreas. 2016. "Stretching Money to Pay the Bills: Temporal Modalities and Relational Practices of 'Getting By' in the Greek Economic Crisis." *Cambridge Journal of Anthropology* 34, no. 1: 45–57.

Tountasaki, Eirini. 2015. *"To Paidi pou tha Megalosei Mesa Sou tha Parei ki Apo Sena": Dorea oarion, Mitrotita kai Siggeneia* ("The child growing inside you will get something from you": Ovum donation, motherhood and kinship). Athens: Patakis. (In Greek)

Van der Zwan, Natascha. 2014. "Making Sense of Financialization." *Socio-Economic Review* 12, no. 1: 99–129.

Vetta, Theodora, and Jaime Palomera. 29 February 2020, early view. "Concrete Stories in Southern Europe: Financialization and Inequality in the Construction Chain." *Antipode*. https://doi.org/10.1111/anti.12620.

Vetta, Theodora. Forthcoming. "Households in Trial: Over-indebtedness, State and Moral Struggles in Greece," in Jelena Tošić and Andreas Streinzer (eds), *Ethnographies of Deservingness: Unpacking Ideologies of Distribution and Inequality*. New York: Berghahn Books.

Vernier, Bernard. 1991. *La genèse sociale des sentiments: Aînés et cadets dans l'île grecque de Karpathos*. Paris: Éditions de l'École des hautes études en sciences sociales.

Weiss, Hadas. 2014. "Homeownership in Israel: The Social Costs of Middle-Class Debt." *Cultural Anthropology* 29, no. 1: 128–49.

12

Financialized Landscapes and Transport Infrastructure

The Case of Ciudad Valdeluz

Natalia Buier

Economic development in Spain between 1995 and 2007 is frequently labeled "the Spanish miracle," as the 4 percent yearly growth of its GDP put Spain well ahead of the majority of the Western economies of the EU, which were struggling to meet the 2 percent mark (López and Rodríguez 2010, 2011). The motor of this growth was the construction sector, with ramifications in the housing market and large-scale infrastructural development, or what David Harvey has dubbed the secondary circuit of accumulation (Harvey 2006). The 2007 crisis brought the collapse of the housing market, and Spain became an emblematic case of the "housing bubble" and an exemplar of the effects of financial speculation. It has been argued that Spain presents one of or maybe even the purest version of the contemporary model of financialized growth (Observatorio Metropolitano de Madrid 2013). While the effects of the collapse of the mortgage market in the United States were widely felt and amply debated, this case is complicated by the more diversified composition of the US economy. Spain, however, is a paradigmatic example of an economy restructured around the marriage of financial and housing assets (see Morell, this volume). Within a few years, millions of homes were empty and foreclosures approached 100,000 annually (Observatori DESC i Plataforma d'Afectats per la Hipoteca 2013).

For those looking for an alternative to the status quo, Spain has offered some reasons for optimism. The strongest response to the housing crisis has been politically articulated on the left. The PAH (Plataforma de Afectados por la Hipoteca—Platform for People Affected by Mortgages) and subsequent developments (Sabaté 2016a, 2016b; Morell and Sabaté Muriel 2017) have firmly put on the agenda a politics that aims to challenge the sacrosanctity of the principle of private property and seeks to give voice to the indebted homeowner as a political subject. The movement has, of course, also met enormous resistance, both institutionally and at the level of everyday political groundwork. In this chapter, I explore this space of resistance. Rather than make any claim about successful political mobilization on the left, I analyze a conjuncture in which, in spite of a profound experience of crisis, the political response remains firmly entrenched in the imaginary of seamless growth. This analysis is couched in a broader discussion about the conditions that have enabled Spain's specific model of financialized growth.

The finance-housing alliance and overaccumulation in the secondary circuit[1] characteristic of the Spanish economy have also depended on a lesser known, less discussed infrastructural boom. The most visible expression of this is the dramatic oversupply of transport infrastructure. Contrary to those who view transport infrastructure development as incidental to structural transformations of the built environment, I argue that the hypertrophy of the infrastructural pillar of the construction sector has had deep consequences for the organization of everyday life in the new spaces of financialized capitalism. I therefore start with a discussion of the relationship between urban development and Spain's impressive high-speed rail network and introduce its specific manifestation in Ciudad Valdeluz—an urban development project connected to the expansion of high-speed rail. I then delve into the geographies of financialized accumulation by investigating the main political response to the experience of crisis in Valdeluz, namely the political platform 40 Compromisos ("40 Commitments"). I argue that the case of Valdeluz is instructive for understanding the specificity of exchange value in relation to the built environment. Unlike commodities produced in the primary circuit, the exchange value of the components of the built environment, in this case housing, are determined in relation to other elements of a spatial configuration. This has profound consequences for the way people understand themselves and organize their lives as property owners. Through the case of Valdeluz, I reveal the political articulation of lived experience as relentlessly future oriented, resolutely conservative, and distinctly vulnerable. Ultimately, this allows to substantiate David Harvey's observation that "there is no politics of space independent of social relations" (Harvey 1976).

Transport and Urban Development

The records established in the Spanish housing sector are easily matched by the lesser known ones in transport. The most impressive is the expansion of Spain's high-speed rail network: at over 3,200 km and with more than a thousand kilometers under construction, today, this is Europe's longest HSR network and globally second only to that of China (European Commission 2017). The inauguration of what is locally known as the AVE (Alta Velocidad Española) took place in 1992, with the Madrid–Seville line. After a relatively sluggish first decade, by the early 2000s, the conditions were in place for a dramatic acceleration. The bulk of today's network was constructed during the 2000s, when dramatic rates of growth translated into a continuously accelerating transformation of the physical environment. While the AVE is certainly the jewel in the crown, it is not a singular development. By 2019, Spain also boasted the longest motorway network in Europe and a spectacular total of forty-seven commercial airports (European Commission 2017).

An in-depth analysis of the relationship between housing and transportation in the contemporary Spanish context is still missing, but inroads have been made in revealing the transport infrastructure boom as a key aspect of accumulation in the secondary circuit (Observatorio Metropolitano de Madrid 2013; Naredo 2010; Segura 2012). By and large, however, existing analysis has treated the expansion of transport infrastructure as derivative of the housing boom. Transport has not been sufficiently integrated into an analysis of the consequences of the financial crisis. Yet transport infrastructure both follows and advances processes of land valorization and urban development. The failure of the promises of mobility and connectivity that accompanied this form of infrastructural growth has resulted in strenuous attempts to salvage the hopes of urbanity. Stereotypical images of hypermobility and connectivity contradict the actual experience of disconnection, forced mobility, and the lengthening of the working day through the journey to work.

One way to characterize the AVE network is to describe it in terms of the central and peripheral locations it connects. In 2019, the forty-seven stops it connects correspond either to central urban nodes or peripheral stations that have enabled the acceleration of urbanization and opened up new areas for development. Valdeluz is one of the latter. Its history begins in 2003, when the location for the new AVE station for Guadalajara was decided. The decision to build the station approximately 10 km outside the city was mired in suspicions of corruption. The suspicions were strengthened by the subsequent announcement that an urban development project (PAU— Proyecto de Actuación Urbanistica) would be attached to the new train station. To make the most of this privileged stop on the Madrid–Barcelona route,[2] the new locality was promoted as a town built from scratch with an almost instantaneous connection to Madrid.

Valdeluz was administratively located within the boundaries of Yebes, a Castilian village of some two hundred inhabitants. It was developed on the property of Teresa Valdés, heir to the marques of Valdés and by marriage related to Esperanza Aguirre, at the time a high profile member of the Partido Popular (PP—Popular Party). It soon became the flagship project of Reyal (later Reyal Urbis), one of the most important construction companies at the time. The company later came to occupy a leading position on the list of spectacular Spanish bankruptcies. The history of Valdeluz is intimately tied to the fortunes of Reyal. Valdeluz was designed as a town for 34,000 people who would occupy about 9,500 housing units. It was intended as a four-phase project to attract middle and upper middle class residents of Madrid, who were promised the advantages of a fast connection to the capital (eighteen minutes to the central station), the pleasures of suburban tranquility, and the benefits of a comparatively low price.

Between 1991 and 2014, the price of property per square meter more than doubled in Spain, going from 700 euros to almost 1,500 euros (González, Mantiñán, and Miró 2016). But in 2006, before the crisis hit, the national figure was almost 2,000 euros. The capital, however, had surpassed all records, and in 2006, prices per square meter had reached 3,000 euros (Maldonado and Pérez 2011). Between 1960 and 2007, the housing stock in Madrid quadrupled (reaching 2.8 million units in 2007); yet prices kept growing. As it has been shown, demographic pressure can hardly account for this, as between 1993 and 2003 population growth in the region of Madrid was 12 percent, while growth in urbanized land during the same years was 47 percent (Díaz Orueta and Lourés Seoane 2012). While aggregate data for prices in Valdeluz is unavailable, my interviews clearly show that those buying property in Valdeluz prior to 2007 were paying exorbitant prices that were still competitive in relation to prices in the capital. The comparatively low price of housing features prominently in most explanations I have encountered regarding the decision to buy a house in Valdeluz. According to interview data, those buying property in Valdeluz were paying a premium in relation to the average price in Castilla La Mancha (in 2007, this was roughly half the price per square meter in Madrid), but still significantly less than for property of comparable characteristics in Madrid: in 2005 the price of a "luxury" one bedroom flat was around 140,000 euros.

When the first residents arrived in 2006 into, according to their own recollections, what was still a gigantic construction site, they were optimistic about the future of the place that had been advertised as "Spain's first town built from scratch." This soon dissolved. In 2008, with housing for approximately ten thousand people completed, the project was brought to a halt. Reyal Urbis, with an estimated debt of 4.6 billion euros, entered a long process of debt restructuring which eventually culminated in a declaration of bankruptcy in 2017. With basic amenities still lacking and only a few hundred residents, Valdeluz seemed destined to become a symbol of speculative urbanization. Western media, with their penchant for depicting the ills of the Southerners, found in Valdeluz the perfect location for illustrating the ghost towns of Spain. With the assistance of *Le Monde* (Bozonnet 2008), *The Guardian* (Chakrabortty 2011), *Süddeutsche Zeitung* (von der Hagen 2013), and the *Daily Mail* (Johnson 2012), "Spain's first town built from scratch" acquired a corrosive notoriety that threatened to push the prices of massively devalued property down even further.[3]

A Double Bind

The financial crisis and its repercussions in the real estate sector brought dramatic developments. As cranes stood still and the numbers of migrant workers commuting daily to Valdeluz to advance its construction grew thinner, the first residents became alarmed. Their small number, surrounded by empty houses and unfinished infrastructure, was the first problem. Numbers were essential to securing essential services, from trash disposal to regular medical facilities. Among the few residents, many were reluctant to give up their previous official addresses, which allowed them to access services in their former places of residence, typically Madrid and its surroundings. Since many of the houses had been sold for speculative purposes in a climate of optimism about forever-rising housing prices, the situation was worsened by the problem of absentee owners. In addition to the problems resulting from actual living conditions in Valdeluz, the situation looked even grimmer because of the devaluation of their assets.

Most first-generation residents[4] of Valdeluz were relocating from Madrid or its outer ring. They were looking for the type of environment stereotypically attractive to middle class families, away from the nuisances and dangers of life in an expanding metropolis. The benefits of suburban living feature prominently in their recollections, yet interviews point clearly to the main selection mechanism: housing prices. The first to buy property in Valdeluz paid precrisis prices, which meant that a three room apartment cost as much as 250,000 euros, while those looking for added comfort paid up to half a million euros for a condo. While in relation to their destination these first-generation residents appear to be upwardly mobile middle class property owners, the moving away from Madrid signaled their exclusion from the housing market in the capital due to prohibitive prices.

Not all newcomers were happy to trade centrality for the comfort of a bigger apartment away, but the location of Valdeluz next to the AVE station promised the impossible: the comforts and accessibility of suburban life only twenty minutes away from Madrid. The first to move to Valdeluz anticipated a subsidized shuttle service ensuring frequent and affordable links to the capital. With Valdeluz reduced to a carcass of speculative development, this plan was withdrawn. By the time of my field research in 2017 the station that had cost 11,000,000 euros had about one hundred daily users, most of whom were not even residents of Valdeluz. The distance between Madrid and Valdeluz remains for most people a time-consuming 60 km drive rather than a swift eighteen-minute ride. Those who moved to Valdeluz with the expectation of a short commute to Madrid have either tried to accommodate their working and family lives to a reality in sharp contrast with what they were promised, or had to look for employment closer to their new home (usually Guadalajara).

Valdeluz is just one example of the challenges of integrating expanding disperse territorial structures. The urban sprawl of financialized growth has been accompanied by an impressive expansion of transport infrastructure. However, mobility patterns have become increasingly polarized: for the few who can afford it, the AVE offers a subsidized luxury transport service, while the majority experience its effects through disinvestment in conventional rail services and ever longer commutes. Rather than freeing up time, for the majority of travelers, the expansion of transport infrastructure has translated into added pressure to move between increasingly distant spaces of production and reproduction. In what follows, I take a closer look at the double bind in which the first-generation residents of Valdeluz found themselves: that any change for the better depended on a growth in the number of residents; but without the dream of a fast connection to Madrid, that increase was unlikely to occur.

40 Compromisos and the Politics of Interrupted Urbanization

In order to understand the particular forms of political organization that emerged in Valdeluz, it is necessary to place them in broader spatial arrangements. In 2011, 40 Compromisos ("40 Commitments") became the main political force in Valdeluz after winning the local election. Just when the 15 M movement (more commonly known internationally as the *Indignados*) was making its powerful appearance, Valdeluz was experiencing its own political revolution. 40 Compromisos is a local political platform that derives from a neighbors association formed by first-generation residents. Its trajectory, from neighbors association to political party, can be explained only by reference to the particular logic of the administrative structure into which Valdeluz was inserted from its beginnings.

Valdeluz is administratively subordinated to the village of Yebes.[5] In 2003, when the location for Guadalajara's AVE station was announced, Yebes was a dying village of 215 residents, like many others in Castille.

Testimony to the length of Yebes' foretold death is the 1972 comedy *Guapo heredera busca esposa*. Yebes is the real location for this movie, which depicts the story of a fictionalized village struggling with the consequences of rural exodus and an aging population. It tells the story of the village shepherd, who, as the last eligible bachelor in the village, can inherit a large amount of land on condition that he marries promptly. Locals still recall the turmoil this produced in the village and their roles as extras. But just like its fictional counterpart, the recent history of Yebes hinges on a conditional opportunity. Yebes is an incarnation of the consequences of the neoliberal model for the decentralization of administration and the entrepreneurial shift in fiscal policy at the local and municipal level. Localities' dependence on revenues from their own entrepreneurial activity, development taxes, and land markets is remarkably expressed in the trajectory of Yebes. With the arrival of Reyal in Valdeluz, the village budget grew from a few thousand euros to over 20,000,000 euros. This bonanza brought with it a wave of optimism; or in the words of Aurelio Sánchez Nicolás, mayor of Yebes between 1983 and 2011, "hope had returned to the village."

Between 2003 and 2011, developments in Valdeluz were overseen from Yebes, and the mayor's job was transformed. Yebes had always been a bastion of the Partido Popular (or, as locals can often be heard saying, *del PP de toda la vida*). In the words of locals, Aurelio "inherited" the office of mayor from his father, who had been the mayor of Yebes for twenty-seven years during Francoism. The PP oversaw the emergence of Valdeluz and concomitant dramatic transformations in the physical landscape of the village of Yebes, where most of the cash surplus generated by development in Valdeluz was spent. Thus, Yebes too was drawn into a frenzy of development: a new multistory building was built to host the mayor's office and a new house of culture, and the construction of a two-million–euro cemetery began. A massive housing project was initiated, comprising several hundred family homes. By 2017, most of these houses lay empty, in an advanced state of dilapidation, while the majority of residents were to be found in the old nucleus. When one asks why the Yebes-based administration did not invest in Valdeluz, villagers and former members of the administration say that "everything was new there," or "everything was already being done there," while their own village had suffered marginalization and disinvestment for decades.

Things looked quite different from Valdeluz, and this difference in perspective was essential for the trajectory of 40 Compromisos. The repercussions of the crisis in Valdeluz started making themselves felt early on: garbage was not collected, letters not delivered, and children could not be taken to the doctor because none was available locally. To make their needs and grievances heard, first-generation residents formed a neighbors association; but their complaints fell on deaf ears in Yebes. According to members of 40 Compromisos, the closed village mentality of the PP-controlled administration was impossible to penetrate; the needs of those living in Valdeluz remained unrepresented. The contingent integration of Yebes and Valdeluz into one administrative unit was rendered more unstable by their physical separation. Valdeluz is 11 km away from Yebes. The connection by road between the two localities passes through the village of Horche. The original project for Valdeluz included plans for a new direct road link, but this never materialized. Between the complications arising from initial planning errors and the unwillingness of farmers from Horche to sell their land to build the road, the distance between the two localities remains approximately as long as that between Valdeluz and Guadalajara. After 2011, however, the power relation was inverted, and it was the turn of the villagers of Yebes to complain.

In Search of Growth: From Neighbors Association to Political Party

Faced with a reluctant local administration that appeared to represent only the interests of the villagers, the members of the neighbors association realized that if anything was to change, they would have to modify the negative reputation that Valdeluz had acquired nationally and internationally. In addition to securing essential services, they would have to counter stigmatization. Managing the reputation of Valdeluz focused on media representations and led to an almost obsessive preoccupation with PR in 40 Compromisos. Recent developments resulting from the collapse of the housing market played into their hands. What from the ownership end looked like entrapment gradually morphed into an attractive opportunity for a different category of future residents. From 2010 onward, population growth resumed at a steady pace as a new generation of customers took advantage of the low property prices. By 2017, the official population had reached 2,652, but unofficial estimates indicate it surpassed 4,000.[6]

In this context, the neighbors association, rebaptized as 40 Compromisos, decided it was time to take part in local elections and finally shift the center of the administration from Yebes to Valdeluz. In the spring of 2011, it won the local elections. Joaquín Ormazabal, a founding member of the former neighbors association, a law graduate and banker of Basque origins with no previous political experience, became the new mayor of Yebes-Valdeluz, thus putting an end to almost three decades of continuous rule by the PP in Yebes. 40 Compromisos had a majority until the 2015 elections, following which it formed a coalition with the PSOE (Partido Socialista

Obrero Español—Spanish Socialist Workers Party), from whose ranks the new mayor, Miguel Cocera, was elected. As its very name suggests, *40 Compromisos* was always an issue-oriented political formation. Its members describe it as eclectic. In their own description, what united them was their desire to organize as neighbors and take matters into their own hands. The ideological spectrum is described as ranging from center-right to a more traditional left, but some individual members resist any pigeonholing. After a convoluted search for a political home, 40 Compromisos eventually joined the UPyD (Unión Progreso y Democracia—Union, Progress, and Democracy). Other established parties were reluctant to be associated with a place that was so deeply enmeshed in stories of corruption. Valdeluz, no longer star project but toxic asset, was also toxic politically. Joaquín Ormazabal's personal sympathy for UPyD, a Spanish nationalist party of Basque origins, played a decisive role.

The political program of 40 Compromisos was based on forty proposals that originated in the experience of daily life in Valdeluz. A few were broadly and abstractly defined, such as, "building around an idea: Valdeluz is the new municipal epicenter" (i.e., as opposed to Yebes); others, such as modifying the urban planning of Valdeluz to attract economic investments, reflected the type of growth strategy the members had in mind; many were concrete, such as building eight ecological islands for recycling, reestablishing the private security service, increasing the number of buses from nine to thirty a day, and reallocating 15 percent of investment to participatory budgeting.[7] One of the major unfulfilled commitments is securing the regional HSR service, referred to as "the shuttles" (*las lanzaderas*), and without which, the initial program stated, "Valdeluz makes no sense." Meanwhile another first-generation resident and party activist in his previous place of residence established the PSOE branch in Valdeluz. The main enemy of 40 Compromisos remains PP—although it has developed its own electoral base in Valdeluz, PP remains identified as the political force that represents the interests of the villagers of Yebes.

The members of 40 Compromisos are united by their experience as first-generation residents. They have all had to reckon with the collapse of their initial expectations and rethink their lives accordingly. Invariably, for those who entered the administration through the electoral process, almost exclusively middle aged men (with one exception), this was also an opportunity for local employment. In a place where opportunities for employment were very limited, electoral victory meant the possibility of a job within walking distance from home. The seeking of personal gain through converting into a paid politician features prominently in the criticism raised against 40 Compromisos. Joaquín Ormazabal, mayor between 2011 and 2015, was accused of breaking his promise not to leave his job at a bank and instead seeking to gain material benefits through his office. Joaquín defends himself by saying that his salary as a mayor was less than he had earned before, and that he had found it impossible to reconcile working at the bank with his duties as a mayor. Interviews with the core members of 40 Compromisos clearly show that the hope of material gain was not the main incentive for their political involvement. But it is true that electoral success of 40 Compromisos offered the paid members of the administration the possibility of meaningful employment at home.

The dominant characteristic of the political imaginary of 40 Compromisos is best described not as apolitical but eclectic. The case of Joaquín is instructive in this regard. After failing to secure his reelection, he decided to withdraw from local politics and return to his job at the bank. Joaquín considers himself "very much to the left" on some issues, such as public education and minority rights, but on the right when it comes to issues such as national unity and urban security. What seems to hold together rather seamlessly the diverse reformist imaginaries is the shared commitment to the scale of the politics of 40 Compromisos, which remains programmatically within the horizon of local politics. Contradictory elements acquire coherence through being integrated into an imaginary of growth. The baseline of the politics of 40 Compromisos is a commitment to restoring Valdeluz to a trajectory of growth, something that finds expression in frequent assertions of the need for long-term planning. For example, the horizon of Vidal, councilor for urbanism and infrastructure, is some twenty to thirty years in the future. Like others, he deplores the search for short-term speculative gain. While members and supporters of 40 Compromisos are profoundly lucid about the issues that have affected their locality, even the most critical of explanations is couched in the language of deviation and exception to normal capitalist growth. Crisis appears as a savage but ultimately exceptional event. In contrast, measured expectations for slower but steady growth, backed by planning from below and aided by expertise, are presented as the only possible basis for sustainable growth. The legitimization crisis into which the dominant political response in Valdeluz is inscribed rests on two pillars: it is future-oriented and conservative, to the extent that change is always a function not of altering social relations but restoring them to an illusory state of equilibrium. However, the peculiarities of the social transformation affecting Valdeluz in the aftermath of the crisis make this particular political expression distinctly vulnerable.

From Ghost Town to a Town of Hope

When the Spanish real estate market collapsed and the price of housing sank to as little as 30 percent of precrisis values, those who had thought real estate would offer a secure form of saving saw their expectations shattered. Matters were made worse in Valdeluz by the situation of interrupted urbanization. Since the project was halted before basic amenities were put in place, living in Valdeluz at the time frequently meant being almost alone in an entire apartment block and that it was almost impossible to resell property. Early efforts of the organized neighbors were therefore directed toward promoting a positive image: the idea that "one lives well in Valdeluz" (*En Valdeluz se vive bien*), a phrase we constantly heard. Following a cue from an online article (Ramón 2013), members of 40 Compromisos in 2017 were likely to present Valdeluz as a story of rebirth: "from ghost town to a town of hope" (*De ciudad fantasma a ciudad esperanza*), "the spirit of Valdeluz" was again infused with a sense of optimism.

This change has come about mostly through people in the region of Guadalajara and those working in the Henares corridor moving to Valdeluz. These "second-generation" residents are taking advantage of the low prices and the banks' willingness to get rid of their housing stock at below-market values. After the developers had declared bankruptcy, most of the empty homes reverted to the banks. Low purchase prices and rental options revived the market. A lease-to-own model gives the renter the option of purchasing the property, with a fraction of the rent paid hitherto being deducted from the final price. A widely circulated newspaper article summed up this dynamic as "Ciudad Valdeluz: From ghost town to paradise of divorcees and *mileuristas*"[8] (Villarino 2015). Unlike first-generation residents, those arriving in Valdeluz in this phase are not mobile middle-class residents relocating from Madrid. Some are working class natives of the region of Guadalajara; others are immigrants who arrived in Spain during the latest cycle of economic growth. Although difficult to quantify numerically, stories abound about people relocating following a disruptive event in their lives, frequently a divorce, thus the image of Valdeluz as a paradise of divorcees. The new residents tend to look at their property not as a form of investment but as the available bargain, and are much less optimistic about their property as a form of investment; they tend to look at it through its use value. Second-generation residents compare what they paid with old catalogue prices while they talk about how in different circumstances, they could not have afforded a paddle court, a pool, or the greater security of a private courtyard.

As Valdeluz began casting off its reputation as a ghost town, things also seemed to improve from the point of view of first-generation property owners. While prices remain well below pre-2007 levels, the slow but steady growth has restored owners' optimistic outlook, many of whom now appear confident that in the not too distant future, the exchange value of their property will be restored to precrisis levels. However, the politics and objectives of 40 Compromisos, firmly rooted in the outlook of first-generation residents, have been increasingly confronted with a different type of problem. While the dynamic of demographic growth has been essential to restoring confidence in the future of Valdeluz, the social differences between first- and second-generation residents have been increasingly expressed in discourses of urban security and aspirations to public order. In the discourse of members of 40 Compromisos, this difference manifests itself through the opposition between *the owner* and *the tenant.* The property-owning citizen appears as the privileged political subject in the political discourse of members of 40 Compromisos, while tenants frequently appear characterized by an excessively entitled attitude. In the words of one of the members of the administration, remembering his response to a woman who had gone to the town hall to complain: "So I asked her, are you an owner?" The difference between owners and tenants does not entirely overlap with the difference between first- and second-generation residents, since second-generation residents are also buying property, but first-generation residents are owners, and it is this experience that has been defining for articulating the political discourse of 40 Compromisos. The figure of the entitled tenant is joined by the figure of the *okupa* (squatter). Members of 40 Compromisos talk about their efforts to cover up stories about the squatting cases that occurred in Valdeluz, since it was believed these would undermine the positive image they were trying to construct. But in spite of the "successful" elimination of the problem, the figure of the squatter still haunts the visions of urban life of members of 40 Compromisos as a constant potential threat to suburban order and civility.

The centrality of the property owner in the political imaginary of 40 Compromisos can be traced back to the actual experience of first-generation residents. Yet, the appeal of this imaginary has not been reduced to first-generation residents, as it also resonates with the fears of working class owners who bought their homes after the collapse of the housing market. Fears of urban insecurity emerge both in relation to stories of relocation, in which immigrant working class neighborhoods of Madrid appear as dangerous and insecure, as well as in the conjuring of the figure of the immigrant as a menacing figure in Valdeluz. Yet, this has not and cannot result in unambiguous support for 40 Compromisos. While the property-owning subject of 40 Compromisos feels equally threatened by those perceived as marginal, the combination of middle-class values and aspiration to cosmopolitanism (as evidenced by Joaquín Ormazábal's progressive sexual and feminist politics) hardly speaks to the working class experience of relocation. The conservative PP has been, in this sense, better positioned to electorally capitalize on such fears, as evidenced by the increase in their electoral support.

As different parties confront each other on the electoral terrain, the difference between first- and second-generation residents remains visibly inscribed in the public spaces of Valdeluz. A visit to the two bars in Valdeluz is almost a laboratory-like reproduction of separation along class lines: affordable prices, ethnic diversity, and rhythms visibly tied to the working day unmistakably remind one that she is in the working class *Moon*. The middle class *Capri* is a reminder of the lifestyle aspirations of a category of residents increasingly outnumbered: central Madrid prices and over-heard conversations about the private businesses of children are conspic-uous signs of markedly different lifestyles. It is probably only a matter of time before class differences in Valdeluz will stop echoing the differences between first- and second-generation residents. While the experiential origins of the politics of 40 Compromisos might be erased together with the fading out of the conflict between first- and second-generation residents, it is unlikely that the underlying vulnerability of this political response will disappear in the process. Even when the memory of the fragility the middle class owner faced with crisis will have subsided, shrinking relative numbers of the same category are likely to render this discourse increasingly inade-quate as an electoral tool.

The Relational Nature of Exchange Value

The brief history of Valdeluz, told through the lens of 40 Compromisos, is a window into the particularities of the exchange value of the components of the built environment. Unlike commodities produced in the first circuit, the value of housing is only determined in relation to other elements of a spatial configuration. Given the fixity of the components of the built envi-ronment, transport plays a crucial role, since connectivity can function as a leveler of difference. In Valdeluz, the AVE was supposed to be the vehicle for creating a prosperous new urban space, rather than a distant urban dormitory. The experience of disconnection has brought with it a return of difference, while the idea that distance can be annihilated by speed has receded into the background. The politics of 40 Compromisos, wed to the initial promise of Valdeluz, maintains the idea of a form of capitalism free of crisis and the stability of its imagined corollary lifestyles. Yet, this particular political response, which carries the ideals of middle class property owners seeking to restore the value of their property, is entirely dependent on the reconfiguration of social relations in the aftermath of the crisis. The middle class property owner is revealed as profoundly vulnerable in the face of the structural instability of financialized growth, and wholly dependent on the crisis-stricken working class, the ranks of which he hoped to escape.

Acknowledgments

This chapter draws on fieldwork carried out in the spring of 2017 and builds on my earlier doctoral fieldwork on the development of Spanish high-speed rail. During my research in Valdeluz, I was accompanied by Diego Ruedas Torres, to whom I am deeply indebted for his practical support and intellectual comradeship.

Natalia Buier obtained her PhD from the Sociology and Social Anthropology Department of the Central European University in 2016. She is currently researching the relationship between infrastructural development, financialization, and the production of nature.

Notes

1. The secondary circuit of accumulation includes the built environment for production (infrastructure) and the built environment for consumption (housing).
2. The Madrid-Barcelona HSR connection was inaugurated in 2008. The connection to the French border was completed in 2013.
3. While the devaluation of housing assets is notoriously difficult to estimate, and exact figures difficult to produce, estimates for the post-2007 collapse of the real estate market point to a 30–40 percent drop in prices as a national average (Vergés 2012; Montalvo 2013; López and Rodríguez 2010). The crisis is also reflected in the drop in the total number of transactions. Estimates for the 2007–2013 period show a 60 percent drop in the total number of real estate transactions in the region of Castilla la Mancha (Montalvo 2013). While aggregate data for Valdeluz is unavailable, my own ethnographic data suggests that the national trends were much more severe in the case of Valdeluz. Real estate advertizing boasts discounts of up to 60 percent as compared to precrisis prices.
4. I use the terms "first generation residents" and "second generation residents" to differentiate between those who moved to Valdeluz before and after the 2007–2008 collapse of the property market.
5. The particular geographical relationship between Valdeluz and Yebes is relevant. Administratively integrated into the municipality of Yebes, Valdeluz is spatially separated from it, thus it is designated as an "exclave" (in the sense of a territorial unit administratively connected but geographically separated from a main region).

6. The difference between the two numbers shows the degree to which locals are still reluctant to give up formal residence in Madrid or Guadalajara, which allows them to access services absent or considered inferior in Valdeluz. The informal estimates are based on data gathered by the municipality on the basis of water bills. However, official registration numbers reveal not only the dynamic of demographic growth (this figure should be cautiously employed as an estimate of precise trends in demographic change), but also the degree to which the municipality's campaign for official registration has been successful. In 2007, there were 37 people registered as officially living in Valdeluz; 197 in 2008; 354 in 2009; while by 2011, this figure had reached 1,276.
7. The process through which a part of the municipal budget is allocated on the basis of direct consultation with citizens and following citizens' initiatives.
8. A term popularized after 2007, literally referring to somebody who earns a thousand euros.

References

Bozonnet, Jean-Jacques. 2008. "Espagne: 'Bienvenidos' à Valdeluz, ville fantôme." *Le Monde*. 22 October. Accessed 6 February 2020. https://www.lemonde.fr/europe/article/2008/10/22/espagne-bienvenidos-a-valdeluz-ville-fantome_1109723_3214.html.

Chakrabortty, Aditya. 2011. "Nightmare for Residents Trapped in Spanish Ghost Towns." *The Guardian*. 28 March. Accessed 6 February 2020. https://www.theguardian.com/world/2011/mar/28/residents-trapped-spanish-ghost-towns.

Díaz Orueta, Fernando, and María Luisa Lourés Seoane. 2012. "Suburbanización y cambio social en la metrópoli madrileña." *Revista de Ciencias Sociales (Cr)* 4, no. 138: 111–24.

European Commission. 2017. "EU Transport in Figures." *Statistical Pocketbook*.

González, Ruben Camilo Lois, María Jose Piñeira Mantiñán, and Sònia Vives Miró. 2016. "539. El proceso urbanizador en España (1990–2014): una interpretación desde la geografía y la teoría de los circuitos de capital." *Scripta Nova. Revista Electrónica de Geografía y Ciencias Sociales* 20: 527–51.

Harvey, David. 1976. "Labor, Capital, and Class Struggle around the Built Environment in Advanced Capitalist Societies." *Politics & Society* 6, no. 3: 265–95.

———. 2006. *The Limits to Capital*. New and fully updated ed. London: Verso.

Johnson, Sarah. 2012. "Eerily Empty Streets of the Spanish Ghost Town Built for 30,000 before Property Crash." *Daily Mail*. 14 September. Accessed 6 February 2020. https://www.dailymail.co.uk/news/article-2203278/Empty-streets-playgrounds-Spanish-ghost-town-built-property-crash.html.

López, Isidro, and Emmanuel Rodríguez. 2010. *Fin de ciclo: financiarización, territorio y sociedad de propietarios en la onda larga del capitalismo hispano (1959–2010)*. Madrid: Traficantes de sueños.

———. 2011. "The Spanish Model." *New Left Review* 69, no. 3: 5–29.

Maldonado, Jesús Leal, and Marta Domínguez Pérez. 2011. "Pasado y futuro del parque de viviendas de Madrid: despejando incertidumbres." *Urban* 14: 80–91.

Montalvo, José García. 2013. "Dimensiones regionales del ajuste inmobiliario en España." *La economía de las regiones españolas en la crisis* 138: 62–79.

Morell, Marc, and Irene Sabaté Muriel. 2017. "Sentidos de la (in)justicia: endeudamiento y espacio urbano en tiempos de crisis." In *Antropologías en transformación: sentidos, compromisos y utopías*, edited by Mª Teresa Vicente Rabanaque, Pepa García Hernandorena, and Antonio Vizcaíno Estevan, 1998–2003. Valencia: Universitat de València.

Naredo, José Manuel. 2010. "El modelo inmobiliario español y sus consecuencias." *Boletín CF+S* 44: 13–27.

Observatori DESC i la Plataforma d'Afectats per la Hipoteca. 2013. "Emergencia habitacional en el estado español: la crisis de las ejecuciones hipotecarias y los desalojos desde una perspectiva de derechos humanos." 17 December. Accessed 6 February 2020. https://observatoridesc.org/es/node/4302.

Observatorio Metropolitano de Madrid, ed. 2013. *Paisajes devastados—Despues del ciclo inmobiliario: impactos regionales y urbanos de la crisis*. Madrid: Traficantes de Sueños.

Ramón, Alberto Ortín. 2013. "Valdeluz, de ciudad fantasma a ciudad esperanza." *Cinco Días*. 25 November. Accessed 6 February 2020. https://cincodias.elpais.com/cinco dias/2013/11/22/empresas/1385142551_676412.html.

Sabaté, Irene. 2016a. "La ruptura de una economía moral y las deslegitimación de las deudas hipotecarias." *Nómadas: Critical Journal of Social and Juridical Sciences* 47, no. 1: 103–17.

———. 2016b. "The Spanish Mortgage Crisis and the Re-emergence of Moral Economies in Uncertain Times." *History and Anthropology* 27, no. 1: 107–20.

Segura, Paco. 2012. "Infraestructuras de transporte y crisis." In *Grandes obras en tiempos de recortes sociales*. Madrid: Libros en Acción.

Vergés, Ricardo. 2012. "Estadísticas de vivienda libre en España. 1987–2011. Series operativas de compraventas y precios." *Estadística española* 54, no. 179: 357–420.

Villarino, Ángel. 2015. "Valdeluz, de ciudad fantasma a paraíso de mileuristas y divorciados." *El Confidencial*. 26 September. Accessed 6 February 2020. https://www.elconfidencial.com/espana/2015-09-26/valdeluz-de-ciudad-fantasma-a-paraiso-de-mileuristas-y-divorciados_1037338/.

von der Hagen, Hans. 2013. "Die unheimliche Stille von Valdeluz." *Süddeutsche Zeitung*. 20 June. Accessed 6 February 2020. https://www.sueddeutsche.de/wirtschaft/geisterstadt-in-spanien-die-unheimliche-stille-von-valdeluz-1.1698469.

13

Housing Financialization in Majorcan Holiday Rentals

MARC MORELL

May it burn all summer
And the rest of the year
The profits of tourism
Deserve our sacrifice …

—Presión, "Arda el Verano"

… a house where no one lives is in fact not a real house …
—Karl Marx, *Grundrisse*, 91

Introduction: The Vanishing Habitation of Holiday Rentals

"I am sandwiched,"[1] exclaimed the twenty-three-year-old resident of an ordinary neighborhood nearby the center of Ciutat (the capital city of Majorca and the Balearic Islands) as he entered the room where the fortnightly assembly of Ciutat per a qui l'habita, no per a qui la visita (Ciutat for those who inhabit it, not those who visit it) was taking place.[2] His peer activists, who had been discussing new trends in gentrification and the tourist commoditization of the city, made room for him. Carlos, a student who at the time was employed as a waiter at a city-center hotel, explained that in the last six months, the tenants of the apartments above and below the one he was renting together with his partner had been asked to make way for holiday rentals. Ever since, the couple has had to deal with confused visitors ringing their bell at all hours, and parties that go on for days.

Yet what annoys Carlos the most is that letting apartments to tourists is happening at all, given its impact on the remaining residential rentals.

For the moment, Carlos and his partner are safe, and they will be able to carry on paying 500 euros rent a month because the owner knows them. But others have had to move out, either because their residential rentals have changed to holiday ones or because the owners demand higher rents in order to make up the difference. Other factors that influence the frailty of rent are the irruption of Real Estate Investment Trusts (REITs) and the lack of social housing. Although the entire tenant population of Ciutat suffers these real estate dynamics, those most vulnerable are students, pensioners, precarious workers, labor migrants without family safety nets, and single-parent families that cannot meet the demanded rentals.[3]

Clearly, for many, the authorities are failing when it comes to ensure affordable housing.[4] Some see the displacement of people as an omen of the very disappearance of the city, a fate imagined by Màrius Verdaguer in his *Ciutat esvaïda* (meaning *Vanished City* [1977]).[5] Surprised that Ciutat could change so dramatically in such a short time, Verdaguer argued that "there is a city for each individual and for each era," and, therefore, "for each individual that disappears, a city also disappears" (Verdaguer 1977: 7). The city of tomorrow, he predicted, was "where the planes, the trains and the great ships of the future are going and our imagination goes too, becoming intoxicated with beautiful dreams" (1977: 7). Half a century later, many Majorcans believe that the bucolic and beautiful dreams of that futurism have ended up in a horrendous nightmare, followed by a huge hangover.

It is within this context that a constellation of movements seeks to limit and even reduce the tourist industry. The list of grievances numbered is long: excessive use of water and energy, massive generation of waste, uncontrolled urban sprawl, labor exploitation based on flexibility and seasonality, the substitution of small local businesses by large corporations, destruction of the fabric of neighborhoods, the saturation of public space, the exorbitant cost of private space due to the conversion of residential housing into tourist accommodation, and the financialization of both. But not everyone shares this negative view. Some benefit from the sixteen million people who in 2018 visited the Balearic Islands, comprising about five thousand square kilometers and just over a million inhabitants.

Besides the care and entertainment of tourists, big money is made from their transportation and accommodation. Over the last six decades, the tourist industry in the Balearic archipelago, exemplifying Spain as a whole, has been led by transport infrastructure development, the building industry, and real-estate speculation (Murray Mas 2015). Holiday rentals are the latest stage of this process, converting residential accommodation into tourist units thanks to digital platforms such as Airbnb. The phenomenon is exacerbated in central areas, driven by the fact that revenues from tourist rentals greatly exceed those obtainable through residential letting (by more than 350 percent for Ciutat's center, according to Yrigoy 2018).

The threat of displacement that hangs over Carlos and his partner, and hence the vanishing of the city they inhabit, is the consequence of the transformation of property into a financialized asset. Ciutat is a good example of the capitalist expansion of the tourist frontier in Europe. With this in mind, my analysis focuses on how platform capitalism and the rentier classes lobby together from the EU all the way down to local government for state regulation of holiday rentals. Yet holiday rentals not only hinder the everyday life of many residents but also evoke contestation. After considering the ways in which holiday rentals have triggered the reorganization of social movements in Ciutat, I shall conclude with a reflection on the consequent changes in class relations within the current dynamics of financialization.

The Tourist Frontier: Capitalist Integration and Class Differentiation

The research team Dret de l'Empresa i Activitat Turística (DEAT, Business Law and Tourist Activity) of the Universitat de les Illes Balears (UIB), explores how to regulate the "sharing economy," which, according to its researchers, is an unstoppable force that is expanding to all productive sectors, including the provision of tourist accommodation.[6] These researchers view holiday rentals as the management of one's own property guided by an entrepreneurial vocation. On this understanding, they say, "There is a market for everybody, [hoteliers] no longer have the monopoly," and, most importantly, "the market will regulate [holiday-rental] provision." Yet, despite the power hoteliers have in the Balearic Islands, the idea that tourist accommodation has always been exclusively theirs is questionable, especially when looking at how the state, not the market, has settled new accommodation typologies.

Authors such as Henri Lefebvre have argued that capital does not function according to its own internal requirements, its logic, and its laws. He maintained that it is the state that encourages the designation of new sectors in which to invest, expand production, and generate surplus (Lefebvre 1976: 322). This has been the case in the Balearic Islands with each successive "tourist boom" and their contribution to the restructuring of capital by spatially fixing the tourist frontier via new types of accommodation (Murray Mas, Yrigoy Cadena, and Blázquez-Salom 2017).[7] This process has to be understood as part of the Spanish brick and mortar accumulation cycle (López and Rodríguez 2011; Coq-Huelva 2013), one that binds social reproduction to the financialization of the built environment and the development of its associated infrastructure (Buier, this volume).

By regulating different types of tourist accommodation in turn, the Spanish and Balearic governments have integrated other built environments and fresh segments of consumption. Each new type of accommodation was approved by the legislator: hotels before 1973, tourist apartments in the mid-1980s, second residences owned by foreign EU citizens in the mid-1990s, agritourist establishments in the early 2000s, and digitally led holiday rentals in the mid-2010s. With the last of these, "tourist booms" have converged with the "waves of gentrification" (Hackworth and Smith 2001). Holiday rentals extend and intensify displacement (Cócola Gant 2016) in gentrification's fifth wave, the other main features of which are the consolidation of real estate as a financial asset, the emergence of large holders in the form of transnational investment funds, the intensification of mortgage debt, and the lack of affordable housing (Aalbers 2019).

Real estate and building industries saw a 54 percent increase from 2016 to 2017, reaching 5,267 million euros (CNMC 2018b: 48). However, recent studies, such as the one conducted by Janoschka, Alexandri, Orozco-Ramos, and Vives-Miró (2019), maintain that the financial extraction of most real-estate growth in Spain is pumped out of its sovereign reach due to the state's promotion of bank disinvestment, while enabling transnational REITs to rearticulate the entire market. This has been simultaneously characterized by a concentration of ownership and property management. In the case of holiday rentals, the 135,291 beds in the Balearic Islands available through Airbnb were managed by only 3,137 agents (sixteen of these managed 22 percent). In 2017, the ten main marketers were based in Germany, the Emirates, the Netherlands, or were simply untraceable (all data gathered from Terraferida 2018).

The centrality of the state in Lefebvre's development on the integration of new sectors is also stressed by Eric Wolf, who draws attention to the ways in which capital resolves its crisis in developing new rounds of surplus extraction by furthering the strategic relation governing the capitalist deployment of social labor. Wolf maintains that each new round involves conflicts between segments of the capitalist class, some of which ally with segments of other classes, including those of the working class (1997: 308). Wolf's differentiation thesis illuminates the reconfiguration of the Balearic owners of the means of accommodation in the tourist industry, as the holiday-rental lobby tries to influence politics to enable its clientele to compete with the hoteliers who control the bulk of the tourist accommodation and who have historically determined Balearic tourism policy (Amer 2005), and have even exported their model abroad (Buades 2014).

These class segmentations and alliances are extremely complex and unsettled since they bring together (among other factors) wage relations, regimes of residence tenure, and debt. Several authors have recently attempted to modify the concept of class by relating it to property and debt. Whereas Lemoine and Ravelli (2017) argue that the democratization of finance (e.g., via shares) leads to generalized impoverishment, Harvey contends that debt generates claims upon future incomes and labor (2018: 450–51), hence locating debt not only as a means of depredation but also of an ongoing original accumulation. But when were classes ever clearly defined? Their legibility is never explicit, especially when the creation and appropriation of value takes rapidly changing forms. It is precisely this shifting nature of the relation of struggle that lies at the heart of how class happens (Kalb 1997, 2015). Perhaps, then, a feasible way for grasping class is to seize the moment when it is on the move (Cox 2013).

I shall revisit class below. First, I must return to my colleagues at DEAT who, with their views on property self-management and their emphasis on the entrepreneurial vocation of the individual, are not particularly interested on social inequalities, let alone how class happens and how to grasp it. What really concerns them is the "sharing economy" pulse found among digital platforms and holiday rentals. There, they believe, is a market that regulates provision. Contra this liberal tenet, in what follows I critique the comforting jargon of the "sharing economy" and examine how its meaning has been transformed. I then focus on how the state has delivered holiday-rental regulation from distant EU offices all the way down to street level by using intermediate levels of state administration as steppingstones.

The Sharing Economy and EU Scaling Policy

On 26 October 2016, Jorge Cuneo, the creator of Hundredrooms, a local company that finds and compares the best holiday rental offers on digital platforms, spoke at the BusinessDMallorca forum held by the main newspaper operating on the island: *Diario de Mallorca*. About fifty mid-aged entrepreneurs managing holiday rentals attended the event. They were worried at the announcement of the Balearic government that this was not a free-for-all, and that legislation would follow. Cuneo portrayed his business as "sharing economy," the "new barter." Hundredrooms' horizon, he boasted, was to achieve a global impact. It seems that the "sharing economy" has shifted from the supposedly invisible hand of individual interest to a strategy of capital accumulation based on a spurious connection between the "digital-technology revolution" and the "another economy is possible" adagio.

The work of Bauwens and Lievens, now collected in a single volume (2015), is foundational. They point out that the economy of exchange between equals (P2P) creates use value through the free cooperation of the producers for a community of users, not for the market. For Botsman and Rogers (2011), the sharing economy includes exchange, barter, trade, rent, and gift, now tuned by new technologies and digital communities of free P2P exchange.[8] Gansky (2010) introduces the concept of "mesh" to connect different nodes so as to coordinate talents, goods, and services, as well as to encourage both sharability and immediacy. Yet the use value purportedly generated outside of the market is, at the end of all this rational optimizing, nothing other than exchange value. This ambiguity has inspired works of very different orientation.

While Rifkin (2014) announces the collapse of the capitalist system due to its crisis of values and the erosion of the rate of growth, Sundararajan (2016) posits a "capitalism of the crowd" based on P2P commercial exchange. For Rifkin, the rise of the sharing commons leads us to a third industrial revolution. By contrast, Sundararajan urges rethinking state regulation of labor markets and social security. Both authors conceptualize the sharing economy as an "epochal" expression of capitalism, but both sow only confusion. Srnicek (2016) approaches the topic by preferring to speak of "platform capitalism." He classifies digital platforms according to the nature of their business. "Lean platforms" (e.g., Airbnb) are purely rentier since everything is outsourced and all that remains is a "control over the platform that enables a monopoly rent to be gained" (Srnicek 2016: 76).[9]

Academic conceptualizations of the "sharing economy" have not only had an impact on emergent entrepreneurs such as Jorge Cuneo of Hundredrooms, but also influence state policy. Since 2016, the European Commission (EC) has produced several reports on the topic of the "collaborative economy," including holiday rentals (e.g., Codagnone, Biagi, and Abdie 2016); even top gurus have provided their services (Sundararajan 2017). Yet the EC's major concern with the sharing economy is not the erosion of labor rights, or social protection, or access to affordable housing, but the use of the data generated (Martens 2016; Easton 2017). In fact, with holiday rentals in mind, EC's reports criticize prohibition and limitation for curbing the generation of income and employment (EC 2016). This last study concludes: "Europe should be open to embracing these new opportunities" (2016: 16).

This is consistent with the Quantitative Easing practices carried out by the European Central Bank, which were intended to stimulate consumption and the integration of new areas of investment (see Kolasa and Wesołowski 2018). Furthermore, the EC reports cited above have been prepared in the context of the Single Market strategy in which the holiday rentals lobbying groups at the EU level (e.g., the European Holiday Home Association that includes both national trade associations and lean platform company members) have been pushing hard for a major liberalization of housing through marketer digital platforms (Haar 2018).

The attitude of the EC toward holiday rentals has strengthened the hand of the Spanish National Commission for the Markets and Competition (CNMC) in disputing the limitations that several regions and towns have activated in order to guarantee affordable residential rentals. For the CNMC, holiday rentals constitute "a true revolution in the accommodation market, generating profit for the users, the citizens and the economy of the cities" (CNMC 2018a: 61–62). It is keen to diminish regional heterogeneity and to avoid local restrictions that impede the "good performance" of the market (CNMC 2018a: 64–66).[10] The crucial measure, though, was the nation-wide "Law on Measures to Relax and Promote the Housing Rental Market" (Law 4 in AE BOE 2013), which modified the "Law on Urban Leasing" (Law 29 in AE BOE 1994) by allowing the use of housing for non-residential purposes.

The Autonomous Community of the Balearic Islands is one of the authorities the CNMC has challenged, because its recently approved regional law "limited" the commercialization of holiday rentals (Parlament de les Illes Balears 2017). However, oppositional movements maintain that the fact of regulation has conferred upon holiday rentals unprecedented recognition. A ceiling of tourist beds has been established (623,624 according to Sáenz 2017, regardless of accommodation type), and each Island Council has negotiated zoning arrangements for holiday rentals with its different municipalities. While the official policy in the Balearic Islands is to curb mass tourism, no budget has been set for inspections.

Ciutat is the capital city. Regardless of the pressure exerted by different lobbies (including trade associations and digital platforms), it has tried to enforce a municipal ban on holiday rentals in all apartments in order to guarantee affordable residential rentals. However, the absence of effective inspections gives rise to abuse. In order to get an idea of the tension generated, I now turn to the role of locally engaged academia with a specific case that illustrates the "mesh" in which the nature of the business does not really matter as long as it is "achieving a global impact."

On Academics, Scams, and Lobbies

Academic engagement works in all directions. The UIB does not speak with one voice. I can recall three conflicts between defenders and detractors of holiday rentals. In 2016, before passing the regional law that regulated them, an agency of the left-wing coalition governing the region at the time financed a UIB business department study of residents' perceptions of holiday rentals (Garau Vadell 2016). The intention was to legitimize a restrictive policy. The results, however, were celebrated by Habtur, the regional holiday-rental trade association, since respondents were explicitly enthusiastic because it was believed holiday rentals would complement increasingly meager incomes while generating employment.

In the second episode another research group from the same business department was commissioned by a government agency to investigate the market. Groizard and Nilsson (2017) argued that there was room for growth, that holiday rentals did not displace tenants, that they combated hotelier monopoly, and spread tourist revenues via rent and new employment opportunities.[11] When these academics presented their findings, a group of around fifteen UIB colleagues opposed to holiday rentals counterattacked in front of rolling cameras. Holiday rentals were not only making rents unaffordable: they were the cause of rising property prices and the widening gulf between owners and tenants. As a result, the report was ridiculed in the media.

Finally, in January 2017, the regional radio announced that the UIB was going to establish an observatory to investigate holiday rentals. It would be led by a permanent lecturer who at that time was the vice-president of Habtur. It only took one hour for the social networks to ignite. The initiative was promptly abandoned.

The role of academics is also important in unmasking predatory practices. Following the complaints of Queta, a member of Ciutat per a qui l'habita, in the spring of 2017, a group of researchers and journalists discovered that three social-housing apartments originally reserved for inhabitants with difficulties of access to housing (one of them occupied by Queta) were each being illegally rented to tourists at 150 euros per night. The apartment block stood in a central area that had been regenerated and gentrified a decade earlier (Morell 2015). The chief operations manager and other workers of the company that managed the social-housing rent contracts offered the apartments on digital platforms. This was a profitable business since the monthly rent of each social-housing apartment was 450 euros. The deeper we dug, the bigger the case got. The owner of the blocks was a real estate company with a portfolio that included several properties in the neighborhood.

Owners and managers had three things in common: (1) a past as executives in the new bank that in 2010 absorbed the saving bank that owned 45 percent of the assets that resulted from the regeneration scheme; (2) a past in that same saving bank; and, surprisingly, (3) active involvement in the transfer of these assets via the Spanish "bad bank" SAREB (Company for the Management of Assets proceeding from Restructuring of the Banking System). Although not representative of the business, these practices not only point to the links between holiday rentals and the financialization of property ownership and management, but also signal the class relation maintained by those who cannot access affordable housing with those who amass their wealth by eliminating such access.

Another less complicated and indeed legal strategy I encountered consisted of using networks of family and friends in small village councils to access information on indebted owners from the days of the economic crisis in 2008 in order to buy them out by means of a bank credit backed by inherited property as collateral. Several fellow villagers murmur this is how the former president of Habtur began his holiday rental business. Before holiday rentals, Joan Miralles was a civil servant working for the Balearic Ministry of Education as a vocational school teacher. Son of a UIB professor in Catalan philology specialized in folklore and of an heiress from an inland village, Miralles received his PhD in sociology after writing a doctoral thesis on the impact on Majorcan culture by second-home foreign EU-citizens in the late 1990s and early 2000s (earlier referred to as the "third tourist boom"). In this study, he had concluded it was better for Majorcan property owners to rent rather than sell, since selling meant Majorcans would lose land ownership (Miralles Plantalamor 2004).

Like most members of Habtur, Miralles has sought to connect with the wider public by asserting the potential trickle-down economics he believes holiday rentals open up (e.g., for caterers, local farmers, etc.). This class differentiation strategy is supposed to undermine the idea that holiday rentals are taking over residential ones, or that they are to blame for rising rents, which has become a mantra at the Foro Vacacional (Vacation Forum) Habtur holds since 2016, to which the operators of digital platforms, tour and service providers, financial companies, lawyers, and members of the Balearic government are invited.

Miralles sees the hoteliers as Habtur's main rivals: "The earlier [the hoteliers] accept we have come to stay, that we represent an important segment of provision for tourists and that we all must negotiate the overall tourism model together, the better.... . The tourism market is not theirs. It is the tourist who chooses" (Hosteltur 2017).[12] While Habtur's rhetoric addresses the interests of owners whose only wish is an additional stream of income (coinciding with the arguments of Spanish federation Fevitur, whose president is from Habtur, and the European Holiday Home Association), most of its prominent members own several properties and are already becoming highly professional, either in adopting new digital marketing strategies or in concentrating property. On one occasion, at a talk I gave in a coastal village, I was approached by a middle-aged businessman who confided that his business was small since he only managed forty holiday rentals.

The Division of Labor between Social Movements

Holiday rentals have not escaped the attention of social movements, many of which denounce and oppose the effects they have on both the environment and society, via various mediatized strategies of awareness and resistance. Some politicians in office agree with these social movements. Take the most recent Mayor of Ciutat, a regional capital city of almost half a million inhabitants. After a careful study of the pros and cons of holiday rentals in apartments, he banned them.[13] This Mayor belonged to a progressive party that was supported by citizens opposed to holiday rentals on the grounds that they cause residential rents to rise and transform the character of the city. He was proud that his own career originated in grassroots movements and wanted to strike a political bargain.[14] Yet his own colleagues in the Majorcan hinterland solicited votes by quietly allowing the continued expansion of this sector.

The challenge was not easy, especially when social movements were organizing protests. The largest demonstration took place on 23 September 2017, a month after the approval of the regional regulation of holiday rentals. Over three thousand people protested against the tourism policy of the Balearic government. With the motto *Fins aquí hem arribat* (We have come so far), the demonstrators—summoned by environmentalist, urban movement groups, and sections of trade unions—demanded courageous measures from the left-wing coalition to put an end to the excessive dependence on tourism.[15] The 23-S platform assembled fifty-two different organizations with diverse claims.

The first set is organizations explicitly addressing the environment. GOB (Balearic Ornithological and Land Protection Group) has been the main conservationist group in the region since its foundation in 1973. It has worked to protect the most sensible environments in the archipelago from urbanization, and it now aims to limit tourism and promote active degrowth strategies. In the eyes of its members, holiday rentals are draining the scarce resources of the archipelago. Because of its experience, GOB's capacity to mobilize is very high.

Terraferida (meaning "Wounded land") is a relatively recent splinter group organization of GOB that is also concerned with the environment. It calls for a stronger opposition and links the predatory economic model promoted by powerful global groups to a local political malaise based upon corruption and the hoarding of public resources by a dominant caste. Seeing the lack of official information on the topic, Terraferida has specialized in offering consistent quantitative data on holiday rentals in the Balearic Islands. Whereas GOB is opened to affiliation, Terraferida is not. Such a stark position also situates Terraferida to be able to reject the compromises struck by the so-called progressive parties, not least in Ciutat, where it was able to verify how the ban of the progressive Mayor was flouted in practice.

In the capital city, residents' associations are particularly strong. FAVP (the federation of Ciutat's residents' associations) can draw on strong communist-led traditions of community activism dating back to the Franco era. Because most of it was coopted in the early times of the so-called democratic transition (especially in the 1980s), it is a funnel for numerous other social movements to access the local corridors of power. Although dominated by senior activists, it has recently reached out to younger generations across the different neighborhoods it controls across the city. Most of these younger people were involved in the local 15 M movements of 2011 that contributed to shattering the structures of federations of residents' associations across many Spanish cities, Ciutat included.[16] The holiday-rental problem has breathed fresh life into the FAVP, in addition to spawning new allied movements, such as Ciutat per a qui l'habita, no per a qui la visita.

This is the group to which Carlos and Queta belong (the activists mentioned above). Its origins lie in a libertarian movement, Tot Inclòs (All Inclusive), that from 2014 to 2017 issued a yearly magazine denouncing tourism's predatory model. Ciutat per a qui l'habita has grown into a fluid intergenerational organization with a fortnight assembly held in a public space when the weather allows. It must be admitted that most of the festive activities it has organized (a tourist trolley march in the Center, a public auction selling Ciutat's neighborhoods, etc.) have attracted more media than activists.

From conservationists who sought to protect the territory to organizations focused on maintaining community integrity and affordability of housing conditions, these diverse movements managed to cooperate through recourse to a division of labor that respected unique trajectories while forging an innovative collective mobilization, conveying a coded expression of class (Kalb and Mollona 2018). It was a point of class convergence that drew these organizations together, one that addressed the social reproduction of life and the transformation of livelihoods.

Conclusion: The State and Movement of Class in Holiday Rentals

In this chapter, I have examined the torchbearer role of the state in the regulation of holiday rentals in Majorca. Combining Henri Lefebvre's integration thesis and Eric Wolf's notions of class differentiation, I have focused on how the expansion of the tourist frontier to holiday rentals has segmented the owners of the means of accommodation while leading them to establish varying alliances with others. This has been made possible by riding on the crest of the public authorities' enthusiasm for the "sharing economy" and its alleged trickle-down effects. I have also argued that platform-led conversion of residential housing into holiday rentals has led to greater concentration of wealth and precarious conditions of residence for citizens. As a result, oppositional movements have coalesced to condemn the latest forms of housing commodification.

Here, financialization, and especially household financialization, is associated with the retreat of public provision, including housing, and with rising inequality (Lapavitsas 2013). Within a Spanish context of housing predation, until now mainly defined by mortgage indebtedness and house repossessions (e.g., Sabaté 2016), holiday rentals are yet another profit-seeking strategy that hinders citizens' access to affordable housing and generates new financial assets.

Lean digital platform companies such as Airbnb can currently gear up for an Initial Public Offering only after raising different rounds of money (Schleifer 2019) that indirectly feed upon property owners like Habtur's former president, who require credit in order to engross their holiday rental business. The flipside of such complex financial maneuvers is that vulnerable people like Queta lose their homes, while Carlos and his partner have to be grateful to their landlord for not increasing their rent or seeking to convert their home into a holiday rental. There is no doubt that holiday rentals reduce the residential stock and raise residential rents, which, in turn, increases the demand for properties as objects of investment. In the long run, residents, whether renting or owning, are displaced.

Returning to Verdaguer's vanishing memoirs, the overall question is not so much what kind of city would be left if all its inhabitants disappeared, but rather to what kind of city does such a vitriolic situation lead us? This is where class comes into the picture. Not being able to dwell because of the emergence of holiday rentals calls to mind Marx's dictum that "a house where no one lives is in fact not a real house" (1973: 91). What remains to be seen is whether the profits of tourism, as the music band Presión sarcastically critiques in the verses also offered in this chapter's epigraph, deserve our sacrifice at all (Presión 2017).[17]

The general principle governing all this framework is the state's defense of private property and its privileging of free commercial use over any social need. Such a strategy leaves unresolved four simultaneous class fronts related to the emergence of holiday rentals and housing: (1) digital platforms that act as monopoly-rent gatekeepers; (2) property owners who make residential rentals difficult; (3) small property owners involved in holiday rentals who yield to the professionalization and ownership concentration of the sector (often involving investment funds); and (4) diverse employers (holiday rentals and hotels) who unite in a pact to keep the working and dwelling conditions of their labor precarious.

The globally induced professionalization of short-term holiday rentals is leading toward a tourist accommodation model that calls for yet wider financialization. We can also observe some new threads of class-formation; but organized opposition is mediated by ideas of territory and community. Take Ciutat per a qui l'habita—it fights against the substitution of residential rentals by holiday rentals, but it also fights for a city that its members build day after day together with many others. There is a struggling city for each individual member of Ciutat per a qui l'habita, and there is even a collective one too. Taken as whole, all these movements are a lively expression of a class on the move, one that tries to fight back the new fusion of social reproduction (housing) with production (tourist accommodation) and the formation of financial assets taking place in the background.

Acknowledgments

This chapter is a product of my research funded by the Programa Margalida Comas 2016 (Conselleria d'Innovació, Recerca i Turisme—Govern de les Illes Balears), and developed at the Department of Geography of the University of the Balearic Islands, where it has contributed to the research project "Overtourism in Spanish Coastal Destinations: Tourism Degrowth Strategies" (RTI2018-094844-B-C31) of FEDER / Ministerio de Ciencia, Innovación y Universidades—Agencia Estatal de Investigación). I dedicate the text to the people who make social movements happen, especially to my comrades of Ciutat per a qui l'habita, no per a qui la visita and their struggle for materializing Ciutat.

Marc Morell received his PhD from the University of Barcelona in 2015. He has been employed as a researcher and lecturer at the University of the Balearic Islands and is currently a researcher in the Department of Social Anthropology of the University of Bergen. His specialization is the class character of the production of space in capitalist society.

Notes

1. All translations from Catalan or Spanish into English are mine.
2. For a dissertation on the names of Ciutat, see Bibiloni (1979). Whereas this author prefers "Palma," I will stick to the more colloquial "Ciutat," since its usage is well spread across the territory. This choice still emphasizes the city rather than the island, although it is possible to conceive the latter as a single urban system (Quintana Peñuela 1979; Mestre Morey 2015). As for Ciutat per a qui l'habita, this is a relatively new organization (September 2016), the main aim of which is to denounce the increasing touristification of Ciutat.
3. In Spain, official data on regimes of tenancy are only updated every ten years via the census of the Instituto Nacional de Estadística. The last census was held in 2011. The Balearic Islands had 586,709 dwellings, of which 73.24% were first homes, 19.95% were second homes, and 16.58% were empty. This data is not available for Ciutat, but we know that out of the 159,316 first homes, 31.5% had been fully bought, 33.25% still had mortgage payments pending, 4.75% had been inherited or donated, 23.87% were rented, 2.15% had been given for free or at extremely low prices, and the remaining 4.48% were occupied under "other" circumstances.
4. The failure of the authorities to ensure affordable rents not only translates into displacement, but also encourages the organization of tenants. Following the example of other cities like Madrid and Barcelona, a new tenant's union has just come into being in Majorca (Bauzà 2019). Besides demanding the authorities for better rental conditions, it will also offer legal advice to its members.
5. Màrius Verdaguer was a man of letters of Minorcan origin mostly based in Ciutat and Barcelona. His book *La ciudad desvanecida*, originally written in Spanish in 1953, was translated into Catalan in 1977. It has become a major literary icon for cultural heritage preservationist groups of Ciutat since the mid-1980s.
6. Interview with members of DEAT by the local newspaper *Última Hora* published in November 2017 (Ginard 2017). Holiday rentals have been a lively topic of public debate in these years, not least through the interventions of the UIB, as I shall show below.
7. "Tourist booms" are to be understood as "spatial fixes" in the sense of David Harvey (2006: 413–45). Spatial fixes address the crises of overproduction generated by capitalism in which the possibilities of profitable investment are exhausted, guiding the process toward the destruction of existing capital through its devaluation or the underutilization of the workforce. Thus, spatial fixes reorganize the built environment through long-term investments in fixed and immobile capital, thereby temporarily averting the accumulation crisis. The state's intervention ensures the conditions of profitability, credit, and finance.
8. Slee (2015) mocks Botsman and Rogers's title to convert *What's Mine Is Yours* into *What's Yours Is Mine*. Slee denounces the new forms of plunder entailed by the "sharing economy," but he does not address its materiality.
9. Although he does not apply his insights to the "sharing economy," Fuchs (2014) offers a solid analysis of the forms of extraction and exploitation found in the digital world.

10. At this point it is important to outline the distribution of competencies between the different levels of state administration in Spain regarding holiday rentals. Residential rentals are ruled by law at a national level, tourism policy is the responsibility of the regional autonomous communities, and town planning is worked out at a municipal level. In the case of the Balearic Islands, each island has a council that harmonizes municipal town planning. As the capital city, Ciutat is an exception to this logic.

11. In the course of my investigation, I was surprised to hear from a working colleague that one of the two authors of the Groizard and Nilsson report (2016) had turned his main home into a holiday rental and had moved with his wife and children to a residential rental where he paid less than his mortgage. Interestingly, he had also turned his second home into a holiday rental. True or not, this gossip suggests the importance of shaming and defaming in this context.

12. Hoteliers fiercely oppose holiday rentals; but if these nonetheless establish themselves, hoteliers will invest in them just as they have done in other accommodation modalities in the past (Magro 2017).

13. By banning holiday rentals in apartments, this Mayor of Ciutat could be taken to court for malfeasance—see Majorca Daily Bulletin Reporter (2019).

14. Such a good relation that in 2017, the Mayor's constituency party wanted to award its annual prize to Ciutat per a qui l'habita. Ciutat per a qui l'habita rejected the prize, claiming that its job was to raise awareness and not to play pork-barrel politics. It therefore insisted on not only completely banning holiday rentals but also on putting a stop to the proliferation of so-called "boutique hotels" across the city.

15. Among other aspects, the protest was motivated by the growing numbers of visitor arrivals, the boom of holiday rentals, and the increase of rental cars. The organizers also criticized the precarious labor conditions the tourist model generated, exemplified by Les Kellys (unionized hotel floor maids).

16. The Plataforma d'Afectats per les Hipoteques (PAH, Platform of People Affected by Mortgages) became an iconic movement in the aftermath of 2011's 15 M in most Spanish cities. It fought against evictions and is still active in Ciutat, specializing in mortgage evictions. One of its splinter groups, STOP Desnonaments (STOP Evictions), specializes in rental evictions, most of which are related to the silent displacement of tenants: i.e., tenants who do not renew their contracts because of disproportionate rent rises that are indirectly influenced by the emergence of the bigger holiday rentals offer. Both PAH and STOP Desnonaments cooperate with the other organizations referred to in this section.

17. This critique calls for reexamining the expansion of surplus labor in the financialization of everyday life. The problem is that it is almost impossible to calculate this kind of displacement. Beyond the numbers (see Wachsmuth and Weisler 2018), there is also a need for an in-depth qualitative research that could show us a way in which to understand, illustrate, and contest the financialization strategy that lies behind holiday rentals from an engagement that makes social anthropology part of a wider political project (Smith 1999).

References

Aalbers, Manuel. 2019. "Introduction to the Forum: from Third to Fifth-wave Gentrification." *Tijdschrift voor Economische en Sociale Geografie* 110, no. 1: 1–11.

AE BOE (Agencia Estatal del Boletín Oficial del Estado). 1994. "Ley 29/1994, de 24 de noviembre, de arrendamientos urbanos." *Boletín Oficial de Estado* 282, 26003.

———. 2013. "Ley 4/2013, de 4 de junio, de medidas de flexibilización y fomento del mercado del alquiler de vivienda." *Boletín Oficial de Estado* 134, 5941.

Amer, Joan. 2005. *Turisme i política: L'empresariat hoteler de Mallorca*. Palma: Documenta Balear.

Bauwens, Michel, and Jean Lievens. 2015. *Sauver le monde: Vers une société post-capitaliste avec le peer-to-peer.* Paris: Éditions les liens qui libérent.

Bauzà, Jaume. 2019. "Nace el primer sindicat de inquilinos de Mallorca." *Diario de Mallorca*. (29 March). Accessed 3 January 2020. https://www.diariodemallorca.es/mallorca/2019/03/29/nace-primer-sindicato-inquilinos-mallorca/1404779.html.

Bibiloni, Gabriel. 1979. "La ciutat de Mallorca: Consideracions sobre un topònim." *Randa* 9: 25–30.

Botsman, Rachel, and Roo Rogers. 2011. *What's Mine Is Yours: How Collaborative Consumption Is Changing the Way We Live.* London: Collins.

Buades, Joan. 2014. *Exportando paraísos: La colonización turística del planeta.* Barcelona: Alba Sud Editorial.

CNMC (Comisión Nacional de los Mercados y la Competencia). 2018a. *E/CNMC/003/18—Estudio sobre la regulación de las viviendas de uso turístico en España.* 19 July. Madrid: CNMC. Accessed 3 January 2020. https://www.cnmc.es/sites/default/files/2133063_1.pdf.

———. 2018b. *Informe anual de la CNMV sobre los mercados de valores y su actuación: Ejercicio 2017.* Madrid: CNMC. Accessed 3 January 2020. http://www.cnmv.es/DocPortal/Publicaciones/Informes/Informe_Anual_2017_.pdf.

Cócola Gant, Agustín. 2016. "Holiday Rentals: The New Gentrification Battlefront." *Sociological Research Online* 21, no. 3: 1–9. Accessed 3 January 2020. https://doi.org/10.5153/sro.4071.

Codagnone, Cristiano, Federico Biagi, and Fabienne Abadie. 2016. *The Passions and the Interests: Unpacking the "Sharing Economy."* Seville: Institute for Prospective Technological Studies, JCR Science for Policy Report. Accessed 3 January 2020. http://publications.jrc.ec.europa.eu/repository/bitstream/JRC101279/jrc101279.pdf.

Coq-Huelva, Daniel. 2013. "Urbanisation and Financialisaton in the Context of a Rescaling State: The Case of Spain." *Antipode. A Radical Journal of Geography* 45, no. 5: 1223–1231.

Cox, Laurence. 2013. "*Eppur Si Muove*: Thinking 'the Social Movement.'" In *Marxism and Social Movements*, edited by Colin Barker, John Krinsky, Laurence Cox, and Alf Gunvald Nilsen, 125–146. Leiden: Brill.

Easton, Catherine R. 2017. "European Union Information Law and the Sharing Economy." In *EU Internet Law Regulation and Enforcement*, edited by Tatiana-Eleni Synodinou, Phillipe Jougleux, Christiana Markou, and Thalia Prastitou, 163–181. Cham: Springer International Publishing AG.

EC (European Commission). 2016. *Communication from the Commission to the European Parliament, the Council, the European Economic and Social Committee and the Committee of the Regions—A European Agenda for the Collaborative Economy.* Brussels: European Commission. Accessed 3 January 2020. https://www.eesc.europa.eu/resources/docs/com2016-356-final.pdf.

Fuchs, Christian. 2014. *Digital Labour and Karl Marx.* New York: Routledge.

Gansky, Lisa. 2010. *The Mesh: Why the Future of Business Is Sharing.* New York: Portfolio / Penguin.

Garau Vadell, Joan Baptista., dir. 2016. *Estudi de la percepció dels residents del lloguer vacacional P2P.* Mallorca: Universitat de les Illes Balears (December). Accessed 3 January 2020. www.caib.es/sites/estadistiquesdelturisme/f/226578.

Ginard, Aina. 2017. "Tras los entresijos de la economía colaborativa." *El Económico. Semanario de la empresa y el turismo de Balears / Última Hora.* (3 November). Accessed 3 January 2020. https://ultimahora.es/noticias/econom ico/2017/11/03/304603/tras-entresijos-economia-colaborativa.html.

Groizard, José Luis, and William. Nilsson. 2017. "Mito y realidad del alquiler vacacional en las Islas Baleares: Análisis y recomendaciones de política turística." *DEA Working Paper Series* 84. Accessed 3 January 2020. http://diari.uib.es/digital Assets/430/430311_2-estudi-complet.pdf.

Haar, Kenneth. 2018. *UnFairbnb: How Online Rental Platforms Use the EU to Defeat Cities' Affordable Housing Measures.* Brussels: Corporate Europe Observatory.

Hackworth, Jason, and Neil Smith. 2001. "The Changing State of Gentrification." *Tijdschrift voor Economische en Sociale Geografie* 22, no. 4: 464–477.

Harvey, David. 2006 [1982]. *The Limits to Capital.* 2nd ed. London: Verso Books.

———. 2018. "Universal Alienation and the Real Subsumption of Daily Life Under Capital: A Response to Hardt and Negri." *tripleC: Communication, Capitalism & Critique. Journal for a Global Sustainable Information Society* 16, no. 2: 449–453.

Hosteltur. 2017. "El recién elegido presidente desvela su plan de acción. Aptur [Habtur]: 'Varios lobbies han criminalizado el alquiler vacacional.' La asociación quiere visualizar los beneficios de esta actividad y ser tratada como un actor de primer nivel." *Hosteltur.* 24 February. Accessed 3 January 2020. https://www.hosteltur. com/120664_miralles-aptur-varios-lobbies-han-criminalizado-alquiler-vacacio nal.html.

Janoschka, Michael, Georgia Alexandri, Hernán Orozco-Ramos, Sonia Vives-Miró 2019. "Tracing the Socio-Spatial Logics of Transnational Landlords' Real Estate Investment: Blackstone in Madrid." *European Urban and Regional Studies*: 1–17. Accessed 3 January 2020. https://doi.org/10.1177/0969776418822061.

Kalb, Don. 1997. *Expanding Class: Power and Everyday Politics in Industrial Communities.* Durham: Duke University Press.

———. 2015. "Introduction: Class and the New Anthropological Holism" in *Anthropologies of Class: Power, Practice and Inequality*, edited by James G. Carrier and Don Kalb, 1–27. Cambridge, UK: Cambridge University Press.

Kalb, Don, and Massimiliano Mollona. 2018. "Introduction: Introductory Thoughts on Anthropology and Urban Insurrection." In *Worldwide Mobilizations. Class*

Struggles and Urban Commoning, edited by Don Kalb and Massimiliano Mollona, 1–29. Cambridge, UK: Cambridge University Press.

Kolasa, Marcin, and Grzegorz Wesołowski. 2018. "International Spillovers of Quantitative Easing." *European Central Bank Working Paper Series* 2229. (27 July). Accessed 3 January 2020. https://www.ecb.europa.eu/pub/pdf/scpwps/ecb.wp2172.en.pdf?6aeb5ce6072587d9d09b8ae10002b67a.

Lapavitsas, Costas. 2013. "The Financialisation of Capitalism: 'Profiting Without Producing.'" *City* 17, no. 6: 795–805.

Lefebvre, Henri. 1976. *De l'État, Tome II: De Hegel à Mao par Stalin (La théorie "marxiste" de l'État)*. Paris: Union Général d'Éditions.

Lemoine, Benjamin, and Quentin Ravelli. 2017. "Financiarisation et classes sociales: introduction au dossier." *Revue de la régulation* 22 (Autumn 2017). Accessed 3 January 2020. https://journals.openedition.org/regulation/12593.

López, Isidro, and Emmanuel Rodríguez. 2011. "The Spanish Model." *New Left Review* 69, no. 3: 5–29.

Magro, Alberto. 2017. "Los hoteleros avisan: Si se apuesta por el alquiler, se pasarán a ese negocio." *Diario de Mallorca*. (26 April). Accessed 3 January 2020. https://www.diariodemallorca.es/mallorca/2017/04/26/hoteleros-avisan-apuesta-alquiler-pasaran/1209634.html.

Majorca Daily Bulletin Reporter. 2019. "Palma Mayor Facing Holiday Rentals Lawsuit." *Majorca Daily Bulletin*. (15 February). Accessed 3 January 2020. https://www.majorcadailybulletin.com/news/local/2019/02/15/54621/palma-mayor-facing-holiday-rentals-lawsuit.html.

Martens, Bertin. 2016. "An Economic Policy Perspective on Online Platforms." *JCR Technical Reports: Institute for Prospective Technological Studies Digital Economy Working Paper* 2016/05. Accessed 3 January 2020. https://ec.europa.eu/jrc/sites/jrcsh/files/JRC101501.pdf.

Marx, Karl. 1973 [1939]. *Grundrisse: Introduction to the Critique of Political Economy*. Translated by M. Nicolaus. New York: Random House.

Mestre Morey, Margalida. 2015. "Ciutat i territori a Mallorca." *Documents d'Anàlisi Geogràfic* 61, no. 2: 351–368.

Miralles Plantalamor, Joan. 2004. "Impactos socioculturales del turismo residencial en España: Análisis comparativo del fenómeno en las diferentes comunidades autónomas a partir del caso mallorquín," PhD dissertation, Universitat d'Alacant.

Morell, Marc. 2015. "When Space Draws the Line on Class," in *Anthropologies of Class: Power, Practice and Inequality*, edited by James G. Carrier and Don Kalb, 102–117. Cambridge, UK: Cambridge University Press.

Murray Mas, Ivan. 2015. *Capitalismo y turismo en España: Del "milagro económico" a la "gran crisis."* Barcelona: Alba Sud Editorial.

Murray Mas, Ivan, Ismael Yrigoy Cadena, and Macià Blázquez-Salom. 2017. "The Role of Crises in the Production, Destruction and Restructuring of Tourist Spaces: The Case of the Balearic Islands." *Investigaciones Turísticas* 13: 1–29.

Parlament de les Illes Balears. 2017. "Llei 6/2017, de 31 de juliol, de modificació de la Llei 8/2012, de 19 de juliol, del turisme de les Illes Balears, relativa a la comercialització d'estades turístiques a habitatges." *Butlletí Oficial de les Illes Balears* 93, Sec. 1: 25.092–25.112.

Presión. 2017. "Arda el verano." In *Estiu d'infern—Un recopilatorio de "canciones del verano."* Various Artists, compilation album. Palma: Discos Polo.

Quintana Peñuela, Alberto. 1979. *El sistema urbano de Mallorca*. Ciutat de Mallorca: Editorial Moll.

Rifkin, Jeremy. 2014. *The Zero Marginal Cost Society: The Internet of Things, the Collaborative Commons, and the Eclipse of Capitalism*. New York: Palgrave Macmillan.

Sabaté, Irene. 2016. "Mortgage Indebtedness and Home Repossessions as Symptoms of the Financialisation of Housing Provisioning in Spain." *Critique of Anthropology* 36, no. 2: 197–211.

Sáenz, Hugo. 2017. "Baleares pone un tope al número de turistas: 623.000." *El Mundo*. (8 August). Accessed 3 January 2020. http://www.elmundo.es/baleares/2017/08/0 8/59899001e2704eb80b8b459f.html.

Schleifer, Theodore. 2019. "Airbnb sold some common stock at a $35 billion valuation, but what is the company really worth?" *Vox*. (19 March). Accessed 3 January 2020. https://www.vox.com/2019/3/19/18272274/airbnb-valuation-common-stock-hoteltonight.

Slee, Tom. 2015. *What's Yours Is Mine: Against the Sharing Economy*. New York: OR Books.

Smith, Gavin. 1999. *Confronting the Present: Towards a Politically Engaged Anthropology*. Oxford: Berg Publishers.

Srnicek, Nick. 2016. *Platform Capitalism*. Cambridge, UK: Polity Press.

Sundararajan, Arun. 2016. *The Sharing Economy: The End of Employment and the Rise of Crowd-Based Capitalism*. Cambridge, MA: The MIT Press.

———. 2017. *The Collaborative Economy: Socioeconomic, Regulatory and Policy Issues*. *In-Depth Analysis for the IMCO Committee*. Brussels: Policy Department A: Economic and Scientific Policy.

Terraferida. 2018. "#Desmuntant Airbnb, estiu 2018." (4 August). Accessed 3 January 2020. from https://terraferida.cat/2018/08/04/desmuntant-airbnb-estiu-2018/.

Verdaguer, Màrius. 1977 [1955]. *La ciutat esvaïda*. Translated by A. Moll. Ciutat de Mallorca: Editorial Moll.

Wachsmuth, David, and Alexander Weisler. 2018. "Airbnb and the Rent Gap: Gentrification through the Sharing Economy." *Environment and Planning A: Economy and Space* (20 June): 1–24. Accessed 3 January 2020. https://doi.org/10.1177/0308518X18778038.

Wolf, Eric R. 1997 [1982]. *Europe and the People Without History*. Berkeley: University of California Press.

Yrigoy, Ismael. 2018. "Rent Gap Reloaded: Airbnb and the Shift from Residential to Touristic Rental Housing in the Palma Old Quarter in Mallorca, Spain." *Urban Studies* (12 December): 1–18. Accessed 3 January 2020. https://doi.org/10.1177/0 042098018803261.

❖ Afterword

Financialization Beyond Crisis

GAVIN SMITH

Money and the Promise of Partners

In 1982, I was contracted by the Central Bank of Peru to study the credit/debit practices of people in the *barriadas* (shantytowns) of Lima. The purpose for my study, I was told, was because loan sharks were making killings from high returns on the loans they made to poor people, and that it was the responsibility of the bank to provide a more equitable service. This was just two or three years after the end of the period of Velasco-Bermudez military rule when inflation was gradually rising, but the recent past gave people memories of very low inflation on the *sol*, Peru's national currency. So off I went to join my contacts in Pamplona Alta, Mariano Melgar, and Villa El Salvador.

What I found was that when Tomas decided he needed a fifteen-year-old pickup to deliver fodder to the pig farm he ran among the sand dunes of Lima's periphery, he asked his neighbor Juan for some cash, which gave Juan a share in Tomas's truck. Tomas did much the same with what turned out to be fourteen other relatives, neighbors, work associates, and members of his football *equipo*. In return, like Juan, they all had shares in Tomas's truck. Some six to nine months later, Geraldo, a shareholder, decided he could run more than one tricycle taxi now that he had three teenage sons, and so he needed money to buy a couple more. So he asked Tomas for his money back plus the same amount he had advanced. Now Tomas had a share in Geraldo's tricycles.

Juan was less fortunate. By 1990, long after I had left and my study was gathering dust in the Central Bank, Peru's rate of inflation was raging.[1]

Around this time, Juan decided to sponsor his daughter to immigrate to the States. He asked Tomas for his share of the value of the truck, plus a similar amount to be used as Tomas's investment in this new enterprise: migration for a better source of income. The problem was, how were Tomas and Juan to calculate the respective values? Unlike Greenspan, their mission in life had not been to reduce the rate of inflation to zero for their friends, as he did for his. So instead, they began by appealing to others in their immediate circle, only to discover that they too were facing similar questions of trust. One or two actually warned Tomas that a couple of years back, these kinds of disputes were settled by calling in Sendero Luminoso (The Communist Party of Peru – Shining Path).

Of course, the Central Bank was picking up on a trend that had developed in the late seventies, but it was probably a little ahead of its time. Now, the mid-nineties might have been a good time to start talking about microcredit; though, when I met the few so-called loan sharks I managed to get to talk to me back in the eighties, I was surprised that their rates of return on loans were about what you would expect given the risks involved and the very limited collateral to which they could lay claim (see also Wolf 1966). So what Tomas, now a somewhat equivocal figure among his buddies, got to learn was that inflation is not good for credit. Of course, the banks knew pretty much nothing about how Tomas managed his household's life back in the eighties. Otherwise, I would have been out of a contract. But their ignorance was not entirely disconnected from the financial problems facing the Peruvian state and its national and, more importantly, its international banks. Failing to have a knowable and hence taxable (for the state) or lendable (for the banks) population, they needed some other kind of collateral. Anything would do; the less noticeable the people involved were, the better—people in the Amazon rain forest, or next to an Andean strip mining operation. Then as now, there was and is a vast difference between the "have-not" financialized states and the "haves" that dominate global finance and a crucial element of that difference is the concern states have for and about their citizens.

The most obvious thing we learn from this story, one that Kalb has already shown us, is that there is nothing new about states and banks wherever they are—all trying to find the means for garnering even the most minute amounts of surplus value from those gathered into their pastoral care; that is to say, in this case, the Central Bank's "responsibility" in respect to the forms of credit available to the poor. But what the story also illustrates is that it is important *what you know*, whether you are the citizen, the state, or the bank. For all concerned, the extent to which your knowledge of the past is valuable relies on the stability that will make the future resemble the present. What *kind of* knowledge you need will depend on what kind of capital (and state) you are entangled in.

But this is not the heuristically most interesting way of thinking about knowledge. Rather, I will try to offset those kinds of accounts that see the projects of the state and banks (in fact, *financialized states*) playing the determining role vis-à-vis livelihood-seeking households by proposing that the conditions of possibility work in all directions. This is not to deny the immense power differentials involved, but rather to explore the triadic dialectic that produces the reciprocal constitution of states, banks, and families in/as households.[2]

So these are the two reflections I will take up in this Afterword: the extent to which it is useful to (over) stress the distinction of a world financialized by capital and one more generally understood as capitalist; and, from the perspective of *critique* (see below), the relative merits of mechanistic narratives of domination as against explorations of the dialectical manner in which social phenomena are constituted.

Break or Continuity

In asking whether recent work has not gone a little too far in characterizing what is distinct about finance capital in comparison to capital in general,[3] I want to stress the distinction that was crucial to Marx's understanding of the task of philosophical *critique* between appearance and reality.[4] He was not at all afraid of providing a convincing description of how the world appeared to those participating in it. He called it "Free-trader Vulgaris." But it was, he said, "the sphere that we are deserting" in favor of the stance of critique—that the most significant thing about appearances was the way they obscure what is actually going on. Here's how he put it:

> This sphere that we are deserting, within whose boundaries the sale and purchase of labor-power goes on, is in fact a very Eden of the innate rights of man. There alone rule Freedom, Equality, Property and Bentham. Freedom, because both buyer and seller of a commodity, say of labor-power, are constrained only by their own free will. They contract as free agents, and the agreement they come to is but the form in which they give legal expression to their common will. Equality, because each enters into relation with the other, as with a simple owner of commodities, and they exchange equivalent for equivalent. Property, because each disposes only of what is his own. And Bentham, because each looks only to himself. (Marx 1976: ch. 6)

For Marx then, the job was not so much to interpret this kind of behavior in its own terms but to critique it.[5] Nonetheless, as Don Kalb notes in the Introduction to this volume, Marx was a product of his age—at least insofar as, finding himself in the world of emergent industry, he identified the key issues of capitalism to be exploitation in production. But the idea was to undermine the "puzzles" he found there through critiquing them—a word for which Marx had a quite restricted meaning (Benhabib 1986: 109; Postone 1996: 87–90; Smith 2014: 18). In the course of this exercise, a series of key concepts arose. He famously started with the commodities that seemed to attain their value by being priced in the market, suggesting that this appearance concealed more fundamental practices and relations.

For the political economists of his time and before him, the foundation on which value might rest was a pressing question. The challenge was not so much to measure it—more of it or less—but to find it. For Marx, it had to be distinguished from the metrics of price. Instead, the value of a commodity arose from a relationship in the sphere of its production: where those who possessed machines and the spaces (factories) they occupied met the laborers who entered the spaces to put the machines to work. This combination of a relation and a practice was what *capital* was—the moment when its value was "realized" on entering the market. It may of course be confined to a different era from ours—one closer to Marx's perhaps. But it was at least a way of starting to strip down the busy world of appearances— production, labor, capital, value. Moreover then (as now) terms such as these, understood dialectically, could not be captured in a dictionary definition but were instead relational and procedural. Take for example my use here of possession (of machines and factories) rather than ownership. Possession refers to control but not necessarily the right to buy and sell.

When I was working in the Andes in the seventies, Andean *haciendas* claimed possession of their highland pasture but sought to avoid legal disputes with peasants over ownership. This was not just because the vast majority of their land was acquired through *force majeur*. It was also because what few deeds they did have granted them title on the specific condition that they not hinder or restrict the free access to pasture by the local inhabitants. Currently, there is some evidence that governmental projects for property registration sponsored by the IMF and World Bank have the effect of obliging people who thought they had possession to enter into legal disputes over ownership (see, for example, Ødegaard 2019; Smith 2018).

So, just as Marx was a product of his age and place, so too were the *hacendados* of the Peruvian Andes in the seventies and the urban squatters or land claimants in Peru today (Smith 2018). If then this is so for Marx, the *hacendados*, and the urban squatters, then it is true for us too. Of course, capitalism has changed since the days of Marx and of course these changes need appropriate conceptualization and critique, but reconceptualizations and revisionist histories are likewise a product of their age. Marx was acutely aware of the historical situatedness of his study, contrasting it to the "Robinsonades" of contemporary political economy who took the conditions they observed in the present to be historical and geographical universals.

When I was preparing a set of essays for a collection soon after 2008 and 2009, I provided the reader at the outset with a kind of guide to a critique of capitalism in the manner of Marx (Smith 2014: 27–64). Then, later in the book, I built on the foundations of this initial analysis, extending the paradigm to explain how a particular kind of politics emerged when finance capital shaped the dominant blocs of many social formations (2014: 177–213). The issue then is not that we are faced with a leap from the Scylla of the concepts used to tackle industrial capital to the Caribdis of finance capital, but rather that there has been a gradual reconfiguration of the earlier concepts. While staying within the Marxian understanding of production, Lefebvre expanded a narrower definition of factory production of commodities whose value was realized as they came to market by pointing out that urban spaces were also produced. People living in those spaces also produced them in part by living their everyday lives. Dialectically then, everyday life was responsible for producing the spaces of daily life while at the same time being produced by them. Subsequently, the use by Italian *autonimistas* of the notion "cognitive labor" expanded earlier meanings of "labor" by suggesting that these kinds of workers didn't carry on their work in a neatly configured space like a factory. Their work, even their leisure, was dispersed, making it hard for those claiming possession of the so-called "means of production" to control them.

The point is that we had already accustomed ourselves to expanded uses of earlier conceptual terms for understanding capitalism before the fashion for studying its specifically financial variant had arisen.

Dominance and Dialectics

A number of anthropologists (Appadurai 2006; Ho 2009) have joined others (e.g., Martin 2002; Roberts 2015; Calkin 2018) and discussed the effects of finance on families and households. But these discussions of financialization and finance capital tend to invoke a causality in which the financialized state *dominates* the world of everyday life to be found among those seeking to put together a livelihood among families in households. A mechanical explanation so evident at the level of appearances obscures the dialectical unfolding that results in the mutual reshaping of the phenomena under study—in this case, the "financialized state" form and the forms of "families" and "households."

Taking inspiration from many of the chapters in this collection, I begin the journey not with banks and hedge funds, then, but rather with families and households. When we read about the indebted households in South Africa, Azerbaijan, Croatia, and Greece, or the denigrated debtors on a British housing estate, we realize that what emerges by no means supports any easy generalizations about the fate of ordinary people subjected to the poison gas that seeps into their lives through financial instruments. Even so, a feature they share, as well, with the people used for incidental jobs in Fujian's "carbon forests" is their devaluing as social persons. In one of the British cases discussed, indebtedness is closely associated with respectability; there are good borrowers, and there are scroungers. This gives the impression that the creditor–debtor relationship precedes the assessment as a social person. But it is also quite evident that any of these predicaments rely on the ideological defining of the person for instrumental reasons. As Robbins makes clear in his chapter, for example, the constitution of the citizen as a self-governing, responsible actor is fundamental to the reproduction through time-of-debt relationships. And yet there are a series of contradictions built into the system that need to be mystified. So, finance capital is not less reliant on the mystifications Marx speaks of in reference to capital in general, and we need to expose the way some of these mystifications work and the kinds of disturbance that result when their underlying relations break down.

In its efforts to overcome all barriers to the generation of wealth, Marx noted that capital transgresses all preexisting forms of reproduction. Yet we now know that there is a caveat. Starting with Rosa Luxemburg (1951), and followed in anthropology by the path-breaking work of Edholm, Harris, and Young (1978), and then taken up by Young, Wolkowitz, and McCulloch (1981), we know that "capitalism needs non-capitalist forms of production" (Luxemburg 1951: 289), much of which takes place in a sphere ideologically characterized as the family to be found in households of various forms. As Melinda Cooper asks rhetorically, "Isn't [capital] compelled in the last instance, to reinstate the family as the elementary legal form of private wealth accumulation?" (2019: 16). The capitalist pursuit of surplus value through expanded reproduction interacts with this sphere of "social reproduction." This is no less true as finance capital becomes dominant than when the argument was made in the context of production capital; but the way capitalism is commonly cast as the dominant player can obscure the dialectical nature of this interaction, so let us look at these things a little closer.

We can be guided by Don Kalb's Introduction. When a state borrows from a bank, the relationship is beneficial to both. The state gets the money it needs at that moment, allowing it to cover a shortfall that might have resulted from insufficient tax revenues, and the bank's security in turn is built on the fact that the state is a reliable guarantor based on its right to collect taxes from its citizenry and of course its assumed ability to do so.[6] Robbins provides us with a nice vignette that helps us to understand how this works, using the case of William III's need for cash, and the bargain he struck in 1694 with James Patterson and what became the Bank of England to get it—the banks' monopoly to print the currency: sovereign money (Robbins, this volume). In that period, there were many ways in which the ruler "taxed" the citizenry. Licenses were sold for the manufacture of soap, for the right to sell salt, to act as a *privateer* (i.e., a licensed pirate) on the high seas, and so on. Henry VIII used a once-off technique now common in neoliberal governance by poaching on goods not hitherto part of his domain—the Catholic monasteries—declaring them his own and then using them for income or selling them off for cash. While all such methods targeted specific groups, they affected the overall population insofar as costs were passed on to them, as Robbins points out.

But, much as we find today, rulers were not about to let the less well-off escape their fiscal responsibilities. For example, in the history of the French Revolution that Jean Jaures wrote in 1900, he provides the ever-increasing list of *tailles* peasant households were subjected to under Louis XVI. These included payments when one used one's own oxen for plowing, for tolls for travel to markets or crossing rivers, for digging a well on one's land (*la garenne*), or for having a chimney in one's house. If tax collectors had a terrifying job as they journeyed through the French countryside, it was not because of its remote barbarity (Corbin 1995), but rather what civilization meant for the peasantry where the royal tentacles extended into peasants' lives: "their clutches over every force of nature, everything that grew, moved, breathed; the rivers with their fish, the fire burning in the oven to bake the peasant's poor bread mixed with oats and barley, the wind that turned the mill for grinding corn" (Jaurès 1969: 76–77). It is hardly worth saying that the tax relationship between a state and its ordinary citizens living as families in households has changed; states have changed, and so have households. Discomfort with teleological history aside, however, and with vastly uneven success between the Global North and the Global South, states have generally found techniques not only for gaining knowledge about households but also for establishing the norms that make them so—proper families in locatable households. For the purposes of today, a neat way for the tax-collector to draw taxes from the citizenry is to find them in households where "families" live. For the purposes of tomorrow, however—that is, for the moment when the state wishes to speak to its banker—there ought to be some stability and uniformity to this dispersed source.

As we have seen, the solvency of the state relies on taxes. Of course, these come through a variety of means (sales taxes, for example) and from different sources (corporate taxes, for example), but the component that comes from taxing working people can most easily be found where they live, which is in households. When states try to "buy time," in Wolfgang Streeck's (2016) words, they can turn to banks who lend them money at relatively low rates of interest because they are reassured by the state's tax-collecting abilities, which rely in turn on finding tax payers. And to the extent that their source is in households, so households are to states what collateral would be to some other kind of borrower.[7] We see here the beginning of the way in which states, banks, and households are to be found in a process of reciprocal constitution.

Of course, reality is by no means as neat as this, but to illustrate the kind of pattern invoked here, I will move on from sovereigns and the Bank of England and turn to the case of Fordism. Along with the Model T that emerged from his assembly line, Henry Ford was very keen on producing the model worker too: reliable, with responsibilities—like a family—and a house, as well as just a wee bit of debt, but not too much. Such a worker could be depended on—something that mattered in those "olden days" when production was not so flexible. Actually the *reliability* of this kind of white American household was good for planning. It made the present neatly foreshadow the future and, with statistics at hand (the word is not unconnected to the word "state"), actuaries could provide reliable estimates of probabilities. So, if we return for a moment to our modern-day William III, the more he can assure the banks from which he borrows that his tax sources are as good in the future as they are in the present, the more he can borrow from them at low interest rates. And thus reassured, the banks can offer credit to their other customers at a stable rate—which they do in the form of money, as we have seen in the Introduction. Moreover, as we learn from Foucault's elaboration of pastoral power, the state itself can follow Ford's example, enhancing the well-being of the citizenry the better for them to pay their taxes.

The story with which I opened this chapter shows how limited such a neat picture of the state–bank–household relationship can be. But we can learn from this by returning to the original "deal" that was struck between the state and the banks. The banks were secured by their association with a supposedly stable state. The state acquired cheap money from the banks on the basis of its reliability in collecting taxes from clearly designated sources, among them households—the more like the Fordist household, the better. In return, the banks had a monopoly in setting the credit rate through money. It is now time to introduce into this Humpty-Dumpty world flexible production, out-sourcing, sub-contracting—in short, what has long been the case in the Global South and has more recently shown itself in North America and Western and Eastern Europe. It was not just by standardizing the tax-paying household that states enhanced their solvency; it was by extending the pattern of the present into the future. Once households became as "flexible" as the new kinds of capitalist firms—households simultaneously enterprises, single-parent families, live-at-home adults, etc.— they could no longer serve the same purpose for the state. Some years back, there was a headline in the British newspaper *The Independent* that read, "One and a half million households in Britain disappear." Reading the text, one discovered that they had mostly disappeared into what was then called "the black economy." This would have been quite alarming for the tax collector. Globally, we might just say that it took the conjunction of a number of factors, most of them connected in some way to the simplified narrative above, to destabilize the state–bank–household arrangement. Once lean production became pervasive, out went that stable family household and with it the auditor's ability to use the present as a model for the future.

And this has an effect too on the monopoly on offering credit as money that arose from the deal chartered banks made with the state. In principle, the traditional chartered bank takes in savings from customers and uses the resulting cash as the basis for offering credit. The bank's security, in other words, derives from two sources: the state acting as "lender of last resort," and the pool of deposited money that provides the basis for leverage.[8] But two things are happening now: (1) the audited reliability of the state's tax sources has become unstable from the bank's point-of-view—it does not guarantee against future risks; and, (2) faced with the hazards of flexible labor and low wages, customers are no longer saving as they used to by depositing in the bank.

Established banks are losing a monopoly that they never really had. After all, controlling money as a means of rapid exchange is one thing, and not one that banks make much money on (as Sohini Kar shows in her chapter); but a monopoly on credit is unachievable (as we have seen in the opening vignette). There is nothing to stop one person from helping out another in this way, and there is nothing to stop the numbers from getting ever larger. So, as traditional banks lost the original major sources of security for their financial practices, they were simultaneously faced with less-formal institutions providing similar services to their own. Unlike the chartered banks, however, these institutions have neither the endorsement of the state nor the protection of its laws. The substitute for the state guarantee and the holding of clients' deposits was to secure their risks by using borrowers' assets as collateral. They could then extend that security by clustering together and passing the security derived from those original assets—houses, cars, and so on—among one another, thereby spreading and diversifying their risk. Faced with this now-open field, the established banks began to form their own clusters in similar manner. Moreover, as the credit arrangements among both chartered and less-formal banks became more widespread, they looked increasingly like money. Indeed, what was emerging with shadow banking was also shadow money.

When banks conventionally used money as a means to make promises to their clients, those promises would "function as a standard against which the value of other promises is made.... [So] the promises that a bank generates *institute[d] an economic norm, a standard of value*" (Konings 2018: 17—emphasis mine). But what we have seen here is that neither states nor chartered banks have been able to retain a monopoly on the prevailing "standard of value." So, while "the production of values is transposed directly onto the exercise of power," the "wedding of the agenda of [finance] to societies and national populations" (Vogl, 2017: 164) has opened finance into a field requiring risk-laden reconstituting of the socioeconomic institutions involved.

Conclusion

If then, as I have argued, we can seek to understand states, banks, and households as caught in an inescapable web in which each eventually constitutes the other—more or less materially, more or less ideologically—the better to achieve their goals, then with states unable to "fix" a standard household, and banks no longer able to make even the pretense of a monopoly on money credit, each of the elements is in flux. However many exceptions we find to this intractable co-constitution, however many messy peripheries there are to this organized core,[9] the fact is that two counter forces have come into play. The legislative and juridical moves states have made to enhance the plasticity of capitalist enterprises have reconstituted the triadic dialectic that made reproduction stable. This has opened the field not only to new forms of banking, but also to new forms of garnering surplus value through outsourcing and the like. As a result of its handiwork, there is no neatly standardized "family" or "household" for the state to tax. Meanwhile, the counter forces that question what constitutes a family, a worker, or a responsible citizen are an emergent result, producing a cluster of counterpolitical forces—among them the one identified by Robbins, but by no means the only one.

Gavin Smith is Professor Emeritus in the Department of Anthropology at the University of Toronto, and Visiting Professor at the National University of Ireland, Maynooth. His ethnographic work in South America and Western Europe has focused on the connection between the ways in which people make a livelihood and their forms of political expression. He currently has a research project with Winnie Lem on Chinese and Latin American migrants in France, Italy, and Spain. His books include *Livelihood and Resistance: Peasants and the Politics of Land in Peru* (University of California Press, 1989) and *Intellectuals and (Counter-) Politics: Essays in Historical Realism* (Berghahn Books, 2014).

Notes

1. It would cost over two million *soles* at the beginning of 1990 to buy what you could buy for a thousand in 1985. https://www.worlddata.info/america/peru/infla tion-rates.php. Accessed 15 November 2019.
2. For an understanding of the dialectic in terms of a triadic set of relations, see Lefebvre (1991) who argues that Marx used it in a similar way in the *Grundrisse*.
3. This is not to deny the importance of the kind of periodization employed by Arrighi (2009) or the global history presented by Kalb in the Introduction. See also McNally (2014).
4. Marx's hermeneutics of suspicion is not especially attractive to anthropologists who see their principle task to be representing "the natives' point-of-view." But the issue may not be quite so clear-cut. In *The Violence of Abstraction* Derek Sayer argues for the need to make a distinction between the terms Marx used for the purposes of critique and those anthropologists would call the "emic categories" of the bourgeoisie— of which the quoted description might be one.
5. Though, as Marx makes clear here, while in the game, you'd be a fool not to play by its rules.
6. It is important to note the temporal nature of the sovereign's shortfall. He needs to obtain money now. He could possibly get it by raising a package of taxes. The historical evidence, however, tends to suggest that it is precisely popular opposition to such measures that could be the last straw. The point is that his turn to the banks is as political as it is economic. In this case, it results from class pressure. See also Note 5 above.
7. Of course, in this case, it is not the banks that repossess on failure to pay, but the state. States tend to have their own sanctions for nonpayment.
8. The reference to leverage here is to note that such banks only use the asset value of their deposits as a percentage of what they are allowed or allow themselves to lend out; let's say from 30–70 percent.
9. A glance at the opening vignette makes clear that virtually none of this fits the set of relationship I have been describing. It would scarcely do so today, though strides have been made to address the issue. The conversion of the tax-farming encomienda system through the eighteenth and nineteenth centuries into haciendas meant shifting from *comunidades de indios* being the collective unit for tribute and tax collection to the *hacienda* acting as a proto-state (Krupa 2015). While these at least had the advantage of recording the sources of state revenue, the unleashing of urban migration in the mid-twentieth century meant that the households once found in peasant communities "disappeared," much as the article in the *Independent* had bemoaned for Britain.

References

Appadurai, Arjun. 2006. *Fear of Small Numbers*. Durham: Duke University Press.

Arrighi, Giovanni. 2009 [1994]. *The Long Twentieth Century: Money, Power, and the Origins of Our Time*. London: Verso.

Benhabib, Seyla. 1986. *Critique, Norm and Utopia*. New York: Columbia University Press.

Calkin, Sydney. 2018. *Human Capital in Gender and Development*. London: Routledge.

Cooper, Melinda. 2019. *Family Values: Between Neoliberalism and the New Conservatism*. Boston: MIT Press.

Corbin. Alain. 1995. *Les villages de "cannibales."* Paris: Flamarion.

Edholm, Felicity, Olivia Harris, and Kate Young. 1978. "Conceptualizing Women." *Critique of Anthropology* 3, no. 9–10: 101–30.

Ho, Karen. 2009. *Liquidated: An Ethnography of Wall Street*. Durham: Duke University Press.

Jaurès, Jean. 1969 [1900–1903]. *Histoire socialiste de la Révolution française*. Vol. 1. Paris: Editions sociales.

Konings, Martijn. 2018. *Capital and Time: For a New Critique of Neoliberal Reason*. Stanford: Stanford University Press.

Krupa, Christopher. 2015. "Cadastral Politics: Property Laws and State Realism in Highland Ecuador." In *State Theory and Andean Politics: New Approaches to the Study of Rule*, edited by C. Krupa and D. Nugen. Philadelphia: University of Pennsylvania.

Lefebvre, Henri. 1991 [1974]. *The Production of Space*. Oxford: Blackwell.

Luxemburg, Rosa. 1951. *The Accumulation of Capital*. London: Routledge and Kegan Paul.

Martin, Randy. 2002. *The Financializtion of Daily Life*. Philadelphia: Temple University Press.

Marx, Karl. 1976. *Capital*. Vol. 1. Harmondsworth: Penguin.

McNally, David. 2014. "The Blood of the Commonwealth: War, the State, and the Making of World Money." *Historical Materialism* 22, no. 2: 3–32.

Ødegaard, Cecilie Vindal. 2019. "Within and beyond the Law: The Ethics of Collective Action in Urban Markets, Peru." *History and Anthropology* [online]. doi: 10.1080/02757206.2019.1669590.

Postone, Moishe. 1996. *Time, Labor and Social Domination*. Cambridge, UK: Cambridge University Press.

Roberts, Adrienne. 2015. "Gender, Financial Deepening and the Production of Embodied Finance: Towards a Critical Feminist Analysis." *Global Society* 29, no. 1: 107–27.

Smith, Gavin. 2014. *Intellectuals and (Counter-) Politics*. Oxford: Berghahn Books.

———. 2018. "Elusive Relations: Distant, Intimate and Hostile." [The 10th Eric Wolf Lecture] *Current Anthropology* 59, no. 3: 247–67.

Streeck, Wolfgang. 2016. *Buying Time: The Delayed Crisis of Democratic Capitalism*. London: Verso.

Vogl, Joseph. 2017. *The Ascendancy of Finance*. Cambridge, UK: Polity.

Wolf, Eric. 1966: *Peasants.* Englewood Cliffs, NJ: Prentice-Hall.

Young, Kate, Carol Wolkowitz, and Roslyn McCulloch, eds. 1981. *Of Marriage and the Market: Women's Subordination in International Perspective*. London: CSE Books.

Index

www.ingramcontent.com/pod-product-compliance
Lightning Source LLC
Chambersburg PA
CBHW070902030426
42336CB00014BA/2297